Print and the Urdu Public

Print and the Urdu Public

Muslims, Newspapers, and Urban Life in Colonial India

MEGAN EATON ROBB

OXFORD
UNIVERSITY PRESS

OXFORD
UNIVERSITY PRESS

Oxford University Press is a department of the University of Oxford. It furthers the University's objective of excellence in research, scholarship, and education by publishing worldwide. Oxford is a registered trade mark of Oxford University Press in the UK and certain other countries.

Published in the United States of America by Oxford University Press
198 Madison Avenue, New York, NY 10016, United States of America.

Library of Congress Cataloging-in-Publication Data
Names: Robb, Megan Eaton, author.
Title: Print and the Urdu public : Muslims, newspapers, and urban life in colonial India / Megan Eaton Robb.
Description: New York : Oxford University Press, 2021. |
Based on the author's dissertation (doctoral)—University of Oxford, 2014. |
Includes bibliographical references and index.
Identifiers: LCCN 2020014198 (print) | LCCN 2020014199 (ebook) |
ISBN 9780190089375 (hardback) | ISBN 9780190089399 (epub)
Subjects: LCSH: Madīnah (Bijnor, India) |
Press—India—Bijnor—History—20th century. |
Urdu newspapers—India—Bijnor—History—20th century. |
Islamic press—India—Bijnor—History—20th century. |
Journalism—Social aspects—India—Bijnor—History—20th century. |
Muslims—Press coverage—India. | Islam—Press coverage—India.
Classification: LCC PN5379.B55 M347 2020 (print) |
LCC PN5379.B55 (ebook) | DDC 079/.542—dc23
LC record available at https://lccn.loc.gov/2020014198
LC ebook record available at https://lccn.loc.gov/2020014199

1 3 5 7 9 8 6 4 2

Printed by Integrated Books International, United States of America

Dedicated to Aiman, Ashel, Asna, and Ella,
who would be good friends

Contents

Preface

This book had its origins in a dissertation project begun at the University of Oxford in 2010 and completed in 2014. The dissertation focused on a single decade of *Madīnah* newspaper and its relevance to the period from the Balkan Wars to the end of the Khilafat Movement. Since 2017 I have approached this project anew to explore the relevance of small-town printing on the wider world.

First and foremost I am indebted to my dissertation supervisor, Francis Robinson, who has remained generous with his time, patience, and resources over the past nine years of work on this project. In the same way, I am particularly thankful to my dissertation supervisor Rosalind O'Hanlon for her incisive critiques and sympathetic encouragement over the past decade. I seek to emulate the model of intellectual generosity they put forward. I have benefited from the guidance of many invaluable mentors, among them Justin Jones, Margrit Pernau, Faisal Devji, Muhammad Talib, Muhammad Akram Nadwi, Farhan Nizami, Nandini Guptu, and Maria Misra, all of whom contributed to the development of the book. I am also grateful to the many friends who offered me valuable support and insightful comments as I presented parts of this book at conferences over the years: Sneha Krishnan, Faridah Zaman, Jennifer Dubrow, Richard David Williams, Layli Uddin, Eve Tignol, Rinchan Mirza, Muhammad Ali Khan Mahmudabad, and Elizabeth Chatterjee, who gave me feedback on parts of the book.

The process of rewriting the project began four years ago after my arrival at the University of Pennsylvania, where I have benefited from colleagues who supported my writing and enriched the argument of my book. I especially appreciate comments made by Jamal Elias, Lisa Mitchell, Karen Redrobe, Ramya Sreenivasan, Heather Sharkey, Donovan Schaefer, Reyhan Durmaz, and Greg Goulding. I am grateful to the Workshop on Material Texts at the University of Pennsylvania for inviting me to present on this book; their insightful questions gave me a broader perspective of the significance of Urdu journalism production processes.

Tasneem Khan and Ahtesham Ahmad Khan merit special mention for the countless hours they spent reading *Madīnah* with me between 2008 and 2018, in Oxford and in Lucknow respectively. I am also grateful to Imre Bangha, SherAli Tareen, Shehnaz Ahmad, Zeba Parveen, Ismail Mathari Porkundil, and Basharat

Husain for their guidance in learning to interpret Urdu primary sources. I also want to thank Abdussaboor Nadwi, instructor at Nadwat-ul 'Ulama, Lucknow, for simultaneously reading *Madīnah* with me and refining my Urdu during my year of residence in Lucknow from 2011 to 2012. Mustafa Menai generously worked with me to revise all translations of *Madīnah* for this volume in the summer of 2019. Any errors in translation or interpretation are my own.

Many offered me invaluable guidance during my archival work in India and became friends in the process—I am grateful to Paramjeet Cheema, Ram Advani, Seema Alavi, Mohsin Ali, Maulwi Nur ul-Hasan Rasheed, Parvez 'Ādil and Muneer Akhtar for their hospitality and guidance. Emma Young applied her fine editor's eye to the manuscript, her feedback improving the manuscript's coherence. Shiny Das, Theo Calderara, and Macey Fairchild at Oxford University Press shepherded the manuscript through the editing and proofing process with care and facility. I am grateful to the anonymous peer reviewers whose insightful questions and perceptive comments strengthened the final product. I presented versions of book chapters at the University of Oxford, University of Pennsylvania, and University of South Carolina, and at the Annual Conference on South Asia in Madison, Wisconsin, and the Annual Conference for the Association for Asian Studies, where constructive critiques enriched the argument.

I completed research for this book with the support of grants from Indiana University's Palmer-Brandon Prize, Oxford University's Clarendon Fund, The Wolfson Graduate Scholarship Fund, The Grimstone Travel Fund, the New College Ludwig Humanities Fund Grant, a grant from the Wolfson South Asia Research Cluster, and a US Department of Education Fellowship to attend the American Institute of Indian Studies' Urdu language program. I have also benefited from an appointment to the Society of Fellows in Critical Bibliography, which gave me access to instruction on typesetting, lithography, and typography. My work also benefited from a postdoctoral position at the Oxford Center for Islamic Studies and a lectureship at the Oriental Institute at the University of Oxford, both held following the completion of my dissertation. The process of revising the dissertation into a book was supported by the Julie and Martin Franklin endowed Assistant Professorship at the University of Pennsylvania and the Research Opportunity Grant at the University of Pennsylvania, where I have worked for the past four years. I am grateful to the library staff at the University of Pennsylvania, the British Library, the National Archives of India, the Uttar Pradesh State Archives, the U.S. Library of Congress, Raza Rampur Library, and University of London, Royal Holloway.

To my Grandmother Katherine Chaudhri, my Grandmama Sara Shelton, my mother Debbie Robb, my father Mike Robb, and my sister Kate Allman, I am thankful for your unconditional love and support. To Simi Appa, thank you for welcoming me into your heart and home in Lucknow; your generosity has made that city into another homeland. To my husband, Terry, I owe the greatest appreciation for his constant affection, strength, and steadfastness, which has enabled us to make a home wherever we are and wherever we may go.

Introduction
A Public Is a Place and Time
Dimensions of an Urdu Public Sphere

In 1912 Bijnor, a small town in northwest United Provinces (UP), a man named Muḥammad Majīd Ḥasan sold his wife's jewelry for the money to found the newspaper *Madīnah*. This newspaper pledged to be "the friend of the *mulk* [the nation], the life of the *qaum* [the Muslim Community]."[1] *Madīnah* went on to become one of the most successful newspapers of any language circulating in North India and the Punjab. This paper's ultimate success is not something most observers could have predicted. It was published in a *qasbah*, an isolated market town with an Islamic hue, and its proprietor, Majīd Ḥasan, was not influential or rich. Nonetheless, despite its isolated beginnings, the paper *Madīnah* went on to become popular across North India and the Punjab and to play an important role in the independence movement. It was so successful in fact that Bijnor *qasbah* became a publishing hub, home to many printing presses. The story of *Madīnah* newspaper and Madīnah Press shows that understanding the relationship between distinctive urban spaces and attitudes to time is important for understanding the early twentieth century public sphere that orbited around the star of Urdu, a sphere that increasingly emphasized ties to Islamic space and time.

The influential voice of *Madīnah* newspaper is not easy to categorize. The product of a family initially relatively low in status, *Madīnah*'s proprietor Majīd Ḥasan hired erudite editors and published established Muslim scholars without having formal educational credentials of his own. The paper's editorial board advocated for the importance of local context even while expanding the geographic horizons of the *qasbah* through coverage of international issues. *Madīnah* was part of a newspaper network that debated the advantages and disadvantages of separatism and after 1937 came out firmly against the exclusivist representational claims of the Muslim League. Published in a far-flung, even backwoods, town, *Madīnah* became an influential source of news read widely in the cities of Delhi, Lucknow, and Lahore. Even for those who were pro-League and pro-Pakistan, its influence was a touchstone that advocated for the relevance of religion in politics and contested sweeping national political narratives.

This book covers a period spanning the end of the Balkan Wars, World War I, the collapse of the Khilafat Movement, the devolution of powers to Indians under the colonial regime, World War II, and the acceleration of calls for independence

Print and the Urdu Public. Megan Eaton Robb, Oxford University Press (2021). © Oxford University Press.
DOI: 10.1093/oso/9780190089375.001.0001

until 1947. The expansion of the geographic horizon of the newspaper public into the *qasbah* context in the years prior to the Balkan Wars brought new voices to a public conversation that would be influential in determining the parameters of Muslim *ashrāf* or elite identity. In this book, I argue that in order to understand this period it is important to pay attention to attitudes toward time and space in delineating the Urdu public sphere. In particular, the case study of the newspaper *Madīnah* challenges the assumption that the *qasbah* stood apart from the vibrant development of the Urdu public in the early twentieth century; in fact, the *ashrāf* of Bijnor *qasbah* capitalized on this marginal status as they engaged with local, national, and international issues, expanding beyond their original geographic limitations while also being protected by them. The history of Bijnor captured in the pages of *Madīnah* demonstrates the importance of the *qasbah* context in preparing its newspapers for increased social resonance: its social and historical proximity to Delhi combined with its relative contemporary isolation from Delhi created the ideal incubator for what would become a significant voice for many of India's Muslims.

What Is a *Qasbah*?

The compelling attraction of any *qasbah* as spiritual heartland and ancestral home remains significant for many contemporary Indians and Pakistanis.[2] A *qasbah* at the turn of the twentieth century was a settlement with a population above several thousand in size, which boasted bureaucratic and market significance and where a significant Muslim minority or majority lived alongside a Hindu population.[3] Scholarship has devoted some discussion to the delineation of *qasbah* as a category. Chris Bayly highlighted the *qasbah* as the source of a cultural tradition parallel to that of Hindu commercial towns, implying that in it perhaps lay the foundations for a type of communalism. Mushirul Hasan considered the *qasbah* primarily as the repository of an idealized, pluralist past, a counterpoint to urban communalist movements. For Rahman, whose work demonstrates the merits of a localized approach to the study of modernity in South Asia, the pluralist, intellectually vibrant *qasbah* has a contemporary legacy grounded in a reverence for space and place. Following in the footsteps of the previously mentioned scholars, what matters for this book more than a particular bracket of population numbers is the sense of distinctiveness coloring the urban category of the *qasbah*.

Ashrāf, the elite descended from educated Muslim migrants and certain Hindu castes, who were based in *qasbahs* experienced rapid fluctuations in fortune over time that led to the formation of identities that emphasized local belonging. *Ashrāf* in these Islamicate small towns successfully garnered state patronage first from the Mughal Empire (1526–1857) and then the British Raj (1858–1947), cultivating a sense of identity through sponsorship of religious festivals, architecture, and art.[4] Endogamy and attention to genealogy records contributed to this sense of distinctiveness among *qaṣbātī* (hereafter *qasbati*) *ashrāf*. At the same time, this identity signifier remained subject to variations in status and prosperity across generations. There was the tendency for wealth to be tied to the *qasbah* itself rather than remaining specifically with individual families.[5] Many prominent Muslim *qasbati* derived their influence from land ownership; their political activism owed much to their agricultural interests.[6] Agriculture provided the main source of livelihood for residents of the Bijnor *parganah*,[7] but the relative lack of influential Muslim landowners in western UP compared to eastern UP resulted in increased tension between communal groups in the region of Rohilkhand.[8] In the East, Kayasth and Brahmin caste organizations often owed their living to Muslim landowners, consolidating common interests that transcended communal alliances. However, in late nineteenth-century and early twentieth-century western UP, Kayasth and Brahmin clerics were more likely to be employed by Hindu men of commerce; Muslim landowners were less predominant and held less influence. This meant that Rohilkhand saw an increasing linkage between politics and religion in matters of municipal governance, compared to eastern UP and Awadh. While in Awadh landed interests tended to cut across communal divisions and discouraged the application of religion to politics, Rohilkhand's dependence on commerce and trade emphasized divisions of interest along the lines of religious community.

The contrast illustrates a crucial point: western UP Muslims' eventual tendency to communalism or separatist nationalism was not necessary or inevitable. It emerged as a result of distinctive patterns of land ownership, the relative poverty of Muslims in the region, the sharp price increases of the late nineteenth century, and the use of elections to settle religious scores.[9] This book adds to that list of influences the development of a vibrant Muslim newspaper culture based in *qasbah*s where these dynamics held sway and spoke to a wider imagined community.

On the one hand, a regionally specific dynamic, incubated in western UP *qasbahs* like Bijnor, became broadly influential through the publication and spread of newspapers like *Madīnah*. On the other hand, *Madīnah* derived its authority from its placement in a *qasbah*, a space that it increasingly presented as being an alternative to the city and the nation. It used the influence of the newspaper to advocate for a nationalist vision that prized the local political context above overarching national narratives. In contrast to studies of newspapers in large cities, significant contributions in their own right, this study of a *qasbah* publication captures an important group of contributors to the twentieth-century Urdu public often overlooked. In making this argument, I am contributing to scholarship that has countered the assumption that influence flowed only from cities to *qasbahs*.[10] Scholarship by Mushirul Hasan, Justin Jones, and M. Raisur Rahman has drawn attention to the significance of cultural, political, and economic history of specific *qasbahs*. Rahman describes *qasbahs* as "alternative sites," meaning places of "strong, autonomous networks of culture, literature, and religion" that are considered "the opposite of cities and urban contexts."[11]

We can certainly find evidence to support arguments that *qasbahs* are a distinct urban form, that they are a microcosm of city life, or both at once.[12] C. A. Bayly established the "*qasbah* as microcosm" model. Mushirul Hasan constructed a model of *qasbah* as an urban form opposite the city. Rahman has tried to reconcile both by stating that the *qasbah* is simultaneously "unique" and a "microcosm of the larger national life." He also argued that the *qasbah* is "more fluid, more cosmopolitan, more adaptive, and more capable of engaging with change" than the city. Of course, we should avoid the assumption that all *qasbahs* share a common culture that can, collectively, contribute to an understanding of the relationship between modernity and Islam in South Asia. This book focuses on the discursive power of a specific set of *qasbati* voices talking about themselves to others. *Madīnah* newspaper addressed a *qasbah* public as opposite to the public of the city, commenting on differences and using them to its advantage. A case study of *Madīnah* demonstrates that the form and content of a lithographic newspaper and temporal, spatial, and social characteristics of the *qasbah* environment that produced it worked hand in hand to create productive alterities to European and nationalist imagined futures.

It may prove useful and justified to move toward a more systematic consideration of colonial cities as centers of religious culture. Even if we relegate all *qasbahs* to the same typological category, however, we should simultaneously give attention to the particular industries and communities that animated them. Other prominent studies have noted the import of the intersection between urban space and religiosity in the subcontinent. Nile Green's *Bombay Islam* considered the "religious economy" of Bombay as one characterized by cosmopolitanism, an inheritance of its port city identity.[13] Munis D. Faruqui has attended to the princely state of Hyderabad, where a pragmatic attitude to Muslim rhetoric characterized the Nizam's politicking between the Marathas and the Mughals, influenced by the shatter zone of Deccani culture as much as by the simultaneous influence of Mughals and Marathas.[14] Stephen Blake has looked at Shahjahanabad, characterizing Islam as "congenial to city life" as a result of the requirement to participate in congregational gatherings with fellow Muslims.[15] Sandra Freitag described Banaras as a city defined not only by auspiciousness and as a pilgrimage center but also as an urban center with a political economy powerful for the agriculturally based hinterland around it.[16] Each of these studies demonstrates how an urban space is defined by a combined attention to ritual significance, economic markets, political negotiations, and geographic placement. Typologies for urban environments have been established to distinguish port cities, political capitals, and cities at the borderlands from *qasbahs*/satellite towns—characterized by their importance as market towns for the sale of agricultural goods and having substantial links to political and economic power. In the late colonial period, rather than seeing this typology upended entirely, we see a new significance that infused the category of the *qasbah*: it begins to appear in periodicals and books as a home of authenticity, a discursive space that corresponded to Walter Benjamin's "homogenous, empty time."

Space and Time

The public is "never simply an empirical object" but is "always also a category of interpretation."[17] Building on this observation made by J. Barton Scott and Brannon Ingram, the account of *Madīnah* and its newspaper conversation given in this book is founded on the theoretical claim that a keystone of any public is a particular relationship to space and time. The public is a category of interpretation with internal significance to South Asia, and the newspaper *Madīnah*, an Urdu newspaper published from 1912 in Bijnor in the then–United Provinces, is a prime example of a periodical that linked itself and the idea of the *qasbah* to a broader Muslim public. In the current political environment, it is difficult to think about the formation of publics without considering their impact on the forms that the nation may take. In India in particular, where Rohit Dasgupta's 2007 statement that "discrimination against people of the Islamic faith and people of the dalit caste has been on the rise" now resonates in the key of prophecy, reflections on the role of Muslims in the historical success of Congress have the potential to be unfortunately controversial. It is thus worth noting that while this book explores an association between Urdu and Islam, it does not argue that this association necessarily led to Pakistani nationalism. Many players in this story saw Urdu as the property of Muslims in the early twentieth century and yet were profoundly pro-Congress and anti-Muslim League. While this book does some work to recover the histories of pro-Congress, political Muslims in North India in the first half of the twentieth century, that is not its guiding aim. Its more important project is to reflect on the significance of space and time in defining the ubiquitous term "public."

Various scholars have responded to Talal Asad's call to engage with temporality in Islam, in particular by exploring reference to the words and deeds of the Prophet as a spatial-temporal frame for action.[18] Daniel Birchok has observed that in Southeast Asia, while the prophetic period is the primary frame of engagement in discourse and practice, it "enters into relationships with the present of different Islamic practitioners through varied, and often local, spatial-temporal paths."[19] These spatial-temporal paths are expressed within a number of spiritual repertoires of Islam. The tradition of *adab*, or "intellectual knowledge, spiritual cultivation, and correct behavior," has been implicitly acknowledged to have a temporal quality by Barbara Metcalf, although its temporal elements in the modern period remain underexplored.[20] Ernest Gellner's work on Morocco[21] and Richard Eaton's work on the shrine of Baba Farid[22] touch on how individual mediated traditions link local practice to other times, sewing them into the fabric of the broader religious tradition. After Faisal Devji's history of Islamic modernism from the perspective of the influential Aligarh Movement,[23] Rahman has reminded us of the significance of local context in understanding how modernity was negotiated at the level of *qasbahs*.[24] This book follows the cue of Rahman in tracing the impact of a group opposed to Aligarh, supportive of Deoband, and grounded in *qasbah*s while speaking to all levels of the urban. Modest in origins and often explicitly opposed to "*jadīdiyyat*," or "novelty," the discourse analyzed in this book nevertheless grappled with the implications of modernity. A social historical perspective emerges from a study of newspaper conversations, which filtered through the daily lives of not only the subaltern and the elite but also the "subalternity of the elite," to use Chatterjee's phrase.[25] Scholarship has acknowledged the impact of the local in Muslim spiritual repertoires and the existence of multiple, overlapping public spheres in and beyond *qasbah*s. Building on this work, there is a need to explore how particular relationships to time could make clearer the significance of spaces like *qasbahs* in modernity.

Sumit Sarkar observed the influence of the imposition of "clock time" on *chakrīs* or office workers in colonial Bengal, inhabitants of a professional position that came to represent a multitude of oppressions by the colonial state.[26] Manu Goswami has considered the coproduction of imperial and national spaces via the railway during the same period, with attention to their Hindu character.[27] This book brings to light the existence of a public space—similarly coproduced with imperial bureaucratic technologies and times—but in this case a public space coded as Urdu-speaking, Muslim, and opposed to the imagined future of Pakistan. This book considers ṭimescapes in its analysis of how *Madīnah* newspaper, along with many other periodicals, engaged with and inflected the Urdu public. In the process this book acknowledges that "temporal frames are not given but chosen" and that "the temporal framework that we impose determines what we can and do see."[28] By sewing the past into the present in the pages of *Madīnah*, the elite of one *qasbah*, Bijnor, embraced a particular Muslim temporal framework and fashioned a usable approach to time relevant to the future of Islam and the *qasbah* space.[29]

Laura Bear, while she does not use the term "timescape," provides a helpful schema of three aspects of time: nonhuman time, social time, and individual time. This book focuses on social time, rather than individual time. It builds on Bear's observations of the way in which "institutions *mediate* divergent representations, techniques, and rhythms of human and non-human time," and it extends Bear's argument to link the concept of time and the imagined community of a "public." Furthermore, Adam has observed that "we cannot embrace time without simultaneously encompassing space and matter, that is, without embodiment in a specific and unique context."[30] By building on this work as well, this book explores how institutions of communication technology and print capitalism interacted with urban spaces to impact the tempo of knowledge transmission.[31] When different levels of urban space were juxtaposed to other matrices of identity—local or national, for instance—that juxtaposition was influenced by contrasting tempos of knowledge production.[32] The departures of the political narratives emerging from the *qasbah* were influenced by the uneven spread of railway and telegraph technologies and their effects on the experience of time and space, as well as by the local legacies of educational institutions and linguistic mediums that shaped the horizons of knowledge for interlocutors.

Space, referring to a physical or geographic location, becomes place, or a social space, through social means.[33] The concept of space overlaps with that of place, and both have been central to the disciplinary conversations of human geography and sociology, which increasingly have been concerned with the question of "how scale, space, and place can help us understand and describe how religious categories emerge and fall apart."[34] In South Asian Studies this way of considering how a physical location becomes related to a spatial imagination has been explored with reference to the city, the emotions, and the printed reproduction of images of Mother India.[35] However, space has not been explicitly linked to discussions on the public sphere, particularly in the reproduction of material texts. *Madīnah* shows how the newspaper conversation and a *qasbah* could coconstitute the same social space or timescape through visual and discursive references linking *qasbah*s to the holy cities of Islam. In describing a *qasbah* timescape with explicit reference to Islam, this book takes its cue from *Madīnah* itself.

Urdu Print Publics

"Print capitalism," or journalism that subsists without government patronage, has been established as an enabling condition for the emergence of a public sphere capable of making demands of the government.[36] David Lelyveld's work spans a period from a moment when the term "print capitalism" in relation to

Urdu was hyperbolic to a period when news print had found its footing, notably demonstrated through the success of the bilingual *Tahzīb ul-Akhlāq*.[37] Syed Ahmad Khan, founder of the Muhammedan Anglo-Oriental College (today Aligarh University), used a combination of English and Urdu models and maintained strong links to the English public and to secular Muslim politics.[38] When it appeared on the scene half a century later, *Madīnah* joined a well-established tradition of lithographic print featuring Islamic aesthetics and focusing on the state of the Muslim community—a community that it defined in terms of the local environment, the international context, and association with a Muslim past.

Inspired by the efforts of European publishers, local presses brought increasing numbers of Urdu readers access to medical, religious, and secular texts previously available only to elites.[39] Building on correspondence and kinship networks, and efficient methods of transmitting knowledge within the Indian *ecumene*, print capitalism transformed this into something constituting a profoundly new iteration of a South Asian public. This public was characterized by an ambivalence in attitudes toward the divide between public and private, religious and secular. Newspapers in urban centers, such as the Urdu language *Āwadh Akhbār*, spoke to an audience delineated by culture and language more than by religion; other newspapers like *Madīnah* would emphasize the Muslim character of the Urdu public. (That is not to say that all public conversations had to choose between a secular or a Muslim approach. Work on Unani or traditional medicine, for instance, has shown that a commitment to secular medical models and the persistent influence of traditional, Islam-inflected medical practices existed simultaneously.[40]) Pioneers of Urdu newspaper publication, usually located in all levels of urban areas with access to lithograph technology, assisted in establishing an early Urdu public characterized by the participation and control of *'ulamā* (scholars) as well as the emergence of a space in which it was increasingly acceptable to challenge that authority.[41] The ambivalence to religion and its coherence with secular rationalism characterized newspapers' (certainly *Madīnah*'s) approach to the authority of scholars generally. As the power of publication increased, the influence of urban publishing networks offering wide audiences and reliable communication grew. *Madīnah* was a significant voice in a network of Urdu newspapers produced by and serving the *ashrāf*, woven through *qasbah*s as much as through large cities.

Because *Madīnah* was published from a *qasbah*, a study of it illuminates an understudied sector of life in the region. Gaining access to different discursive perspectives on life in the *qasbah*, in contrast to life in urban areas, has been a persistent challenge in historiography of the *qasbah*. Colonial documents necessarily focused on *qasbahs* as economic and administrative units.[42] Descendants of *zamīndārs* and *t'āluqdārs* dating from the Mughal period retained their land rights under the British, who viewed landed ownership as a mark of leadership.[43] As a result, British records of vernacular newspapers tended to emphasize the influence of landed newspaper editors who boasted landed wealth over that of publishers who could not claim links to Mughal or British state patronage.[44] *Madīnah* was controlled by a family that had relatively little wealth or land at the time when the newspaper was founded; it was perhaps for that reason that the colonial apparatus initially underestimated its potential impact. The family gained wealth, prestige, and a measure of political power through their journalistic activities. Indeed, rather than any formal educational qualification, it was Majīd Ḥasan's publishing endeavors that conferred on him the honorific title of "Maulānā."

Scott and Ingram have pointed out that the public as a category of interpretation is "internal to the self-understanding of colonial and post-colonial South Asia." Ingram has evaluated separately the central importance of the boundaries of a "*pablik*" in South Asia in his work on pamphlets, showing how study of this "ephemeral" genre assists in tracing the evolution of Muslim publics in South Asia.[45] Francesca Orsini has demonstrated the role of Devanagari script in consolidation of a Hindi public sphere.[46] These influential historical approaches have helped us understand that a person or group does not simply use media to propagate specific ideas. Instead, media and shared symbols influence what can be said and in the process delineate the boundaries of the public. In selection of source material, this book focuses on the quotidian, the literature that defined the rhythms of everyday life. Published more regularly than books or literary magazines, newspapers show the same editorial teams and their respondents commenting regularly on the same sets of issues over time. There is some advantage to looking at *akhbārāt* or newspapers rather than the more literary *rasā'il* (periodicals or magazines). Through the quotidian we gain direct access to a *qasbah*'s discursive response to the challenges of early twentieth-century modernity.

It is of course important to emphasize that Bijnor was not representative of "the *qasbah*" in South Asia. *Qasbah* contexts varied widely in the nineteenth and twentieth centuries. As we will explore in chapter 2, Bijnor *qasbah* was typical of many urban localities in that it had a telegraph connection in the 1880s but was unusual in that it lacked a direct railway connection until 1930, and these facts shaped the distinctive timescape that *Madīnah* projected. Bijnor was also distinct in that it developed an unusually dense concentration of printers and newspapers, influenced by the prominence of *Madīnah*. Likewise, while *Madīnah* was surprisingly influential, it cannot be taken to represent the entire Urdu public sphere or even the entire Urdu newspaper conversation. To avoid the pitfalls of generalizing one example to characterize the whole, this book contextualizes *Madīnah* as one set of voices in a set of noisy exchanges between Urdu periodicals and the Urdu-speaking public, drawing on a wide range of archival material, including colonial government records, *tazkirahs*, Urdu secondary scholarship, and a range of rarely available Urdu newspapers and periodicals. A thick description of *Madīnah* yields rich benefits: the newspaper's archives track the public reception of volatile issues, shine light on the familiar yet hazy character of urban life, and establish a narrative history of Bijnor that provides familial and local context for these insights. Most importantly, because *Madīnah* emerged from a distinctive time and place, it provides a good case study to demonstrate the benefits of looking at the public as a category with temporal and spatial resonances. With this in mind, it is important to note that the Urdu public, of which *Madīnah* formed a significant voice, was limited in geographic expanse and in sociological composition. Spanning from Punjab in the North to Lucknow in the East, the heartland of the North Indian Urdu public lay in the United Provinces.[47] Readers would have been mostly men, mostly Muslim, and mostly educated in Urdu, as well as some Persian and Arabic.

Could There Be a Pious Public?

The Urdu language and Muslim identity in some circles were becoming more closely associated in the first half of the twentieth century, and popular publications like *Madīnah* reflect a crystallization of this association. Increasingly the use of Urdu, Persian, and Arabic as well as use of calligraphy and visuals were linked directly to Islam; this occurred alongside the continuation of an Indo-Persianate tradition previously more closely allied to Mughal political norms than religious ideals.[48] *Madīnah* not only invoked an Indo-Persianate tradition but simultaneously linked analysis of Muslim reformist social issues to a burgeoning regional political identity. Significantly, opinions expressed in the paper reflected the continued elision of the two, previously separate identity strands of language choice and religion.

This book highlights how Islam could and did function as an aspect of the common language employed to consolidate an Urdu public sphere. Scholarship has explored Muslim engagement with mass media as a form of pious practice. Gail Minault formed an important foundation for this work when she established the importance of shared symbolic language in enabling the widespread success of the Khilafat movement in the twentieth century.[49] Margrit Pernau's work on *akhbārāt* challenged what had previously been assumed to be the central significance of British newspaper models on South Asian journalist publications.[50] Barbara Metcalf's work on the Deoband madrasa made clear the significance of print, and indeed training in scribal work and calligraphy, to that reformist project.[51] This work has been key to extending genealogies of the public beyond the arc defined by Benedict Anderson, who was primarily concerned to document the decline of cosmopolitan sacred languages, leaving open the question of how vernacular languages were tied to the rise of new sacred imagined communities.[52]

Both typological and genealogical approaches to the public sphere have tended to overlook the term "religion," assuming that it can refer only to a "distinctly modern concept" that is necessarily ill-suited to an analysis of South Asian cultures. That assessment is indicative of strains of historiography that assume that the term "religion" must privilege its doctrinal dimensions, or imply a clear distinction between sacred and secular.[53] Scholarship in South Asian studies has long since disproved any facile distinction between sacred and secular in the South Asian context. Nevertheless, while avoiding sacred/secular dichotomies there emerged a trend of sidestepping religion as a category of analysis, no doubt in part because religious studies had been one influential origin point of this unhelpful dichotomy. Of course, there is much to be gained from considering alternatives to the term "religion," when other terms better conceptualize authority, power, and identity.[54] There is much to be gained considering other conceptual categories in studies of public formation in the twentieth century as well. However, the relevance of religion is too clear to be ignored in this conversation among Urdu newspaper publishers. This book discusses interlocutors who have become aware of discourse on religion—through exposure to colonial census structure and racialization of religious communities—and who engage with the English, Urdu, Hindi, and Arabic terms relevant to the English term "religion" as substantive in the negotiation of boundaries of the public.

In the process of engaging with this category of analysis, we must of course avoid assumptions that religion is defined by doctrine recorded in master texts, a hallmark of Max Müller–era Orientalist studies of South Asian religions, which bolstered a tendency to overemphasize the separation between the sacred and the secular.[55] To refer to religion as a category of analysis in a study of the public sphere, without assuming that religion is merely a mask for other motives or an impenetrably sui generis category, is also to contradict any presumed inconsistency between religion and modernity and to transcend a simple equivalence of religion with doctrine or text.[56] Engaging with "religion" as a conceptual category important to the histories of public sphere construction necessarily leads us to consider the social, institutional, emotional, and material dimensions of religion alongside the legal and doctrinal dimensions. These are the dimensions of religion with which this study is concerned, rather than with legal or doctrinal aspects.

This book is published at a moment when a new interest in religion and its study has emerged in a range of disciplines. Scholars have embraced the porousness of the categories of sacred and secular in analysis of artifacts, rituals, and beliefs in South Asia.[57] In disciplines like geography, this category, which for a time disappeared, perhaps in response to the relegation of the academy by Habermas to the domain of the secular, has regained visibility.[58] In sociology, recent attempts to circumvent the discipline's old "insistence that religion is a sui generis analytical category" of little interest and to "export" the category of religion into other subdisciplines have sought to portray religion as a "site through which religious actors can be studied."[59] In the discipline of history we have seen a shift from reductionist or essentialist approaches; in this work religious practice, material sites, and emotions can be generative of modern, authentic forms of identity in South Asia. At the same time, there has remained a Marxist reluctance to acknowledge the Weberian observation that religion has the capacity to generate new identities rather than serve primarily as an epiphenomenon. Sumit Sarkar wrote in 1997 of his suspicions that the turn away from Marxist thought had seen religion go from something that appeared in history as "interacting with class, gender, power structures, etc." to being a determining feature, something that "communities are defined *by*."

> A two-fold displacement has occurred: from colonial domination to Western cultural conquest; and from subaltern, usually peasant consciousness (often marked by the centrality of religion, but not detached from questions of class, exploitation, and power) to affirmations of community consciousness in effect *defined* by religion and abstracted from indigenous power relations (other than those embodied in that alleged quintessence of post-Enlightenment rationality, the bureaucratic nation-state).[60]

Acknowledging that religion can be generative of new identities in a Weberian sense does not require an abstraction of that social context from relations of power. This book recounts the formation of a community consciousness defined at least partially by religion while avoiding the temptation to abstract religion from "indigenous power relations."

This book contributes to this rehabilitation of the conceptual category of religion in the historiography of South Asia, and relates that category to an enhanced understanding of the public in South Asia. Human geographers such as Catherine Brace and her colleagues argue that we must acknowledge the possibility of the central role of religious practices in the "constitution and reconstitution of society."[61] On the other hand, Margrit Pernau has cautioned us, rightly in the case of South Asia, that we must not presume the importance of religion as a hegemonic conceptual category.[62] This book tacks between these two approaches; it certainly does not argue for Islam's hegemonic importance in all cases for Muslims in South Asia. However, the evidence in *Madīnah* and the publication's popularity suggests that in the first half of the twentieth century Islam was a conceptual category of significance for many Muslims, who saw a vital connection between Islam and Urdu. In taking this approach I also build on the work of Benedict Anderson, who observed the impact of the decline of sacral languages like Latin and Sanskrit but left open the question of how the rise of vernaculars like English, Hindi, and Urdu could be tied to the rise of imagined communities in which religion was an important feature. Studying the early twentieth-century Urdu public as one inflected by Islam illustrates one such complex and fascinating case.

Public, Pious or Not

In 1993 Chatterjee pointed out the limitations of the Habermasian definition of the public, dependent as it was on the preexistence of "individual" and "audience-oriented" subjectivities in the eighteenth-century European context.[63] Since then, while studies of "the public" in South Asia have worked toward provincializing that category, these approaches have circulated alongside historiography that reinforced the dichotomy between material and spiritual domains.[64] Das-Chaudhuri reaffirmed the approach of Chatterjee in 2007 when he wrote, in response to Anderson's assertion of the significance of modular forms of nationalism in Bengal, that what saved the region's imagination from "forever [remaining] colonized" was that Bengal had a "spiritual inner domain, which unlike the material outer domain was not monopolized by or annexed to the colonizing West."[65] Responding to work that has observed lack of clarity over the applicability of the term "public" in South Asia, as well as Scott and Ingram's renewed call to write "South Asian genealogies" of the public, this book offers both an important data point and a methodological model: a granular account of a local newspaper's contributions to an Urdu public that informed Muslim political identity.[66]

The term "public sphere" here refers to a North Indian arena, with substantial interlocutors across the subcontinent and the world, where constituents simultaneously built consensus about the common good and negotiated the boundaries of what constituted "common" space. The construction of this space required an agreement on a "common language of debate."[67] In this case, that common language was not just Urdu but also an attitude to Urdu that saw it as intertwined with Islam. Also important was the quality of plasticity, or an expectation that matters of public concern would be determined via "discursive contestation."[68] This approach is typological rather than genealogical.[69] This means that there is no presumption that the admittedly limited public of intellectuals or "subaltern elite" emerged only alongside European-inflected print capital. However, it is certainly true that the public composed of *akhbārāt* and correspondence networks took on a new form in the nineteenth century, inflected by print capitalism and colonial-era technologies of communication. The self-conscious concept of the "public" as a conceptual category was also crystallized in the late nineteenth and early twentieth century, formed both in opposition to and in cooperation with the colonial state, the Hindi public sphere, and informal social and political institutions.[70] A necessary component for public space is the existence of "specific means for transmitting information and influencing those who receive it"[71] as well as a common language used to communicate that information.

This contribution can also be read in light of Chatterjee's attempt to record "the numerous fragmented resistances to that normalizing project" of nationalism.[72] An important vector of resistance was an orientation of a public. To some extent, the story of *Madīnah* provides a front-row seat to the formation of an imagined community. However, this book is also an account of a fragmented resistance to nationalism: a newspaper published from a *qasbah* that both contributed to nationalism and at the same time resisted normalizing, even Russifying (to use a term from Benedict Anderson) efforts to build national political parties out of the Indian National Congress and the Muslim League. If we pay attention to the orientation of a public in time and space, it becomes easier to understand the ways that this public, this community, was a contributor to but also opposed to normalizing practices that elided the historic particularity of small urban spaces. It is when we pay attention to the relationship between public, space, and time that we grow more attuned to "the twists and turns, the suppressed possibilities, the contradictions still unresolved" in the formation of publics, communities, and nations.[73]

I begin the book by immersing the reader in the history of *Madīnah*, an influential and understudied Urdu newspaper, through analysis of new archival material. The first chapter includes a description of the proprietor, editors, and circulation of this previously overlooked publication through analysis of a wide range of Urdu- and English-language archives across three continents, including rare copies of *Madīnah* itself. The significance of *Madīnah* is shown to be positioned at the crossroads of the cultural prestige of *qasbah* intellectual networks and the increasingly marginal importance of the *qasbah* in colonial India.

The second chapter focuses on the impact of penetration of new technologies on the formation of the distinctive timescape of *Madinah*. It argues that Bijnor *qasbah* hosted alternate geographies and temporalities that allowed it to construct itself as a site of authentic protest to national trends in early twentieth-century South Asia. The alterity of this *qasbah* timescape was tied to the early adoption of the telegraph and the late adoption of the railway. This timescape assisted Bijnor *qasbah* in establishing a claim to a future alternative to the national in South Asia.

The third chapter pays attention to the materiality of the newspaper and its production. Visual analysis of *Madīnah* newspaper and its calligraphy, along with archival research recounting the process of newspaper production in a *qasbah*, will show that its written text, even if explicitly "secular" in content, could simultaneously be religious in form. This religious quality derived from the newspaper's visual elements, its visual and discursive association with holy spaces, and its calligraphy.

In the fourth chapter, I turn from the material production of the paper to its discursive content. The subordinated elites participating in the Urdu newspaper conversation became aware of the increasingly precarious balance of power in Europe in the early twentieth century; evidence from *Madīnah* demonstrates how the Muslims contributing to its pages used discussion of Europe to hash out the boundaries of an Urdu public with global proportions. Through its coverage of the European martial and political landscape *Madīnah* focused attention on Islam and arbitrated debates on the lines between the religious public and the political public. *Madīnah* was a prominent public forum that placed the voices of *'ulamā* alongside representatives of explicitly political aims. Publications like *Madīnah* also provided opportunities to literate *ashrāf* in *qasbah*s who were later inclined to pursue local political power, promoting political mobility for a generation of *ashrāf* involved in journalism.

The fifth chapter unpacks the paper's attitude to Europe, tracing four examples of *Madīnah*'s engagement with local issues from the 1910s until the 1930s, demonstrating that the paper used its discursive position to present alternatives to national narratives. This attempt met with varying levels of success. Ultimately, the alterity of the *qasbah* enabled the paper to make a key transition: from promoting League–Congress cooperation to justifying cooperation with Hindus in Islamic terms. The case study of the 1937 Bijnor by-elections shows how conversations in Bijnor *qasbah* both exposed fault lines in Muslim identity and instituted a separation from the national matrix of Congress–Muslim League alignment.

What emerges in this book is a close view of the fabric of daily life and experience of Muslims engaging through Urdu journalism in the project of renovating a modern, Urdu public. *Madīnah* newspaper and press was characterized by a commitment to Urdu and the reformation of a public in the modern age of lithographic journalism, safe within the *qasbah* whose walls stretched to encompass the world in a new way. Chapter 1 begins with an introduction to the grand project of *Madīnah*, its proprietor Maulānā Majīd Ḥasan, and his star-studded stable of editors.

Notes

1. The English translation is "friend of the country, life of the nation." The Urdu transliteration is: "*mulk kā rafīq, qaum kā* (*sic*) *jāṉ*." Majīd Ḥasan, Title Page, *Madīnah*, May 1, 1912, 1.

2. For further exemplary discussions of this attraction, see M. Raisur Rahman, *Locale, Everyday Islam, and Modernity* (Delhi: Oxford University Press, 2015), 9–11; Gyanendra Pandey, "'Encounters and Calamities': The History of a North Indian Qasba in the Nineteenth Century," in *Selected Subaltern Studies*, ed. Ranajit Guha, and Gayatri Chakravorty Spivak (Oxford: Oxford University Press, 1988); Mushirul Hasan, "Qasbas: A Brief in Propinquity," *A Leaf Turns Yellow: The Sufis of Awadh*, ed. Muzaffar Ali (New Delhi: Rumi Foundation / Bloomsbury Publishing India, 2013), 110; Mushirul Hasan, "The Qasbah Culture—I," *The Hindu*, July 22, 2002.
3. This number is based on discussion by M. Raisur Rahman and C. A. Bayly. M. Raisur Rahman, *Locale, Everyday Islam, and Modernity* (New Delhi: Oxford University Press, 2015), 10; C. A. Bayly, *Rulers, Townsmen and Bazaars: North Indian Society In the Age of British Expansion, 1770–1870*, 3rd ed. (New Delhi: Oxford University Press, 2012), 111. Bayly defines a *qasbah* as any urban center with more than three thousand people in the late eighteenth and nineteenth centuries. British colonial-era gazetteers echo awareness of their bureaucratic significance. E.g., *Gazetteer of the Province of Oudh*, vol. 11 (Lucknow: Oudh Government Press, 1877–1878), 312.
4. M. Raisur Rahman, *Locale, Everyday Islam, and Modernity* (Delhi: Oxford University Press, 2015); Mushirul Hasan, *From Pluralism to Separatism* (Oxford: Oxford University Press, 2007).
5. C. A. Bayly, *Rulers, Townsmen and Bazaars: North Indian Society in the Age of British Expansion, 1770–1870*, 3rd ed. (New Delhi: Oxford University Press, 2012), 190.
6. E.g., Munshī Ehteshām 'Alī (Kakori); Syed Nabiullah (Kara); Ḥasrat Mohānī (Mohan); Rafī Aḥmed Kidwaī (Masauli); 'Abdur Raḥmān Bijnorī (Bijnor); Dr. Mukhtar Aḥmad Anṣārī (Yusufpur); 'Abdul 'Azīz Anṣārī (Bara Banki); Maulvī Syed Iltifat Rasūl (Jalalpur); Ḥusain Aḥmad Madanī (Deoband). Names found in Francis Robinson, *Separatism among Indian Muslims: The Politics of the United Provinces' Muslims 1860–1923* (Cambridge: Cambridge University Press, 2007), 365–415.
7. A group of towns in India constituting an administrative subdivision.
8. In the early twentieth century, the main crops were rice, wheat, barley, bajra, and gram.
9. Francis Robinson, "Municipal Government and Muslim Separatism in the United Provinces, 1883 to 1916," *Modern Asian Studies* 7 (1973): 407, 409–413.
10. Justin Jones, "The Local Experiences of Reformist Islam in a 'Muslim' Town in Colonial India: The Case of Amroha," *Modern Asian Studies* 43, no. 4 (2009): 871–908; Mushirul Hasan, *From Pluralism to Separatism: Qasbahs in Colonial Awadh* (New Delhi: Oxford University Press, 2004); M. Raisur Rahman, "Qasbah: Network, Everyday Islam, and Modernity in Colonial India," PhD diss., University of Texas at Austin, 1–30; Parvez 'Ādil, "Madīnah Akhbār," PhD thesis, University of Najibabad, 2013.
11. M. Raisur Rahman, *Locale, Everyday Islam, and Modernity* (New Delhi: Oxford University Press, 2015), 27, 52.
12. C. A. Bayly, *Rulers, Townsmen and Bazaars: North Indian Society in the Age of British Expansion, 1770–1870*, 3rd ed. (New Delhi: Oxford University Press, 2012). Also see Mushirul Hasan, "The Qasbah Culture," *The Hindu*, July 22, 2002. See M. Raisur Rahman, *Locale, Everyday Islam, and Modernity* (Delhi: Oxford University Press, 2015), 7, 11.

13. Nile Green, *Bombay Islam: The Religious Economy of the West Indian Ocean* (Cambridge: Cambridge University Press, 2011).
14. Munis D. Faruqui, "At Empire's End: The Nizam, Hyderabad and Eighteenth-Century India," *Modern Asian Studies* 43, no. 1 (2009): 5–43.
15. Stephen P. Blake, *Shahjahanabad: The Sovereign City in Mughal India, 1639–1739* (Cambridge: Cambridge University Press, 2010).
16. Emperor Aurangzeb had attempted to impose a *qasbah* "cultural style" on Banaras by razing and rebuilding the city and renaming it Muhammadabad, all changes that failed to take root. Sandria B. Freitag, *Culture and Power in Banaras: Community, Performance, and Environment, 1800–1980* (Berkeley: University of California Press, 1992), 3.
17. J. Barton Scott and Brannon Ingram, "What Is a Public? Notes from South Asia," *South Asia: Journal of South Asian Studies* 38, no. 3 (2015): 360.
18. Talal Asad, "The Idea of an Anthropology of Islam," Presentation at the Center for Contemporary Arab Studies, Georgetown University, Washington, DC, 1986; Pnina Werbner, *Pilgrims of Love: The Anthropology of a Global Sufi Cult* (London: Hurst, 2003); Nancy K. Florida, *Writing the Past, Inscribing the Future: Exile and Prophecy in an Historical Text of Nineteenth-Century Java* (Durham: Duke University Press, 1995); Zareena A. Grewal, "Imagined Cartographies: Crisis, Displacement, and Islam in America," PhD diss., University of Michigan, 2006; Engseng Ho, *The Graves of Tarim: Geneaology and Mobility across the Indian Ocean* (Berkeley: University of California Press, 2006); Mikaela Rogozen-Soltar, "Managing Muslim Visibility: Conversion, Immigration, and Spanish Imaginaries of Islam," *American Anthropologist* 114, no. 4 (December 2012): 611–623; Roschanack Shaery-Eisenlohr, "Territorializing Piety: Genealogy, Transnationalim, and Shi'ite Politics in Modern Lebanon," *Comparative Studies in Society and History.* 51, no. 3 (July 1, 2009), cited in Daniel Andrew Birchok, "Sojourning on Mecca's Verandah: Place, Temporality and Islam in an Indonesian Province," PhD diss., University of Michigan, 2013, 4.
19. Cited in Daniel Andrew Birchok, "Sojourning on Mecca's Verandah: Place, Temporality, and Islam in an Indonesian Province," PhD diss., University of Michigan, 2013, 4.
20. Metcalf writes that although *adab* is characterized by what transmits from above, or a "superregional, cosmopolitan culture," it is also shaped by local and regional traditions that equate to "one's past" (Barbara Metcalf, "Introduction," in *Moral Conduct and Authority: The Place of Adab in South Asian Islam*, ed. Barbara Metcalf [Berkeley: University of California Press, 1984], 15). Some work on time and Islam focuses on phenomenology of time; see, e.g., Anna-Teresa Tymieniecka, *Timing and Temporality in Islamic Philosophy and Phenomenology of Life* (Dordrecht: Springer, 2007).
21. Gellner and Eaton both write that lineages of holy men embodied tradition rather than being interpreters or transmitters of it. Each holy man offers a direct access to authority connected to the time of the Prophet and the creation of the Qur'an. Or we might say that the holy men, while being of a specific time, are timeless. See Ernest

Gellner, *Saints of the Atlas* (Chicago: University of Chicago Press, 1969); Richard Eaton, "The Political and Religious Authority of the Shrine of Baba Farid," in *Moral Conduct and Authority: The Place of Adab in South Asian Islam*, ed. Barbara Metcalf (Berkeley: University of California Press, 1984), 333–56.

22. Richard Eaton, "The Political and Religious Authority of the Shrine of Baba Farid," in *Moral Conduct and Authority: The Place of Adab in South Asian Islam*, ed. Barbara Metcalf (Berkeley: University of California Press, 1984), 333.
23. Faisal Devji, "Apologetic Modernity," *Modern Intellectual History* 4, no. 1 (2007): 61–76.
24. M. Raisur Rahman, *Locale, Everyday Islam, and Modernity* (Delhi: Oxford University Press, 2015), 13–18.
25. Partha Chatterjee, *The Nation and Its Fragments: Colonial and Postcolonial Histories* (Princeton: Princeton University Press 1993), 37.
26. Sumit Sarkar, *Writing Social History* (Delhi: Oxford University Press, 1997), 176, 182, 190.
27. Manu Goswami, *Producing India: From Colonial Economy to National Space* (Chicago: University of Chicago, 2004), 1–3.
28. Barbara Adam, "Of Timescapes, Futurescapes and Timeprints," lecture at Lüneburg University, June 17, 2008.
29. Faridah Zaman has demonstrated how we can look at approaches to the past in the context of contemporary public upheavals as ways of accessing productive visions for the future Islam. Zaman, "The Future of Islam, 1672–1924," *Modern Intellectual History* 5, no. 1 (2008): 1–31.
30. Barbara Adam, "Of Timescapes, Futurescapes and Timeprints," lecture at Lüneburg University, June 17, 2008.
31. See Laura Bear, "Doubt, Conflict, Mediation: The Anthropology of Modern Time," *Journal of the Royal Anthropological Institute* 20, no. S1 (2014): 3–30.
32. Margrit Pernau, *Ashraf into Middle Classes: Muslims in Nineteenth-Century Delhi* (Oxford: Oxford University Press, 2013), 154. Sandip Hazareesingh's work demonstrates how early twentieth-century Bombay became "an authorized space for contesting and negotiating the colonial present and possibly political futures of South Asia." It also points out the intimate connection between the development of the newspaper and the new language of "civic rights" centered on the category of urban life. See Sandip Hazareesingh, "Colonial Modernism and the Flawed Paradigms of Urban Renewal: Uneven Development in Bombay, 1900–24," *Urban History* 28, no. 2 (2001): 235–55, quoted in Eric Lewis Beverley, "Colonial Urbanism and South Asian Cities," *Social History* 36, no. 4 (2011): 482–97; see also Sandip Hazareesingh, *The Colonial City and the Challenge of Modernity: Urban Hegemonies and Civic Contestations in Bombay City, 1905–1925 (Delhi: Orient Black Swan, 2007).*
33. Yi-Fu Tuan, *Space and Place: The Perspective of Experience* (Minneapolis: University of Minnesota Press, 1977), 6, cited in Razak Khan, "The Social Production of Space and Emotions in South Asia," *Journal of the Economic and Social History of the Orient* 58, no. 5 (2015): 617.

34. Elizabeth Olsen, Peter Hopkins, and Lily Kong, "Introduction—Religion and Place," in *Religion and Place: Landscape, Politics and Piety*, ed. Peter Hopkins, Lily Kong, and Elizabeth Olson (New York: Springer, 2013), 5. Any discussion of space takes its cue from Henri Lefebvre, who argued that social space is socially produced. Henri Lefebvre, *Production of Space* (Hoboken, NJ: Wiley-Blackwell, 1992), 33, cited in Razak Khan, "The Social Production of Space and Emotions in South Asia," *Journal of the Economic and Social History of the Orient* 58, no. 5 (2015): 617.
35. Marcia Hermansen, "Imagining Space and Citing Collective Memory in South Asian Muslim Biographical Literature (Tazkirah)," *Studies in Contemporary Islam* 4, no. 2 (2002): 1–21; Razak Khan, "The Social Production of Space and Emotions in South Asia," *Journal of the Economic and Social History of the Orient* 58, no. 5 (2015): 611–33. Sumathi Ramaswamy unpacks the intersection of visual images of Mother India and the spatialization of the nation in *Goddess and the Nation: Mapping Mother India* (Durham: Duke University Press, 2010).
36. Benedict Anderson, *Imagined Communities: Reflections on the Origin and Spread of Nationalism*, rev. ed. (London: Verso, 1991), 55–60; Jürgen Habermas, *The Structural Transformation of the Public Sphere: An Inquiry into a Category of Bourgeois Society* (Cambridge: Polity, 1989), 26–30.
37. David Lelyveld has provided a history of the development of Urdu presses from the earliest papers, one of which had only thirty-nine readers when it closed, to the success of "print capitalism" in the early twentieth century. David Lelyveld, "Sir Sayyid's Public Sphere: Urdu Print and Oratory in Nineteenth Century India," *Cracow Indological Studies* 11, no. 11 (2009): 237–67.
38. Sir Syed's literary world, linked closely to communication channels among the British government, was characterized by an unusual departure from lithographic print and adoption of type, a shift from ornate to simple formats, and a focus from general issues to those specific to the Aligarh College. See David Lelyveld, "Sir Sayyid's Public Sphere: Urdu Print and Oratory in Nineteenth Century India," *Cracow Indological Studies* 11, no. 11 (2009): 237–67.
39. Seema Alavi, "Unani Medicine in the Nineteenth-Century Public Sphere: Urdu Texts and the Oudh Akhbar," *Indian Economic and Social History Review* 42 (March 2005): 118–19.
40. While Guy Attewell demonstrates that the colonial intervention coded Unani Tibb as a Muslim area of medicine, Seema Alavi emphasizes the internal center of gravity of these debates. Arnav Bhattacharya demonstrates the simultaneous impact of secular, rational medical discourse and Unani Tibb in work on sexuality in Bengali. On the other hand, Alavi shows that in the debate over medical licensing in *Āwadh akhbār*, the use of traditional medicine was justified on the grounds of the *mulk*, or nation, rather than religion. Seema Alavi, "Unani Medicine in the Nineteenth-Century Public Sphere: Urdu Texts and the Oudh Akhbar," *Indian Economic and Social History Review* 42 (March 2005): 118–19; Guy Attewell, *Refiguring Unani Plural Healing in Late Colonial India* (New Delhi: Orient Longman, 2005), 4; Abul Hasanat, *Sachitra Jouno Bigyan* [Illustrated Sexual Science], vols. 1 and 2 (Kolkata: Mullick Brothers, 1936); Arnav Bhattacharya,

"Sexual Science and Unani Medicine: Exploring Islam, Gender and Sexuality in Abul Hasanat's *Sachitra Jouno Bigyan* [Illustrated Sexual Science]," unpublished paper, 2018.

41. Margrit Pernau, "The Delhi Urdu Akhbar: Between Persian Akhbārāt and English Newspapers," *Annual of Urdu Studies* 18, no. 1 (2003): 105–31; Seema Alavi, "Unani Medicine in the Nineteenth-Century Public Sphere: Urdu Texts and the Oudh Akhbar," *Indian Economic and Social History Review* 42 (March 2005): 101–29; Francis Robinson. "Technology and Religious Change: Islam and the Impact of Print," *Modern Asian Studies* 27, no. 1 (February 1993): 229–51; C. Ryan Perkins's work has documented the emergence, in the early twentieth century, of "the printing press' new-found role as one of the main forums for public debate." As described by Perkins, the representative voices of the vigorous public debate over Brijnarayan Chakbast's (1882–1926) publication of a new edition of Pandat Daya Shankar Kaul Nasīm's (1811–1843) *Gulzār-i nasīm* were newspapers located in Lucknow, Gorakhpur, Kanpur, and Hyderabad. C. Ryan Perkins, "From the Meḥfil to the Printed Word: Public Debate and Discourse in Late Colonial India," *Indian Economic and Social History Review* 50, no. 1 (January–March 2013): 47–73.
42. M. Raisur Rahman, *Locale, Everyday Islam, and Modernity* (Delhi: Oxford University Press, 2015), 31–37.
43. M. Raisur Rahman, *Locale, Everyday Islam, and Modernity* (Delhi: Oxford University Press, 2015), 31–37.
44. Department of Criminal Intelligence, *Statement of Newspapers and Periodicals Published in the United Provinces during the Year 1912 [with Index]* (Simla: Government Central Branch Press, 1913), Uttar Pradesh State Archives.
45. Brannon Ingram, *Revival from Below: The Deoband Movement and Global Islam* (Berkeley: University of California Press, 2018); Brannon Ingram, J. Barton Scott, and SherAli K. Tareen, *Imagining the Public in Modern South Asia* (New York: Routledge, 2016); Brannon Ingram, "Crises of the Public in Muslim India: Critiquing 'Custom' at Aligarh and Deoband," *Journal of South Asian Studies* 38, no. 3 (2015): 403–18; Brannon Ingram, "The Portable Madrasa: Print, Publics, and the Authority of the Deobandi 'Ulama'," *Modern Asian Studies* 48, no. 4 (2014): 845–71.
46. Francesca Orsini, *The Hindi Public Sphere* (Oxford: Oxford University Press, 2009).
47. This geographic space overlaps significantly with the "Hindi heartland" Orsini identifies. Francesca Orsini, *The Hindi Public Sphere* (Oxford: Oxford University Press, 2009), 6–12.
48. Francesca Orsini, *The Hindi Public Sphere, 1920–1940* (Oxford: Oxford University Press, 2009), 4–5.
49. Gail Minault, *The Khilafat Movement: Religious Symbolism and Political Mobilization in India* (New Delhi: Oxford University Press, 1982).
50. Margrit Pernau, "The Delhi Urdu Akhbar: Between Persian Akhbārāt and English Newspapers," *Annual of Urdu Studies* 18, no. 1 (2003): 105–31.
51. Barbara Metcalf, *Islamic Revival in British India: Deoband, 1860–1900* (Princeton: Princeton University Press, 1982).
52. Benedict Anderson, who described the rise of the nation as "the most universally legitimate value in the political life of our time," linked the rise of "nation-ness" to the existence of three trends: a decline in the belief that sacred texts have privileged

access to or exclusively embody truth, the decline of belief in a central monarch ruling by divine right, and the development of a sense of shared experience of time among a group of people separated geographically. He presents late-stage, anticolonial, nationalist movements as a form of productive "piracy" of colonial imaginings of the nation, as seen through the interaction of the quintessentially colonial institutions of the census, the map, and the museum. These colonial imaginings, in Anderson's formulation, were a manifestation of a "modular" form of nationalism developed already in Europe, and before that in the colonial Americas. The case studies, most convincing in the Southeast Asian context, have drawn critique for their lack of applicability to the South Asian context beneath the level of English-educated, English-speaking elites. Benedict Anderson, *Imagined Communities: Reflections on the Origin and Spread of Nationalism*, rev. ed. (London: Verso, 1991), 1–8, 21–36, 160–66, 167. For critiques, see Partha Chatterjee, *The Nation and Its Fragments: Colonial and Postcolonial Histories* (Princeton: Princeton University Press, 1993), 5.

53. J. Barton Scott and Brannon D. Ingram, "What Is a Public? Notes from South Asia," *South Asia: Journal of South Asian Studies* 38, no. 3 (2015): 360.

54. An example of this approach is the excellent work by A. Azfar Moin, *The Millennial Sovereign: Sacred Kingship and Sainthood in Islam* (New York: Columbia University Press, 2012), cited in J. Barton Scott and Brannon D. Ingram, "What Is a Public? Notes from South Asia," *South Asia: Journal of South Asian Studies* 38, no. 3 (2015): 360.

55. Significant in establishing this particular use of the terms "sacred" and "secular" was the work of the sociologist Emile Durkheim, who predicated his analysis of religion on his understanding of individuals as understood chiefly in relationship to social facts or groups. For Durkheim, the distinction between the terms "sacred" and "secular" referred to a range of processes by which meanings were constituted in religion. Where religion was "the soul of society," the term "sacred" referred to things set apart and that affirm the status of the social group. Durkheim's approach came under criticism for many reasons: its reduction of religion to a social practice, its exclusive emphasis on the exogenic aspects of religion, the lack of accounting for individual subjectivity, and most crucially the fact that the sacred and secular are of course, in many cases, blurred. Emile Durkheim, *The Elementary Forms of Religious Life*, trans. and with an introduction by Karen E. Fields (New York: The Free Press, 1995).

56. "The question of whether or not the workers had a conscious or doctrinal belief in gods and spirits was also wide of the mark; after all, gods are as real as ideology is—that is to say, they are embedded in practices." Dipesh Chakrabarty, *Provincializing Europe: Postcolonial Thought and Historical Difference* (Princeton: Princeton University Press, 2000), 78.

57. For an example of this approach, see Vidya Dehejia, *The Body Adorned: Sacred and Profane in Indian Art* (New York: Columbia University Press, 2009).

58. Jürgen Habermas, "Notes on a Post-Secular Society," signandsight.com, cited in Elizabeth Olsen, Peter Hopkins, and Lily Kong, "Introduction—Religion and Place—Landscape, Politics, and Piety," in *Religion and Place: Landscape, Politics, and Piety*, ed. Peter Hopkins, Lily Kong, and Elizabeth Olson (New York: Springer, 2013), 3.

59. Jeffrey Guhin, "Religion as Site Rather Than Religion as Category: On the Sociology of Religion's Export Problem," *Sociology of Religion* 75, no. 4 (2014): 579–93.
60. Sumit Sarkar, *Writing Social History* (New Delhi: Oxford University Press, 1997), 43.
61. Catherine Brace, Adrian R. Bailey, and David C. Harvey, "Religion, Place and Space: A Framework for Investigating Historical Geographies of Religious Identities and Communities," *Progress in Human Geography* 30, no. 1 (2006): 29.
62. Margrit Pernau, *Ashraf into Middle Classes: Muslims in Nineteenth-Century Delhi* (New Delhi: Oxford University Press, 2013), xiii.
63. Partha Chatterjee, *The Nation and Its Fragments: Colonial and Postcolonial Histories* (Princeton: Princeton University Press, 1993), 74.
64. Dipesh Chakrabarty discussed the potential risks in translation, namely the assumption of false equivalence of the term "public" across language and culture. See Dipesh Chakrabarty "Open Space/Public Place: Garbage, Modernity, and India," *South Asia: Journal of South Asian Studies* 14, no. 1 (June 1991): 15–31, quoted in J. Barton Scott and Brannon Ingram, "What Is a Public? Notes from South Asia," *South Asia: Journal of South Asian Studies* 38, no. 3 (2015): 358.
65. R. Das-Chaudhuri, "The Nationalist Imagination," in *A South Asian Nationalism Reader* (New Delhi: Worldview, 2007), 68–69, cited in Rohit K. Dasgupta, "Remembering Benedict Anderson and His Influence on South Asian Studies," *Theory, Culture and Society* 33, no. 7 (2016): 335.
66. Scott and Ingram's work is a recent and important contribution to a long-standing conversation established by Sandra Freitag in 1991, when she called scholars to unearth the "indigenous bases onto which Western European notions of the public' could have been grafted." Sandra Freitag, ed., "Aspects of 'the Public' in Colonial South Asia," special issue, *South Asia: Journal of South Asian Studies* 14, no. 1 (June 1991), quoted in J. Barton Scott and Brannon Ingram, "What Is a Public? Notes from South Asia," *South Asia: Journal of South Asian Studies* 38, no. 3 (2015): 359.
67. Francesca Orsini, "Introduction," in *The Hindi Public Sphere, 1920–1940: Language and Literature in the Age of Nationalism* (Oxford: Oxford University Press, 2002).
68. Nancy Fraser, "Rethinking the Public Sphere: A Contribution to the Critique of Actually Existing Democracy," *Social Text*, no. 25/26 (1990): 56–80. Quoted in Francesca Orsini, "Introduction," in *The Hindi Public Sphere, 1920–1940: Language and Literature in the Age of Nationalism* (New York: Oxford University Press, 2002), fn. 17.
69. J. Barton Scott and Brannon Ingram, "What Is a Public? Notes from South Asia," *South Asia: Journal of South Asian Studies* 38, no. 3 (2015): 357–70.
70. Francesca Orsini clarifies that the "public sphere" refers to a social arena consisting of spaces for debate common to many people, and featuring an evolving set of norms of comportment that reflect awareness of these spaces as public. For descriptions of the development of the Hindi public sphere in the early twentieth century, see Francesca Orsini, "Introduction," in *The Hindi Public Sphere, 1920–1940: Language and Literature in the Age of Nationalism* (New York: Oxford University Press, 2002), 4–5; Vasudha Dalmia, *The Nationalization of Hindu Traditions: Bhāratendu Hariśchandra and Nineteenth-Century Banaras* (Delhi: Oxford University Press, 1999). For a study

focusing on the role of Islam in the public sphere, see Dietrich Reetz, *Islam in the Public Sphere* (Delhi: Oxford University Press, 2006).

71. Jürgen Habermas, *The Structural Transformation of the Public Sphere: An Inquiry into a Category of Bourgeois Society* (Cambridge: Polity Press, 1992), 49.
72. "Now the task is to trace in their mutually conditioned historicities the specific forms that have appeared, on the one hand, in the domain defined by the hegemonic project of nationalist modernity, and on the other, in the numerous fragmented resistances to that normalizing project." Partha Chatterjee, *Nationalist Thought and the Colonial World: A Derivative Discourse* (Minneapolis: University of Minnesota Press, 1993), 13.
73. Partha Chatterjee, *Nationalist Thought and the Colonial World: A Derivative Discourse* (Minneapolis: University of Minnesota Press, 1993), 22.

1
Putting the Public House of *Madīnah* on the Muslim Map

In Urdu histories of journalism's key role in the independence movement, *Madīnah* already holds a prominent place.[1] At a time when reading and discussing newspapers were already key components of social life, the proprietor of *Madīnah* targeted a popular audience with a stable of star editors. The initial readers of *Madīnah* were Muslim gentry, or *ashrāf*, thinly spread across *qasbah*s and cities in North India and the Punjab. In a time and place with a literacy rate of less than 5 percent, the newspaper gained increasing popular appeal and became widely known, for a strong oral tradition circulated newspapers among those who could not read. News also spread rapidly by word of mouth, sometimes haphazardly. Men often gathered outside of mosques in the evening to discuss the day's news.[2] Workers at railway stations or eateries picked up stories and passed them on. In Sa'ādat Ḥasan Manṭo's short story "*Nayā qānūn*,"[3] a *ṭāngā*[4] driver transmits distorted versions of current events picked up from his paper-reading customers.[5] Women heard conversations about national and international issues discussed at home and on the streets. Thus, the group of people influenced by newspapers included people both literate and nonliterate in the Urdu script, and the recorded number of subscribers at any time represents but a fraction of the newspaper's audience.

The newspaper was one space in a public sphere characterized by public gatherings, associations, and spaces of transportation as well as other types of printed texts. The *ashrāf* in Bijnor, like those in other *qasbah*s across Awadh and Rohilkhand, would have conducted regular *mushā'arah*s, or poetry recitations.[6] During these readings connoisseur audiences, composed of both Muslims and Hindus, assembled to recite original poetry and classic works in an extemporaneous style. Poetry was recited, not silently read. Shouts of praise echoed around successful performances. This interactive mode of sharing poetry found a correspondent in the tea stalls and sitting rooms in North India, where readers gathered to share the day's news. The popular gathering place to read newspapers varied. In Aminabad, Lucknow, locals sat at the local bookstore Danish Mahal or gathered in hotels; in Bihar people flocked to *chāi-khānā*s (tea stalls); in Bijnor, local houses provided the best environment for conversation. At the *chāi-khānā*s the literate read aloud newspapers to other patrons in lively gatherings called

Print and the Urdu Public. Megan Eaton Robb, Oxford University Press (2021). © Oxford University Press.
DOI: 10.1093/oso/9780190089375.001.0001

aḍḍā bāzī.[7] Children in Patna received free tea for reading news to older patrons of the local *chāi-k͟hānās.*[8] In this way the newspaper overlapped with other significant institutions and physical spaces in South Asia.

Madīnah earned a reputation as a "popular" publication—it was widely read in Lucknow and Lahore and Kabul, and in Lucknow at least its content helped to shape readers' political education.[9] Contributing authors came from *qasbahs* scattered across the United Provinces, including: Amroha, Deoband, Basti, Etawah, Shairkoṭ, and Bacchraon. Furqān Aḥmad Ṣiddiqī, historian of Bijnor, realized the international significance of the ubiquitous publication of his childhood once he grew older:

> Afterward I realized that, aside from India, *Madīnah* circulated in every corner of Afghanistan, Iran, Burma, Sri Lanka, Malaya, and South Africa. Although Maulānā Azad's *al-Hilāl* and *al-Bilāg͟h* were the beloved papers of a special class, *Madīnah* was the most popular paper of the common people.
>
> *ba'd mein̲ ma'lūm hū'a kih Madīnah Hindūstān ke 'alāvah Afg͟hānistān, Īrān, Burmā, Srī Lankā, Malāyā, aur Janūbī Afrīqah ke kone mein̲ jātā thā. Maulānā Āzād ke al-Hilāl aur al-Bilāg͟h agar mak͟hṣūṣ tabqa ke maḥbūb ak͟hbār the to Madīnah 'avām kā maqbūltarīn ak͟hbār tha.*[10]

While Maulānā Azad's publications were the pinnacle of a publishing genre that targeted a traditional *ashrāf* newspaper-reading public, *Madīnah* was a new type of paper that tapped into the values of the gentry while also targeting a broad readership not limited to the traditional elite, nor even to the cosmopolitan urbanite. The annual subscription fee in 1912 was graduated, reflecting an awareness of social stratification and revealing a varied target readership that spanned *zamīndārs* (leasing landowners), *madrasahs* (Islamic educational institutions), and civil servants.[11]

To a lesser degree, *Madīnah* spoke to another significant audience: British officials who held sway over government policies and other crucial resources. The editors of *Madīnah* initially showed awareness of British surveillance through explicit deference to British officials; for instance, Majīd Ḥasan cited the *ijāzat* (permission) of the Magistrate and Collector of Bijnor, G. B. Lambert, in its inaugural issue.[12] This attentiveness to British intelligence materialized more obliquely in a few ways: self-censorship, editorials protesting government censorship of other Urdu newspapers, and bold articles rebelling against the censors.

Origins and Vision

The proprietor of *Madīnah*, Majīd Ḥasan, was born in Bijnor in 1883. His father taught him Arabic using the Qur'an and Persian through Sa'adi's *Gulistān* and

Bustān, as well as the *Sikandarnāmah*.[13] He left Bijnor to begin his training—by some accounts to train as a *qāẓī*, or judge, in Lahore, and by other accounts to train as an apprentice publisher. The increasing frailty of his *phūphā*, or uncle, Aḥmad Ḥasan, required him to abandon his training to return to Bijnor to assist with the running of the family newspaper, *Ṣaḥīfa*.[14] Following the death of Aḥmad Ḥasan, Majīd Ḥasan stayed in Bijnor, caring for his aunt's children and continuing to run the newspaper. *Ṣaḥīfa*'s modest following had begun to wane already when Majīd Ḥasan married Muḥtarmā Kanīz Fāṯimah, a daughter of a wealthy family, around 1910.[15] At that point he dreamt of a bright moon shining in the sky. From behind the first moon, another moon appeared and drifted away from it, becoming brighter, larger, and more impressive than the first. Majīd Ḥasan interpreted this dream as a message to start his own paper, which he decided to call *Madīnah*.

The earliest documentation of the dream narrative comes in the publication of the silver jubilee edition of *Madīnah* in 1939. It represents not personal idiosyncrasy but an extensive tradition of dream interpretation. The first editor of *Madīnah*, Maulvī Syed Nūr ul-Ḥasan Ẕahīn Karatpūrī, a renowned journalist, was also famously a dream interpreter. The tradition considers some dreams very straightforward, requiring little interpretation, while others require substantial interpretation. Among those dreams that require interpretation, we find four types, determined by the number of people who are affected by the dream: *k͟hāṣṣah*, dreams that concern only the dreamer; *mushtarikah* ("common"), dreams that relate to the dreamer and one other person; *ru'yā manṣubah ila majami' min al-nās*, dreams that relate to a group or groups; and *'ālamīyyah* (literally "universality"), dreams that relate to all people—this final category of dream is one in which we would expect to see celestial symbols such as the moon, sun, and stars[16] and is the category in which Majīd Ḥasan's dream would have fallen.[17] An example of this type of dream is that of Joseph in which the moon, sun, and planets bowed to him, predicting his rule over nations (Qur'an 12:4). Another example in the Ottoman context is the dream of 'O̱smān G͟hāzī, the man who would become the namesake of the House of 'O̱smān; in this dream 'O̱smān G͟hāzī saw a moon rise from the sheikh Edebali, move toward him, and enter into his own chest. At the moment it entered him, a tree sprouted from his navel and cast a shadow all over the earth. This image symbolized the future spiritual and temporal authority of the House of 'O̱smān or the Ottoman Dynasty. The significance of the moon's appearance in the dream would have indicated that the endeavor the dream presaged would have an impact on all Muslims.

It is not clear who exactly interpreted Majīd Ḥasan's dream; the account suggests that he interpreted it himself, although his reading may later have been reaffirmed by Karatpūrī, the first editor of *Madīnah* mentioned earlier. A dream could carry both philosophical and motivational import for specific action. In the case of Maulānā Majīd Ḥasan, it motivated him to take the risk of founding his newspaper; its prophetic interpretation may have justified the unusual move to his family.

The name of the newspaper, *Madīnah*, simply means "city" in Arabic; this is an ironic choice considering that the paper was based in a *qasbah* with a population of only twenty thousand, hardly a city. The choice may reflect something of the paper's ambitions: to provide a link with or even conjure that holy city of Islam through its visual and material presence. On the other hand, an orthodox vision or dream experience was often associated with a stay in a holy city. By choosing the name *Madīnah*, Majīd Ḥasan was implying that the reading of the newspaper took readers on a spiritual journey without the necessity of terrestrial travel.

Ibn ʿArabī (1165–1240 CE), a Muslim philosopher, scholar, and poet who came to be acknowledged as one of the most important Sufi teachers, linked his most important visionary experiences to great written works.[18] While in significance Maulānā Majīd Ḥasan was far from an Ibn ʿArabī figure, his dream of the two moons is also linked to a body of written work that followed. Majīd Ḥasan did not claim, as Ibn ʿArabī did about his *Futūḥāt al-makkīyya,* that the resulting text was equivalent to divine dictation; however, through the interpretation of the dream the founding of the newspaper was associated with divine will. This was particularly important to establish, considering Majīd Ḥasan ultimately founded a newspaper that would eventually outshine and lead to the closing of the existing family newspaper, *Ṣaḥīfa*. While *Madīnah* and *Ṣaḥīfa* both remained relatively well-known papers in North India for a time,[19] judging from departures in tone and political approach in the later editions, it seems likely that Ḥasan passed the reins of *Ṣaḥīfa* to other editors in the mid-1910s before that paper shut down completely.

The privilege of addressing the *qaum*[20] was conferred by the community itself, rather than by any formal qualification that Majīd Ḥasan had achieved.[21] He did at first appear quite impoverished in terms of credentials. He was not a "true" Maulvī, in the sense of a person educated formally; he eventually earned the honorific of "Maulvī" through his achievements as a newspaper editor. Ḥasan's level of education was not impressive by early twentieth-century standards, and although he had the family publishing business, he had few connections and little wealth. The claim that he had a popular mandate is appealing, but it would be more accurate to say that Majīd Ḥasan built his publishing business as an entrepreneur, motivated by considerable ambition (Figure 1.1).

Perhaps convinced by the compelling vision of her husband's dream, Muḥtarmā Kanīz Fāṯimah offered her wedding jewelry to assist her husband Majīd Ḥasan in starting *Madīnah*. Even including that money, the capital used to start *Madīnah* was nominal when compared to resources marshaled by other

Figure 1.1 Majīd Ḥasan. Undated photo, family archives.

ashrāf-run newspapers in large cities.[22] Majīd Ḥasan described his condition when starting *Madīnah* as a desperate one: "Aside from sincerity, service, and trust in God, I had no other wealth."[23] Majīd Ḥasan made his declaration registering his newspaper for publication on July 10, 1912.[24] The dream of two moons proved prophetic; *Madīnah* eclipsed *Ṣaḥīfa* to become a prominent voice for Muslims and eventually a particular perspective of the nationalist cause associated with the Jam'īat 'Ulamā. Majīd Ḥasan continued to work assiduously for the progress of *Madīnah* until his death in 1966.[25] While *Madīnah* was the most famous publication of Madīnah Press (or, as it was sometimes called, Madīnah Book Agency), the press also published many books, several of which were advertised in the paper.[26]

Claiming Afghani heritage as a Shaikh, Majīd Ḥasan was a picture of pious health. Taking care to walk to the local mosque five times a day, rain or shine, he demonstrated self-conscious perfection in his habits and took great care with his appearance. He wore a crisp white kurta each day; he visited the barber twice weekly to maintain his trim beard and to cut his nails.[27] Majīd Ḥasan set a high bar for moral conduct. He was known to observe the correct method of ablution even in the dead of winter. Preferring simple food, he frowned on indulgence even among his children. In fulfilling his duties to the poor he was equally conscientious, living by the motto "if there be even a little money in your pocket, do not deny the questioner."[28] His fastidiousness in appearance and conduct translated to his work on *Madīnah*.

Majīd Ḥasan was involved in every aspect of the newspaper's production: he wrote articles, proofread contributions, and edited the calligraphy on the lithographic stone used for printing. Having some skill in calligraphy, he took a hand directly to the master copy of the paper etched onto the lithographic stone.[29] The newspaper was edited in Majīd Ḥasan's home compound, with editors living on site during their work. The paper was printed and prepared for delivery in the home's courtyard (Figure 1.2). In other words, Majīd Ḥasan's involvement in *Madīnah* was total.

Figure 1.2 The courtyard that formed the nucleus of Madīnah Press in Bijnor, Uttar Pradesh. Photo by author, July 2018.

Muḥtarmā Kanīz Fāṯimah, Majīd Ḥasan's first wife (Figure 1.3), proved an intelligent and capable assistant to newspaper production, despite the fact that she could not read.[30] Matching her husband's piety, she maintained strict purdah while assisting in the paper's daily management.[31] A woman renowned for her altruism, Muḥtarmā Kanīz Fāṯimah assisted in arranging marriages of poor girls in her neighborhood calling to mind the paragon Asg͟harī in Nazīr Aḥmed's *Mirāt-ul ʿUrūs* (The Bride's Mirror).[32] Her deference toward her husband and children was legendary.[33] After her union with Majīd Ḥasan produced four daughters, she arranged her husband's second marriage to a daughter of a man named Tawhīd Ḥassan in order to ensure a male heir. Majīd Ḥasan's second wife had two sons, including Syed Ak͟htar, who inherited Madīnah Press. Muḥtarmā Kanīz Fāṯimah's involvement in the newspaper and the links made between her work and the agenda of *Madīnah* newspaper highlight the sense that maintaining the newspaper was more than simply a family business; it was a legacy and a duty.

Figure 1.3 Muḥtarmā Kanīz Fāṯimah, at home. Undated photo, private archive.

A Voice of the *Ashrāf*

Publications like *Madīnah* may have provided opportunities to literate *ashrāf* in *qasbahs* who were later inclined to pursue local political power, promoting political mobility for a generation of *ashrāf* involved in journalism. Journalism provided new opportunities for advancement among the unpropertied *ashrāf*. Texts such as Gerhard Herklots and Jafar Sharif's book *Qānūn-i Islām* [The Laws of Islam] made the distinction between *ashrāf*, or "noble" Muslims, and *ajlaf*, or "common" people. *Ashrāf* ancestry was divided into four categories, formally based on either geographic origin or links to the early leaders of Islam: Syeds (descended from the Prophet), Shaikhs (descended from the first three Caliphs), Mughals (descended from immigrants from Persia or Central Asia), and Pathans (claiming heritage in Afghanistan). Plenty of genealogies were falsified in order to claim membership in the *ashrāf*, a porous social category.[34] Interestingly, the proprietor of *Madīnah* was listed as a Shaikh in official colonial records, yet one of his contemporary biographers in India, Parvez 'Ādil, mentions he claimed Afghani heritage, which would have made him a Pathan. It is possible that the colonial records were incorrect. It is also possible that Majīd Ḥasan's family edited their heritage in order to claim membership among the local elite and thereby augment the newspaper's influence.

Mirzā Muḥammad Ḥasan Qatīl's 1811 history *Haft tamāsha* describes the social intrigues involved in claiming *ashrāf* identity in the early nineteenth century. According to Qatīl, qualification as *sharīf* could be obtained either through claims to noble birth or social status, expressed through influence or wealth. Hindus tended to emphasize birth status while Muslims tended to emphasize social status as the basis for marital unions.[35] Himself a Khattri[36] by birth, Qatīl converted to Islam at the age of seventeen before being enlisted to write this ethnography of local customs for a visiting ruler from Karbala. His text emphasizes the interdependence of Muslim and Hindu customs in the area. He also discusses the vulnerability of many claims to *ashrāf* status. The designations of Shaikh and Pathan could disguise a variety of origins, with genealogies often representing aspirational claims rather than fact. The designation of *ashrāf*, even if based on an adopted name and invented genealogy, remained a source of power, albeit one vulnerable to accusations of fraud. Qatīl was a contemporary and rival of Ghalib, who undermined his competition by constantly referring to him as "Diwali Singh, the Khattri from Faridabad."[37] The category of *ashrāf* in the early nineteenth century, rather than being a formal register with legal implications, was a flexible way of claiming status and prestige across the generations.[38] A century after Qatīl's book came out, *Madīnah* made a concerted effort to equate *ashrāf* identity with Islam, and in the process provided opportunities for its proprietor and editors to consolidate their elite status.

Editors and Their Influence

Madīnah's community of editors, subeditors, and proprietors illustrate the interconnected network of professionals working on newspapers across North India, with a shared commitment to confounding censorship laws. Editors of *Madīnah* were products of *qasbahs* and lived in Bijnor or nearby while employed by the publication. At least one assistant editor, Ḥamīd Ḥasan "Fakīr" Bijnorī (1903–1991), was a relative, having married Majīd Ḥasan's daughter in the 1910s before he became the editor of Madinah Press's children's magazine Ghunchah after 1922. Ḥamīd Ḥasan would later be listed as an assistant editor from 1930 to 1935 and even take over as editor for several months when the need arose in 1945.[39] When a new editor took over the work of *Madīnah* and was not already resident in Bijnor, he would move into the Ḥasan compound, which acted as the administrative office of the paper.[40] Several small apartments attached to the main verandah, so editors could live in comfort with their families, remaining accessible to the newspaper office while maintaining privacy. Maulānā Majīd Ḥasan's name, along with the name of the current chief editor, always appeared on the paper's title page. At any given time there could be up to three editors of the paper, with the chief editor being referred to as "*mudīr-i mas'ūl*."[41]

Although Majīd Ḥasan's proprietorship provided continuity for the newspaper, its different editors influenced the paper's tone and focus. The turnover between editors could be rapid when legal troubles emerged. For instance, in 1924, when the editor Qāẓī Badrul Ḥasan Jalālī (1891–1956) was prosecuted by the British Raj for an article, he resigned his editorship, but he stepped back into his position once the dust of government scrutiny had settled.[42] If Majīd Ḥasan attracted too much scrutiny from government surveillance, he could retreat from view behind the shadow of his prominent editors, continuing to exert the same influence behind the scenes. This allowed his outfit to survive draconian censorship measures while retaining the continuity essential to the newspaper's success.

When he launched the newspaper in 1912, Majīd Ḥasan had little local influence. The only person of significance attached to the newspaper initially was a prominent journalist of the period, Nūr ul-Ḥasan Zahīn, who wrote for *Ṣaḥīfa* as well. Colonial censors initially dismissed *Madīnah* as a "bigoted Muhammadan organ, inclined to make trouble between Hindus and Muhammadans." *Madīnah* first earned the ire of colonial administrators by criticizing the headmaster of Bijnor High School for complying with the British Educational Code.[43] This was only the first of many encounters with censorship legislation.

Maulvī Syed Nūr ul-Ḥasan Zahīn Kiratpūrī, a Bijnor district man by birth, was the first and third editor of *Madīnah*. He had been educated at a local madrasah in his *qasbah*, Kiratpur, near the city Naginah.[44] A blind man renowned more for his wisdom than his formal education, he attracted a refined and pious stratum of *qasbah* society. While Majīd Ḥasan led the daily organization of the staff and handled the writing of news items and other general articles, Nūr ul-Ḥasan Z̲ahīn Kiratpūrī was in charge of editorials and assisted with administration.[45] He composed poems under the *takhallus*, or pen name, *Mattīn bijnorī* ("Strong Bijnori").[46] Kiratpūrī's poetry focused on the decline of Islam in an age of European influence. *Madīnah*'s first subeditor was Syed Muḥammad Lā'iq Ḥussain Qavī "Zammarud-raqam" Amrohavī, who also came on board during this period. His *takhallus* "Zamurrud-raqam" meant "emerald pen," referring to his calligraphic skill and poetic ambitions (see chapter 3 for an in-depth discussion of the importance of calligraphy to the paper's overall project). Between the end of 1912 and the beginning of 1913 Nūr ul-Ḥasan Z̲ahīn Kiratpūrī departed as editor of the newspaper but continued to contribute. *Madīnah* briefly went without an official editor until M. Āg̲h̲ā Rafīq Bulandshahrī arrived sometime in 1913.

M. Āg̲h̲ā Rafīq Bulandshahrī served as editor between 1913 and 1915.[47] He was born in Bulandshahr, a northwestern district of Uttar Pradesh near Bijnor known as an exemplar of *sharīf* culture.[48] One of the defining issues of his tenure was the Kanpur Mosque controversy of 1913, which saw the Urdu press deliberating the fate of Muslim places of worship as monuments to spiritual and national identity.[49] In the first half of 1913, the municipal board in Kanpur prepared to destroy the outer part of a mosque in order to widen a road, specifically the *dalal,* or location where worshippers conducted ritual ablution before their prayers. The *dalal* was not formally part of the mosque, but Urdu newspapers, including *Madīnah, al-Hilāl, Comrade*, and *Zamīndār*, spoke out against the destruction as an attack on the Muslim community. *Madīnah* was not the first Urdu paper to comment on the Kanpur issue, but it was instrumental in framing the destruction as an attack on the sacred space of Islam.[50] Āg̲h̲ā Rafīq engaged with English-language newspapers as well, arguing against the *Pioneer* newspaper's advice that Muslims should not see the construction project as an attack on their religious community.[51]

Under Āg̲h̲ā Rafīq, *Madīnah* continued to develop its persona as an invigilator of Muslim sacred symbols, increasingly laying claim to be a representative voice of the Muslim community. According to Majīd Ḥasan and his editors, *Madīnah* and other Urdu-language newspapers, like mosques, had become monuments of import to the Muslim community.[52] *Madīnah*'s popularity slowly increased, as did the frequency of publication; beginning in 1914 it issued twice a week.

In 1916 and 1917, the paper again came under the editorship of Nūr ul-Ḥasan Z̲ahīn. World War I coverage saw reporting on regular news from the front with an emphasis on the Ottoman Empire. April 1917 marked the beginning of Editor Maẕhar ud-Dīn Shairkoṭī's tenure, and the newspaper's shift to publishing more explicitly political, anti-British stances. Shairkoṭī, a novelist as well as a journalist, was born in the Shairkoṭ *qasbah* of Bijnor in 1888. Initially educated by Maulānā 'Abdul Qayūm Arshāq and Miyānji Sa'ad Allah Sahib, he had attended Deoband as a pupil of Maulānā Mahmud ul-Ḥasan Asīr Mālṭā, known as Shaikh ul-Hind.[53] After completing his education at Deoband, Maẓhar ud-Dīn returned to Shairkot, where he worked on the newspaper *Dastūr* under the management of Ḥakīm Asrār ul-Nabī and on the newspaper *Nagīnah*. Among his many credentials, Shairkotī also had experience editing a daily paper called *Risālat* and had been a subeditor of the Calcutta newspaper *al-Balāgh*, edited by Maulānā Azad after the closing of his paper *al-Hilāl*. After *Nagīnah*'s closure Maẓhar ud-Dīn began his stint at *Madīnah* on April 28, 1917, with an article on Qur'anic surahs.

Maulānā Majīd Ḥasan saw Maẓhar ud-Dīn's affiliation with the newspaper as the beginning of a new period of commitment to the Muslim community[54] and wrote an illustrious introduction for his new editor. Majīd Ḥasan's message in his introduction was clear: he had brought in a power player to man the ship of *Madīnah*, a man who indubitably linked the paper to a network of powerful publications and individuals. The new editor transformed *Madīnah* into a more explicitly political entity. Maẓhar ud-Dīn associated with prominent political Muslims of the period, including Syed Ḥasan Imām, who presided over the Indian National Congress's consideration of the Montagu-Chelmsford Reforms in Bombay in 1918.[55] His other associates included Nawab Muḥammad Ismā'il Khān. He was, along with Khalīquzzamān, a key organizer of the UP Muslim League, and a prominent member until 1947; he remained in India after independence. Descended from Nawab Muṣtafa Khān "Shefta," the friend and patron of Ghalib, Khān lived at Mustafa Castle in Meerut. Maẓhar ud-Dīn also associated with Syed Habīb Shāh, a Lahori Muslim who toured Northern Punjab to mobilize support for the Khilafat Committee.[56]

After the end of World War I in November 1918, discussions of independence and postwar reality in India began in earnest.[57] The state of Islam, and the progress of both national and local branches of organizations such as the Muslim League and Congress, became matters of intense concern.[58] Mohandas Karamchand "Mahātmā" Gāndhī (1869–1948) featured in several articles musing on the way forward for political Muslims.[59] In addition, discussions of the fall out of World War I in Turkey and the caliphate took center stage.[60] Under Maẓhar ud-Dīn's leadership, the newspaper emphasized the connection between the fate of Indian Muslims and of those in Turkey and other nations with significant ties to Islam.[61]

Maẓhar ud-Dīn presided over *Madīnah*'s publication of an article critical of the government's role in the Jallianwallabagh massacre, which led to a dramatic conflict with the British Raj.[62] In April 1919 *Madīnah* published an article criticizing Lieutenant Governor Sir Michael O'Dwyer's (1864–1940) endorsement of the actions of Colonel Reginald Dyer, who had overseen the disproportionate response at Jallianwallabagh. The article minced no words:

> His honour O'Dwyer's government of Panjab, from the very beginning, kept as the foundation of its policy a despotic course of action [. . .] This was his honor O'Dwyer's last period of government; therefore it was necessary that he make amends for his past course of actions. This was the time when, instead of extinguishing the fire with the water Of gentleness and kindness, he inflamed the hearts of the *ahl-i Punjab*. Perhaps it could be said that he did not put out the fire with water, but instead doused it with oil. If that were not the case, then why would he at the conclusion of his reign, give orders that were so repellent, so far from resembling affection that they approximated hate?[63]

It was actually illegal at this point in time to question the motives of the colonial government; thus, the final statement of the quotation accusing O'Dwyer of "hate" fell afoul of censorship laws. The government banned *Madīnah* from circulating in the Punjab as a result of this piece. Maẕhar ud-Dīn and Majīd Ḥasan's response was defiant: in August 1919 they renamed the newspaper *Yas̱rab*, an Arabic synonym of *Madīnah*, as a bid to evade censorship.[64] On the cover of each issue of *Yas̱rab* an Iqbal couplet appeared, a knowing wink to its readership base:

> The dust of Madinah is better than both worlds
> How wonderful is the city where the beloved is.
>
> *Kẖāk-i yas̱rab az do ʿālam kẖūshtar ast*
> *Āʾe kẖunak shahre ke ānjā dilbar ast.*[65]

The couplet hinted at the paper *Yas̱rab*'s true identity, offered praise for the paper's unpretentious popularity, and emphasized the link between the newspaper and the city Madīnah. *Madīnah*'s proprietor and editors were men who wore their few educational laurels lightly. More important than formal education was the ability to use that knowledge in the service of Indians generally and Muslims particularly. Unsurprisingly, the attempt at flouting the circulation ban was quickly detected. The paper reverted back to the title *Madīnah* after a few weeks, and the ban on circulation was lifted eventually.[66] *Madīnah* was a space offering a figurative point of access to the community of Islam, the *qaum*, and it was a space increasingly under siege of colonial censorship laws.

Madīnah had been only one of many significant voices in the press commenting on the Jallianwallabagh fiasco. As the UP fortnightly report complained, "[The] occurrences in the Punjab [. . .] practically absorbed the entire attention of the press." Along with *Madīnah/Yasrab*, the British excluded from Punjab *al-Khalīl* of Bijnor, *The Independent* of Allahabad (a Nehru paper), *Hamdam* and *Akhuwat* of Lucknow (Farangi Mahalli papers), *Swadesh* of Gorakhpur, and *Amrita bazar patrika* of Calcutta. The government demanded securities, or large sums of money as surety against future crimes of sedition, from papers in Bengal, Nagpur, Lucknow, and Madras.[67] *Madīnah*'s inclusion in this censorship was a testament to its growing influence; its subterfuge demonstrated a growing sense of urgency in its mandate to reach readers and an emerging resolve to flout British restrictions.

In the 1920s, *Madīnah* focused on coverage of the Muslim League and the Indian National Congress, showing a preference for Congress.[68] It was perhaps Maẓhar ud-Dīn's affection for the League that motivated him ultimately to resign from *Madīnah* in 1921. It is also possible that Maẓhar ud-Dīn's taste for politics pulled him closer to Delhi and toward the League after the political awakening accompanying the Khilafat Movement. It was common for editors to move around among different *qasbah*-based newspapers, and after leaving *Madīnah*, Maẓhar ud-Dīn joined Munshī Safīr Aḥmed's Naginah-based paper *Almān* as its first editor; he was instrumental in relocating that paper to Delhi. He later became close to the leadership of the All-India Muslim League, including Muḥammad 'Alī Jinnāh. In the 1930s he founded a paper entitled *Vaḥdat* (*Unity*) in order to assist the propagation of Muslim League ideals. When Maulānā Shabbīr Aḥmed 'Usmānī, a Deobandi who supported the creation of Pakistan, resigned from the pro-Congress Jam'īat 'Ulamā and declared his allegiance to the Muslim League and Jinnah, he did so from Maẓhar ud-Dīn's office.[69] This demonstrated *Madīnah* was one node in an important network of political power and publishing prestige in this period and had to make considered choices when it came to balancing shifting political alliances.

Maẓhar ud-Dīn Shairkoṭī had arrived in *Madīnah* already a man of high stature. His three years there were some of the most formative for a new generation of nationalists, when *Madīnah* newspaper and other periodicals embraced a role as simultaneously political and Muslim voices. *Madīnah*'s dramatically increasing readership gave Maẓhar ud-Dīn Shairkoṭī a large platform to practice bold journalism, whetting his appetite for direct political action. His politics diverged from that of *Madīnah* in the two decades following his departure. Maẓhar ud-Dīn was eventually assassinated in 1939 while representing the Muslim League at conference on the Palestine issue. Muḥammad 'Alī Jinnāh (1876–1948) wrote a letter, published in *Almān*, expressing his shock at his associate's death. Maẓhar ud-Dīn was awarded a posthumous Pakistan Movement Gold Medal in 1989 for his efforts in promoting the founding of Pakistan.[70] Significantly, the positions of *Madīnah* editors on the question of separatism were varied. This reflected both a tendency for *Madīnah* to emphasize the inclusion of a range of political approaches in its pages and also highlights how rapidly political alliances transformed in the middle of the twentieth century.

The last year of Maẕhar ud-Dīn's tenure as chief editor saw Qāẓi Muḥammad 'Adīl "Abāsī" (1898–1980) join the editorial board briefly. Already committed to the Khilafat Movement following his enrollment in the University of Allahabad, 'Adīl became convinced that journalism was his path to exert positive influence on the "Turkish question." He saw an advertisement for members of the editorial board for Madīnah Press in a paper and sent in an application. We know from family diaries that as a member of the editorial board he was paid 60 rupees a month, 10 of which was deducted for food and accommodation in the extended household of Majīd Ḥasan.[71] Majīd Ḥasan disliked the amount of time that 'Adīl spent dedicated to Congress activities alongside his work, so 'Adīl did not last long in Bijnor. Before the year was out 'Adīl wrote to Lahore and received a job at Lahore's *Zamīndār*. After he was appointed a delegate for the Indian National Congress's Ahmedabad Conference in late December 1921, he traveled from Bijnor to the conference, and instead of returning to his work on the staff of *Madīnah* he made his way to Lahore instead. Eventually 'Adīl would become chief editor of *Zamīndār* in 1922.

After Maẕhar ud-Dīn's departure from *Madīnah*, in 1921 Moradabad-born Qāẓī Badrul Ḥasan Jālālī, B.A., took up the mantle of the *Madīnah* editorship. Maulvī Nūr ul-Raḥmān would later refer to the period of Jālālī's tenure as a "foundational era" (*imtīyāzī 'ehdah*) for the newspaper.[72] Like Shairkoṭī, Jalālī found himself in the crosshairs of colonial sedition laws. He was prosecuted in 1924 under section 124A of the Indian Penal Code as a result of an article he wrote on the British in Kabul. Following his prosecution, he issued an apology and resigned; within a year he resumed his post. Majīd Ḥasan became so worried by the prosecution that he nominally resigned as proprietor to avoid government attention, while keeping control of the newspaper behind the scenes. Much like the *Yas̱rab* renaming strategy, this attempt at subterfuge was unsuccessful and Ḥasan quickly renamed himself proprietor.[73]

In the same year, Maulānā Naṣrullah K͟hān "'Azīz" (1897–1967), a Punjabi in his early forties, was named subeditor; he would go on to become head editor in 1929. He was already part of the transregional Urdu newspaper network: before coming to *Madīnah*, 'Azīz had worked on the staff of the *Sufī* in Punjab. By this time *Madīnah* newspaper already had a reputation for anti-British sentiment, affinity for Turkey, and antipathy to the Hindu-driven Shuddhī and Sangaṭhan movements. Its influence was growing outside of Bijnor, especially in the Punjab, but was still limited in Bijnor itself.[74] The growing prestige was assisted by employing editors and assistant editors from a wide range of prestigious educational institutions and local *madrasas*. Although the newspaper had a reputation strong enough to draw graduates from prestigious institutions, only from the 1930s onward did *Madīnah*'s popularity translate into local prestige for its proprietor.

Madīnah gave several young journalists their start in the industry. One of these, Ḥamīd Ḥasan "Fakīr" Bijnorī, who would go on to marry the proprietor's daughter, was contributing poems to *Madīnah* in his childhood. Not only contributors but even the editors could be fresh graduates from prominent *madrasas*. Maulānā Amīn Aḥsan Iṣlāḥī (1904–1989) came to Bijnor after graduating from Madrasatul Iṣlāh, the educational institution founded by Maulana Shiblī in 1914. He was an assistant editor with *Madīnah* and also worked with the children's magazine *Ghunchah*. His name appeared as a third-in-command "joint editor" in December 1922 at the age of eighteen. He was so young, in fact, that when he started work in Bijnor, many were of the opinion that he did not look the part of a scholar of Arabic. When he arrived in Bijnor, a group of men showed up at the press, excited to meet the erudite new editor newly arrived from Madrasatul Iṣlāḥ. The *mālik*, or manager of the press, 'Abdul Ḥamīd, pointed them to a room where he said Iṣlāḥī was at work on an editorial. The men came back to 'Abdul Ḥamīd, thinking there was some mistake—a boy was sitting in the room instead of the newspaper's new editor. 'Abdul Ḥamīd said, "Oh brother, that *is* Maulānā Amīn Aḥsan Iṣlāḥī. He confuses whoever comes to meet him because his facial hair hasn't grown in yet."[75]

Another young journalist who credited *Madīnah* as his introduction to journalism was Nūr ul-Raḥmān, B.A. (1894–1972). In 1928 the thirty-two-year-old became editor after having worked for the newspaper as a reporter. A *zamīndār* and a Shaikh, he hailed from Bacchraon, where he received his initial education.[76] He then enrolled in Madrasa Awliyā Rampur, followed by Muslim High School Utavah and Aligarh Muslim University. He received his B.A. with distinction from Aligarh, but in 1920 separated himself from the institution over differences in attitude on the "Turkish question." In that same year he wrote in an article in *Madīnah* that the newspaper had influenced him: "The beginnings of my journalistic life happened with the famous, community (*qaumī*) newspaper of that time, '*Madīnah*.'"[77] Qāẓī Badrul Ḥasan Jālālī's personal clerk had been Naṣrullah Khān 'Azīz, who became so key to the editor's work that his name also appeared on the cover page alongside that of Nūr ul-Raḥmān, even though the latter man remained the head editor.[78] Another subeditor during Nūr ul-Raḥmān's tenure was Moḥammad Aḥsan, also a Shaikh from Bacchraon *qasbah* in Amroha, who had worked as an administrative clerk in government service.[79] After leaving *Madīnah*, Nūr ul-Raḥmān joined Jamia Millia Islamia library and became the head editor of the periodical *Jām'ah*, filling a number of important administrative roles: Secretary for the Muslim Chairman of Commerce, Calcutta; Joint Secretary for the Anjuman-i Taraqqī-yi Urdū. An author himself, he was secretary of the society honoring Qāẓī 'Abdul-Ghaffār.[80] He also reportedly did some secretarial work for Maulānā Muḥammad ʿAlī Jauhar, emphasizing the associations between the ʿAlī brothers and *Madīnah*'s journalism network.[81]

In 1929, the editorship was assumed by Naṣrullah Khān "ʿAzīz," who was promoted after several years as an assistant editor.[82] He was the son of Muḥammad Sharīf Ullah Khān. There were multiple subeditors during his tenure: Muḥammad Aḥsan and Maulānā Abūllais Iṣlāḥī Nadvī (1913–1990), who would become the first *amīr* of the Jamāʿat-i Islāmī Hind, were among these. Less than a year after taking up his post, Naṣrullah Khān was prosecuted under section 124A of the Indian penal code. Khān pled "not guilty" to the charge of "[attempting] to excite disaffection to the government" and was convicted and sentenced to fifteen months' rigorous imprisonment.[83] The objectionable pieces that led to Khān's prison sentence were an article titled "*Faṣl-i bahār* [Spring Season]" and a poem headed "*Paighām-i ambal* [Call to Action]." In "Spring Season" an invection against the Rowlatt Act concluded with a striking couplet breathtaking in its daring:

> In the night of cruelty I will take it out from the middle of my Caravan
> Oh, my fire will be scattered; my breath will be the raining flames
>
> *Main ẓulmat-i shab mein le ke niklūngā apne darmāndah-yi kārvān ko*
> *Sharar fishān hogī āh merī, nafs merā shʿolah bār hogā*[84]

As a result *Madīnah* was required to deposit a large security under the Indian Press Act, indicating the paper's increasing determination to challenge censorship legislation in the service of nationalism. The text that follows is the translation of "Call to Action" provided to British officials in the confidential documentation of the prosecution; the text was circulated in domestic intelligence channels as evidence of *Madīnah*'s rabble-rousing.

> "*Paighām-i ambal* [Call to Action]"
> The manner in which the moths burn themselves on the candle,
> In the same way self-sacrificing people lay down their lives for the sake of their country.
> Brave to the intoxication of the wine of patriotism.
> I go about in such a way as if I were carrying a public house on my shoulders.
> *The door of the public house has opened, come ye who may like to have a drink.*
> *This is what the old tavern-keeper is telling those who drink.* [emphasis mine]
> Come. Young men, there is again a stir in the field of action.
> How long is this merry-making to go on? How long this indulgence in drinking?
> The garden of our country has been laid waste through plunder,

The country now possesses neither that bloom nor glory.
May, O Lord! the tree of the objects of him who has in this way devastated
the garden of (our) country be also cut out by the root.
Captivity in English prison is a prelude to the joys of heaven,
That is to say the door of the jail of the country opens in Paradise.
Is there any enjoyment or pleasure even greater than martyrdom?
What are you thinking? Arise young men of the country.
May spring come afresh over the garden of liberty.
O, blood of martyrs of the country, flow like a river.

Madīnah was this public house, and the editor the tavern-keeper. Playing off of the established Sufi trope of the tavern and the tavern-keeper, it presented the public house as a place symbolic of transgression in the service of enlightenment. Those who kept company in the newspaper, according to this poem, were transgressors of colonial orthodoxy, in this case law breakers, acting in the service of enlightenment. Accompanying notes cited the article's references to violent insurrection in support of Khān's conviction. His prison sentence did not prevent him from resuming his editorship of *Madīnah* following his release from prison in 1932; in fact, during his imprisonment his name was kept as a badge of honor on the title of page of *Madīnah*, above even the name of Ḥāmidul Anṣārī Ghāzī, who was the chief editor during Khān's absence.[85] Perhaps because of Khān's return, in 1934, *Madīnah* was again forced to deposit a large security–this time under the updated Press Ordinance of 1931. *Madīnah* had gained a reputation as a pro-Congress paper and by now had finally achieved popularity at the local as well as national level.[86] Khān's second term as editor yielded yet more controversy, which only reinforced its popularity among readers. In 1935, the paper was forced to forfeit its 1,000-rupee security in punishment for an article harshly criticizing the government response to the Quetta earthquake.[87] *Madīnah* complied with the government's punitive demand for an additional 2,000-rupee deposit as a security against future violations. Many newspaper presses closed their doors after being charged with criminal activity, or after receiving an invoice for such a cripplingly large security.[88] The fact that *Madīnah* was able to meet this substantial demand is evidence that the paper was extremely profitable, an assessment supported by colonial surveillance of the paper from the 1920s.[89]

Naṣrullah Khān, having overseen *Madīnah*'s escalating penchant for nationalist drama and protest, remained the editor until the end of 1935 or early 1936, when 30-year-old Maulānā Ḥāmidul Anṣārī "Ghāzī" (1906–1992) rose to the editorship. Anṣārī, the son of M. Mansūr Anṣārī, was a Shaikh of Ambhattā in the district Saharanpur. Anṣārī had been educated first at Dar ul-'Ulūm Ma'īnīyah in Ajmer and then Dar ul-'Ulūm Deoband, where he received instruction from the scholarly luminaries Anwar Shāh Kashmīrī, Maulānā Shabīr Aḥmed 'Usmānī, Maulānā Ibrāhīm Balīyavī, and Maulānā 'Azaz 'Alī Amrohavī Shaikh ul-Adab. At Deoband he was particularly attached to his teacher *'ulamā* Anwar Shāh Kashmīrī, later calling himself that teacher's "*ākhrī shāgird*" or "final student." During his studies Anṣārī worked at the weekly periodical *Gul bāgh* (later to be renamed *Bahār bāgh*) and on the staff of *al-Mahmūd*, a weekly periodical in honor of Shaikh ul-Hind Maḥmūd ul-Ḥasan. After completing his Deobandi qualifications quickly at the age of twenty, he worked on the Urdu publications *Muhājir* and *al-Jam'īat*, the paper of Jam'īat 'Ulamā-i Hind, until he took up his position with *Madīnah* in 1931.[90]

As Anṣārī's links to Deoband suggest, the 1930s saw a significant overlap between the editorial staff of *Madīnah* and *al-Jam'īat*. For instance, Maulānā Muḥammad Usmān Fāraqlait (1897–1967) served on *Madīnah*'s editorial board for a year in the early or mid-1930s, seeking refuge from the wave of arrests of journalists in Delhi. He worked in Bijnor until Maulānā Ḥusain Aḥmad Madanī traveled to Bijnor in person to ask Majīd Ḥasan to give Fāraqlait permission to return to his work on *al-Jam'īat*.[91] Majīd Ḥasan, aware that he could not refuse, readily gave Fāraqlait leave to return to Delhi. In 1939, Fāraqlait arrived in Lahore, where he oversaw editorials at the publication *Zamzam*, which ran afoul of the colonial government until it was closed for a year in the early 1940s. In Lahore, Fāraqlait continued to be renowned for his fiery, anticolonial rhetoric.[92] The Sunni nature of the paper was clear. A conflict between chief editor Bazmī and the *Nigār* editor Nīyāz Fatehpūrī centered around the use of the word "*kufr*," or infidel, in articles referring to Shī'a Muslims.[93] Someone, perhaps 'Allāmah Mashriqī, the founder of the Khaksar movement, wrote out verbatim several 1939 articles in *Madīnah* covering Sunni–Shī'a conflicts over processions in Lucknow.[94]

By 1937, the newspaper had clearly aligned itself with Congress, the Jam'īat 'Ulamā-i Hind, and Deoband; it was critical of the Muslim League, the Hindu Mahasabha, and the Shī'a community. Anṣārī was involved with *Madīnah* over the next thirteen years; he passed the editorship to Abū Sa'īd Bazmī (1910–1951) in 1937 and then resumed it in 1945 after Bazmī's departure.[95] In the interim period after leaving *Madīnah*, he became briefly involved in the publication of Tājūr Najībābādī's periodical *Adabī dunīyā* before quitting and moving to Delhi. There he founded Nadwatul Muṣannefīn, a publishing company in Delhi, with Muftī 'Atīq ul-Raḥmān 'Usmānī, Maulāna Ḥāfiz ul-Raḥmān Sihvāravī, and Maulānā Sa'īd Aḥmad Akbarābadī.

Abū Sa'īd Bazmī arrived at *Madīnah* in January 1937, overlapping with Ghāzī. After Ghāzī separated from the newspaper in May 1937, Abū Sa'īd Bazmī became the *mudīr-i mas'ūl* (chief editor).[96] He had been born in Bhopal to a poor family who nevertheless prized education. Undeterred by his family's meager financial resources, he achieved the distinction of passing exams in Farsi, Arabic, Urdu, and English (in the latter subject he achieved a bachelor's and master's degree).[97] He received government employment, and finding that unfulfilling he started his own newspaper, titled *Rehnumā*, which was controversial enough that the government eventually closed it down. After taking up the head editorship, Bazmī led *Madīnah* through a period of increased scrutiny as a result of the 1937 Bijnor by-elections. Under Bazmī's guidance *Madīnah* was sharply critical of the Muslim League and the Hindu Mahasabha.[98] In September 1940 he was arrested in Bhopal under the Defense of India Act and convicted to twenty-one months' imprisonment. During his period of imprisonment, no editors were listed on the cover of *Madīnah*. After Bazmī returned to his editing responsibilities, he was photographed with the local Congress stalwart Ḥāfiẓ Moḥammad Ibrāhīm following the Nationalist Muslim Conference at Lucknow, along with a leader of the Khaksar movement. The image, shown in Figure 1.4, underlines what had become clear associations between *Madīnah* and two political alternatives to the League: Congress and the Khaksar movement. After Bazmī left *Madīnah*, he took up positions in Lahore as the editor of two newspapers named *Zamzam* and *Shahbāz*. Following independence, even though he had remained sharply critical of Partition, he remained in Pakistan and became the editor of another paper called *Aḥsān*.[99]

While *Madīnah* criticized the League and the call for Pakistan, it also boldly questioned the direction of Congress policies when they impeded perceived Muslim interests. As D. P. Mukherji, censor for the British government, had observed in 1936, "[*Madīnah*] wields a great influence in all circles."[100] Majīd Ḥasan's dream continued to exert its force. British assessment of the paper in 1945 described *Madīnah* as both a voice for Muslims and stubbornly independent:

> [A] nationalist Muslim paper, believes in political principles of the Congress, but its criticism of the treatment of Muslims by the Congress has been bitter. It does not spare the Muslim League either and is against the Pakistan scheme. Attitude towards the present War neither favourable nor hostile to the British. Very popular with Muslims, Congress and Ahrar.[101]

Resisting easy categorization, *Madīnah* was linked to a range of divergent visions for the future of Muslims in South Asia. It was perhaps this editorial autonomy that earned the respect and loyalty of readers. Above all, the paper sought to be an explicitly Muslim forum for discussion. The British were concerned by *Madīnah*'s boldness. As independence neared, the British watched *Madīnah*

8 THE PIONEER Friday, October 12, 1945

NEWS FROM THE U.P. DISTRICTS

From Our Own Correspondents

PROSECUTION OF 'UJALA' EDITOR DROPPED

REVIEW OF KUMAUN DISTRICT BOARDS

SABHA ELECTION BOARD FORMED

'VARSITY COUNCIL MEETING

ALMORA

50 CONGRESS MANDALS ORGANISED

AZAMGARH

LEAGUE ELECTION CAMPAIGN

JAUNPUR

TEACHERS' CONFERENCE

UNAO

CLOTH FOR RURAL AREAS

MEERUT

GONDA

ROW-MORE-FOOD CAMPAIGN

MUSLIM LEAGUE ELECTION MEETING

CLUB DINNER

NATIONALIST MUSLIM CONFERENCE AT LUCKNOW—From L. to R.: Mr. Abu Said Bazmi, editor, the 'Madina'; Hafiz Mohammad Ibrahim, ex-Congress Minister, UP, and Mr. Mohammad Saied, a Khaksar Leader, snapped when they were leaving the conference Pandal.

MORE and MORE HIND CYCLES ... ARE AVAILABLE NOW

HIND CYCLES

HIND CYCLES LIMITED, 250, WORLI, BOMBAY.

Managing Agents—BIRLA BROS. LTD.

THE TOOLS THEY NEED. . .

Many million hands are busy working for the Industrial and Agricultural Development of India. We supply every kind of tool for these willing hands, for Government and Civilian uses.

We manufacture hammers, augers, vices, hand-band and circular saws, axes, beaters, shovels, powrahs and agricultural implements of every kind. All our tools are made from correct steel and are finally tempered.

For full particulars apply to India Metal Sales Ltd., Navasari Chambers, Fort, Bombay.

KAMANI METAL INDUSTRIES

MENTION THE PIONEER WHEN WRITING TO ADVERTISERS

Figure 1.4 See photograph on bottom right. Ḥāfiẓ Moḥammad Ibrāhīm (center), *Madīnah* editor Abu Said Bazmī (left). *The Pioneer*, October 12, 1945, 8. Microfilm. British Library.

closely, prohibiting it from circulating internationally out of fear that it would provide fodder for enemy propaganda.[102]

In 1945 Maulānā Ḥāmidul Anṣārī "Ghāzī" was once again called to be the chief editor of *Madīnah* and remained at his post until 1950. Originally chief editor from 1931 to 1937, Anṣārī had left to work briefly at the Najibabad publication *Adabī Dunīyā* before moving to Delhi and cofounding the publisher Nadwatul Muṣannifīn.[103] Anṣārī shepherded *Madīnah* through the tumultuous period of Partition, leaving *Madīnah* finally in 1950, when he shifted to Bombay and became chief editor of the daily *Jamhūrīyat.*[104] When he had a disagreement with the paper's leadership, he broke off in 1956 to form his own weekly version of *Jamhūrīyat,* which ran until 1962. A career journalist, Anṣārī demonstrated the peripatetic tendencies of Urdu journalists as well as a tendency to return to *Madīṇah* after breaks to edit other publications.

Not only *Madīnah*'s editors but also its contributor journalists had a reputation for commitment to the art of journalism. They also demonstrated the interconnectivity of the journalism enterprise in North India: how journalists simultaneously wrote for publications in far-flung locations, in both *qasbah*s and large cities, and frequently shifted locations. As a case in point, a writer for *Madīnah* named Qadūs Ṣahbā'ī, a man who had first studied journalism with Maulānā Shaukat 'Alī, gained a reputation as a particularly committed journalist, who contributed not only to *Madīnah* but also to *Khilāfat* (Bombay), *Āzād hind* (Calcutta), *Musulmān* (Delhi), *Ṣobaḥ vaṯan* (Bhopal), and *Niẓām* (Delhi).[105] Historian of *Madīnah* Parvez 'Ādil writes: "On the field of journalism he was such a youth[106] as was not made prisoner by the vicissitudes of the time; until his final breath he loved his way of conduct (*maslak*) in the same way that the lover loves the beloved [*Voh maidān-i ṣaḥāfat ke aise shāhīn the jin ko nairangī-yi daurān bhī asīr nah banā kisī dam-i ākhir tak apne maslak se usi ṯaraḥ moḥabbat karte rahe jis ṯaraḥ 'āshiq apne maḥbūb se kīyā karta hai*]."

Madīnah's popularity in North India and the Punjab steadily declined after independence. The paper was never the same after 1947, as prominent authors and editors migrated to Pakistan, and those remaining saw Urdu replaced by Hindi as the state language in the new state of Uttar Pradesh. Without new generations of readers growing up reading, speaking, and working in Urdu, the paper faded from its former glory. *Madīnah* had been one of the most prominent newspapers in South Asia. After independence, the running of the paper transformed from profitable enterprise to labor of love. Majīd Ḥasan's family handled the running of the newspaper until the last editor, Syed Ḥasan, stopped the presses of *Madīnah* quietly in 1975, a few years after Majīd Ḥasan's death in 1972. In the twenty-first century only a handful of issues of the newspaper and the empty veranda where the printing press stood remain of what once was one of the most prominent, unlikely newspapers in the subcontinent.

Structure, Content, and Format

Although *Madīnah* targeted a Muslim readership, it discussed issues relevant to both Muslims and non-Muslims. Printed using lithographic technology, the newspaper varied in length; it would be anywhere from eight to fifteen pages long. It included a range of genres in poetry and prose. The focus of the content spanned the local, regional, and international. The cover occasionally displayed striking images of the city of Madīnah and the Prophet's Mosque in Madīnah or *al-Masjid an-nabawī*.[107]

Madīnah featured original poetry as well as accounts of recent *mushā'irahs*, or poetic performances, that reprinted some of the greatest hits of the gathering.[108] Hard news came in a few forms. The section "*'ām a<u>kh</u>bār aur 'ām tār*" (general news and telegrams) featured snippets of regional news received by telegraph; this section included notices of local issues including robberies, deaths, prominent visitors to the area, and updates on the state of roads for travelers.[109] National and international political news appeared, in the form of commentary on municipal governance regulations, reports on colonial policies, and speeches printed or translated verbatim from colonial officials, Indian National Congress, the Muslim League, or other organizations.[110] International news gained prominence in times of war, during the Khilafat Movement, and in times of key debates regarding self-governance in England—news of war came accompanied by elaborate maps.[111] There were also regular updates on the state of important Muslim institutions, like Nadwah, Deoband, Aligarh Muslim University, and Jamia Millia Islamia.[112] The paper's association with Deoband and the followers of Maulānā Ḥusain Aḥmad Madanī was most marked.

Editorials written anonymously or with the bylines of prominent *'ulamā* offered advice on relevant social issues or current affairs; readers could write with pressing spiritual questions to receive guidance remotely, including on matters of Qur'anic interpretation.[113] A number of prominent authors of the period wrote for *Madīnah*, with and without bylines. For instance, two scholarly accounts state that Maulānā Syed Abūl A'la Maudūdī (1903–1979) wrote columns for *Madīnah* between 1918 and 1923.[114] This means that Maudūdī received some of his earliest education in journalism from Majīd Ḥasan and the staff of *Madīnah*; following this work he went on to work for *Tāj* (Jabalpur) and *Muslim* (Delhi) and ultimately became an editor of Jam'īat 'Ulamā's newspaper *Jam'īat*.[115] Any article without a byline would have been written by the editorial team, one of the editors, or the proprietor himself; these entries constituted the majority of the newspaper's content.

Between 1912 and 1915 a women's page, or *A<u>kh</u>bār-i nisvān*, frequently appeared on one of the last pages of *Madīnah* (just before a page or two of advertisements). The women's page, intended to interest and instruct honorable Muslim women,[116] included editorials and creative pieces written by both male and female authors. Political news items and advertisements related to women tended to appear in the main section of the paper.[117] During these first three years of publication, when an issue shorter than the full-length version of fifteen pages appeared, the women's section was almost always omitted. In the latter half of 1915 a frenzy of media coverage on World War I combined with a change in editorial leadership caused the women's section to disappear, although individual articles on women's education and health continued. The final page of the paper remained unofficially reserved for women's issues, when the need arose. As World War I drew to a close and the Khilafat Movement crested the horizon, *Madīnah* used the women's section to underscore a distinctive, authoritative Muslim voice.[118] The women's section included editorials, short stories, poems, advertisements, and news items targeted at cultivated Muslim women.[119] While men always edited and often authored columns,[120] this section of the paper identified itself as a space ostensibly for women, with particular attention to mothers. In many cases overtly, in some cases covertly, men wrote in the voices of women.[121] This section may have been the immediate predecessor of Madīnah Press's magazine Ghunchah, founded in the early 1920s just as *Akhbār-i nisvān* disappeared from *Madīnah*. In other sections of the paper, stories of women warriors fighting in the Italo-Turkish War of 1910–1911 and later in the Balkan Wars were framed to shame men into acts of courage. As I have written elsewhere, "threaded through each of these expressed and cultivated emotions was the presence of the newspaper as a new confessional space, offering anonymous intimacy among its readers."[122]

Advertisements abounded in *Madīnah*, selling bicycles, hair dye, impotence cures, medical texts, copies of the Qur'an, and even other newspapers. The advertisements indicated a readership spread across North and Central India; companies advertising in the paper were flung as far afield as Bombay, Lahore, and Karachi. Other ads courted customers closer to home in Bijnor, Naginah, Delhi, and Lucknow. Notes selling advertising space in *Madīnah* show that printing ads was a source of income for Majīd Ḥasan alongside subscriptions and the trade books that his press also produced, contributing to the paper's sustainability.[123]

By providing news of the same standard as papers in large cities, *Madīnah* and other remarkable *qasbah*-based newspapers, including *Zulqarnain* (Budaun), *Nagīnah* (Naginah), and *Najat* (Bijnor), set themselves apart from the previous incarnation of the *qasbah* newsletters, which had focused on local, agricultural matters. One aspect of *Madīnah*'s self-presentation was its emphasis on the *qasbah* as a preserver of Muslim tradition in the decades preceding independence. While *qasbah* newspapers shared with urban center papers an emphasis on the *ashrāf* as a social category, they were distinctive in couching their credibility in part in their geographical placement in the *qasbah*. The emergence of an influential newspaper grounded in a *qasbah* signaled the arrival of a distinct voice into the Urdu public: a nationally and internationally aware voice in dialogue with urban publics but based in *qasbah* life, expressing particular concerns of the *ashrāf*, including the place of religion in politics, maintenance of an Indo–Persian tie, and importance of Urdu as embodying that tradition.

Circulation and Perception

Madīnah newspaper had begun in 1912 with a circulation of merely 350 copies. By 1915, circulation had increased only to a modest 450.[124] From its inception the newspaper took seriously its role as a source of information and guidance. *Madīnah* emphasized punctuality and consistency. The newspaper experienced so few irregularities in its distribution that we can pinpoint exactly two delays—in 1913 and 1916. The delayed issue of April 22, 1913, sent three days late due to Ḥasan's illness, came accompanied with a profuse apology.[125] In 1916 *Madīnah* issued twice in one week because of scheduling problems and a desire to release fresh news of World War I in a timely manner. Majīd Ḥasan explained the anomaly in a lengthy article, eager to emphasize that *Madīnah* usually ran on schedule.[126] When *Madīnah* threatened to run late a third time, in November 1917, due to Majīd Ḥasan's delayed return from a trip to Lucknow, the crisis was only narrowly averted. The issue was only missing his contribution, which had been lost in transit. In the dead of night Majīd Ḥasan sat and wrote the article again from scratch. After all, he wrote, "a newspaper should publish on its own time, not when the sun rises."[127] With this statement, he suggested that the newspaper, and other publications like it, established rhythms of time with a gravity separate from celestial bodies. *Madīnah* created its own time, punctuated by the predictable rhythms of its publication, distribution, and reading aloud in gatherings.

After the advent of the Khilafat Movement and the arrival of its star editor Maẓhar ud-Dīn Shairkoṭī, *Madīnah* found its niche as a voice for political Muslims sympathetic to the Indian National Congress. Majīd Ḥasan capitalized on his paper's involvement in Khilafat politics. By 1922, *Madīnah*'s circulation had increased to a remarkable 12,500 issues twice a week. Those circulation numbers made the paper the most widely distributed nationalist paper in any language in UP in that year.[128] Only Kanpur's Hindi-language *Pratāp* (10,000) and *Hind kesārī* (4,000) gave the paper distant competition. By 1931, *Madīnah*'s circulation had leveled out at a respectable 6,000, bested in circulation by the nationalist Hindi-language *Pratāp* (Kanpur), *Bhavishya* (Allahabad), and *Chānd* (Allahabad).[129] Over the 1930s *Madīnah*'s circulation increased again to 8,000, where it remained until the year following Partition, when circulation saw a significant decline.[130]

Having begun—literally—as a dream, by the 1920s and 1930s *Madīnah* had grown into one of the most influential papers of dissent in India.[131] During the 1920s and 1930s Majīd Ḥasan recommended himself as a local Muslim leader, using the political capital gained from increased circulation of *Madīnah* to become a member of the municipal board.[132] In *Madīnah* he protested a redrawing of electoral lines in Bijnor and commented on proposed construction works in the city.

Madīnah and Majīd Ḥasan's influence grew apace through the 1930s and 1940s. When Maulānā Ḥusain Aḥmad Madanī (1879–1957), a prominent Islamic scholar of the Deoband school, objected to a 1938 letter to the editor published in *Madīnah*, he initiated a meeting between *Madīnah*'s editors and concerned scholars to submit a correction in the newspaper.[133] Madanī's concern reflected *Madīnah*'s currency among literate Muslims. Other letters to the editor and contributing articles demonstrated an attempt to reach out to a readership that embodied contemporary *sharīf* values in relation to religious and vernacular education and reforms, as well as concerns with obtaining government patronage. The paper, and increasingly Majīd Ḥasan himself, remained influential as a Muslim space more than a space for a specific political perspective.[134] To make reference to the above poem, the public house of *Madīnah* offered a roof over both Islam and language in the context of colonial rule. The placement of *Madīnah* in a *qasbah* was linked to the paper's transformation into a space, both literal and abstract, for a conversation regarding the place of Islam among the *ashrāf* and the nationalists.

Of course, both Muslims and Hindus were counted alike among the readership of Urdu newspapers, including *Madīnah*; Urdu literacy was a sign of a general education, especially among Kayasth Hindus and landowners. However, *Madīnah* was distinct from the many other Urdu newspapers that were edited and run by Hindus–like Kanpur's *Zamānah* (edited by Munshī Dayā Narāyan Nigam, a Kayasth Hindu) or Bareilly's *Shuʿāʿ* (edited by Rāja Bahādur, also a Kayasth Hindu) or Agra's *Musāfir* (edited by Pandit Tārā Dat). *Madīnah* joined these publications in advocating for Hindu–Muslim unity in support and critique of Congress politics, but its self-conscious identity gave it a unique character. It projected this identity both explicitly and also implicitly through its use of Arabic, Persianate Urdu, references to North Indian Muslim cultural practices, and editorials targeted at Muslims. In other ways the paper also spoke to a broader Indian readership, through its coverage analyzing cultures external to South Asia.[135] Even so, *Madīnah* encouraged its readership to see the Urdu newspaper conversation as protective of Muslim interests.

Madīnah showed some editorial coherence, and the proprietorship of *Madīnah* stayed in the hands of a single family, the Ḥasan family, from its inception in 1912 until the doors of the press closed in the 1970s. *Madīnah* was not a monolith, however. It did not imbibe a party line and transmit it unfiltered to a national audience. *Madīnah*'s character and focus transformed significantly according to editorial leadership and writer contributions, often publishing conflicting views on specific issues to cultivate a rich conversation. And the editors and writers who worked for *Madīnah* went on to enact dramatically divergent visions of South Asian Islam's future. Working within a network of publications that traded writers and editors regularly, *Madīnah* became a recognizable, distinctive publication that represented a Muslim voice from the *qasbah* context, a set of voices that gained influence precisely because they resisted easy categorization.

In this chapter I have sketched an outline of the world of *Madīnah* and its intertwining with the broader Urdu newspaper conversation in the early twentieth century. Chapter 2 establishes the significance of space and time in the influence wielded by the paper, contributing to the creation of the discursive category of the *qasbah* as an authentic voice in the Urdu public.

Notes

1. Syed Muḥammad Aqīl Rizvī, ed., *Intik̲h̲āb-i Madīnah Bijnor* [Selections of Madīnah Bijnor](Lucknow: Uttar Pradesh Urdu Academy, 1988), 5, 9; Syed ʿAqīl Ḥaidar, "Uttar Pradesh mein̲ Urdū Ṣaḥāfat [Urdu Journalism in Uttar Pradesh]," *Nayā Daur: Urdū Ṣaḥāfat* (June/July 2011): 144–45.

2. Furqān Aḥmad Ṣiddīqī, *Z̤ilaʿ Bijnor ke Javāhir* [The Jewelry of Bijnor] (Delhi: Jade Press, 1991), 40–43.

3. Saʿādat Ḥasan Manṭo, "*Nayā Qānūn* [New Law]," in *Manṭo ke numāyandah afsāne* (Aligarh: Ejūkeshnal Buk Hāʾus, 1977), 13–45.

4. Cart drawn by a single horse.

5. Saʿādat Ḥasan Manṭo, "Nayā Qānūn," in *Readings in Urdu: Prose and Poetry*, ed. C. M. Naim (Honolulu: East-West Center Press, 1965), 49–64, Digital South Asia Website, http://dsal.uchicago.edu/digbooks/dig_toc.html?BOOKID=PK1975.N18.

6. Munibur Rahman, "The Mushaʾirah," *Annual of Urdu Studies* 3 (1983); Syed Nūr ul-Ḥasan Hashimi, *Eik Nādir Roznāmchah* (Lucknow: n.p., 1954), 4; for reference to Allahabad, see Mushirul Ḥasan, "Qasbas: A Brief in Propinquity," *A Leaf Turns Yellow: The Sufis of Awadh*, ed. Muzaffar Ali (New Delhi: Rumi Foundation / Bloomsbury Publishing India, 2013), 110.

7. Derived from the Hindi word *aḍḍā*, meaning "roost," *aḍḍā bāzī* describes lengthy gatherings accompanied by food and conversation.

8. Ahtesham Khan, conversation, Lucknow, India, March 30, 2013.

9. For reference to readers of *Madīnah* in Lucknow, see Parvez ʿĀdil, "Madīnah Ak̲h̲bār" (PhD thesis, University of Najibabad, 2013), 14. For reference to readers in Lahore, see Furqān Aḥmad Ṣiddīqī, *Z̤ilaʿ Bijnor ke Javāhir* [The Jewelry of Bijnor] (Delhi: Jade Press, 1991), 40–43; Muḥammad Zakariyā Kāndhlavī, *Āp Bītī* (Lahore: Darul Ishāʿt, 2003). G̲h̲ulām Ḥusain reported learning of an attack by reading *Madīnah* or *Zamīndār* in Kabul. See "Conviction of Muzaffar Ahmad Shaukat Usmani, as a Danger and Nalini Gupta in the Bolshevik Conspiracy Case. Withdrawal of Prosecution against G̲h̲ulām Ḥussain and Singaraveln Chetty," July 11, 1923, 21, Home Political 1924 F-261 kw, National Archives of India.

10. Furqān Aḥmad Ṣiddīqī, *Z̤ilaʿ Bijnor ke Javāhir* [The Jewelry of Bijnor] (Delhi: Jade Press, 1991), 40–43.

11. The standard fee was 3 rupees, with discounts for madrasahs and a surcharge for landed *zamīndārs*. To understand the meaning of the subscription rates, note that

books sold for a few annas in this period and 16 annas made a rupee. The landed paid about double the normal subscription fee at any time. *Madīnah*, May 1, 1912, 1.

12. "*Akhbār Madīnah ka vajah-yi tasmiyah* [The reason for the naming of *Madīnah*]," *Madīnah*, May 1, 1912, 1.
13. Parvez ʿĀdil, personal correspondence with author, October 15, 2013.
14. Muneer Akhtar, personal conversation, Bijnor, April 14–16, 2013. N.B.: The honorific *phūphā* refers to a paternal aunt's husband.
15. ʿAbad Samīʾ ul-dīn, quoted in Parvez ʿĀdil, "Madīnah Akhbār" (PhD thesis, University of Najibabad, 2013), 46.
16. Daldanius Artemidorus, *Kitāb Taʿbīr al-rūʾyā*, ed. ʿAbd al-Munʾim al-Hafni and Ḥunayn bin Isḥāq (Cairo: Dar al-Rashad, 1991), 18–19, cited in M. Amanullah, "Islamic Dreaming: An Analysis of Its Truthfulness and Influence," in *Dreaming in Christianity and Islam: Culture, Conflict, and Creativity*, ed. Kelly Bulkeley, Kate Adams, and Patricia M. Davis (New Brunswick, NJ: Rutgers University Press, 2009), 100–101.
17. Gottfried Hagen, "Dreams in Biographical, Historical, Theological, Poetical, and Oral Narratives, and on the Internet," in *Dreams and Visions in Islamic Societies*, ed. Özgen Felek and Alexander D. Knysh (Albany: State University of New York Press, 2012), 104.
18. Nile Green, "The Propriety of Poetry: Morality and Mysticism in the Nineteenth Century Urdu Religious Lyric," *Middle Eastern Literatures: Incorporating Edebiyat* 13, no. 3 (December 16, 2010): 299.
19. Nūr ul-Ḥasan Rashīd, conversation with author, Kandhala, India, April 2013.
20. Literally "nation, people, race, or tribe," the meaning of the term *qaum* was subject to dramatic shifts in the first half of the twentieth century. For a short reflection on these shifts, see Ali Usman Qasmi and Megan Eaton Robb, "Introduction," in *Muslims against the Muslim League*, edited by Ali Usman Qasmi and Megan Eaton Robb (New Delhi: Cambridge University Press, 2017), 7–8.
21. Parvez ʿĀdil, *Tārīkh-i Madīnah Bijnor* (Rampur: Applied Books, 2018), 133–40.
22. "That son of Bijnor who started up the newspaper *Madīnah* with so little capital yet through his skill and worthiness made it into a distinguished Indian newspaper. Maulwi Sahab, with his prudence, discipline, order, and moderation, was taught that through belief in God a man can start a project with a small measure [of resources] and God will bestow good fortune and progress so that it can become an example for the entire world. Maulvī Majīd Ḥasan Sahab's newspaper *Madīnah* also became an example for the entire world." Farzānah Mashmulah, *Roznāmah-yi ʿAvām* [People's Daily], January 30, 1996.
23. Quoted by Zīyā al-Ḥasan Farūqī, *Do Māhī* [Bimonthly] (Lucknow: n.p., 1981), 74, cited in Parvez ʿĀdil, "Madīnah Akhbār" (PhD thesis, University of Najibabad, 2013), 30.
24. Department of Criminal Intelligence. *Statement of Newspapers and Periodicals Published in the United Provinces during the Year 1912 [with Index]*. Simla: Government Central Branch Press, 1913.
25. Farzanah Khalīl Mashmulah, *Roznāmah-yi ʿAvām* [People's Daily], January 30, 1996.
26. E.g., Moḥd ʿAbdul Shāhīd Khān Sherwānī, ed., *Karvān-i Khayāl* [Caravan of Thoughts] (Bijnor: Madīnah Press, 1946). For a sample list of books, see "*Madīnah Buk Eijansī kī Qābil-i Qadar Kitābein*" [Madīnah Book Agency's Distinguished Books], *Madīnah*, April 13, 1937, 16.

27. Farzanah Khalīl Mashmulah, *Roznāmah-yi ʻAvām* [People's Daily], January 30, 1996, cited in email correspondence with Parvez ʻĀdil, September 4, 2008.
28. "*Jeib mein chand paise bhī hon to sā'il si inkār mat karo.*" ʻAbad Samī' ul-dīn, cited in Parvez ʻĀdil, *Tārīkh-i Madīnah Bijnor* (Rampur: Applied Books, 2018), 133–40.
29. Parvez ʻĀdil, *Tārīkh- i Madīnah Bijnor* (Rampur: Applied Books 2018), 133– 40.
30. Parvez ʻĀdil, *Tārīkh- i Madīnah Bijnor* (Rampur: Applied Books, 2018), 133– 40.
31. Parvez ʻĀdil, *Tārīkh-i Madīnah Bijnor* (Rampur: Applied Books, 2018), 133– 40.
32. *Mirāt-ul ʻUrūs* [The Bride's Mirror] was published by Nawāl Kishor Press in the 1880s. The book, inspired in part by similar texts in Victorian Britain, encouraged reform of Muslim women's education and manners. Nazīr Aḥmed compares the fates of two sisters. Akbarī, the eldest, personifies ignorance and greed. Asgharī, the younger sister, is a paragon of virtue. For an Urdu copy of the text, see Nazīr Aḥmed, *Mirāt-ul ʻUrūs* (Lucknow: Nawal Kishore Press, 1881).
33. ʻAbad Samī' ul-dīn, quoted in Parvez ʻĀdil, "Madīnah Akhbār" (PhD thesis, University of Najibabad, 2013), 30.
34. Margrit Pernau, *Ashraf into Middle Classes: Muslims in Nineteenth-Century Delhi* (New Delhi: Oxford University Press, 2013), 59.
35. Qatīl, 1968, 77–79, 83–84, 86–87, 92–93, 96, cited in Margrit Pernau, *Ashraf into Middle Classes: Muslims in Nineteenth-Century Delhi* (New Delhi: Oxford University Press, 2013) 59–60.
36. Khattri refers to a Hindu caste from the northern Indian subcontinent.
37. Margrit Pernau, *Ashrāf into Middle Classes: Muslims in Nineteenth-Century Delhi* (New Delhi: Oxford University Press, 2013), 62; Ralph Russell and Khurshidul Islam, *Ghalib 1797–1869: Life and Letters* (Delhi: Oxford University Press, 1994), 47.
38. Margrit Pernau, *Ashrāf into Middle Classes: Muslims in Nineteenth-Century Delhi* (New Delhi: Oxford University Press, 2013), 64.
39. Majīd Ḥasan, "*Ẓarūrī guzārish* [Necessary Announcement]," *Madīnah*, September 21, 1927; Parvez ʻĀdil, *Tārīkh-i Madīnah Bijnor* (Rampur: Applied Books, 2018), 358.
40. Muneer Ḥasan Akhtar and Parvez ʻĀdil, conversation, Bijnor, April 14–16, 2013.
41. Parvez ʻĀdil, WhatsApp correspondence, August 3, 2018.
42. *Statement of Newspapers and Periodicals Published in the United Provinces during 1926* (Allahabad: Supt., Govt. Press, 1927), British Library.
43. Department of Criminal Intelligence, *Statement of Newspapers and Periodicals Published in the United Provinces during the Year 1912 [with Index]* (Simla: Government Central Branch Press, 1913), Uttar Pradesh State Archives.
44. *Madīnah*, May 12, 1912, 1; Parvez ʻĀdil, telephone conversation with author, June 18–25, 2013.
45. Parvez ʻĀdil, "Madīnah Akhbār" (PhD thesis, University of Najibabad, 2013), 52.
46. Parvez ʻĀdil, "Madīnah Akhbār" (PhD thesis, University of Najibabad, 2013), 64; *Madīnah*, April 18, 1913, 9.
47. *Indian Newspaper Reports*, March 13, 1915; *Madīnah*, March 1, 1913, 1.
48. Parvez ʻĀdil, telephone conversation with author, June 16, 2013; H. R. Nevill, *Bulandshahr: A Gazetteer* (Allahabad: Supt., Govt. Press, 1903); for a more detailed

exploration of Bulandhshahr's architecture, which reveals elements of heritage present in the last half of the nineteenth century, see Frederic Salmon Growse, *Indian Architecture of To-day as Exemplified in New Buildings in the Bulandshahr District* (Allahabad: North-Western Provinces and Oudh Government Press, 1885–1886).

49. Santhi Kavuri-Bauer, *Monumental Matters: The Power, Subjectivity, and Space of India* (Durham: Duke University Press, 2011), 111–14.
50. *Madīnah*, April 23, 1913.
51. *Madīnah*, September 8 and September 15, 1913.
52. *Indian Newspaper Reports*, July 1, 1914. Also see chapter 4 of this volume.
53. Parvez ʿĀdil, "Māhī," *Tārīkh-i Madīnah Bijnor* (New Delhi: Applied Books, 2018), 311–13.
54. At this time the newspaper began to print on its cover page a list of words describing its ideological priorities on its header: "*Islāmī, sīyāsī, ʿilmī, akhlāqī, tamadanī* [Islamic, Political, Educational, Ethical, Cultural]."
55. *Madīnah*, April 28, 1917, 1.
56. Satish Chandra Mittal, *Freedom Movement in Punjab, 1905–29* (Punjab: Concept Pub. Company, 1977), 184; Parvez ʿĀdil, "Madīnah Akhbār" (PhD thesis, University of Najibabad, 2013), 40.
57. "*Teḥerīk-i āzād ka pehelā shahīd* [First Martyr in Freedom Movement]," *Madīnah*, November 5, 1918, 6.
58. "*Payām-i aman: sulah kānfarans kā ineqād* [Message of Peace: The Holding of the District Conference]," *Madīnah*, January 25, 1919, 2; "*Āll Inḍia Muslim Līg aur maslah-yi khilāf* [All India Muslim League and the Issue of the Khilafat]," *Madīnah*, October 9, 1919; "*Vafād Muslim līg kī tāzah ʿarzdāsht be-khidmat vazīr-i ʿāzim* [The Loyal Muslim League's Latest Request to the Prime Minister]," *Madīnah*, October 9, 1919, 5.
59. "*Gereftār aur Mahātmā Gāndhī kā payām* [Arrest and the Message of Mahātmā Gāndhī]," *Madīnah*, April 13, 1919, 7; "*Mahātmā Gāndhī Amritsar mein* [Mahātmā Gāndhī in Amritsar]," *Madīnah*, November 13, 1919, 5.
60. E.g., *Maslah-yi Turkī* [The Issue of Turkey] *Madīnah*, January 25, 1919, 4; "*Khilāfah-yi Aval kī Tajārat-o Sakhāvat* [The Economic Generosity of the First Caliphate]," *Madīnah*, February 13, 1919, 1.
61. "*Islām aur Naishanalizam: Islāmī Qaumī-yi Hurriyāt aur Musāvat* [Islam and Nationalism: The Freedom and Equality of the Muslim Community]," *Madīnah*, October 21, 1919, 2.
62. *UP Government Poll: Report for Fortnight Ending 30-4-1919*, Internal Government Correspondence, 1919, National Archives of India.
63. "*Panjāb Gavarnmanṭ kā tarz-i ʿamal: Lāhor-o-Amritsar kī nāzak hālat Panjāb kī khabron par ānsar muqarar dīyā gayā* [Panjab Government's Course of Action: The Delicate Condition of Lahore and Amritsar, Censorship Established for Panjab's Newspapers], *Madīnah*, April 18, 1919.
64. *Yasrab (Madīnah)*, August 25, 1919.
65. *Madīnah*, September 13, 1919, 1. Thank you to ʿAli Noori for discussing this translation with me.

66. "At the end of August the *Yasrab* (a new incarnation of the *Medina*) was excluded." Report on the Punjab Disturbances, Home Political A, 1920 APR 126–164, 31, National Archives of India.
67. *UP Government Poll: Report for Fortnight Ending 30-4-1919,* Internal Government Correspondence, 1919, National Archives of India.
68. Department of Criminal Intelligence, *Statement of Newspapers and Periodicals Published in the United Provinces 1934* (Allahabad: Supt., Govt. Press, 1935), British Library.
69. Mohammad Mohiuddin Qāẓī, "*Hazār sāl jad-o jehed* [*Thousand Year Struggle*] (n.p., n.d.), 242, cited in Parvez 'Ādil, *Tārīkh-i Madīnah Bijnor* (Rampur: Applied Books, 2018), 315.
70. *Almān*, "Martyr of the Community," May 1939, 5, cited in Parvez 'Ādil, "Madīnah Akhbār" (Ph.D. thesis, University of Najibabad, 2013), 14; Qāẓī, *Thousand Year Struggle*, 262, cited in Parvez 'Ādil, *Tārīkh-i Madīnah Bijnor* (Rampur: Applied Books, 2018), 315.
71. Muḥammad Irshād 'Abāsī, *Āyina shab-o roz: Zātī dā'irī* [The Mirror of Days and Nights: Personal Diary], cited in Parvez 'Ādil, *Tārīkh-i Madīnah Bijnor* (New Delhi: Applied Books, 2018), 330.
72. Parvez 'Ādil, *Tārīkh-i Madīnah Bijnor* (New Delhi: Applied Books, 2018), 324.
73. "The proprietor took alarm at the prosecution and resigned the post of publisher and printer and substituted a man of straw. However he still controls the policy." Department of Criminal Intelligence, *Statement of Newspapers and Periodicals Published in the United Provinces* (Allahabad: Supt., Govt. Press, 1924), British Library.
74. Department of Criminal Intelligence, *Statement of Newspapers and Periodicals Published in the United Provinces,* (Allahabad: Supt., Govt. Press, 1926), British Library.
75. 'Abdul Raḥmān Nāṣir, special issue on Maulānā Amīn Aḥsan Iṣlāhī, *Shahanshāhī 'Ulūm ul-Qur'ān Aligarh* 13–15 (January 1998–December 2000): 563, cited in Parvez 'Ādil, *Tārīkh-i Madīnah Bijnor* (Rampur: Applied Books, 2018), 361.
76. Parvez 'Ādil, *Tārīkh-i Madīnah Bijnor* (Rampur: Applied Books, 2018), 324–27.
77. *Madīnah*, September 21, 1928, 1, quoted in Parvez 'Ādil, *Tārīkh-i Madīnah Bijnor* (Rampur: Applied Books, 2018), 324.
78. *Madīnah*, September 12, 1928, 1, quoted in Parvez 'Ādil, *Tārīkh-i Madīnah Bijnor* (Rampur: Applied Books, 2018), 324.
79. Department of Criminal Intelligence, *Statement of Newspapers and Periodicals Published in the United Provinces,* 1928 (Allahabad: Supt., Govt. Press, 1929), British Library.
80. Qāzī 'Abdul Ghaffār was the publisher of *Payām* (Hyderabad) in 1940 and the author of three notable books: *Laila ke Khatūt, Majnū kī Dā'iry*, and *Ajīb*. He was involved in the creation of the "Sundar Lal Report" on the 1948 massacres following police action in Hyderabad, which was so inflammatory it has remained classified by the Indian government. Rafat Alam, "Qazi Abdul Ghaffar—My Maternal Grandfather (Nana Abba)," Rafat Alam's blog, http://www.rafatalam.com/Qāẓī-abdul-ghaffar-my-maternal-grandfather-nana-abba. Also see Syed Ali Mujtaba, "Hyderabad's Fall and Sunderlal Report," CounterCurrents.org, https://www.countercurrents.org/mujtaba290913.htm.
81. 2010 interview between Parvez 'Ādil and the son of Nūr ul-Raḥmān, Asad al-Raḥmān, cited in Parvez 'Ādil, "Madīnah Akhbār" (Ph.D. thesis, University of Najibabad, 2013), 214.

82. There were multiple subeditors during his tenure; Muḥammad Aḥsan and Maulānā Abūllais̱ Iṣlāḥī Nadvī (1913–1990), who would become the first amīr of the Jamā'at-i Islāmī Hind, were among these.
83. "Statement of Prosecutions and Convictions under Sections 121-A, 124-A, 153-A, and 295-A of the Indian Penal Code. During the months of January, February, March and April 1930," Home Political 1930 F-173-1 Part li, 196–208, National Archives of India.
84. "*Faṣl-i Bahār* [Spring Season]," *Madīnah*, March 17, 1931, 3.
85. For example, see *Madīnah*, December 1, 1930; December 5, 1930; December 9, 1930; December 13, 1930; December 17, 1930; December 21, 1930; December 25, 1930; December 28, 1930. In 1931, the newspaper stopped distinguishing between the different roles of its administrators, merely listing K͟hān, G͟hāzī, and the assistant editor.
86. Department of Criminal Intelligence, *Statement of Newspapers and Periodicals Published in the United Provinces*, 1934 (Allahabad: Supt., Govt. Press, 1935), British Library.
87. Department of Criminal Intelligence, *Statement of Newspapers and Periodicals Published in the United Provinces*, 1935 (Allahabad: Supt., Govt. Press, 1936), British Library.
88. Among the most prominent of these papers were *Oudh Punch*, *al-Hilāl*, and *al-Bilāg͟h*. See Department of Criminal Intelligence, *Statement of Newspapers and Periodicals Published in the United Provinces during the Year 1912 [with Index]* (Simla: Government Central Branch Press, 1913), 388–89, Uttar Pradesh State Archives. Department of Criminal Intelligence, *Statements of Newspapers and Periodicals Published in India and Burma during the Year 1914* (Delhi: Supt., Govt. Printing, India, 1916), Home Political A 1916 MAR51, National Archives of India.
89. "Majīd Ḥusain, Sheikh, Sunni, age about 41 years; a man formerly of no position and of limited means, and was formerly employed in some press in the Punjab. Has now made a lot of money out of his press and acquired considerable influence among local Muhammadans." Department of Criminal Intelligence, *Statement of Newspapers and Periodicals Published in India and Burma during the Year 1924* (Delhi: Supt., Govt. Printing, India, 1925). Home Political 1925 F-204-lv-25, National Archives of India.
90. Parvez 'Ādil, *Tārīk͟h-i Madīnah Bijnor* (Rampur: Applied Books, 2018), 339–42.
91. Parvez 'Ādil, *Tārīk͟h-i Madīnah Bijnor* (Rampur: Applied Books, 2018), 348.
92. Note that 'Ādil lists this retirement date at 1973, which is likely a clerical error since 'Ādil records that Fāraqlaiṯ died in 1967. Parvez 'Ādil, *Tārīk͟h-i Madīnah Bijnor* (Rampur: Applied Books, 2018), 349.
93. Parvez 'Ādil, *Tārīk͟h-i Madīnah Bijnor* (Rampur: Applied Books, 2018), 353.
94. The eighteen-page file is labeled "az 'Allāmah Mashriqī," suggesting that Allāmah Mashriqī, the founder of the Khaksar movement, was the one keeping the reading notes. Raza Rampur Library, *Madīnah*, May 1, 1939.
95. Department of Criminal Intelligence, *Statement of Newspapers and Periodicals Published in the United Provinces*, 1936, 1950 (Allahabad: Supt., Govt. Press, 1937, 1951), British Library.
96. Ẓīyā ul-Ḥasan Farūqī, *Risālah Do-māhī* (Lucknow: Uttar Pradesh Urdu Academy, 1981), 89; Parvez 'Ādil, *Tārīk͟h-i Madīnah Bijnor* (Rampur: Applied Books, 2018), 316.
97. Naẕīr Reḥmānī, G͟hunchah 30 (October 1, 1951), 3–4; cited in Parvez 'Ādil, *Tārīk͟h-i Madīnah Bijnor* (Rampur: Applied Books, 2018), 316–18.
98. *Madīnah*, July 25, 1940, 2; *Journal* 113 (September 1998): 13; cited in Parvez 'Ādil, *Tārīk͟h-i Madīnah Bijnor* (Rampur: Applied Books, 2018), 319.

99. Parvez ʻĀdil, *Tārīkh-i Madīnah Bijnor* (Rampur: Applied Books, 2018), 319–20.
100. Department of Criminal Intelligence, *Statement of Newspapers and Periodicals Published in the United Provinces*, 1936 (Allahabad: Supt., Govt. Press, 1937), British Library.
101. *List of Newspapers and Periodicals in the United Provinces*, 1945.
102. "As stated by Sir R. Tottenham in his noting of 19.2.42, the primary consideration in granting or refusing export permits is the question of military security. Amongst information which in war time must be denied to the enemy is that which can be made into valuable propaganda material by the enemy." "Proposal that Home Department Should in Future Deal with Question Affecting the Refusal of Export Licenses to Newspaper Etc., And That the C.C.I. Should Refer Such Cases for Orders of the Home Department through the D.I.B," 14, Home Political I 1941 F-33-26 41; "List of Newspapers to Which Bureau of Public Information is Subscribing for the Year 1940–1," Home Political 1 1940 F-33-11 40, National Archives of India.
103. Anṣārī's colleagues in founding Nadwatul Muṣannifīn were Maulānā Muftī ʻatīq al-Raḥmān ʻUs̱mānī, Maulānā Ḥafẕ ul-Raḥmān Saiyūhārvī, and Maulānā Sʻaīd Aḥmad Akbarābādī. Parvez ʻĀdil, *Tārīkh-i Madīnah Bijnor* (Rampur: Applied Books, 2018), 341.
104. Parvez ʻĀdil, *Tārīkh-i Madīnah Bijnor* (Rampur: Applied Books, 2018), 342.
105. ʻĀrif ʻAzīz Matbūʻa, *Ẕikr-i jamīl* (Bhopal: Madhīyah Pradīsh urdū ākādamī, 1995), 72, cited in Parvez ʻĀdil, *Tārīkh-i Madīnah Bijnor* (Rampur: Applied Books, 2018), 321–23.
106. The term *shāhīn*, literally falcon, was used by Iqbal as a symbol for Muslim youth.
107. E.g., *Madīnah*, May 1, 1913; August 1, 1913; December 15/22, 1914; April 15, 1915; January 22, 1916.
108. E.g., The report of the Meerath Circle Educational Week mushairah in 1937. "*Tahzib-i maghrib*," *Madīnah*, February 5, 1937, 1.
109. E.g., "*ʻĀm akhbār aur ʻām tār*," *Madīnah*, May 22, 1912, 10.
110. E.g., "*Anjuman-i tarqī-yi taʻlīm kā sālānah jalsah* [The Annual Meeting of the Organization of the Advancement of Education], *Madīnah*, March 8, 1919, 2.
111. E.g., "*Naqs̄hah-yi Yurop* [Map of Europe]," *Madīnah*, August 22, 1914, 8.
112. E.g., "*Nadwat ul-ʻulamā' ke arākein* (sic) *mein bāhamī ikhtilāf* [Differences among the Members of Nadwah]," *Madīnah*, August 15, 1913, 8; "*Nadwah*," *Madīnah*, May 5, 1917, 4.
113. E.g., "*Fatāwe mutaʻliq masjid machhlī bāzār kānpur* [Fatwas Relating to the Machli Bazar Mosque, Kanpur], *Madīnah*, August 15, 1913, 8; "Fatāwe," *Madīnah*, August 22, 1916, 8; October 15, 1916, 8; October 22, 1916, 8; November 1, 1916, 8; January 1, 1917, 8.
114. Raḥīm Bakhsh Shāhīn, "Maulānā Maudūdī" (unpublished manuscript), 118–19, cited in Parvez ʻĀdil, *Tārīkh-i Madīnah Bijnor* (Rampur: Applied Books, 2018), 335–38. According to ʻĀdil, Maudūdī contributed to *Madīnah* at the same time as he was contributing to the newspapers *Tāj* (Jabalpur) and *Muslim* (Delhi).
115. Raḥīm Bakhsh Shāhīn, *Maulānā Maudūdī* (unpublished manuscript), 118–19, cited in Parvez ʻĀdil, *Tārīkh-i Madīnah Bijnor* (Rampur: Applied Books, 2018), 335–38.

116. *"Ya'anī mulkī ta'līmyāftah mo'azaz k̲h̲awātīn ke liye ak̲h̲bār madīnah kā mak̲h̲ṣūṣ ṣafhah* [For Honorable, Educated, Indian Women, a Special Page]," *Madīnah*, February 8, 1913, 8.

117. E.g., *"Ak̲h̲bār-i nisvān* [Women's Newspaper]," *Madīnah*, August 8, 1913, 9.

118. For more on *Madīnah* 's Women's Newspaper, see Megan Eaton Robb, "Women's Voices, Men's Lives: Masculinity in a North Indian Urdu Newspaper," *Modern Asian Studies* 50, no. 5 (2016): 1441–73.

119. See, for example, *"Al-Nisvān Madīnah: Y'anī mulkī ta'līmyāfta k̲h̲avātīn ke līye ak̲h̲bār Madīnah ka mak̲h̲ṣūṣ ṣafḥa* [For the Women of Madinah: Meaning the Newspaper Madinah's Special Page for the Educated Women of the Country]," *Madinah*, February 8, 1913, 8.

120. Muneer Akhtar, interview, Bijnor, Uttar Pradesh, April 14–16, 2013.

121. Megan Eaton Robb, "Women's Voices, Men's Lives: Masculinity in a North Indian Urdu Newspaper," *Modern Asian Studies* 50, no. 5 (2016): 1441–73.

122. Megan Eaton Robb, "Women's Voices, Men's Lives: Masculinity in a North Indian Urdu Newspaper," *Modern Asian Studies* 50, no. 5 (2016): 1445.

123. E.g., *Madīnah*, February 5, 1937, 1.

124. "Medina, March 13, 1915." *Selections from Indian Owned Newspapers Published in the United Provinces 1914–1916* (Nainital: United Provinces Government, 1917), 298, Uttar Pradesh State Archives.

125. *Madīnah*, May 8, 1913, 5.

126. *"Ak̲h̲bār madīnah mein hafte mein do bār* [*Madīnah* Newspaper Twice in One Week]," *Madīnah*, December 1, 1916.

127. *Madīnah*, November 5, 1917, 3.

128. Gyanendra Pandey, *The Ascendancy of the Congress in Uttar Pradesh, 1926–34: A Study in Imperfect Mobilization* (Delhi: Oxford University Press, 1978), 64.

129. Gyanendra Pandey, *The Ascendancy of the Congress in Uttar Pradesh, 1926–1934: A Study in Imperfect Mobilization* (Delhi: Oxford University Press, 1979), 64.

130. Department of Criminal Intelligence, *Statement of Newspapers and Periodicals Published in the United Provinces, 1936, 1950* (Allahabad: Supt., Govt. Press, 1937, 50), British Library.

131. Gyanendra Pandey, *The Ascendancy of the Congress in Uttar Pradesh, 1926–34: A Study in Imperfect Mobilization* (Delhi: Oxford University Press, 1979), 64.

132. Department of Criminal Intelligence, *Statement of Newspapers and Periodicals Published in the United Provinces in 1926* (Allahabad: Supt., Govt. Press, 1927), British Library.

133. Muḥammad Zakarīyā Kāndhlavī, *Āp Bītī* (Lahore: Darul Isha'at, 2003).

134. *Memorandum submitted by the Government of the United Provinces to the Indian Statutory Commission*, vol. 9 (London: Indian Statutory Commission, 1930), 209, OP-RC/116A, British Library.

135. A serialized article on the people of Siam [modern Thailand] reviews in detail how Siamese women are different from Indian women. It describes the "horrible" smell of the food that they prepare and the "strange" way that they dress their hair. Despite these observations, the editors encouraged female readers to accept Siamese women into their kinship groups if their brothers chose a Siamese wife. *"Sayām*: Part I," *Madīnah*, October 1, 1913, 8; *"Sayām*: Part II," *Madīnah*, October 22, 1913, 9.

2

Back to the Future *Qasbah*

The Timescape of Bijnor

This chapter delves into the role of space and time in the formation of the public. Statements in *Madīnah* linked Bijnor's physical isolation to a temporal distance, a spatial-temporal rift that allowed it to define a segment of the Urdu public that stood at odds with the "Westernized city" and from this position also to reach out and connect with a broader Muslim *qaum*. This chapter explores the power of alternate temporalities, enabled by nostalgia, as a mechanism of power. Statements about the passage of time were irruptive, enabling the construction of an alternative *qasbah* timescape, and with this alternative timescape, an alternative public.[1] While the *qasbah* has more recently been tied to an idealized past, close analysis of the discourse of *Madīnah* newspaper reveals an early twentieth-century voice that saw the present, past, and future as productively intertwined in the *qasbah*. This argument proceeds with reference to the way *Madīnah* newspaper positioned itself in response to the spatial disruptions of the telegraph and the railway, as well as biographical and periodical writings on prominent *qasbati*s with links to Bijnor that explicitly discuss the past. It is this form of cosmological production that helps define the public to which *Madīnah* addressed itself, and that ultimately undergirded the paper's production of political alterities described in chapters 4 and 5.

The Speed of Time

Poets, philosophers, and journalists were preoccupied with the subject of time in late nineteenth- and early twentieth-century British India. Ghalib wrote that *raftār-i ʿumr*, a span of a life, "means traversing a path of restlessness/the calculation of a year is a flash of lightning, not the sun."[2] While time and its passage are implicit in the metaphor *raftār-i ʿumr*, the poetic trope *raftār-i zamānah* or "the speed of time" or "swiftly changing time" linked time explicitly to reflections on religion, society, and politics. Majrooh Sultanpuri (1919–2000) penned the following couplet that touched on the nature of time:

> Time takes its speed from those voices, whose lyrical flower is the world;
> With those voices we prisoners harmonize

Print and the Urdu Public. Megan Eaton Robb, Oxford University Press (2021). © Oxford University Press.
DOI: 10.1093/oso/9780190089375.001.0001

raftār zamānah le jin kī, gītī hai gul-i naghma jin kā
ham gāte hain un āvāzon se āvāz milā'e zindān mein[3]

As in all ghazals, the meaning here was open to interpretation. The voices mentioned in the second line established the rhythm of time itself and produced the world through its lyrics. By joining with the melody the listeners could harmonize with the speed of time from within the walls of oppression, which could be a reference to the timeless strictures of mortality or to something as specific as the British Raj. In the couplet, all listeners were inmates of prison. The imagery of music called to mind, on the one hand, time's separation from its listeners and their helplessness to change its inexorable path. On the other hand, important in the couplet was the chance to contribute to the melody of time by harmonizing with it.

Poets and scholars were not the only ones preoccupied with time and our relationship to it; it was also an important concern for journalists writing in Urdu. Majīd Ḥasan and other upstart journalists in the first half of the twentieth century bemoaned the passage of time and sought to harmonize with it. A telling poem appeared in *Madīnah*'s first issue. Titled *raftār-i zamānah* or "speed of time," it expressed regret over the irrelevance of Islam in a changing era.

The carousel of the world[4] has brought with it a wonderful change
Muslims are dozing in a dream of ignorance these days.

rang lāyā hai nirālā charkh gardan ājkal
so rahe hain khwāb-i ghaflat mein musalmān ājkal

[. . .]
If there could be the assistance of the Holy Prophet,
Then the unmindful Muslims might come awake.

gar madad beher Muḥammad Muṣtafa islām kī
hosh mein ā jā'en ghāfil musalmān ājkal[5]

This poem was a *marṣiyah*[6] for times past, mourning the lost importance of Islam and invoking the Prophet to "wake up" Muslim readers. Following Sultanpuri's metaphor, the speed of time was singing a melody, but in this poem Muslims remained asleep to its sound. The Prophet was not in himself Time but the agent who could shake Muslims out of their stupor and make them aware of, and perhaps bring them into harmony with, Time. Becoming aware of time related to key goals relevant to *ashrāf* ideals: cultivating *itifāq*, or unity; *'ilm*, or knowledge of the Qur'an; and *ḥadīth*, which comprised modesty in thought and expression as well as correct wardrobe choices. Time had a role in the formation of the Muslim public, as the arena in which unity and knowledge were expressed, ranges of acceptable dress and expression determined, and the history of a community made.

In *adab*-based traditions there is the process of continuously relating the present to the past. Holy words, authoritative individuals, and auspicious gaps in time and space serve as the threads sewing present and past into one coherent timescape. There was also from the eighteenth century on an anxiety to separate the public and private spheres—with religion belonging to the private—Nazīr Aḥmed being one of the most prominent of those reformist thinkers affirming this division.[7] As Metcalf stated, "Most of the time, perhaps, individuals live without self-conscious attention to the integrity and coherence of their values, but in times of crisis and change, lines are drawn and values explored."[8] Or to extend the above metaphor, the seams linking past to present are sometimes tested, torn, or intentionally ripped out and sewn again. In the early twentieth century, the rise of new technologies of transport and communication, and the vicissitudes of the nationalist movement and its factions' attitudes toward religious identity, prompted such "crisis and change." This preoccupation with time in the face of historical change helps account for statements of increased nostalgia for Islam during a period when Islam was, counterintuitively, actually increasing in importance as a distinct social and political category in South Asia.

One distinctive aspect of this *zamānah*, or period, was the increasing prominence of newspaper conversation. While recent work has considered the role of print in the reformation of public spheres, this work has not adequately considered periodicals produced by Muslims as Muslims.[9] While it is important to note that the voice that Bijnor *qasbah* developed in this period is not equivalent to a singular voice for Islam, it is fair to say that Islam was relevant to social and political concerns of the public that emerged as the world of Muslim *qasbati*s began to overlap with the audience of Urdu newspapers. Through the lens of its newspaper discourse, in this chapter we see how a part of the Bijnor community refashioned itself by tearing apart and sewing together layers of Indo-Persian administrative culture, Urdu print formats, and the Muslim *qaum* with a subset of the existing Urdu print public that emphasized Islam. Social time was an implicit and explicit aspect of this print public, in which the past and present were primary materials used in the construction of the future.

Introduction to a Rohilkhand *Qasbah*: Bijnor Pre-1857

While settlements named *qasbah*s exist in various corners of the Muslim world—particularly North Africa and the Middle East—the connotations of the word vary. Used in North Africa to describe the quarters of a city where native Arabs live,[10] the word *qasbah* derives from the Arabic root meaning "to divide, cut up." The same root contributes to the words in contemporary Arabic meaning "city," "town," and "citadel." References to *qasbahs* first emerged in texts in the sixteenth century, when Abū Fazl described them as small towns within Mughal-controlled provinces. Muslims who claimed origins in the Middle East and Central Asia settled in North India and other regions from the eleventh century, gradually imbuing previously non-Muslim settlements with Islamic influence.[11] Mughal servants and Muslim migrants interacted with upper-caste Hindu kinship groups, such as the Kayasths, who also benefited from government patronage, contributing to the creation of a mobile, elite group based in the *qasbah*. While *qasbahs* appeared across the subcontinent, the largest and most distinctive belonged to North India.[12] *Qasbahs* in the United Provinces (hereafter UP) benefited from their proximity to Delhi, which gave them access to the Mughal imperial center and therefore court patronage.[13] North Indian *qasbahs* tended to cluster near Delhi, Lucknow, and Faizabad—the major centers of power during the Mughal period. Rohilkhand was a prominent region boasting several *qasbahs*.

Scholarship has defined a South Asian *qasbah* in a number of ways.[14] One perspective refers to the *qasbah* as a "market town," larger than a village but surrounded by agricultural producers who travel to the town regularly to exchange goods.[15] This definition prioritizes the economic character of the *qasbah*. This kind of "kasbah" appears in several colonial-era glossaries, where the word refers to a small settlement serving as a market for a particular district. The *ganj* and the *qasbah* were interchangeable in these sources, in contrast to current understandings that emphasize how their origins and affiliations to colonial power differed.[16] Under the Mughal Empire, the word *qasbah* became a term signifying a unit of administration.[17] Districts were separated into *parganahs*, of which *qasbahs* served as capital cities. British officials later adopted *qasbahs* as capitals of *tahsils*, local units created to enable efficient administration. *Qasbahs* often served as centers for revenue collectors, magistrates, and other colonial officials.[18]

A *qasbah* at the turn of the twentieth century was a settlement with a population above several thousand in size that boasted bureaucratic and market significance and where a significant Muslim minority or majority lived alongside a Hindu population.[19] For this study, what matters more than a bracket of population numbers is the sense of distinctiveness coloring the urban category of the *qasbah*. The compelling attraction of the *qasbah* as spiritual heartland and ancestral home remains significant for many contemporary Indians and Pakistanis.[20]

The region known as Rohilkhand, where Bijnor *qasbah* is located, earned its name during the eighteenth century when a series of independent rulers asserted dominance in the face of Mughal decline. ʿAlī Muḥammad's (1706–1748) establishment of sovereignty in the mid-eighteenth century during the reign of Emperor Muḥammad Shah (1702–1748) transformed the region previously known as Kuttaher to Rohilkhand, literally "the land of the mountain-dwellers," a reference to an influx of Afghan or Pathan immigrants during ʿAlī Muḥammad's period of rule. ʿAlī Muḥammad expanded the reach of Pathan or Rohilla governance in the area north of the Kotdwara mountains through action against the Raja of Kumaon, while west of the Ganges he expanded through military action against Qutb al-Mulk, the Mughal paymaster general (*ba<u>kh</u>shī al-mamālik*) under Muḥammad Shah.[21] Rohilkhand became an independent area only nominally loyal to the Mughals from the mid-eighteenth century. Rohilkhand was later subdued by the Marathas, who invaded in retaliation for Rohilla involvement in the Panipat war; it was then annexed by the Nawab of Audh in 1774 and by the East India Company in 1799. After 1799 the area controlled by ʿAlī Muḥammad's descendants, the Princely State of Rampur, remained limited to the small area around Bareilly. Even so, Bareilly and the rest of Rohilkhand remained rich in links to administrative positions and in patronage of the literary arts. In this region, first the East India Company and then the British Raj continued to depend on *qasbah*s as administrative centers for the collection of agricultural revenues.[22]

The Company separated Bijnor from Moradabad in 1817 to form a separate division.[23] The center of the new district was Naginah, until in 1824 the collector Mr. N. J. Halhed (who was also a key character in early operations against the "thugs") moved the headquarters to Bijnor, possibly in order to place the center closer to the military station at Meerut.[24] In 1837 the district's name changed from Moradabad to that of its administrative center, Bijnor. Rapid transfers of power, and the regular migration of the elite from locality to locality within the district, were not unique to Bijnor. Rather, in this regard, Bijnor was a characteristic example of the cumulative influence of migration on which the success of *qasbati* families and the character of individual *qasbah*s were built.

*Qasbah*s hosted markets for nearby villages and attracted early Sufi devotional figures before their significance as market towns for agricultural goods attracted Mughal investment in the form of administration and patronage.[25] As *qasbah*s grew from their origins as market towns and regional centers for agricultural areas, they retained strong roots in agriculture.[26] For the *ashrāf*, it was rights to agricultural revenue that defined possession. Population and resources shifted from large urban centers to medium and small urban centers over the course of the eighteenth century, reflecting the decline of imperial centers and the success of the Rohillas' model of political power. The *ashrāf* benefited from the revenue-free land grants of rulers, which often remained tied to the *qasbah*s where they had been conferred even if the ruler changed, creating institutional continuity despite constant migration. This happened in large cities such as Allahabad

(Shahjehani Sufis) and Lucknow (Firangi Mahal), as well as in *qasbahs*. This "digging in" occurred between 1690 and 1830, leading to a development of, in C. A. Bayly's words, a "[*qasbah*] culture which ran parallel to, though not yet in opposition to, that of the Hindu commercial towns."[27] This process established a persistent community of Muslim and also Hindu Kayasth *ashrāf* who survived the vicissitudes of specific regimes to consolidate institutional gains and gain land ownership. It also laid the groundwork for conflict once regional states declined in power and "changes in outlook" occurred that emphasized difference over solidarity.[28]

Bijnor *Qasbah* Post-1857

Bijnor features in one of the few detailed literary accounts of a district's response to the rebellion of 1857, written by Sir Syed Ahmad Khan, who was a subordinate judge in Bijnor district at the time. During the Uprising of 1857, Bijnor district demonstrated sharp division between Hindus and Muslims and participated in an overthrow of British authority after English administrators and their families fled across the Ganges. The Nawab of Najibabad, who was charged with the protection of the government and the treasury in the absence of the British, promptly took control of both after the English fled.[29] Bijnor only returned to English control through British military intervention. With the final dissolution of the Mughal Empire and the withdrawal of patronage from Muslims following 1857, *qasbahs* including Bijnor drew on their own administrators, artists, and scholars "to recreate a world in their own image."[30]

After 1857, the *'ulamā* of Delhi left the city for ancestral *qasbahs*. Disillusioned by the sacking of Delhi and the final disintegration of the Mughal Empire, and facing a sudden lack of patronage in the city, they fell back on well-maintained familial networks in their ancestral homes.[31] In *qasbahs* the demand for *ashrāf* administrators was still high. Barbara Metcalf has mentioned Deoband, Saharanpur, Kandhlah, Gangoh, and Bareilly as a few places that experienced an influx of *'ulamā* in this period.[32] The movement was merely one chapter in a longer trend of migration to and from *qasbahs*, dating from at least the eighteenth century. Members of the Sayyid, Shaikh, and Paṭhān communities leveraged their Mughal and colonial service backgrounds to obtain administrative service positions in either the new colonial government or in Hyderabad.[33] For example, Kakori residents secured employment at the district headquarters of Lucknow while simultaneously maintaining their roots in Kakori *qasbah*.[34]

For the service gentry, a migratory lifestyle had long been the norm. The Mughal Empire usually rotated local administrators every three years. The British colonial government adopted the same model.[35] The influx of financial support to the community in the form of revenue-free grants and institutions tended to outlive any individual *qasbati*.[36] Migration between localities, both between other *qasbah*s and between the *qasbah* and the city, were part and parcel of the life of a *qasbati*. This peripatetic lifestyle and the tendency of financial benefit to attach to the *qasbah* rather than to individuals contributed to the constancy of attachment to the ancestral *qasbah*. The advent of metaled roads, the telegraph, and the railway made it easier to consolidate existing networks of correspondence and travel, closing the gap between the *qasbah* and the city. At the same time, and perhaps as a result, the significance and distinctiveness of the latter category seemed to come under threat, and that very distinctiveness became a badge of authenticity in the new public conversation that was being defined, to a significant degree, by newspapers.

The Telegraph: Closing the Gap, Keeping the Distance

The fates of the railway, telegraph, and periodical technologies were linked in South Asia.[37] This was particularly the case in *qasbah*s and other localities outside of urban centers. In Bijnor, the confluence of these three technologies brought the *qasbah* into the same frame as the domestic and international city. It is generally understood that these technologies facilitated military-imperial objectives, but as we will see, they also enabled the production of other identity-constitutive spaces that could compete with those objectives.[38]

*Qasbah*s had long formed one of the first levels of urban life in a predominantly agricultural context; its administrators, scholars, and Sufis filled a mediating role, remaining apart from the city but simultaneously exerting (or attempting to exert) influence over it.[39] In the early twentieth century, the spread of new communication technologies shrank the distance between the *qasbah* and imperial centers. However, the distance shrank at different rates for different *qasbah*s according to imperial policy. As the fate of the railway, telegraph, and periodical technologies were all tightly linked in the life of the *qasbah*, the tension between connectivity and disconnectedness created a new discursive place for "the *qasbah*" in Bijnor.

Let us begin with the telegraph. This innovation transformed trade, railway schedules, industrial corporations, warfare, and of course the newspaper. A brief recital of communication timings demonstrates the irruptive power of the telegraph. For instance, in 1840, sending a message from Bombay to London took five weeks. In 1868, a telegraph sent from Calcutta to Karachi took 17 hours and 48 minutes to transmit. By 1870, the same message transmitted in a blistering speed of 4 hours and 43 minutes.[40] In 1875, a telegraph was transmitted from London to Bombay in five minutes. With the opening of the Red Sea line, international communication via telegraph between India and Britain became dependable.[41] Jawaharlal Nehru later proclaimed the telegraph had been the "herald of the New Age."[42]

The dramatic expansion of the telegraph caused reflection on the nature of time and space among its Indian and British users. Telegraph lines diminished the time required to transmit messages, making distant spaces seem nearer.[43] In response to the expansion of the telegraph globally, London's *Daily Telegraph* published a report that "[time] itself is telegraphed out of existence."[44] Rudyard Kipling wrote in his poem "The Deep-Sea Cables" that "they have killed their father Time."[45] The telegraph was a precondition of the existence of daily or weekly newspapers in India.[46] Until recently, however, we have had access to relatively more scholarship regarding the European response to the telegraph's impact on time than the South Asian response. By the early twentieth century, the telegraph had penetrated deeply enough into the subcontinent to include several far-flung *qasbahs* in its network, informing *qasbatis* of the political developments of Delhi, Calcutta, London, New York, and Moscow.[47] Perhaps in response to the competition posed by the informal networks described by Bayly as *ecumene*,[48] in 1872 the government ensured concessions for members of the press to encourage their use of the telegraph and to enable further surveillance of its conversations.[49]

From its inception, the telegraph was a government-owned service, in contrast to both the telephone and the railway industries, which began as private enterprises.[50] The first experimental telegraph lines had appeared in India in 1839, enjoying widespread use from the 1850s.[51] The telegraph was useful to the Raj during the 1857 riots; the telegraph lines became targets of "mutineering" soldiers as a result.[52] After 1857, concerns about India's isolation from Britain grew, catalyzing the emergence of the first telegraph line connecting India (Bombay) to Britain in January 1865. Manu Goswami has demonstrated that railway production was a method of conceiving space, to use Henri Lefebvre's term, in order to homogenize the constituent parts of an imperial nation.[53] Goswami's work demonstrates the ironic coproduction of imperial and nationalist spaces using the example of the railway; state-financed projects intended for homogenization of imperial subjects simultaneously established the boundaries of a conceived space of nationalism. In a similar way, while the telegraph and various newspaper surveillance technologies enacted institutional influence on the *qasbah*, they also enabled *qasbah* periodicals to produce and speak to a public beyond the boundaries of Bijnor.[54]

Telegraph expansion to Bijnor was slightly delayed. In 1875 the first telegraph line arrived in the district: a tributary line linking the nearby city of Naginah and Bijnor.[55] In 1883, as a result of negotiations between the Postal and Telegraph Departments, the latter agreed to construct and maintain short branch lines to "outlying postal offices" like Bijnor.[56] A Government Telegraph Office appeared in Bijnor by 1891.[57] The fact that Bijnor's telegraph station was a tributary rather than a throughline from 1875 until 1891 meant Bijnor had remained relatively isolated from the rapid transmission of news and messages compared to other small towns that had been connected earlier.[58] Once the telegraph was in place, Bijnor's inhabitants made prodigious use of it.

Bijnor punched above its weight in volume and variety of literary output. The same year that forty-two periodicals and newspapers were circulated from Lucknow, Bijnor *qasbah* produced ten publications.[59] In other words, despite having less than 7 percent of Lucknow's population, Bijnor *qasbah* was producing almost a quarter as many publications as Lucknow in 1912; this established a trend that was to continue in the following decades. Among those publications that took advantage of the transformative potential telegraph communication was the Bijnor publication *Zamīndār wa Kāshtkār* (*The Landowner and Cultivator*), owned by Muḥammad Yakub, which dealt with local and agricultural matters until 1909, when it used greater access to international affairs to rename itself *al-Khalīl* (*The Friend*) and shift its focus to include more extensive commentary on government and political topics.[60] Muḥammad Yakub also owned the periodical *Risāla-i Tāza naẓā'ir* (*Fresh Periodical of Venerable Men*), which reported only on the rulings of the high courts.[61] Also present among Bijnor's Urdu periodicals were Aḥmad Ḥusain's *Mashriq-ul-'ulūm* (*The House of Knowledge of the East*) and M. Jairaj Singh's *Tohfa-i hind* (*Gift of India*), which was explicitly opposed to *Madīnah* and its sister publication *Ṣaḥīfa* (*Page*), reportedly standing for the "Hindu side as against the Muhammadan."[62] *Mu'allim-i 'ām* (*The Common Man's Teacher*), published by Bahār-i hind Press, which was also owned by the same M. Jairaj Singh, struck a different tone and sought to "avoid all religious controversies."[63]

Madīnah used the telegraph to receive national and international news from English sources—the structure of telegraph tariffs particularly encouraged communication with the Ottoman Empire, because Britain was concerned to strengthen the empire's failing infrastructure as a security against growing instability in Europe.[64] *Madīnah* also subscribed to the Reuters service, which transmitted news from international centers like New York and London. The paper also invited correspondents to send in information directly. Anyone could send a telegram to the "manager of Madina newspaper, Bijnor," since that entry was listed in the Public and State Abbreviated Address book, distributed widely across India.[65] Editorials from correspondents across the globe appeared, and whole sections of the newspaper were dedicated to telegrams received, demonstrating that readers accepted this invitation to submit news themselves.[66] The inclusion of *Madīnah* in the Public and State Abbreviated Address Book reinforced *Madīnah*'s particular dependence on the telegraph.[67] Its national and international news section was initially titled *'ām akhbār aur 'ām tār* (general news and telegrams) or *barqīyāt* (literally, "electricity"). Particularly at the start of the paper, the "fresh" nature of the news was emphasized in the title of this section—for example, in May 1912 the telegram news section was entitled "*tāzah bi-tāzah-yi nū bi-nū*" (literally, "the up-to-date of the very latest").[68] Information that arrived via telegraph was naturally breaking news; the brisk write-ups were kept brief and to the point, like telegrams. While telegraph communication was costly, in 1904 and 1905 the fees for press telegrams and registration fees were lowered, contributing to the diffusion of news throughout the subcontinent.[69] By the 1930s, although *Madīnah* no longer had a section nominally dedicated to telegrams, its "Muslim world" section included information likely garnered via telegram. By contrast, in its "letters to the editor" section, complaints about the handwriting of submissions implied that it was still more common to handwrite those letters.[70]

The case of *Madīnah* suggests that newspapers published in *qasbah*s depended primarily on the post office to send out issues of the paper, the same office used to transmit and receive telegrams for content. The post office, which had been well established for a century already, thus remained Bijnor's key link to other municipalities in the early 1900s. Post office transport included horse- and camel-driven mail carts, runners, and steamer services operating via sea and river; eventually rail became the primary means.[71] In the late nineteenth and early twentieth centuries, the Postal Department experienced a huge upswing in the number of newspapers sent using its services in the UP; this corresponded to the already well-documented increase in the production of newspapers in Indian languages.[72]

Like other communities of the period, Bijnor *qasbah* was transformed by the introduction of the telegraph after the 1870s. While the telegraph enacted institutional influence on the *qasbah*, it also enabled *qasbah* periodicals to produce and speak to a public beyond the boundaries of Bijnor. Meanwhile, in another sense Bijnor remained at a spatial-temporal remove, for it was not connected to the railway system until 1930, much later than other *qasbahs*. In going without a railway connection for so long Bijnor *qasbah* incubated an alternate timescape specific to that locality, while simultaneously making use of the telegraph and the postal service to sew itself into the fabric of the international world, receiving news and transmitting its own influential perspective far afield.

The government regularly surveilled "vernacular language" of newspapers using the telegraph; the British Raj exempted the Indian language press from the telegraph tariff so that the government could keep abreast of developments by monitoring its messages.[73] In 1910, the Government of India expanded a directive to UP, encouraging censorship of post and telegraphic messages used by newspapers. In 1931, when the British Raj added a telegraph tariff to raise revenue, the Indian language press remained exempt so that the government could keep abreast of developments by monitoring its messages.[74]

Newspapers in turn employed the telegraph to protest censorship, or to evade censorship by sending objectionable messages simultaneously to several newspapers. Perhaps in response, one policy forbade the reprinting of another newspaper's content less than 24 hours after its reception by telegraph to slow down information transmission.[75] Policies like this aimed to slow down the swift transmission of news, ensuring that neither government censorship nor time were "telegraphed out of existence."

The Railway: Bijnor a World Away

In the early twentieth century, the distance between Bijnor and imperial centers like Delhi and Lahore was shrinking. Distance, however, and its partner, time, shrank at different rates for different localities according to imperial policy. While in other places telegraph and railway development came hand-in-hand, or perhaps in lock-step, in Bijnor over half a century passed between the arrival of the telegraph and the arrival of the railway. The ensuing tension between connectivity and disconnectedness created a new discursive place for "the *qasbah*" in Bijnor; *Madīnah* interpreted this division in a way that not only opposed "Western" influence but also inculcated a link between Islam, time, and public life.

These linkages were not automatic. It is important to note that other Bijnor periodicals also cultivated a sense of distinctiveness that capitalized on that *qasbah*'s distance from "Westernized" cities, but without invoking Islam. Hindi periodicals *Saddharm pracharak* and *Vedic Magazine* and *Gurukul samachar* similarly interpreted Bijnor's character in a way that opposed Western influence, and M. Jairaj Singh's Urdu-language *Tohfa-i hind* was a self-designated representative of Hindu interests in the locality.

Railway expansion was touted as a symbol of scientific and cultural progress by some and viewed with suspicion by others.[76] By the early twentieth century the railway had become a bone of contention between the Bijnor *ashrāf* and the colonial government. Bijnor *qasbah* remained one of the few district headquarters without direct access to a railway line until 1930. This neglect was surprising considering that other cities, less central to the administration of Bijnor district, enjoyed railway access from the 1870s onward; all of the district's main commercial centers (Seohara, Dhampur, Naginah, and Najibabad) were located directly on the railway line. It is even more surprising when we consider the frequency of Bijnor *qasbatis*' calls for railway expansion. *Madīnah* and other newspapers in Bijnor continued to assertively advocate railway expansion for Bijnor for almost two decades before achieving success.[77] Bijnor inhabitants submitted a petition specifically requesting a light-gauge railway line between 1907 and 1910.[78] *Madīnah* called for the spread of the railway in terms of business, reputation, and public health, acting as spokesman for rural India and all locations "of the smallest measure."[79]

> As bubonic plague had become visible in *qasbah*s and villages, where cases are continuing to occur in that fashion [. . .] a request has been made of the government for a light railway so that in locations of every such district [even] of the smallest measure [people], if they feel the need to, may be brought out from there. In the district Bijnor also this movement is continuing during a holiday of the government.
>
> *jin baʿẓ qasbāt-o dīhāt mein̠ t̠āʿūn namūdār hūʾā thā vahān bī-dastūr kais hote rehete hain̠ [. . .] gavarnminṭ se tajvīz kī gaʾī hai kih eik halkī reilwe sab se choṭe paimāne kī har aise ẓilaʿ ke maqām par jis jagah uskī ẓarūrat mihisūs ho nikālī jāʾe, ẓilaʿ bijnor mein̠ bhī gavarminṭ kī eik chuṭhī par uskī tihirīk ho rahī hai.*

Before the advent of the railway to the district, the sugar export trade thrived in Meerut and Muzaffarnagar, but the railway had shifted the focus of the sugar trade to towns with access to rail transport.[80] Towns that experienced railway expansion in the early decades of the twentieth century (Naginah, Dhampur, and Najibabad) enjoyed increased trade, while the Bijnor *qasbah* declined in economic importance. These transformations fueled the feelings of insecurity among *qasbatis* in Bijnor and shaped the priorities of political appointments and municipal board representation.

The disruption of the railway was not limited to the economic sphere. One writer in *Madīnah*'s pages captured the sense of almost metaphysical disruption when he described the Dehra-Dun to Rajputanah railway line as shortening a length of eight miles to five and a half feet.[81] In other words, the railway was associated with a collapse of space because of its ability to shorten the time spent traveling between two places. It had the power to convert measurements of distance from large to small, and in trade terms to transform the significance of localities from small to large. So the deferment of railway expansion accompanied a growing disillusionment with the colonial government in Bijnor. As localities surrounding Bijnor saw large distances shrink and transport times disappear into thin air, the *ashrāf* in Bijnor, and the staff and editors of *Madīnah*, unsuccessfully tried to conjure this power that could link them more closely to the world for which they spoke.

The isolation of Bijnor *qasbah* was simultaneously overstated and keenly felt. On the one hand, even now, Bijnor and other *qasbah*s remain physically isolated—trains rarely stop there, and the roads leading in to the city are often in disrepair and difficult to navigate. Moreover, the Sufi tradition of Gogā Pīr common in Bijnor and surrounding districts indicates an isolation from mainstream spiritual networks such as the Chishti Sufi tradition.[82] Displaced individuals from Bijnor are unusual among *qasbati*s in not relating to a distinctive local shrine, indicating that Bijnor *qasbah* is an outlier in an urban context often dominated by specific Sufi traditions.[83] However, the isolation of *qasbah*s like Bijnor has also been exaggerated. The Gogā Pīr spiritual tradition was part of a family of ritual traditions that spread southwest into Rajasthan; in that sense the region was far from a spiritually disconnected hinterland even in the premodern period.[84] Migration of *qasbati*s out of the *qasbah*s into the city in the first half of the twentieth century created and reinforced the interconnected nature of familial and professional networks across *qasbah*s in North India. Mushirul Hasan has observed that the increasingly frequent emigration of male landed gentry in search of opportunity facilitated the growing influence of the *qasbah*s in the popular imagination.[85] Colonial records show that Bijnor *qasbati*s were leaving for other districts in UP by the hundreds each year.[86] Emigrants from the *qasbah* moved in search of jobs or migrated seasonally. And of course, the railway and the telegraph were not the only roads out of the *qasbah*; metaled roads saw the growing presence of buses and automobiles as modes of transport and trade.[87]

Yet, while Bijnor's perceived isolation was in some sense belied by the wide circulation achieved by its journalists, in the early twentieth century *Madīnah* newspaper increasingly turned the circumstance into a point of solidarity with the concerns of other municipalities across North India. (Perhaps in an extension of this principle, current inhabitants of difficult-to-access *qasbah*s use the inheritors of the telegraph's legacy, the Internet and mobile phone, to access news and correspondence and send their own messages outside the walls of the home and the *qasbah*.[88]) Anxieties regarding the sustainability of the local economy, particularly related to the impact of railway construction on manufacturing, artisanal work, and agriculture, influenced coverage of urban India and the evolution of a public that spoke for Muslim *qasbati*s. In this period *qasbati*s began increasingly to define their environment as the antithesis to the city environment and its "chicanery, hypocrisy and competitive spirit."[89]

As *qasbati*s continued to migrate around the region in the early twentieth century, the distinctiveness of an Indo-Persian, Arabic-inflected public was amplified: a public that transcended a specific geographic locale and was committed to the touchstones of the *qasbah* and Islam. By the 1930s newspaper and telegraph networks linking *qasbah*s to the national and international horizon were entrenched, and even Bijnor *qasbah* had the long-desired railway connection. Space and time in Bijnor had caught up with the world beyond. But by now, the newspaper conversation even more adamantly expressed an anxiety for the passage of time to obey Muslim rhythms.

The Rhythm of Islam, the Rhythm of the Future

In the pages of *Madinah*, we find accounts of historical figures, scholarly editorials, and even advertisements that indicated the link between the past and the future of Islam. Articles on historical figures were sprinkled throughout the paper alongside accounts of current events; their lessons were often explicitly connected to contemporary social and political challenges.[90] In news coverage of the war being waged between Italy and Turkey in 1912 prior to the breakout of the First Balkan War, the news correspondent digressed from his criticism of Italy's distribution of deceptive propaganda to declaim:

> It is true that the nation (*qaum*) that becomes the ruler of a country is one in whose hand there is a sharp sword. But civilized nations (*mohazzab qaumein*) fulfilled their promises, otherwise how could rulers gain authority over the common people? In this regard, however much pride and glory Islam displays, it will merit that. Since the time of the Prophet Muḥammad, may blessings be upon him, until recent times, all promises have been thoroughly fulfilled by Islamic rulers.[91]
>
> *yih sach hai kih mālik-i mulk voh hī qaum hotī hai jis ke hāth mein shamshīr taiz ho. Magar mohazzab qaumein apne ʿahd-o paimān kī ẓarūr pābandī kartī hain varnah bādshāhon ko ʿavām par kyā fauqīyat ḥāṣl ho saktī hai. is amr mein islām jisqadr fakhr-o mabāhāt kare usko munāsib aur zeibā hai. janāb sarvar-i ʿālam ṣallallāhu ʿalayhi-va sallam se lekar tā zamānāh-yi hāl tamām ʿihd-o paimān salāṭein-i islāmīyā kī ṭaraf se mazbūṭī ke sāth nibāhe gaye.*

The term *qaum*, here translated as "nation," should not be confused with the more recent interpretation of the term as similar to the modern *nation-state*. Nevertheless, this passage attempted to argue that the history of rule by Muslims justified the Ottoman Empire's moral claim to victory in the Italo-Turkish War of 1912. In the same issue *Madīnah* contracted its own commitment to accuracy with the reporting of *The Rome Star*, a major news source emanating from Rome, which according to *Madīnah* had published false propaganda about the death of Turkish leaders. In this way, coverage of contemporary events was woven throughout with reflections on the past to create a case for Muslim victory.

At the conclusion of the first Balkan War—after battles waged between Turkey and the Balkan League and shortly after the Treaty of London had been brokered with the assistance and advice of the United Kingdom—an account of Chānd Bībī, the sixteenth-century regent of Bijapur, appeared in *Madīnah* to "bring it into a new light."[92] In this account, Chānd Bībī, after attempting to oppose Akbar's troops by taking the advice of others, had decided "what was to be done now, it was right that she do it according to her own opinion only."[93] The article emphasized the importance of Chānd Bībī's commitment to Bijapur, recounting the opinion of British historian Colonel Meadows-Taylor that Chānd Bībī was not only a contemporary of Queen Elizabeth but also had an empire equal to hers in "*shān-o shaukat*," or "glory and power."[94] As during the Italo-Turkish War, the example of Chānd Bībī was held up in *Madīnah* to advocate for Turkey's independence in brokering terms of peace.

Aside from political commentaries and historical biographies, scholars appeared in *Madīnah* entering into a theological debate on the future of Muslims in relation to God's knowledge. Important to the debate was the relationship between transmitted knowledge and the future. A tract had appeared in *Tahzīb ul-akhlāq*, an Urdu newspaper published from Aligarh, stating that religious truth admits to no alteration or inconsistency. In response, *Madīnah* published a critique of the assumption of "fixed knowledge":

> The summary of the aforementioned honored scholar's writings is this that all future actions exist and are established in the knowledge of God, encircling all details and certainty in such a way that in no matter is there a possibility for trifling differences, nor is there any possibility of any alteration or shortcoming in God's knowledge.
>
> But he presents the argument: What does God have to do with the servant's lack of control; only through foreknowledge can we prove the slave's helplessness and disability. And giving the example of the railway timetable the praiseworthy scholar has clarified that matter by [saying,] "look, here are all the times and the placement of the car at every station, and its arrival and departure, all has already been established." But aside from those foreknowledges, the railway timetable can never have an effect on the nature and power of the drivers, and on the effects of water and fire on them.[95]
>
> *fāẓil-i mauṣūf kī taḥrīr kā k̲h̲ulāṣah yih hai kih jumlah umūr-i āyand ʿilm-i ilāhī mein̲ maujūd aur moʿayyan hain̲ aur ʿilm-i ilāhī sab ko ʿalāʾ al-tafṣīl aur ʿalāʾ yaqīn aisā muḥīṭ hai kih kisī chīz mein̲ adna naqqādat kā iḥtimāl aur allāh ke ʿilm mein̲ kisī qism kā tag̲h̲ayyūr yā nuqsān hargaz momkin nahin̲.*
>
> *magar farmāte hain̲ kih usko bandah kī majbūrī se kyā ʿilāqah aur ṣirf taʿayyun ʿilmī se bandah kī be-ik̲h̲tiyārī aur maʿzūrī kaisī s̲ābit aur qābil taslīm ho gayī.*

Aur relve ṭā'im ṭaibal kī miṣāl bīyān karke fāẓil-i mamdūḥ ne us amr ko vāẓih kar dīyā kih dekho yahāṉ jumlah auqāt aur har ṣṭaishan par gāṛī kā qayām aur uskā pahunchā aur chalā jānā sab mo'ayyan ho chukā hai magar bāwajūd un tamām ta'ayyunīyāt ke unkā ko'ī aṣr gāṛī chalāne-vāloṉ kī qudrat aur ikhtīyār aur pānī aur āg kī ta'aṣṣur par hargaz nahiṉ paṛtā."

Future actions, or *"umūr-i āyand,"* would not obey a railway timetable, the article in *Madīnah* argued, even if God's knowledge was similar to a railway timetable in clarity and accuracy. If the Qur'an was a timetable for Muslims, it certainly did not exist independently from those Muslims who interacted with it. The future was not something derived from the simple sum of past and present. Instead, the future would result in the "effect of all the scheduling on the nature and power of the drivers," or the discursive relationship between the believers and the text. This model emphasized the power of the believer along with the past models of transmitted knowledge.

Through advertisements in *Madīnah* we see that even everyday experiences of time could take on a Muslim hue. In late 1937 an advertisement began to appear in *Madīnah* for a "Muslim wristwatch for faithful Muslims" that included an image of the crescent, Arabic writing, and roman numerals.[96] The same advertisement mentioned a Muslim pocket watch and a locket, small mementos of Islam that could be worn on one's person, forming one of many threads of everyday life woven into the timescape of Islam.

An even more powerful binding thread than these trinkets was the arrival and reading of *Madīnah* itself. Bijnor author Furqān Aḥmad Ṣiddīqī included Majīd Ḥasan in his biography of local luminaries because Majīd's newspaper united locals and spanned the globe. One of his childhood memories included *Madīnah*:

> During my childhood my honorable Grandfather received the newspaper [*Madīnah*] that was published every three days. In the evening when the gathering (*mahfil*) was assembled, there would be discussions (*tabṣire*) of its news, editorials, and articles.[97]

bachpan kā zāmānah thā qiblah dādā ṣāḥab ke pās yih akhbār jo sih rozah thā āyā kartā thā. shām ko jab meḥfil jamtī to is akhbār kī khabroṉ, idārīyoṉ aur maẓāmīn par tabṣire hote the.

The newspaper marked the end of the day, the end of the evening's prayers, and the daily connection between members of this local congregation. This daily interpretation of the news through a community framework, an Islamic framework, both defined a local literati linked to a single, local mosque and wove them into a global tapestry of newspaper readers who would never meet. They were also, significantly, linked by a sense of closeness between the time of the Prophet and the contemporary political milieu, which lent an urgency to the conversations.

Other poems and songs appeared that did not explicitly invoke Islam or time but were nonetheless evocative of *Madīnah*'s exceptionalism.[98] A commentary on the Khilafat and noncooperation movements, this poem spoke with the voice of an old spinning wheel that though old and decrepit kept spinning:

> My skeleton is dry wood / go on, count my each and every bone[99]
> But even so I sit deliberately / But even now I keep my neck stiff
> *ghūn̲ ghūn̲ ghūn̲ ghūn̲ ghūn̲ ghūn̲ ghūn̲ ghūn̲*
>
> *d̲hānch hai merā sūk̲h̲ī lakrī / gin lo merī eik eik pakhuṛī*
> *phir bhī jamā'e baiṭhā hūn̲ pat̲rī / gardan ab bhī rahatī hai akar̲ī*
> *ghūn̲ ghūn̲ ghūn̲ ghūn̲ ghūn̲ ghūn̲ ghūn̲ ghūn̲*

In this way, the daily rhythms of newspaper consumption and discussion spun together past and present. The poem on the spinning wheel of *Madīnah*, likely sung or recited by readers, whose childlike rhythms decorated the front page of a 1921 newspaper, reinforced what Laura Bear has called a time-map: while it "only [had] a partial relationship to the passage of real time . . . it mediated and shaped personal experiences of it."[100] Print recorded time; it advertised the implements to measure it, but it also shaped the experience of time through the rhythms of its dissemination, its selection of subject matter, and its own contributions to the conversation.

Correspondence Networks: An Old Technology Meets a New Century

The evidence in *Madīnah* suggests that the conversation in and among newspapers published in *qasbahs* was characterized not only by the influence of long-standing newspaper models but also by *ashrāf* correspondence networks, which included large cities like Lucknow and Lahore as well as *qasbahs*. At the same time, through the newspaper, correspondence found expression in a new form that included more interlocutors and a larger audience. Thus, new technologies and formats facilitated rather than superseded previously established networks of communication and identity, both mundane and spiritual—and thus the space produced by the newspaper conversation was both a departure from and a continuation of the past.

The small section of Indian society literate in Urdu, much of which had substantial links to *qasbahs*, had been engaged in a vibrant newspaper conversation since the mid-1800s. Research on the newspapers *Āwadh Akhbār* (Awadh Newspaper, Lucknow), *Dehlī Urdū Akhbār* (Delhi Urdu Newspaper, Delhi), and *Jam-i Jahān Numā* (*Mirror of the World,* Calcutta) has described this discourse as a continuation of *akhbārāt* or handwritten-newsletter culture of the eighteenth and nineteenth centuries,[101] an invocation of English printing models,[102] and an elision of journalism and spiritual guidance.[103] The vibrant letters to the editor sections in *Āwadh Akhbār* often hinted at insider knowledge that emphasized that the letters were only one part of an ongoing, long-standing conversation among the *ashrāf*; the papers were built on existing networks of correspondence in nineteenth-century Lucknow.[104] In the early twentieth century, when *Madīnah* joined the well-established tradition of lithographic periodicals, the typical tone of those publications' readers' response sections also suggest that they may have mapped onto existing correspondence networks.[105]

The evidence indicates not a wholesale invention of a print public but rather an extension of a public established among *ashrāf* networks via correspondence and post prior to the arrival of the telegram. In a similar way, the modern technologies of lithography and telegraph were not incompatible with miraculous communication but could exist alongside them. While James Douglas wrote about late nineteenth-century Bombay, "[the] truth is, the electric telegraph has flashed this class of spirits out of existence," and while some miracle stories of communication across large distances and stormy seas among Muslims died out with the arrival of the telegraph, other evidence points to the enchantment attaching to industrial technologies.[106] Adding to the evidence provided by Nile Green on this count, telegraph reports brought far-off spiritual experiences closer to readers. *Madīnah* published images of the holy city of Madīnah that left at least some readers inspired spiritually, as well as *fatwe*, or legal judgments by Deobandi *'ulamā*, in response to readers' letters.[107] *Madīnah* even printed a report in its telegraph section of King George's visit to a martyr's tomb (in its very early days, when more than a tinge of loyalism marked its pages).[108] Significantly, endorsements by Deobandi *'ulamā* in its early issues portray the paper as enabling, not displacing, spiritual experience.[109] Chapter 3 explores how *Madīnah* captured a layer of spiritual meaning in its material form.

While placing emphasis on the importance of the *qasbah* as a source of traditional, Indo-Persian culture and values, inhabitants of *qasbahs* emphasized their distinctiveness not only in terms of locality but also in terms of a specific relationship with the history of Islam in the subcontinent.[110] This public as promulgated in Bijnor cultivated a distinctive temporal quality that linked past and present as indicators of virtue and prestige. Following 1857, with the decline of patronage to Muslims in cities (and quite contrary to the colonial rhetoric about the "barbarism" that lay beyond the city walls), *qasbahs* had become a place of refuge for administrators, scholars, and religious leaders alike.[111] The shift of the *sharīf* social status group and its discourse from large urban centers such as Delhi to the *qasbahs* that formed the foundation of much of its culture at first seems to correlate with a more abstract shift of Islam from the secular public space to the domestic, private sphere. According to this view, in *qasbahs*, the legally defined public space of Islam could remain "religious" in a way that was impossible in more central urban areas, where religion had been relegated to the private sphere. This interpretation has led to arguments that characterize *qasbahs* as providing syncretic, and more recently pluralistic, models for communal harmony. But what is more significant to note is the way that the local context was reified as a referent for a public space; this *qasbah*-centered public incorporated Western education and colonial processes to an extent, while retaining emphasis on Indo-Persian and Arabic influences. Those voices then could transmit and become influential beyond the *qasbah* walls. *Madīnah*'s distribution and reception shows that process at work. In the *qasbah* local pasts overlapped and mingled with the present; the influence of that timescape transmitted from the *qasbah* to larger urban centers.

The biography of Bijnor district luminary Nazīr Aḥmed Dehlvī (1831–1912) began with this quotation from the subject: "I have great pride on this point, that by my ancestors I am a hereditary Muslim, and in my pedigree are included the names of *'ulamā* and shaikhs tied directly to the conclusion of the Delhi Sultanate."[112] It is for this reason that Nazīr Aḥmed's *nisba*—or the use of a locality as a part of one's name—is Dehlvī rather than Bijnorī, despite his having been born in Bijnor. The *nisba* convention, commonly referring to a *qasbah*, does not necessarily indicate the village, city, or *qasbah* of birth but instead indicates a connection to a locality that retains the past in the present. By the same token, a *tazkirah* (or geneaology) of Bijnori luminaries includes families who have not resided in the *qasbah* or district of Bijnor for several generations.[113] The echoing of origin among *qasbati* Muslims in the choice of name threads several human timelines together into a single timescape characterized by authority and legitimacy. This timescape contests nationalized narratives of communal belonging that deny the significance of local spaces and local temporalities.

Dialogue within the *qasbah*, instead of being an extension of the propaganda pushed outward by *sharīf* Indians in major urban centers, remained a source of original debate that interpreted the applicability of Islam to the modern project. *Madīnah*'s contributors sought to define an Urdu-speaking, Muslim public in which the *qasbah* featured prominently as a source of authenticity. For example, in response to the publication of the seminal Progressive Writers' Movement book *Angāre* in 1933, *Madīnah* laid out the personality of the *qasbah* in contrast to the city:

> We are grateful to exalted God that he has allowed us to live in a remote township to perform the duties of journalism, a township that is safe from the piety-destroying and faith-removing elements of civilization, where neither the gaieties and frivolities of youth and poetry strike with lightning the granary of patience and steadfastness, nor the tumultuousness of beauty breaks the bonds of faith, and where the fierce and fiery winds of atheism and apostasy cannot burn the rose-garden of faith and religion.
>
> No calamity can reach the place of solitude.[114]
>
> *ham allāh-ta'allah ke shukr-guzār haiṉ kih us ne farā'iẓ-i ṣaḥāfat adā karne ke liye hameiṉ eik aisī bastī meiṉ iqāmat-guzīṉ hone kā mauqah dīyā hai jo dūr uftādah aur tihzīb-o ḥaẓārat ke taqva-shikan aur īmān rubā 'anāṣir se maḥafūz̤ hai, jahāṉ nah shi'r-o shabāb kī rangīnīyāṉ k̲h̲irman-i ṣabr-o s̱abāt bijlīyāṉ girātī haiṉ nah ḥusan-o jamāl kī mahshar ārāyīā shīrāzah-yi īmān ko dar ham bar ham kartī haiṉ aur ilḥād-o zandaqah kī tund aur ātishīṉ havā'īṉ gulshan-i dīn-o īmān ko jhulas saktī haiṉ.*
>
> *hīch āfat na rasad gausha-yi tanhā'ī rā.*

Madīnah set Bijnor apart as a place isolated from the worldly knowledge touted in cities, characterized by steadfastness. The editors of *Madīnah* saw its entries as a part of an Indo-Persian discourse aligning the present and the past in "the rose-garden of faith and religion." The newspaper conversation reaffirmed a Muslim public that was an extension of the *qasbah* and its history; this timescape acted as a representative of Muslims to British observers as well as an admonishment to readers to consider their Muslim identity, if not their *qasbah* roots, as an invaluable feature of their public identity.

On the one hand, *qasbati*s advocated for the significance of local context, in contrast to Westernized cities but also increasingly against Muslims who insisted that "Islamic culture" required membership in the Muslim League. On the other hand, the *qasbati*s in Bijnor remained connected to Muslims beyond their immediate locality and found it necessary to encourage right action among the mass of Muslims beyond Bijnor. Further, *Madīnah* in particular was a mass publication; it did not target a special group like the literary magazines of those days but sought, distinctively, to speak to the "common" Muslim.[115] This otherness was key to *Madīnah*'s influence in the Khilafat movement—the paper was the most widely distributed newspaper of any language for a brief period in the early 1920s. It also emerged center stage in Bijnor locals' objections to the infamous 1937 primary election in Bijnor, discussed in detail in chapter 5, which saw Ḥāfiz̤ Ibrāhīm forced to run for re-election after switching affiliations from the Muslim League to Congress.

Bijnor's character in this period was distinctive in its particular combination of agricultural advantage, its lack of a manufacturing industry, and its isolation from trade networks (until the 1930s); on the other hand, it was typical of North Indian *qasbahs* in its proximity to Delhi and its rich history of administrative and scholarly networks dating from the earliest days of the Mughal period. Its past served in many ways as an exemplar of the common past of the *qasbahs,* and, like many *qasbah*s, Bijnor defied the mold of the colonial capitalist timescape. Its newspapers, particularly *Madīnah,* reflected engagement with political challenges and an ambition to reach the ears of an increasingly national and international public while retaining the cultural capital earned through its incubation of a distinctly local Indo-Persian tradition. Bijnor's *Madīnah* shaped a mass Urdu public conversation through the invocation of the past as an active element of the present.

The Binding Nostalgia of the *Qasbah*: Tugging at the Present with the Past

In a *tazkirah* of Bijnor Furqān Aḥmad Ṣiddīqī wrote accounts of literary figures in Bijnor district, describing their accomplishments. In his description of the book he distanced himself from nostalgic writings, dismissing those types of books as the "*padram sulṭān būd* [my paternal grandfather was a sultan]" genre:

> This book was not written with the feeling of "my paternal grandfather was a Sultan." In this period this sort of thing has no importance, and in all truth it never had any importance. In reality the purpose of this book is to praise to the new generation those great values, of those who had to struggle with great difficulty and torment to achieve honor, wealth, reputation, and knowledge. It was not all of a sudden or coincidentally that successes came within their reach.
>
> *yih kitāb 'padram sulṭān būd' ke iḥsās ko sāmne rakhkar nahīn̠ likhī gayī. is daur mein̠ is bāt kī ko'ī ahammīyat bhī nahīn̠ hai aur sachī bāt to yih hai kih kisī daur mein̠ bhī nahīn̠ thī. dar aṣl is kitāb kā maqṣad nayī nasl se un 'aẕīm hastīyon̠ kā ta'āruf karānā maqsūd hai jinhon̠ ne 'ilm, shohrat, daulat, aur 'izzat ḥāṣil karne ke līye baṛī baṛī taklīfiyon̠ aur aẕiyyatein̠ jheilī hain̠. kāmyābīyān̠ achānak un ke gale kā hār nahīn̠ banī thī.*

This book exhorts readers to read the past as more meaningfully linked to the present and future. The preface goes on to talk about how the "jewels of Bijnor" demonstrate the heights of success that are only accessible to those who undergo hardships but display hard work and devotion (*kaṛī, mehenat aur lagan*).[116] The values of hard work, devotion, honor, and reputation imbued Bijnor's ancestors and should be reflected in present and future Bijnoris—the virtues of the past and the present woven together to array a public simultaneously new and old.

There is a distinct impression today that *qasbah*s have disappeared, leaving behind little legacy but nostalgia and influential surnames.[117] *Qasbah*s as influential networks of bureaucratic power and universal prestige in the form in which we found them in the late nineteenth and early twentieth centuries are certainly a thing of the past. However, a legacy of *qasbah*s persists: what were previously networks of influential judicial authority have become communities with substantial links to urban, national, and international networks and elite education. Far from leaving behind no legacy at all, the *qasbah* and its networks survive in resistance to national(ized) narratives and an emphasis on locales constructed over and against national identities.

While the *qasbah* has long been tied to an idealized past, in the late nineteenth and early twentieth centuries it was simultaneously engaged in a project of refashioning Islam for the future. The *idea* of the *qasbah* was dependent on a nostalgia that decried the decline of its culture in a time when, ironically, its cultural and political relevance increased.[118] Historical documents like *Madīnah* are not the accounts of witnesses documenting an inevitable process of unraveling but are voices actively engaged in tearing out the seams of a *qasbạti* public and sewing present, past, and future together in a new form.

Jamal Malik has observed that the *qasbah* witnessed a cultural renaissance in the nineteenth century even as its commercial prospects continued to decline.[119] In the same vein, the early twentieth-century *qasbah,* as an alternate timescape and landscape persisting on the threshold of modern urban life, contributed a steady stream of advice on how Muslim readers should think about themselves. The nostalgia associated with the qasbah was something other than a longing for the past, indicating the need for a sufficiently complex framework to understand the temporal relations that produced it. In the nostalgic rhetoric of *Madīnah*, the past was one of many contested spaces in a project that aimed to refashion the foundation of the public.

Keeping Time

"The *qasbah*" was a subject of nostalgia and even sociopolitical authenticity for which *Madīnah* sought to speak. *Madīnah* made general claims about the nature of *qasbah* life from this distinct context, appealing to an idealized *qasbah* culture that overlapped with the figurative space of the newspaper and resonated with Muslims, as the popularity of the newspaper indicated. The statements of "the *qasbah*" were no less irruptive for their elision of the distinctions between the distinctive localities in which its widespread readers lived.

To put this argument in terms of an extended metaphor referenced at the beginning of the chapter, to sing in harmony with the *raftār-i zamānah* of the twentieth century required extensive knowledge of the prison in which one lived, an imagined commonality among all inmates, and understanding of the songs inmates had sung in its confinement. In the poem, as in the public conversation among *qasbatis* in Bijnor, time was an aspect of the public space under contestation. It was unacceptable to ignore one's fellow inmates, fall asleep, and ignore the passage of time. Singing in harmony required a deep understanding of the song and cooperation with others to make music. In the same way, the accounts of *qasbatis* linked to Bijnor demonstrated how the public was formed through an alignment of time and space. It was not only time but also its passage. Every few days a new volume of sheet music arrived with the newspaper, holding in its pages the "music" of the passage of time, cueing Muslims' entry into the public song of the age.

Although the telegraph connected Bijnor to the rest of India and the world, the delay in railway expansion and *Madīnah*'s response to it highlighted a sense of perceived isolation. This isolation, alongside its foundation on longstanding *ashrāf* correspondence networks and *akhbārāt* formatting models, became marks of authenticity in *Madīnah*. Both the isolation and the connectivity of the *qasbah* community influenced a perception of a connection between the space of the *qasbah* and Indo-Islamic time in *Madīnah*. Chapter 3 turns to the materiality of *Madīnah*, to demonstrate how its particular applications of lithographic technology helped pull its readers inside that Indo-Islamic timescape.

Notes

1. I take my cue from Foucault's *Archaeology of Knowledge* here, in resisting an approach to statements as an expression of a deeper, already existing, silent statement or belief. Instead the emphasis is on statements "as and when [they] occur," allowing for the irruptive potential of statements. Michel Foucault, "The Unities of Discourse," in *Archaeology of Knowledge* (New York: Routledge, 1972), https://www.marxists.org/reference/subject/philosophy/works/fr/foucault.htm.
2. Using the same trope, Haidar Ali Aatish (1778–1847) wrote, "This sound comes from the span of a life, a horse / that horse also needs some hunter [to ride it]." [*yeh sadā ātī hai raftār-i samand-i 'umr se / vo bhī ghoḍā hai koī jis ko ki koḍā chāhiye*].
3. While *āvāzo̱n se āvāz milnā* means "to bring into concord with, be harmonious," the phrase *malnā'e 'alā* means "angels or inmates of heaven." This could be a play on words. Many thanks to Abdul Manan Bhat for catching a typo in the Rekhta.org transcription

of this poem, which lists "*gītī*" instead of "*gātī*." Tāj Syed, comp., *Kulliyāt i majūh sultānpūrī* (Lahore: Al-Hamd Publications, 2003), 142.

4. *charkh gardan*.
5. Raqamzadah Mulk ul-kalām Syed Muḥammad Lā'iq Ḥussain Ṣāhab Qaumī "Zamarudraqam," "*Raftār zamānah* [The Speed of Time]," *Madīnah Akhbār*, May 1, 1912.
6. Lamentation or mourning of a tragedy.
7. Nazīr Aḥmed, *Mirāt ul-'Urūs* (Dihlī: Kitābī Dunīyā, 2003).
8. Barbara Metcalf, "Introduction," in *Moral Conduct and Authority*, ed. Barbara Metcalf (London: University of California Press, 1984), 17.
9. For instance, Isabel Hofmeyr's study has provided a useful methodological model, using a multilingual model to look at the pamphlet as emblematic of the public of Gāndhī's *satyagrahis*. Isabel Hofmeyr, *Gāndhī's Printing Press* (Cambridge, MA: Harvard University Press, 2013); Anne K. Bang in her discussion of Hofmeyr has called for more work on Islamic periodicals. Anne K. Bang, "Pondering the Text as Change Maker," *Comparative Studies of South Asia, Africa, and the Middle East* 35, no. 2 (2015): 376. Nile Green has explored links between the spread of print technologies and the rise of print publics in early Qajar Iran, providing a methodological model for this type of study. Nile Green, "Persian Print and the Stanhope Revolution: Industrialization, Evangelicalism, and the Birth of Printing in Early Qajar Iran," *Comparative Studies of South Asia, Africa, and the Middle East* 30, no. 3 (2010): 473–90. Jennifer Dubrow has looked at an earlier period of print, with attention to identity matrices other than religion, contrasting religious identity with the cosmopolis of the Urdu language itself. Jennifer Dubrow, *Urdu Cosmopolis* (Honolulu: University of Hawai'i Press, 2018).
10. M. Raisur Rahman, *Locale, Everyday Islam, and Modernity: Qasbah Towns and Muslim Life In Colonial India* (New Delhi: Oxford University Press, 2015), 31.
11. M. Raisur Rahman, *Locale, Everyday Islam, and Modernity: Qasbah Towns and Muslim Life In Colonial India* (Delhi: Oxford University Press, 2015), 3.
12. M. Raisur Rahman, *Locale, Everyday Islam, and Modernity: Qasbah Towns and Muslim Life In Colonial India* (Delhi: Oxford University Press, 2015), 4; *Qasbahs* flourished from the seventeenth century in Punjab, Gujarat, Malwa, Deccan, Rajasthan, Bihar, and Kashmir. Rahman has provided this list of locations, with a detailed bibliography of references to *qasbahs* in these areas. Selected citations include, for Punjab: Muhammad Qasim Zaman, *The Ulama in Contemporary Islam: Custodians of Change* (Princeton: Princeton University Press, 2002), 125; for Gujarat: Makrand Mehta, ed., *Urbanization in Western India: Historical Perspective* (Ahmedabad: Gujarat University Press, 1988), 73–77; for Malwa: Norbert Peabody, *Hindu Kingship and Polity in Precolonial India* (New York: Cambridge University Press, 2003), 96–98; for Rajasthan: Shail Mayaram, *Against History, against State: Counterperspectives from the Margins* (New York: Columbia University Press, 2003); for Bihar: Anand Yang, *Bazaar India: Markets, Society, and the Colonial State in Bihar* (Berkeley: University of California Press, 1998); for the Deccan: Burton Stein, *Thomas Munro: The Origins of the Colonial State and His Vision of Empire* (Delhi: Oxford University Press, 1989), 75. For a complete list of references, see M. Raisur Rahman, *Locale, Everyday Islam, and Modernity: Qasbah Towns and Muslim Life In Colonial India* (Delhi: Oxford University Press, 2015), 4.

13. M. Raisur Rahman, *Locale, Everyday Islam, and Modernity: Qasbah Towns and Muslim Life In Colonial India* (Delhi: Oxford University Press, 2015). Those *qasbahs* in the United Provinces that have benefited from the light of scholarship include Deoband: Barbara Metcalf, *Islamic Revival in British India: Deoband, 1860–1900* (Princeton: Princeton University Press, 1983); Amroha: M. Raisur Rahman, *Locale, Everyday Islam, and Modernity: Qasbah Towns and Muslim Life In Colonial India* (New Delhi: Oxford University Press, 2015), 63–85, and Justin Jones, "The Local Experiences of Reformist Islam in a 'Muslim' Town in Colonial India: The Case of Amroha," *Modern Asian Studies* 43, no. 4 (July 2009): 871–908; Bara Banki: Mushirul Hasan, *From Pluralism to Separatism: Qasbahs in Colonial Awadh* (New Delhi: Oxford University Press, 2004); Rudauli, Bilgram, and Budaun: M. Raisur Rahman, *Locale, Everyday Islam, and Modernity: Qasbah Towns and Muslim Life In Colonial India* (Delhi: Oxford University Press, 2015), 63–85; and Sihali: Jamal Malik, *Islamische gelehrtenkultur in Nordindien: Entwicklungsgeschichte und Tendenzen am Beispiel von Lucknow* (Leiden: Brill, 1997).
14. C. A. Bayly was the first to define the *qasbah* as an urban unit distinctive to South Asia in his 1983 chapter on Kara in Allahabad district. C. A. Bayly, "The Small Town and Islamic Gentry in North India: The Case of Kara," in *The City in South Asia: Pre-modern and Modern*, ed. Kenneth Ballhatchet and John Harrison (London: Curzon, 1980), 20–48.
15. Manasori Sato and B. L. Bhadani, eds., *Economy and Polity of Rajasthan: Study of Kota and Marwar* (Jaipur: Publication Scheme, 1997), 2–3.
16. "The *qasbahs* are almost universally the headquarters of parganas, and from them the pargana used to be administered under the native rule." *Gazetteer of the Province of Oudh*, vol. 11 (Lucknow: Oudh Government Press, 1877–1878), 312; M. Raisur Rahman, *Locale, Everyday Islam, and Modernity: Qasbah Towns and Muslim Life In Colonial India* (Delhi: Oxford University Press, 2015), 31–37.
17. H. R. Nevill, *Bijnor: A Gazetteer* (Allahabad: Supt., Govt. Press, 1908), 214–17.
18. Several *qasbahs* could exist in a single *parganah*, however. Manasori Sato and B. L. Bhadani, eds., *Economy and Polity of Rajasthan: Study of Kota and Marwar* (Jaipur: Publication Scheme, 1997), 2–3.
19. This number is based on discussion by M. Raisur Rahman, C. A. Bayly, and Ravidendar Kumar. M. Raisur Rahman, *Locale, Everyday Islam, and Modernity: Qasbah Towns and Muslim Life In Colonial India* (Delhi: Oxford University Press, 2015), 10. Bayly defines a *qasbah* as being any urban center with more than 3,000 people in the late eighteenth and nineteenth centuries. C. A. Bayly, *Rulers, Townsmen and Bazaars: North Indian Society in the Age of British Expansion, 1770–1870*, 3rd ed. (New Delhi: Oxford University Press, 2012), 111. British colonial-era gazetteers echo awareness of their bureaucratic significance. E.g., *Gazetteer of the Province of Oudh*, vol. 11 (Lucknow: Oudh Government Press, 1877–1878), 312.
20. For further exemplary discussions of this attraction, please see M. Raisur Rahman, *Locale, Everyday Islam, and Modernity: Qasbah Towns and Muslim Life In Colonial India* (Delhi: Oxford University Press, 2015), 9–11; Gyanendra Pandey, "'Encounters and Calamities': The History of a North Indian Qasba in the Nineteenth Century," in *Selected Subaltern Studies*, ed. Ranajit Guha, and Gayatri Chakravorty Spivak (Oxford: Oxford

University Press, 1988); see also Mushirul Hasan, "The Qasbah Culture—I," *The Hindu*, July 22, 2002.

21. Charles Hamilton translated into English from Persian a history of Rohilkhand written during the reign of Shah Alam II (r. 1759–1806). Charles Hamilton, comp. and ed., *Historical Relation of the Origin, Progress, and Final Dissolution of the Government of the Rohilla Afghans in the Northern Provinces of Hindostan. Compiled and edited by Charles Hamilton*, 2nd ed. (London: J. Debrett, 1788).
22. M. Raisur Rahman, *Locale, Everyday Islam, and Modernity: Qasbah Towns and Muslim Life In Colonial India* (New Delhi: Oxford University Press, 2015), 175.
23. H. R. Nevill, *Bijnor: A Gazetteer*. (Allahabad: Supt., Government Press, 1908), 180.
24. H. R. Nevill, *Bijnor: A Gazetteer*. (Allahabad: Supt., Government Press, 1908), 124.
25. C. A Bayly, *Rulers, Townsmen and Bazaars: North Indian Society in the Age of British Expansion, 1770–1870*, 3rd ed. (New Delhi: Oxford University Press, 2012); Mushirul Hasan, *From Pluralism to Separatism: Qasbas in Colonial Awadh* (Oxford: Oxford University Press, 2004); M. Raisur Rahman, *Locale, Everyday Islam, and Modernity:* Qasbah *Towns and Muslim Life in Colonial India* (New Delhi: Oxford University Press, 2015).
26. C. A. Bayly, *Rulers, Townsmen and Bazaars: North Indian Society in the Age of British Expansion, 1770–1870*, 3rd ed. (New Delhi: Oxford University Press, 2012).
27. C. A. Bayly, *Rulers, Townsmen and Bazaars: North Indian Society in the Age of British Expansion, 1770–1870*, 3rd ed. (New Delhi: Oxford University Press, 2012), 190.
28. C. A. Bayly, *Rulers, Townsmen and Bazaars: North Indian Society in the Age of British Expansion, 1770–1870*, 3rd ed. (New Delhi: Oxford University Press, 2012), 193.
29. C. A. Bayly, *Rulers, Townsmen and Bazaars: North Indian Society in the Age of British Expansion, 1770–1870*, 3rd ed. (New Delhi: Oxford University Press, 2012), 183; Syed Ahmed Khan, *Tārīkh-i sarkashī-yi ẓila‘-yi Bijnor*, trans. Hafiz Malik and Morris Dembo (New Delhi: Idārah-i Adabīyat Dillī, 1982).
30. Mushirul Hasan, "Qasbas: A Brief in Propinquity," in *A Leaf Turns Yellow: The Sufis of Awadh*, ed. Muzaffar Ali (New Delhi: Rumi Foundation / Bloomsbury Publishing India, 2013), 112.
31. Mushirul Hasan, "Qasbas: A Brief in Propinquity," in *A Leaf Turns Yellow: The Sufis of Awadh*, ed. Muzaffar Ali (New Delhi: Rumi Foundation / Bloomsbury Publishing India, 2013), 112.
32. Barbara Metcalf, *Islamic Revival in British India: Deoband, 1860–1900* (Princeton: Princeton University Press, 1983), 73, 76, 82, 85.
33. Justin Jones, "The Local Experiences of Reformist Islam in a 'Muslim' Town in Colonial India: The Case of Amroha," *Modern Asian Studies* 43, no. 4 (2009): 876.
34. Claudia Liebeskind, *Piety on Its Knees: Three Sufi Traditions in South Asia in Modern Times* (Oxford: Oxford University Press, 1998).
35. K. G. Subramanayam and Muzaffar Alam, *Writing the Mughal World* (New York: Columbia University Press, 2012).
36. Chris Bayly pointed out that the shifting of "urban material" from one place to another was a natural aspect of South Asian urban life from the eighteenth century, reflecting changes in political status and the models of political power of the Rohillas. He also observed that institutions benefiting from the revenue-free grants of rulers

often remained in *qasbahs* following the departure of a particular ruler, creating institutional and theological continuity. This process of "digging in" was most notable between 1690 and 1830. Chris Bayly, *Townsmen and Bazaars: North Indian Society in the Age of British Expansion, 1770–1870*, 3rd ed. (New Delhi: Oxford University Press, 2012), 190.

37. Ulrike Stark, *An Empire of Books: The Naval Kishore Press and the Diffusion of the Printed World in Colonial India* (New Delhi: Permanent Black, 2008), 364–65; Jennifer Dubrow, *Cosmopolitan Dreams: The Making of Modern Urdu Literary Culture in Colonial South Asia* (Honolulu: University of Hawai'i, 2018), 8–9; Marian Aguiar, "Introduction," in *Tracking Modernity: India's Railways and the Culture of Mobility* (Minneapolis: University of Minnesota Press, 2011), 1–23.
38. I have been inspired here by the approach of Manu Goswami, *Producing India: From Colonial Economy to National Space* (Chicago: University of Chicago, 2004).
39. M. Raisur Rahman, *Locale, Everyday Islam, and Modernity: Qasbah Towns and Muslim Life In Colonial India* (New Delhi: Oxford University Press, 2015), 2.
40. "Approximate average time occupied by Messages between the principal stations and the distances of various routes." Correspondence from D. G. Robinson to the Secretary to the Government of India, July 24, 1871, LI (1871): 361, 35, Bodleian.
41. *Administrative Reports of the Indo-European Telegraph Department*, 1872–3 to 1894–5, Report for 1872-3, 3. V/ 24/ 4289, Bodleian.
42. Jawaharlal Nehru, "Foreword," in Krishnalal Jethalal Shridharani, *Story of the Indian Telegraphs: A Century of Progress* (New Delhi: India Posts and Telegraphs Department, 1953).
43. Krishnalal Jethalal Shridharani, *Story of the Indian Telegraphs: A Century of Progress* (New Delhi: India Posts and Telegraphs Department, 1953), 65; Amelia Bonea, "Telegraphy and Journalism in Colonial India, c. 1830s to 1900s," *History Compass* 12, no. 4 (2014): 387–97.
44. Claude S. Fischer, *America Calling: A Social History of the Telephone to 1940* (Berkeley: University of California Press, 1992), 97, cited in Adam Burgess, *Cellular Phones, Public Fears, and a Culture of Precaution* (Cambridge: Cambridge University Press, 2004), 58.
45. Cited in Matthew Goodman, *Eighty Days: Nellie Bly and Elizabeth Bisland's History-Making Race around the World* (New York: Ballantine Books, 2013), 194.
46. Where telegraph technology arrived in India, telephones followed in the 1880s.
47. C. A. Bayly, *Empire and Information: Intelligence Gathering and Social Communication in India, 1780–1870* (Cambridge: Cambridge University Press, 1996), 180–211, cited in Mark R. Frost, "Pandora's Post Box: Empire and Information in India, 1854–1914," *English Historical Review* 131, no. 552 (2016): 1046.
48. C. A. Bayly, *Empire and Information: Intelligence Gathering and Social Communication in India, 1780–1870* (Cambridge: Cambridge University Press, 1996), 180–211, cited in Mark R. Frost, "Pandora's Post Box: Empire and Information in India, 1854–1914," *English Historical Review* 131, no. 552 (2016): 1046.

49. Krishnalal Jethalal Shridharani, *Story of the Indian Telegraphs: A Century of Progress* (New Delhi: India Posts and Telegraphs Department, 1953), 65.
50. Krishnalal Jethalal Shridharani, *Story of the Indian Telegraphs: A Century of Progress* (New Delhi: India Posts and Telegraphs Department, 1953), 85.
51. Krishnalal Jethalal Shridharani, *Story of the Indian Telegraphs: A Century of Progress* (New Delhi: India Posts and Telegraphs Department, 1953), 2.
52. Krishnalal Jethalal Shridharani, *Story of the Indian Telegraphs: A Century of Progress* (New Delhi: India Posts and Telegraphs Department, 1953), 63.
53. Manu Goswami, *Producing India: From Colonial Economy to National Space* (Chicago: University of Chicago, 2004).
54. While Goswami's conceptualization of coproduced space of India is influential to this book's understanding of the impact of telegraph and railway technologies, in *Madīnah* the spatial demarcation of India is just as much essentially Muslim as it is Hindu. For that matter, in *Madīnah* the Indian space was just as crucially grounded in the *qasbah* as it was grounded in the city.
55. India Office of the Accountant General, Posts, and Telegraphs, *Skeleton Map of India Illustrating the Lines of Telegraph in 1870* (Dehra Dun: Survey of India, 1870), Bodleian Library, University of Oxford; Survey of India, *Telegraph Map of India: Correct to Sept. 30th 1914* (Dehra Dun: Survey of India, 1914), Bodleian Library, University of Oxford; Survey of India, *India Shewing Telegraphs* (Dehra Dun: Survey of India, 1892), Bodleian Library, University of Oxford.
56. William Stevenson et al., *Imperial Gazetteer*, vol. 8 (Oxford: Clarendon Press, 1911), 440.
57. India Office of the Accountant General, Posts, and Telegraphs, *Skeleton Map of India Illustrating the Lines of Telegraph in 1870* (Dehra Dun: Survey of India, 1870), Bodleian Library, University of Oxford; Survey of India, *Telegraph Map of India: Correct to Sept. 30th 1914* (Dehra Dun: Survey of India, 1914), Bodleian Library, University of Oxford; Survey of India, *India Shewing Telegraphs* (Dehra Dun: Survey of India, 1892), Bodleian Library, University of Oxford.
58. The lines were constructed alongside metaled roads rather than along a railway line, as was typical in larger urban centers. *Report of the Telegraph Committee* (Calcutta: Supt., Govt. Press, 1907), 109–10, British Library.
59. Lucknow had a population of 264,049 according to the 1901 Census, and Bijnor had a population of 17,583 in the 1901 census. H. R. Nevill, *Lucknow: A Gazetteer* (Allahabad: Supt., Govt. Press, 1908), 214.
60. Department of Criminal Intelligence, *Statement of Newspapers and Periodicals Published in the United Provinces during the Year 1912 [with Index]* (Simla: Government Central Branch Press, 1913), 6–7, Uttar Pradesh State Archives. Other documented Hindi-language publications issuing from Bijnor in 1912 included the Hindi-language Saddharm Prachārak Press, Kangri, which published *Saddharm prachārak* (*Promoter of Sublime Doctrine*), *Vedic Magazine*, and *Gurukul samachar* (*Gurukul News*) and emphasized the importance of countering Western influence in particular. These two latter periodicals shifted to Lahore in April 1912. Dharam Divākar Press published the Hindi-language *Abla hitkārak* (Ill Favored), which intended to encourage widow remarriage.
61. Department of Criminal Intelligence, *Statement of Newspapers and Periodicals Published in the United Provinces during the Year 1912 [with Index]* (Simla: Govt. Central Branch Press, 1913), 112–13.

62. Department of Criminal Intelligence, *Statement of Newspapers and Periodicals Published in the United Provinces during the Year 1912* [with Index], issued by the Director of Criminal Intelligence (Simla: Govt. Central Branch Press, 1913), 71.
63. Department of Criminal Intelligence, *Statement of Newspapers and Periodicals Published in the United Provinces during the Year 1912* [With Index], issued by the Director of Criminal Intelligence (Simla: Govt. Central Branch Press, 1913), 103.
64. Krishnalal Jethalal Shridharani, *Story of the Indian Telegraphs: A Century of Progress* (New Delhi: India Posts and Telegraphs Department, 1953), 65; Jorma Ahvenainen, *The History of the Near Eastern Telegraphs: Before the First World War*, ed. Suomalainen Tiedeakatemia (Helsinki: Academia Scientiarum Fennica, 2011), 176–77.
65. "Public and State Abbreviated Addresses," in *Post Office Guide: India* (Calcutta: Government Press, 1910–1920), 680, British Library.
66. For example, in *Madīnah*, May 22, 1912, this section published breaking news from St. Petersburg and Italy. Italy's news was reported as coming from "*āj kā tār*" (today's telegram).
67. "Public and State Abbreviated Addresses," in *Post Office Guide: India* (Calcutta: Government Press, 1910–1920), 680, British Library, IOR/V/25/760.
68. *Madīnah*, May 22, 1912.
69. D. K. L. Choudhury, "Sinews of Panic and the Nerves of Empire: The Imagined State's Entanglement with Information Panic," *Modern Asian Studies* 38, no. 4 (2004): 975–76, cited in Daniel Headrick, "Double-Edged Sword: Communications and Imperial Control in British India," *Historical Social Research* 35, no. 1 (2010): 59.
70. Compare "*i<u>tt</u>ilā'ı̄*" (communications), *Madīnah*, December 1, 1934, 10; "*Duniyā-i Islām*" (The World of Islam), *Madīnah*, December 28, 1934, 1.
71. Appendix I, "Statement showing, according to postal circles (1) the number of post officers, letter-boxes and village postmen, and (2) the distances over which mails were conveyed by Railway, mail carts, runners and steamers at the close of the year 1902–3 and of the preceding year," India Post Office, *Annual Report of the Post Office of India: 1902–1903* (Calcutta: Supt., Govt. Press, 1903), 24, Bodleian Libraries, University of Oxford.
72. Kirti Narain, *Press, Politics and Society in Uttar Pradesh, 1885–1914* (New Delhi: Manohar, 1998), 1–15.
73. Krishnalal Jethalal Shridharani, *Story of the Indian Telegraphs: A Century of Progress* (New Delhi: India Posts and Telegraphs Department, 1953), 61.
74. Krishnalal Jethalal Shridharani, *Story of the Indian Telegraphs: A Century of Progress* (New Delhi: India Posts and Telegraphs Department, 1953), 61.
75. Kirti Narain, *Press, Politics and Society in Uttar Pradesh, 1885–1914* (New Delhi: Manohar, 1998), 24–26.
76. Laura Bear has written about the ways in which the Indian railways "restructured experiences of landscape, space, and time." This restructuring was also characterized by efforts to discipline and contain those who shifted "places and strata of origin" in a period of fluidity. The railway's arrival in Bijnor district impacted the development of agriculture and manufacturing industries, as well as transmission of periodicals. The selective expansion of rail augmented the fortunes of some cities and undermined the economic advancement of other settlements. Work on the railway bureaucracy has emphasized

the ways that institutions shaped the emergence of national trends. Laura Bear, *Lines of the Nation: Indian Railway Workers, Bureaucracy, and the Intimate Historical Self* (New York: Columbia University Press, 2007); Robert Gabriel Varady, "Rail and Road Transport in Nineteenth Century Awadh: Competition in a North Indian Province," PhD diss., University of Arizona, 1981, 221. Aparajita Mukhopadhyay has pointed out that authors of travelogues in both Hindi and Bengali appropriated the railway as a method of tourism and religious pilgrimage for Hindus. Relatively few travelogues were written on train travel by Muslims or in Urdu. Train travel presented several social challenges to traditions of gender separation, for women across traditions. In the 1870s, responding to complaints about women's proximity to men, Awadh Railways responded by creating separate railway cars for women. Women of privilege in particular became concerned about the necessity of mixing with women from lower social status. Aparajita Mukhopadhyay, "No Land for Muslims: Railway Travel and Imagining India," presentation, SOAS, London, October 28, 2013. For a selection of maps representing the state of the Indian railroad throughout the early twentieth century, see Sarat Chandra Ghose, *A Monograph on Indian Railway Rates* (Calcutta: Supt., Govt. Press, 1918). Nalinaksha Sanyal, *Development of Indian Railways* (Calcutta: University of Calcutta, 1930), 380; Jogendra Nath Sahni, *Indian Railways: One Hundred Years, 1853–1953* (New Delhi: Ministry of Railways, 1953).

77. *Selections from the Vernacular Newspapers Published in the Punjab, North Western Provinces, Oudh, and the Central Provinces* (1900–1925), 1911, 905; 1909, 859, National Archives of India.
78. "Petition from the Inhabitants of Bijnor," Department: Railway Department, Branch: Railway Construction, 1907–10, File No. 79–84, National Archives, New Delhi, India.
79. "*Tā'ūn ẓila' bijnor mein̲ lā'iṭ railwe kī tajvīz* [The Proposal for a Light Railway in the Town and District Bijnor]," *Madīnah*, May 1, 1913.
80. William Stevenson Meyer et al., *Imperial Gazetteer*, vol. 8 (Oxford: Clarendon Press, 1911), 198.
81. "*Is bāt kī manẕūrī hadāvar kar dī gayī ki jamā'at intiẕāmīyah rohilkhanḍ reilwe dīrdūn asṭeishan har davār dhera reilwe se rajpūtānah tak sāṛhe pānch fiṭ peimānah kī eik relwe kī peimā'ish kare jiskā ṭavīl āṭh mīl hogā. Yih kām dehrah dūn rājpūtānah relwe kā nām mashhūr ho gayā*," *Madīnah*, May 15, 1912.
82. Bijnor's tradition in reverence of Gogā Pīr appealed to both Hindu and Muslim inhabitants of *qasbahs*. Celebrations commemorating a Sufi of regional significance named Gogā Pīr, also called Zahīr Pīr or Zahīr Dīwān, occurred annually. The districts and cities surrounding Bijnor, including Muzaffarnagar, Saharanpur, Bidauli, and Meerut, boasted some connection to the spiritual tradition of Zahīr Pīr, but the rituals revering the Sufi were limited to Muslims. Bijnor's Zahīr Pīr following was characterized by the involvement of both Hindus and Muslims. A small fair named "Chhair Zahīr Diwan" usually involved approximately 250 people, occurring once a year in Bijnor on the ninth day of the Hindu month Bhaadra or Bhadrapada. This would have put the festival at the beginning of September.

83. Francis Robinson, e-mail to the author, August 7, 2017.
84. H. R. Nevill, *Muzaffarnagar: A Gazetteer* (Allahabad: Supt., Govt. Press, 1903), 105, Bodleian Libraries, University of Oxford.
85. Mushirul Hasan, "Qasbas: A Brief in Propinquity," in *A Leaf Turns Yellow: The Sufis of Awadh*, ed. Muzaffar Ali (New Delhi: Rumi Foundation / Bloomsbury Publishing India, 2013), 110, 112.
86. Edward Gait, *Census of India, 1911: United Provinces of Agra and Oudh*, vol. 15, part 2 (Calcutta: Supt., Govt. Press, 1911).
87. Stefan Tetzlaffi, "The Motorisation of the 'Mufassil': Automobile Traffic and Social Change in Rural North India, c. 1925–70," PhD diss., University of Gottingen, 2015.
88. For instance, I exchange correspondence via WhatsApp with women who rarely leave their home in Kandhala *qasbah*.
89. Maulvī 'Abdul Ḥaq Bilgrāmī, *Māsir al-ikram* (Hyderabad: n.p., 1910), paraphrased in Mushirul Hasan, "Qasbas: A Brief in Propinquity," in *A Leaf Turns Yellow: The Sufis of Awadh*, ed. Muzaffar Ali (New Delhi: Rumi Foundation / Bloomsbury Publishing India, 2013), 108.
90. *"Chānd Bībī," Madīnah*, June 1, 1913, 9; *"Chānd Bībī," Madīnah*, June 22, 1913, 9; *"Chānd Bībī," Madīnah*, July 1, 1913, 9; *"Chānd Bībī," Madīnah*, July 8, 1913, 9; *"Chānd Bībī," Madīnah*, July 22, 1913, 9; *"Hasrat rabi'a naṣrī," Madīnah*, August 8, 1913, 9.
91. "*Jang-i Iṭalī-o Ṭurkī* [The War of Italy and Turkey], *Madīnah*, May 1, 1912, 3.
92. *Madīnah*, June 1, 1913, 9.
93. "*Jin kī hālāt agar roshnī mein lā'e jā'enge to eik nayā manẓar ānkhon ke sāmne phir jā'egā* [If her (Chānd Bībī's) condition is brought into light, then it may be seen in a different perspective]" *Madīnah*, June 1, 1913, 9; "*ab jo kuchh kīyā jā'e voh apnī hī rā'e se karnā sachhā hai* [what was to be done now, it was right that she do it according to her own opinion only]," *Madīnah*, July 8, 1913, 9.
94. *Madīnah*, July 8, 1913, 9.
95. "*Tihzīb-i akhlāq se taṣīḥ 'aqā'id aham hai* [Correcting your beliefs is more important than culture and morals]," *Madīnah*, May 8, 1912, 3.
96. *Madīnah*, October 28, 1937, 8.
97. Furqān Aḥmad Ṣiddīqī, *Ẓila' bijnor ke jauvāhir* [Jewels of Bijnor] (New Delhi: Jade Press, 1991), 40–43.
98. "*Purāne charkhe kā rāg* [The rāg of the old spinning wheel]," *Madīnah*, July 25, 1921, 1.
99. "*Pakhuṛī*: s.f. Petal, flower-leaf; the shoulder-blade," see John T. Platts, *A Dictionary of Urdu, Classical Hindi, and English*, Digital Dictionaries of South Asia, https://dsal.uchicago.edu/dictionaries/platts.
100. Laura Bear, "Doubt, Conflict, Mediation: The Anthropology of Modern Time," *Journal of the Royal Anthropological Institute* 20, no. S1 (2014): 3–30.
101. Margrit Pernau, *Ashraf into Middle Classes: Muslims in Nineteenth-Century Delhi* (New Delhi: Oxford University Press, 2013), 116.
102. Ulrike Stark, "Politics, Public Issues and the Promotion of Urdu Literature: Avadh Akhbar, the First Urdu Daily in Northern India," *Annual of Urdu Studies* 18 (2003): 66–94.

103. Margrit Pernau, "The Delhi Urdu Akhbar: Between Persian Akhbarat and English Newspapers," *Annual of Urdu Studies* 18, no. 1 (2003): 122.
104. Jennifer Dubrow, *Cosmopolitan Dreams: The Making of Modern Urdu Literary Culture in Colonial South Asia* (Honolulu: University of Hawai'i, 2018), 86, 88, 90–91.
105. E.g., "*Iṯṯilā'-t-i k͟husūsī: Maktub*" (Particular Communication: Letters), *Madīnah*, April 1, 1928, 11.
106. J. Douglas, "Anglo-Indian Ghosts," in *Bombay and Western India: A Series of Stray Papers*, vol. 2 (London: S. Low, Marston & Company, 1893), 363–66, cited in Nile Green, conclusion of *Bombay Islam: The Religious Economy of the West Indian Ocean, 1840–1915* (Cambridge: Cambridge University Press, 2011), 235. For Green's approach to enchantment of industrial communications, see Nile Green, "The Enchantment of Industrial Communications," in *Bombay Islam: The Religious Economy of the West Indian Ocean, 1840–1915* (Cambridge: Cambridge University Press, 2011), 90–118.
107. E.g., see the letter celebrating publication of *Madīnah* by Syed Mohammad Mustajāb ul-Dīn Ṣabr, May 1, 1912; for *fatwe*, see *Madīnah*, May 8, 1912.
108. "*'Ām ak͟hbār aur 'ām tār: haẓūr mālik-i mo'aẓẓam Jārj panjam aur mushāhid muqaddas kā vāq'aya* [general news and telegrams: the honorable King George the fifth and the experience of the sacred tomb of the martyr]," *Madīnah*, May 22, 1912, 10.
109. *Madīnah*, May 8, 1912.
110. *Madīnah*, May 8, 1912; Muḥammad Walī ul-Ḥaq Anṣārī, "*Farangī mahal kī 'ilmī, adabī aur siyāsī k͟hidmāt*," *Nayā Daur* (February–March 1994): 48; Muḥammad Ināyatullah Anṣārī, *Taẕkira-yi 'ulamā-yi farangī maḥalī* (Lucknow: Ishā'at ul-'Ulūm Barqī Press, c.1930–31), accessed online via Rekhta.org, https://www.rekhta.org/ebooks/tazkira-e-ulama-e-farangi-mahal-mohammad-inayatullah-ebooks.
111. *Madīnah*, May 8, 1912.
112. Ashfāq Aḥmed, 'Azmī, *Nazīr Aḥmed: Shakṣīyat aur kārnāme* (New Delhi: Muktabah Shāhirāh, 1974), 9.
113. Furqān Aḥmad Ṣiddīqī, *Ẓila' Bijnor ke jauvāhir* [Jewels of Bijnor] (New Delhi: Jade Press, 1991).
114. *Madīnah*, February 13, 1933; translation published in Shabana Mahmud, "*Angāre* and the Founding of the Progressive Writers' Association," *Modern Asian Studies* 30, no. 2 (May 1996): 447–48, with the exception of the translation of the Farsi couplet concluding the passage, which I have slightly altered from Shabana Mahmud's initial translation, "No calamity can reach the seclusion of solitude."
115. Furqān Aḥmad Ṣiddīqī, *Ẓila' Bijnor ke jauvāhir* [Jewels of Bijnor] (New Delhi: Jade Press, 1991), 40–43.
116. Furqān Aḥmad Ṣiddīqī, *Ẓila' Bijnor ke jauvāhir* [Jewels of Bijnor] (New Delhi: Jade Press, 1991), 1–10.
117. Ḥāmid Anṣārī stated at a release of M. Raisur Rahman's book, "I am very delighted to read such a valuable book which is in fact a chapter of North-Indian history on Qasbahs. History should be recorded as to why the institution of Qasbahs has suddenly started declining and has almost disappeared. One reason could be that people had to leave their places to earn livelihood." *Janta Ka Reporter*,

July 21, 2015, http://www.jantakareporter.com/india/vice-president-releases-a-book-on-qasbahs-locale-everyday-islam-and-modernity/7584. Mushirul Ḥasan stated, "Qasbah as a social and cultural entity is not only a lost idea but has vanished without leaving behind any substantial legacy." Mushirul Ḥasan, "The Qasbah Culture—I," *The Hindu*, July 22, 2002. Francesca Orsini at a talk at the University of Pennsylvania mentioned that the surname Bilgrāmī was useful to indicate a certain literary and academic pedigree. University of Pennsylvania lecture series, Department of South Asian Studies, Spring 2017.

118. Faridah Zaman has written that nostalgia is indicative of "temporal and spatial ambivalence in historical moments." See Faridah Zaman, "Beyond Nostalgia: Time and Place in Indian Muslim Politics," *Journal of the Royal Asiatic Society* 27, no. 4 (October 2017): 627–47.
119. Jamal Malik, *Islam in South Asia: A Short History* (Leiden: Brill, 2008), 266.

3
Urdu Lithography as a Muslim Technology

In content and in appearance, *Madīnah* imbued itself with value to Muslims particularly. Not only discursively but in its choice of imagery, calligraphy, and form, *Madīnah* emphasized its links between the present and the past. *Madīnah*'s first cover displayed a dramatic image of the city of Madīnah and the boat that brought King George V to India for his Darbar in 1911, surrounded by palm trees (Figure 3.1). The inclusion of the boat may have been an oblique reference to the newspaper's support of the Hajj, one of the key rituals of Islam, and its campaign for government-sponsored transport to Mecca. The cover mixed elements of Urdu, Persian, and Arabic. The city of Madīnah would have appeared as "*al-Madīnah*" if written in Arabic; here it is simply "*Madīnah*." At the same time, the title includes diacritic marks usually reserved only for Qur'anic Arabic. While the text included several words in Arabic, the grammar of the sentences remained for the most part in Urdu or Persian. This manner of mixing three languages rendered Arabic words understandable to South Asian Muslim readers, even if they did not read the language, while linking *nastaʿlīq* calligraphy to Qur'anic practices and Persian heritage. This mixing of modes infused the Urdu with sacred import.

During World War I the newspaper's covers featured large representations of the city of Madīnah accompanied by Arabic embellishments. In Figure 3.1, the cover is crowned with a pair of flags bearing the crescent of Islam, which bore a striking resemblance to the flag of the Ottoman Empire. The Arabian desert appears on each cover behind a dramatic eagle's eye view of the *masjid* in Madīnah. A crescent moon hangs watchfully over the scene, and the sky is dotted with stars above the rolling sand dunes. Below the picture, at the bottom of the encircled vignette of Madīnah, appears a phrase of blessing to the prophet in Arabic, written using the *naskh* calligraphic form.

Scholarship on the transmission of oral knowledge to print in Islam has identified a dichotomy between the way traditional manuscripts preserved the written word—requiring a stamp of approval, or an *ijazat*, before it could be finalized—and the impersonal way that print is seen as preserving the written word—mass produced, industrialized, bureaucratized. *Madīnah*, and the many other Urdu newspapers that used the lithograph to preserve Urdu calligraphy, formed a bridge between the intensely personal manuscript tradition and the world of mass print. Neither manuscript nor soulless copy, *Madīnah* invoked

Print and the Urdu Public. Megan Eaton Robb, Oxford University Press (2021). © Oxford University Press.
DOI: 10.1093/oso/9780190089375.001.0001

Figure 3.1 Cover of *Madīnah*, March 22, 1915, 1. Library of Congress, Washington, DC.

the personalized correspondence networks of the past in a mass-produced form. In this way, it married Persianate newsletter models with images referencing an Arab-inflected pan-Islam: the forms on the page targeted a Muslim readership just as precisely as the Urdu language targeted an Urdu public. Visual and structural analysis of *Madīnah* shows that even explicitly "secular" content could simultaneously be religious in form. This religious quality derived from the newspaper's visual elements, its association with holy spaces, and its calligraphy. Far from illustrating a clear divide between the sacred and the secular, the case study of *Madīnah* argues against the utility of drawing a strict boundary between the two categories in descriptions of the public sphere in South Asia. In the early twentieth century the English-language category of *religion*, like that of the *public*, was increasingly in conversation with multilingual concepts and experiences of North Indians, in a fashion productive of new identities. That dynamic bore out in visual references to Muslim spaces and literary publics.

Scholarship on the lithographic press has focused primarily on books—in particular, on the print traditions emanating from large cities like Lucknow.[1] While printers used lithography to make books look more like manuscripts, Urdu newspaper publishers used lithography to make newspapers look like the mass-produced correspondence that had previously bound together *ashrāf* social networks. *Madīnah* was not only an example of commercial publishing following "its own imperatives of entertainment and profit," in Orsini's words.[2] It deserves consideration also as a manifestation of piety. Journalism was a *farẓ*, or duty, to the proprietor and editors of *Madīnah*.[3] The example of *Madīnah* suggests that we must consider this potential dimension of other Urdu newspapers as well.

This is not to say that all Urdu newspapers were Muslim in precisely the way that *Madīnah* was; it is not the case that all Urdu newspapers claimed to represent Islam, nor were they viewed as representatives of Islam in the first half of the twentieth century. In this period there were many Urdu newspapers run by Hindus, or teams comprised of both Hindus and Muslims, that made no claims to represent a religious community. By the same token, there were many Hindi-language newspapers run by Muslims that avoided references to Hindi as the language for Hindus. There is a serious risk of overstating the clarity of the alliance between Urdu and Islam during this period if we look through the teleological lens of modern-day Pakistan and the place of Urdu in that state. On the other hand, the familiar affiliation between Urdu and Islam was rooted in what came before: it was not a magical occurrence on the eve of Partition, nor was it entirely the result of top–down policies imposing an artificial alliance between language and religion. Certainly, policies that mandated Urdu as the language of governance in Pakistan had a role to play in promoting links between that language and Islam, just as policies that mandated Hindi as the language of governance in the United Provinces (UP) demoted the formal status of Urdu in that province. The case study of *Madīnah* offers us the opportunity to explore how North Indians were experiencing these linkages prior to Partition: the ways that visual, emotional, historical references in public culture had already provided some of the scaffolding that allowed Muslims to build a single roof over language and religion.

In contrast to approaches that treat media merely as neutral instruments of effect, this book treats mass media as one part of a larger process of mediating reality, consistent with constructivist approaches to religion. In chapter 2 we learned how *ashrāf* in Bijnor *qasbah* used telegraph technology to compile content from a rapidly expanding geographic horizon, influencing perceptions of time. Lithography visualized *Madīnah* in a way that coded the paper to Islam. In the case of lithographic newspapers, the medium was an important part of the message.

Script and Visual Culture of Print in Islam

To understand the visual character of Persian script in Urdu newspapers and other forms of publishing we need an understanding of the iconic significance of the Arabic and Persian scripts in Islam. Jamal Elias has written about the use of text as a form of religious imagery in Islam in the earliest histories: reproducing the Arabic script "well and carefully" is linked to the pardon of sins in an early *ḥadīth* transmitted via the authority of Wahb ibn Munabbih (d. c. 732).[4] Elias demonstrated that "writing possesses the quality of acting as a visual signifier much in the same way that pictures or objects do."[5] In other words, writing and reading are modes of somatic engagement with oral language in the same way that the rocking motion of madrasa students memorizing scripture is. As the mass media came to complement the manuscript tradition in the early twentieth century, the significance of calligraphy persisted, and its links to Islam became more visible.

Once the form of the communication and the content of the communication are distinguished from each other, the mode of representation transforms from discursive to figurative representation, as David Morgan has said, and "it begins to perform rather than defer" meaning.[6] In other words, the form becomes visible as a second point of access to meaning rather than a passageway to the actual meaning of the words. The *nastaʻlīq* script, the particular type of calligraphy in which Urdu is written in South Asia, typically operates by deferring meaning, mobilizing, as Baudrillard stated, "by virtue of its very lack of signification . . . an entire imaginary collectivity."[7] But when we distinguish the form of the Urdu newspaper from its content, it becomes clear that in a market of news offered in multiple languages and scripts, the mass-produced calligraphy of these papers began to *perform* as a figurative as well as a discursive medium in South Asia in the first half of the twentieth century. It is important to note that when giving an account of piety it is a mistake to focus exclusively on textual evidence (as demonstrated by David Morgan, Peter Burke, and Ivan Gaskell).[8] However, my purpose here is simply to uncover the strands of piety expressed in a textual source and to show how the visual form of written Islam contains untapped analytical potential. My analysis extends a theoretical framework initially applied to images of people, animals, and scenes of life to figurative, handwritten text and its channels of production and distribution in South Asia.[9] Lithography and its role in the expansion of print demonstrate the power not only of the discursive content of the text but also that of the visual form of the written word.

The addition of print technologies to repertoires of oral technologies of transmission was a key turning point in the character of authority in Islam.[10] For Muslims in North India, the engagement with print resulted in a gradual shift from a view in which humans were the sole embodiment of knowledge in Islam and print was a mere aid to memorization, to a perspective in which the printed word, distinct from the hand-copied manuscript, held the ability to impart knowledge. Debates have been marked by reflection on how the shift from oral to print media either changed religiosity for Muslims in British India or demonstrated continuity with past traditions.[11] Muhammad Qasim Zaman has demonstrated that there are key continuities in the diversity of approaches that *ʿulamā* took and continued to take before and after the introduction of print, indirectly making an argument for continuity in the context of change.[12] *ʿUlamā* not only used print technology, but the technology of print also influenced commentaries by creating an impetus for scholars to "find an audience in the greater Muslim world."[13]

The aesthetics of *Madīnah* and other lithographic newspapers played a vital role in their construction of a distinctive Muslim, Urdu public space and temporality in early twentieth-century India. *Madīnah* engaged in world-building based on the religious valence of preexisting literary and social networks, and in turn underpinned a conversation in those networks that increased associations between religion, printed symbols, and language. Historical or cultural studies scholarship looking at the relationship between print and religious identity either has overlooked newspapers or has limited its focus to newspapers' content and political affiliation.[14] This chapter focuses on the visual culture of newsprint as a technology that possessed irruptive power, influencing patterns of community formation, knowledge transmission, and the texture of knowledge. In particular, technologies of print production and institutions of news distribution influenced "rhythms of human and non-human time."[15] Urdu newspapers like *Madīnah* through their visual form—their preservation of *nastaʿlīq*, and visual associations between the holy city and the newspaper as a space—became metonyms for the presence of the Muslim past in the present.

In contrast to approaches that treat media merely as neutral instruments of effect, this book treats mass media as one part of a larger process of mediating reality, consistent with constructivist approaches to religion.[16] In chapter 2 we learned how *ashrāf* in Bijnor *qasbah* used telegraph technology to compile content from a rapidly expanding geographic horizon, influencing perceptions of time. Lithography visualized *Madīnah* in a way that coded the paper to Islam. Rather than assume that a newspaper has always been a newspaper in exactly the same way, I argue that the early twentieth-century Urdu newspaper had the ability to invoke Islam, and sometimes did. In the case of lithographic newspapers, the medium was an important part of the message.

Nafis Nasta'līq: Exquisite *Nasta'līq*

Handwriting has long been connected to virtue, art, and statecraft in Islam. Writing is particularly central to Islam; after all, it preserves the Divine Word of the Holy Qur'an, it distinguishes mankind from other animals, and learning to write well helps humans realize their intended nature.[17] A manuscript attributed to the Iraqi philosopher Abū Ḥaiyān al-Tawḥīdī (d. after 1009–1010) penned in the tenth century brings together a representative range of reflections on the power of the reed pen and handwriting. His account laid out in detail the importance of the selection of the pen (or in Latin, *calamus*), the angle of the nib, and the correct reproduction of each Arabic letter in a variety of calligraphic forms. Handwriting is compared in this treatise to a form of fine art, akin to the production of beautiful textiles. "The embroidered cloth of handwriting is its evenness, its design, its shape, its color, the well-measured arrangement of the black (writing) on the white (paper of the page)," al-Tawḥīdī recounted.[18] Handwriting indicated virtue and personality. Hishām b. al-Ḥakam states, "Handwriting is jewelry fashioned by the hand from the pure gold of the intellect. It liquefies and founds the content of the heart and fashions the ingots of the part of the body in which thought and feeling are situated."[19] Handwriting has been the substance of prophecy as well; the calligrapher Ibn Mukla was described as a "prophet in the field of handwriting." The art "was poured upon his hand, even as it was revealed to the bees to make their honey cells hexagonal."[20] Later texts like the *Golistān-i honar* (*Calligraphers and Painters*) continued to present the occupation of calligraphy as prestigious and even sacred.[21]

In nineteenth-century South Asia, calligraphy was still a manifestation of spirituality. Deoband permitted vocational training in calligraphy for its *'ulamā* from its inception as a reflection of this connection and in order to expand the influence of scholars in the increasingly important lithographic press.[22] The early twentieth century saw the embrace by Chishti Sufis like Ḥakīm Faqīr Muḥammad Chishtī, as well as scholars and activists like Maulānā Ghulām Rasūl Mehr (1895–1971) and Muḥammad Iqbāl (1877–1938), of the continued development of a distinct style of Urdu calligraphy that would be linked to Islam.[23] This style was specifically connected to Lahore, where Majīd Ḥasan received his first journalistic training and where *Madīnah* was also widely read. Urdu calligraphic manuals indicate a continuation of this connection between Urdu and the calligraphic tradition, embracing calligraphy as a manifestation of spirituality in the twentieth century.[24]

The form of writing in the Arabic script most closely associated with Urdu is the *nasta'līq* script. In comparison to *naskh*, the Arabic script most commonly employed across the Middle East, *nasta'līq* had a distinctive role and significance in Muslim visual culture in the South Asian subcontinent.[25] Appropriately, the word *nasta'līq* is a compound, indicating a hybrid combination of *naskh* with another form called *ta'līq*. Its invention is attributed to Mīr 'Alī Tabrīzī (d. 1420 CE), the fourteenth-century Persian calligrapher. Persian scribes employed this method of writing with nonsacramental texts; nonetheless, the elegant formation of the script indicated virtue and even proximity to God.[26] The man in whom *nasta'līq* reached its zenith in quality was Maulānā Sultān 'Alī Mashhadī (c. 1440–1520), about whom the sixteenth-century Persian poet Qādī Aḥmad wrote that his mastery of writing indicated a closeness to 'Alī.[27] Furthermore, to those who aspired to become calligraphers, Qādī Aḥmad wrote, "Purity of writing proceeds from purity of heart. / Writing is the distinction of the pure."[28] In this analysis, the writing on the page was a divine metaphor for correct action on earth.

While popular tradition has it that the Mughals brought *nasta'līq* to South Asia, two manuscripts copied in *nasta'līq* demonstrate that this mode of calligraphy was in fact already thriving during the sultanate period. Edinburgh University Library has a copy of the Persian Bible that was copied in Agra in 1450 using *nasta'līq*.[29] The Bibliothèque Nationale in Paris has a *nasta'līq* copy of the *Tāj al-mā'aṡir* (*Exploits of the Crown*) copied in India in 1465, approximately two decades before the birth of Babur (1483–1530).[30] By the Mughal period, then, *nasta'līq* was well developed as a South Asian mode of writing; certainly by the time of Babur, the ability to write Persian in *nasta'līq* had become closely associated with virtue and elite connoisseurship. A poem well-penned would rise in value, according to Emperor Babur's description of the poetry of Baisunghur Giāt al-Dīn Mirzā.[31] *Nasta'līq* was the favorite style of Emperor Akbar (1542–1605) and the most fashionable style of the Mughal period. Meanwhile, *naskh* continued to be used for the copying of sacramental works like the Qur'an and the copying of any Arabic.[32] In fact, calligraphers at Akbar's court were frequently expert in both modes of writing.[33] Since calligraphy was a high-stakes affair, commentaries on *nasta'līq* appeared that laid out criteria for the selection of the reed pen, paper, and ink and the angle at which the pen should be cut, as well as emphasizing that maintaining virtuous behavior was essential to developing as a calligrapher. Today in the Hast-o-Neest Institute at Lahore, calligraphy instruction begins with instruction on how to cut the nib of the calligrapher's first pen.

Contemporary scholarship on the power of calligraphy in Islam almost always refers to Arabic, *naskh*, and other writing in the Middle East broadly defined. For instance, Brinkley Messick's *The Calligraphic State* explores contrasts in the transition from a state apparatus founded on calligraphy to a modern bureaucratized authority, as demonstrated by a shift from handwritten manuscripts and letters to the print production of modern legal texts in Yemen.[34] There are many significant differences between the Yemeni context and the South Asian context, however, that explain the divergent influences that the introduction of print had in each region. Yemen was characterized by a state-controlled publishing culture, which experienced significant diversions into small-scale printing presses in the nineteenth century.[35] This is in contrast to South Asia, where publishing was a decentralized endeavor from the beginning of the print era. In addition, missing in the Yemeni case was a profoundly important element of the South Asian context: the early introduction and wide adoption of lithographic technology, a technology that actually supported the continued importance of handwriting, and in particular *nasta'līq*, rather than undermining it. These differences also distinguish South Asia from the late Ottoman Empire, a context that has been explored by Zoe Griffith.[36] The existing scholarship on calligraphy in Islam, on the one hand, tends to assume that the metropole of Islam is the Middle East, despite the majority of the world's Muslims residing in South and Southeast Asia. Work focusing on digital calligraphy, on the other hand, assumes that handwriting and print were always mutually exclusive in the Islamic context.[37] Neither of these assumptions is useful to an understanding of the Urdu press in North India. In this respect, the work of Jamal Elias and Jürgen Wasim Frembgen, who have both focused on *nasta'līq* calligraphic traditions in Pakistan, demonstrates the value of questioning those assumptions.[38]

Scholars have observed that, in the early twentieth century, Urdu-speaking Muslims were turning toward Arabic and English models of intellectual production. Francis Robinson has demonstrated how the reformist turn of the nineteenth century in South Asia was characterized by a shift in emphasis to Arabic sources, particularly *ḥadīth*, with renewed attention to *maulid* (birth of the Prophet) ceremonies and biographies of the Prophet. The accompanying concern to translate Arabic sources into Urdu also characterized much of the print activity of the nineteenth century.[39] Seema Alavi has demonstrated that in the eighteenth and nineteenth centuries, Unani *ḥakīm*s shifted from Mughal understandings of health as an aristocratic virtue to Unani Tibb[40] as a science supported by Arabic literature.[41] Frances Pritchett has shown how the nineteenth century saw a reaction against the elaborate and artificial Persian models for Urdu prose and poetry, to the extent that Persian was blamed for Indians' problems grappling with English.[42] Moḥammad Ḥusain Āzād, the author of *Āb-i ḥayāt*, said in a speech in the nineteenth century that instead of the artifice of Persian, speakers of Urdu should turn toward English: "New kinds of jewelry and robes of honor, suited to the conditions of the present day, are shut up in the storage-trunks of the English—which are lying right here beside us, but we don't realize it."[43] For Āzād, English provided a refuge from the deceptive elegance of Persian models.

From Hali's *Musaddas*, in which poetry is bequeathed to Urdu as a "legacy" by the Arabs, to his *Introduction to Poetry and Poetics*, in which Persian poetry is not mentioned once in the entire book, there is plenty of evidence to demonstrate that Urdu speakers were distancing themselves from Persian models of intellectual production and embracing Arab and English models instead.[44] Ironically, this was the same period when, having done away with the illusion that they were exercising power through the Mughal emperor, the British Raj leaned ever more heavily on Mughal models of governance.[45] In slight counterpoint to these observations, this chapter explores how the aesthetics of newspapers *did* continue to draw on Persian influence. While many areas of life were characterized by a turning away from Persian influence, and in certain respects this included the newspapers, the calligraphy and the aesthetic models on which the papers were built preserved its legacy. This is particularly apparent in their continued emphasis on calligraphy and specifically calligraphy in *nastaʿlīq*.

While Arabic quotations in *Madīnah* and other Urdu newspapers would appear in *nas<u>kh</u>*, the lithographic newspaper's emphasis on *nastaʿlīq* calligraphy revealed the formation of a distinctive set of visual referents combining Arabic and Indo-Persian influences. Its form was not as exaggerated in depth or in perpendicularity as the Lahori *nastaʿlīq* associated with Muhammad Iqbal's publications that would be developed after 1928. Because the publication was a regularly published newspaper, rather than a book, the clarity of the calligraphy is also naturally less than that expected in a published book of poems, where the publisher enjoyed the luxury of time in copyediting. However, the calligraphy in *Madīnah* already illustrates some of the calling cards of Lahori *nasta'līq*. The characters *nūn* and *'ayn* had great depth in comparison to those characters in Persian *nasta'līq*, and the characters of *alif* and *lām* are perpendicular to the horizontal line, rather than slightly slanted as in Persian *nasta'līq*.[46] According to oral history, Muḥammad Iqbāl chose the perpendicularity of the calligraphic script to "subtly embody the spirit of the times," making reference to the boldness of form and exaggerated length and bolt-uprightness of vertical characters.[47] *Madīnah* demonstrates that some of these features were already a part of the Urdu calligraphic lexicon, which Muḥammad Iqbāl may have emphasized in his efforts to create a distinctive graphic footprint for Lahori *nasta'līq*.

The Template of the Printed Newspaper in South Asia: *Akhbārāt*

Until Margrit Pernau's work on the subject, the origins of Urdu newspapers in the *akhbār navīs* tradition were obscured, permitting the assumption that the European printing press and newspaper models guided the development of Urdu print. As Margrit Pernau and, more recently, Michael Fisher have demonstrated, there are significant continuities between the Persian-language *akhbārāt*—or newsletters of the Mughal period, penned by *akhbār navīs*—and Urdu *akhbārāt*—or newspapers.[48] Indeed, both as physical artifacts and imagined links binding the Muslim community, twentieth-century newspapers and their distribution networks were an extension of correspondence networks that had flourished long before their arrival.

The *akhbār navīs* method of knowledge exchange was established in the sixteenth century. Emperor Akbar tasked clerks with recording court diaries for the reference of government servants and courtiers, as well as to reflect the emperor's symbolic significance as the embodied spirit of the empire. These news writers called *akhbār navīs* emerged at the same time; they also collected records at the central court and in this case were employed by either an individual or a group of "subscribers" to transmit the information to Mughal outposts.[49] In this way, regional leaders and interested parties could keep tabs on developments at the center without jeopardizing their hold over state matters at home. Kinship groups associated with the role of *akhbār navīs* correlate with trends in the *ashrāf* more generally.[50] Many of these *akhbār navīs* or *wāqi'a navīs* would have been Muslims of Central Asian heritage; there were of course also many who were not Muslim. The eighteenth-century Maratha powers' collection of *akhbārāt* reveals that most *akhbār navīs* under Peshwa rule hailed from "Islamized" Hindu castes—Kayasth and Khattri—known for their membership in the scribal elite.[51]

The East India Company adopted the Mughal network of *akhbār navīs*, and the British eventually institutionalized and bureaucratized the system to suit their purposes. By the early twentieth century, the British had come to depend on newspapers to do the type of information-gathering legwork that *akhbār navīs* had done previously.[52] Meanwhile, newspapers originating in and speaking to local communities, including *Madīnah*, self-consciously claimed the tradition of the *akhbār navīs* through their titles, section headings, and use of Persian.

Persian and then Urdu newspapers of the nineteenth and twentieth century claimed connection to the heritage of the *akhbār navīs* through linguistic links in three main ways.[53] First, articles in these newspapers incorporated the term *akhbār* into the title of the publication. *Madīnah* always referred to itself as *Madīnah Akhbār* in the newspaper bylines and editorials, establishing a verbal link between the *akhbār navīs* tradition and the Bijnor publication. Second, published articles often referred to the "*akhbār*" of specific locations when reporting news from other localities. For instance, *Madīnah* often refers to the "*akhbār*" of Indian provinces and foreign countries, entitling the section of each newspaper discussing national and international news "*'ām akhbār aur 'ām tār*" or "general news and telegrams." This wording makes clear that *akhbār* is being referred to in the sense of private correspondence between the writer and the editor of *Madīnah*. The mode of presentation implied that *Madīnah* was publishing news gained from a network of *akhbār navīs* placed across India and the world. *Madīnah* also refers to *payām*, or messages, noting down the source and date of each transmission to underline its authenticity as fresh correspondence.[54] Finally, Fisher points out that many newspapers of the period employed Persian language and terminology to establish another link between their publication and the rich tradition of *akhbār navīs*. *Madīnah* regularly published Persian poetry, and its editors as well as correspondents often wrote in heavily Persian-inflected Urdu.[55]

Madīnah presented itself as the early twentieth-century incarnation of the *akhbār navīs*, using the telegraph to gather information from "personal" sources in order to keep readers abreast of developments at the center and abroad. This identification with the tradition of the *akhbār navīs* justifies the intensity of *Madīnah*'s frustration at the failure of both the All-India Muslim League and the Congress to disseminate regular reports regarding their activities. In 1917, a particularly virulent article lambasted both groups for not submitting a credible report on their activities for almost two years.[56] This withholding of information would have seemed even more threatening considering *Madīnah*'s self-defined role as *akhbār-navis* for the Muslim *ashrāf*.

However, in contrast to the *akhbār navis* models of the Mughals and the Company, *Madīnah*, like other Urdu newspapers in the twentieth century, increasingly targeted Muslim subscribers and marketed itself as a Muslim source of *a<u>kh</u>bār*. Although Islam influenced the practice of *a<u>kh</u>bār* collection and record-keeping under the Mughal state, *a<u>kh</u>bārāt* were tools local leaders used to build an arsenal of information for a range of purposes, rather than a means to address a particular religious community. The evolution of Urdu-language newspapers invoking Persianate traditions, including *Madīnah,* marked a sea change in information dissemination and in Islam's link to identity among *ashrāf* in North India. Pernau goes so far as to call the network of news writers in the nineteenth century the "nucleus of the public sphere."[57] Extending that central status to writers of *a<u>kh</u>bārāt* in the twentieth century, an emphasis on the association between language and religion in this nucleus of the public would have been influential. If a public is a space and time, as this book argues, the Urdu public as it appeared in *Madīnah* was mapped by roads linking the *qasbah* with the holy cities of Islam, the *ashrāf* with the global Muslim community, and a thorough mixing of the present with Persianate and Arabic pasts.

The Newspaper as Muslim Network

The *akhbārāt* networks had traditionally approached matters without distinguishing between secular and religious content. The colonial government, however, insisted on this distinction, and when papers like *Madīnah* failed to stay in the lane of exclusively "religious" content they earned the suspicion and ire of the colonial surveillance agencies.[58] As early as 1912, a list of publications under surveillance in UP in 1912 included several publications in *qasbahs*, several of which violated this rule and were labeled "bigoted Muhammadan organ[s]."[59]

Majīd Ḥasan was linked, through preexisting kinship networks, with the editors of other prominent small-town newspapers across North India. His newspaper reprinted articles from other small-town as well as some big-city newspapers, commenting on their approaches and engaging them. His staff were, like him, products of *qasbah* culture, drawn from surrounding small towns, linked together by generations of kinship and professional ties. The editors lived with Majīd Ḥasan while they worked on the paper. In this way, *Madīnah* built on existing relational networks as it shaped a public sphere anchored in Urdu.

Many of the newspapers demonstrated commonalities in editorial leadership as editors shifted from publication to publication. In large cities, it seems to have been more common to shift between publications in the same city; for example, in Delhi Ḥāfiẓ Syed 'Azīz Baqā'i shifted from the *Ḥurīyat* to the *Paishwā* editorial team.[60] In the world of the *qasbahs* individuals more frequently followed publications from one *qasbah* to another. Maẓhar ud-Dīn Shairkoṭī (editor of *Madīnah*, 1917–1921), for instance, completed his education at Deoband, worked on the newspaper in Shairkot *qasbah* named *Dastūr*, edited *Nagīnah* in

Naginah, then shifted to *Madīnah* in 1917, and in 1921 went on to edit the paper based in Naginah called *Almān*. This regular rotation reinforced the sense, despite natural competition for readership, of a common newspaper landscape that journalists shared.

Majīd Ḥasan also established relationships with the editors of other leading Urdu newspapers by reprinting columns from their publications, including several from large cities: *Hamdard, al-Hilāl*, and *Zamīndār*.[61] A 1917 article in *Zamīndār* invoked the name of *Madīnah* along with those of other like-minded papers in solidarity with a position on the fate of the Ottoman Empire.[62] *Madīnah* also linked itself to other *qasbah*-based newspapers by reprinting material as well as, as we have seen, regularly exchanging staff.[63]

There is additional evidence in the predecessors of newspapers to suggest that this network of twentieth-century Urdu journalists and publishers was also an extension of existing *zamīndār* or landowner networks. Many prominent Muslim *qasbatis* derived their influence from land ownership; their political activism owed much to their agricultural interests.[64] Chapter 2 mentions the newspaper *Zamīndār wa kāshtkār* (*The Landowner and Cultivator*), which initially targeted landed gentry with a basis in the region around Lahore and later changed its name and shifted focus to political issues.[65] There may have been other cases in which small newsletters circulated between landowners locally renamed themselves and marketed themselves as general interest papers, ultimately transforming into more explicitly political publications.[66] The self-consciously Muslim Urdu newspapers that cropped up in small towns or *qasbahs* across North India in the early part of the twentieth century existed as complements to networks of correspondence and existing news traditions rather than as straightforward replacements.

The network of individuals within each printing press also reproduced traditional social structures. While there were some books on printing sourced in Europe and available in libraries in urban centers, most journalists and printers learned their skills on the job through apprenticeships, which contributed to their social network. Majīd Ḥasan himself trained in two areas of the Punjab. Majīd Ḥasan's business was incorporated into a household characteristic of the South Asian *qasbah* context, with the staff in separate subhouseholds clustered around the central courtyard containing the printing shop and offices, on the same pattern as any traditional extended household in the region.

The period between 1900 and 1925 was a golden age for the expansion of local newspapers in South Asia. While letterpress was relatively quicker and easier than lithographic printing, it required access to a huge store of typeset letters unavailable outside of a few cities in North India. Some Urdu language papers used letterpress, such as Maulānā Azad's paper *al-Hilāl*, based in Calcutta, and the Mohammadan Social Reformer of *Tahẕīb ul-akẖlāq* that ran from 1871 to

1877, later renamed and published as the *Aligarh Institute Gazette*. Letterpress papers would have looked professional and expensive; this technology was more frequently available in large cities like Calcutta, Delhi, and Bombay. Aligarh College was a significant exception to this trend. Lithography, on the other hand, was the technology behind most other newspapers and periodicals published in Urdu.[67] As *Madīnah* established its reputation, its use of lithographic nastaʿlīq calligraphy created an immediate visual link that reinforced its association with the world of the *qasbah*.

Mobilizing the Newspaper Network: A 1938 Controversy in Maẕāhir ʿUlūm

A controversy regarding the head of Saharanpur's Maẕāhir ʿUlūm madrasah, Maulānā Zakarīyyā Kāndhlawī, who had connections to Deoband and Maulānā Madanī, provides an excellent illustration of how newspapers interlaced and competed with correspondence networks. It is also a good case study of how the correspondence that appeared in newspapers like *Madīnah* was selectively edited. In 1938 Maulāna Jāib al-Raḥmān Ṣāḥab Ra'īs al-Aḥrār, while in Lahore, read a story in *Madīnah* criticizing the leadership of Maulānā Zakarīyyā Kandhlawi, who was then the head of a madrasah, Maẕāhir ʿUlūm.[68] The editor of *Madīnah* in that period, Abū Saʿīd Bazmī, had a young friend or relative who was a student at the madrasah, who had many complaints against Maulānā Zakarīyyā.[69] In 1938 this relative and his friends wrote multiple letters of complaint against Maulānā Zakarīyyā, which Bazmī printed in *Madīnah*. Maulānā Madanī wrote a letter in response to the complaints, addressed to Bazmī, stating that he had known Maulānā Zakarīyyā since he was a child of twelve years old, when he had lived with Zakarīyyā's family, and insisting that the charges of mismanagement were certainly baseless. Several other individuals joined the defense with their own letters mailed to the newspaper: the president of Jamʿīat ʿulamā Hind, Maulānā al-Ḥāj Muftī Kafāyat Allah; and two scholars, Shaikh al-Ḥadīth and Maulāna Jā'ib al-Raḥmān Ṣāḥab Ra'īs al-Aḥrār.

Bazmī refused to publish any of these letters of response. He did write back to Maulānā Madanī, no doubt unable to ignore him because of his spiritual prestige, to say that he had received many letters of complaint against Maulānā Zakarīyyā, more than he was able to print. In response, Madanī wrote to command the presence of editor Bazmī and Majīd Ḥasan in Saharanpur on a day he had appointed to discuss the charges against Maulānā Zakarīyyā. Maulānā Zakarīyyā, as well as the students who had brought the complaint against him, were also brought to the meeting.

What ensued in Saharanpur appears to have been a *munāẕara*, or debate, in which Maulānā Madanī presided. He asked the students about their complaints, which boiled down to the charge that Maulānā Zakarīyyā had paralyzed the administration of the madrasah. Madanī asked the students for examples or proof of the complaint, which they did not provide. Someone at the meeting mentioned that the students were "overawed" by the presence of Madanī ("*Ḥaẕrat se mar'ūb hai*"). Madanī acknowledged that his presence may have had an extreme effect on the young students, but he ultimately reaffirmed his intention to explore the charges in person, asking "Well, how else are we supposed to look into the matter?"

Madanī asked the secretary or head administrator of the madrasah, Maẕāhir 'Ulūm, whether he felt that his work was paralyzed by Maulānā Zakarīyyā. The administrator passionately negated the allegations. At the behest of Madanī, the group then collaborated on a joint statement, penned by Bazmī, saying that the complaints made against Maulānā Zakarīyyā were baseless and untrue. The statement was signed by: Abū Sa'īd Bazmī, editor of Madīnah; Nang Islāf Ḥussain Aḥmed Ghafalah (his identity is unclear); Muḥammad Majīd Ḥasan, the owner of *Madīnah* newspaper; Jā'ib al-Raḥmān Ludhiānvī Ṣadr-i Aṣrār (president of the Ahrar); and Rashīd Aḥmed 'Afi 'Ana (the administrator of Maẕāhir 'Ulūm Madrasah). The recorded statement that emerged from the inquiry was published in the June 1938 issue of *Madīnah*. The immediate and pointed response of a leading Deobandi scholar, Maulānā Madanī, to a story printed in *Madīnah* confirms that it was a newspaper of substance, whose account was taken seriously by leading scholars of the day. Zakarīyyā, whose reputation had been threatened by *Madīnah*, was not dissuaded regarding the cultural importance of newspapers. In fact, he would record later in life his despair about his students' unwillingness to read newspapers.[70]

The Lithographic Print Process

The nineteenth century had seen the proliferation of print, and the runaway success of lithography. Metal type arrived in India by the 1550s, and a more substantial wave of moveable type technology arrived in North India in the late 1700s and early 1800s.[71] Lithography was invented in the late eighteenth century in Europe and arrived in India in the 1820s.[72] As Francesca Orsini has written, in South Asia moveable type was not commercially viable because it required a large capital outlay. Instead, the success of print as a commercial endeavor came about with the spread of lithography.[73] It became attractive to publishers of Urdu because of its unique ability to preserve the characteristic beauty of *nasta'līq*. The popularity of egg-white emulsion transfer methods and evidence from an Urdu lithographic manual suggest that local printers quickly began experimenting in ways that suited the local environment. While it was well established that the albumen found in egg-whites could bind photographic chemicals to paper, in Europe this technique was rarely applied in the service of printing written script.

The art of printing using European lithographic techniques and practices was thus adapted to the South Asian context. By extension, we see how this process of adaptation complicates the link between print capitalism and the public sphere in the subcontinent. Lithographic printing required significant technical training. A matter worthy of "*afsos*" or "regret," according to the first known lithographic manual published in Urdu in South Asia, was the delay in putting to press the technical knowledge required for the art, or *fann*, of lithographic printing. According to the author of the manual, Muḥammad Aḥīuddīn, who was also the proprietor of Nizāmī Press in Budayun *qasbah*, the delay in putting lithographic knowledge in print had led to a stagnation of the development of the print industry in South Asia.[74] Dependence on oral or "*sīnah-ba sīnah*" methods of transmission meant that individual printing presses gathered knowledge of printing technology through the migration of individuals proficient in the technology. In this sense, the art and science of printing clearly depended on a connection between teacher and student.[75] This "*sīnah-ba sīnah*" method of knowledge transmission dominated lithographic printing presses. On the other hand, industry experts sought to universalize lithographic technologies in order to make them competitive in the early twentieth century. Significantly, Aḥīuddīn makes no mention of calligraphy, instead focusing on the technologies of transmitting the written word from a piece of paper to the lithographic stone, and from the stone to a piece of paper.[76] He sought to separate the work of calligraphy from the work of printing. We know from work done by Ulrike Stark and Barbara Metcalf, as well as Muḥammad Qāsim Nānautvī's Urdu history of Deoband titled *Sawāniḥ Qāsmī*, that training and employing calligraphers and printers for work with lithographic printing presses was important to the mission of Nawal Kishore Press in Lucknow, and to that of the madrasah in Deoband.[77] Gianni Seviers's work demonstrates the link between Aḥīuddīn and Aligarh's contribution to the marrying of lithographic print and Muslim interests. In the *sīnah-ba sīnah* method of calligraphy instruction, there was far less of a boundary between the art of calligraphy and the art of print. It seems that this boundary firmed up over time, if we are to judge from the appearance of handbooks like that of Aḥīuddīn in the early twentieth century. Calligraphy was an important aspect of *Madīnah*'s reputation, and the editor's proficiency in calligraphy a feather in its cap. Additional examples make clear that *Madīnah* was not alone in seeing the connection between lithography, calligraphy, and the fate of the Muslim *qaum*.

A great deal of technical knowledge was required to oversee a lithographic newspaper, despite its relative cheapness and ease of access relative to letterpress technology. Knowledge of chemistry and calligraphy were paramount. A lithographic press required, in addition to the skilled writing and editing required by all papers, access to plentiful labor both manual and skilled in the printing process, as well as skilled calligraphers. The importance of newspaper production in Bijnor is attested by the fact that Bijnor district alone boasted at least five lithographic presses in the first decade of the twentieth century, a disproportionate concentration considering Lucknow had twenty-five presses in the same period.[78]

In lithography designs were first drawn with crayon or a grease-based ink—either by calligraphers directly onto a piece of paper that was then placed onto the stone by egg-white emulsion transfer, or through direct writing by a specialized calligrapher who was capable of mirror-writing, an art form perfected in Lucknow. Ink was developed locally in South Asia, rather than imported. Aḥīuddīn describes the popularity of a Kanpuri touche, referred to as *kāpī kī roshnā'ī*, or "printing ink," created according to a recipe of ingredients readily available in South Asia.[79] *Madīnah* primarily used the egg-white emulsion transfer method, in which heat was applied from above the paper and also from below by heating the stone, facilitating the transfer of the ink from the treated paper to the stone itself. From that point on, any errors were corrected by acid treatment and painting directly on the stone using mirror-writing.[80] This approach allowed the publisher to circumvent the need for the skill-intensive task of mirror-writing until the last stage of the process. Majīd Ḥasan was himself skilled enough in mirror-writing to personally execute corrections, according to his grandson Muneer Akhtar, who trained in publishing and personally observed the workings of the newspaper in his early life.[81] For the addition of color, Aḥīuddīn's lithographic manual indicates that even though the names used were often English ("Vermillion" or its lightened version "Red Lake"), the pigments themselves were initially taken from local soil.[82] By 1924, the limitations in color had disappeared:

> Earth red vermillion "Vermilion" (*sic*) and a few other expensive lightened red pigments such as "Red Lake" were gathered from the earth but after twenty years of chemical experiments and striving in pigment crushing and readying we have prepared a sum of [chemical] red colors, which aside from being strong are also excellent [in appearance].

At least at Nizami Press, the pigments for printing were never imported; instead, print technicians learned how make their own pigments and then passed that knowledge on to their students (Figure 3.2). These indigenous, chemically

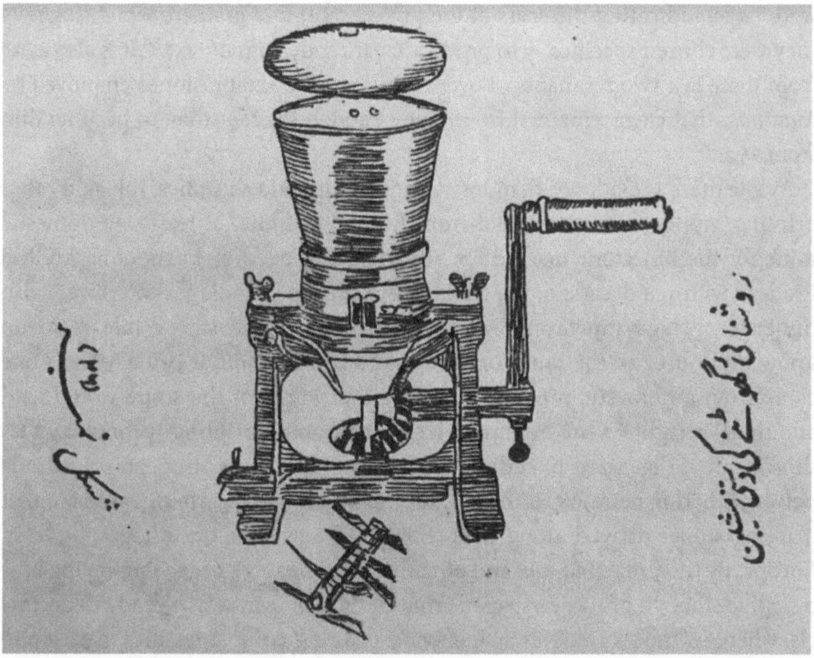

Figure 3.2 An image of a hand-press for the creation of inks. From: Muḥammad Aḥīuddīn, *Lithogrāfī: Fann t̤abāʿat par Urdū mein̲ kār-āmad aur pahalī kitāb* (Budaun: Mat̤buʿa Niẓāmī Press, 1926), 181.

derived inks were also given English names: "Indian Varmillion Red" or "*Inḍiyan varmiḷiyan reiḍ*" and "*Reiḍ orak*" or "Red Ochre."[83] While Aḥīuddīn had solicited help in developing an Urdu lexicon for lithography at the translation department of Osmania University in Hyderabad, he was unsuccessful.[84] Nevertheless, we see through this handbook a demonstration that the tools of lithographic printing were adapted to the South Asian landscape, literally and figuratively.

According to Muneer Akhtar, two types of printing press were used by Madīnah Press: a Ratcliffe and an unknown brand, both shipped from England.[85] Stones were used, rather than offset lithography. Most of the lithographic stones in circulation in the late nineteenth and early twentieth century were mined out of southern Germany, and much of the lithography ink or touche was sourced from France—since France had the monopoly on the production of gum arabic, a key component of lithographic ink, due to its colony in Senegal. While it is not possible to tell from a lithographic image itself whether it was created using limestone, marble, or onyx, judging from the two stones left in storage at the Madīnah Press headquarters, now the family home of Muneer Akhtar in Bijnor, it is clear that stones used for the printing of *Madīnah* were limestone. These blocks were large, indicating the scale of the project, and fine grained, which suggests they were chosen specifically to produce clear renderings of text.[86] It is also clear from these last two remnants of over two dozen lithograph stones employed by *Madīnah*, that each remained in use long enough for the stone to become thin from wear.[87]

While there is evidence demonstrating that lithograph stones, ink, and other printing supplies were imported from Europe to India, at least one domestic mine for the limestone needed for lithography opened in Kurnool in Andhra Pradesh within a decade of the technology's arrival in India.[88] Stones were also mined from Jaggayyapeta and Dachepalle in Andhra Pradesh.[89] While we do not know the source of the limestone employed by *Madīnah*, it is likely the stone came from a domestic mine. Confirming the source of the stone would lend additional weight to the argument that lithographic printing technology was thoroughly indigenized in India. Another option is that European print trade networks had penetrated to the level of the *qasbah*; it is certainly possible that printing stones arrived along with technical knowledge on lithography from Europe. By the time *Madīnah* and other local newspapers began employing lithographic stone to print newspapers, this method of print was already in decline elsewhere in the world. Newspapers and printing companies in America and Europe were jettisoning their stones just as Madīnah Press was amassing its impressive collection.[90]

By the 1920s, several presses also began looking for replacements to the stone processes, looking to employ offset lithography using aluminum sheets rather than stones. Aluminum sheets could be bent around rollers, eliminating the complex mirror-image process. Instead, writing could be done directly onto a chemically prepared sheet and the reverse offset process would turn the image into a mirror image by placing that image onto another roller before it placed the final impression onto the printed page. It seems that *Madīnah* never employed offset lithography, based on existing evidence: the Ratcliffe produced an electric version of a single-press lithography machine, and oral histories and material evidence point to a sole dependence on stone lithography even as late as the 1960s. Like many publishers working with Urdu, this old-fashioned form of printing outlasted the utility it offered in North America and Europe because of the distinctive requirements of Urdu calligraphy.

The process of graining a stone, smoothing the surface to prepare it for printing, was long and laborious. Two lithographic stones could be placed on top of one another, with the bottom remaining stationary and the top spun to speed up the grinding process; this work would have been performed by manual laborers. Stones could weigh anywhere from several dozen pounds up one hundred pounds.[91] At Madīnah Press, the process was probably made extremely efficient by the plentiful availability of skilled and unskilled laborers in the *qasbah*.

Newspapers and printing presses could become a cottage industry for small towns and neighborhoods, employing dozens of people. Eyewitness accounts confirm that *Madīnah* at one point printed using a collection of over two dozen large stones, the majority of which might be in use at any given time for newspaper and book projects.[92]

Before the etching process, a light coat of two fine powders—rosin and talcum—are used to prepare the image on the stone for the application of gum arabic. In order to fix or "etch" the image that has been painted or written onto the stone, the artisan would paint a combination of gum arabic and acid over the image. A combination of nitric and acetic acid was used, in order to capture the characteristic nuances in lithographic art prints. A strong acid was not desirable in the etching process for newspapers, since the acid would cause the transmission of minute irregularities in the ink distribution in calligraphy to the paper. While in Europe acetic acid was derived from the active ingredient in vinegar, in South Asia we see from Aḥīuddīn's manual that local alternatives were employed instead, specifically the "dried extract of sour mangoes or lemons."[93]

As soon as the gum arabic/acid combination was painted onto the areas treated with grease (touche, crayon, or ink), the acid in the solution began a chain reaction that acted on the grease. This chemical reaction drove the grease from the touche into the stone and created grease reservoirs a few millimeters deep in the stone, changing the chemical composition of the limestone further. On the positive areas of the matrix—meaning where there was text or image—the gum arabic created grease reservoirs in the stone that were ready to repel water and soak in ink. On the other hand the change in the chemical composition of the negative or untreated areas of the stone made those negative areas soak in water and repel ink. This process, called etching, could be time-intensive. Once it was complete, the stone and image were buffed with a soft cloth and prepared for printing. A petroleum-based substance was then used to strip the stone of the ink while preserving the greasy reservoirs created by the etching process. While we know from Aḥīuddīn's manual that paraffin oil was usually employed for this purpose, even petrol or kerosene could be used.[94] At that point the image was ready for inking and printing. First, a bead of ink was spread onto a palette, often an old, decommissioned stone, and "rolled up" onto an ink roller, or *sīyā kā belan*—today the roller is usually wrapped in suede, which picks up the ink nicely. Aḥīuddīn also makes reference to a wooden or stone pin covered in skin, since his directions for preparation of the ink roller for use involves treating it with ink and repeatedly rolling the stone to soften its *masāmmāt*, or pores.

Once the roller was evenly covered with ink, the process of inking the stone began. This involved either one or two people carrying out two tasks. First a thin layer of water was wiped onto the stone so that the negative areas of the stone would soak in the water while the greasy areas of the stone would repel the water.

The second step was rolling on the ink, which the negative areas, saturated with water already, would repel. The positive, greasy areas would soak up the ink, creating a dark image eventually dark enough for printing multiple copies. Multiple applications of water and ink were required before the greasy reservoirs had soaked up enough ink to allow for the printing of a copy of the text onto paper. Different strategies were employed depending on whether the job called for inking in black only or inking in multiple colors. *Madīnah* was typical in employing at least red and green on a regular basis by the 1930s. Printing in multiple colors required the same sheet of paper to be run through the hand-press or the electric press multiple times. For this purpose, reconciliation lines or *milān ke nishān* were written on the printed image to help the printers keep track of the correct placement of the paper on the press (Figure 3.3). Multiple people with specialized knowledge of printing were required to oversee the production of multiple newspaper and book runs. As the late arrival of manuals indicates, the mode of transmission was dependent on the migration of individual printers and personal instruction.

Only after all of these steps did the stone enter the printing press, with a blank sheet of paper placed onto the stone. The paper might be prepared with special marks used to keep positioning consistent if there were to be multiple runs to create a multicolored image. The paper was always smaller than the stone, since a larger piece might be easily marred by the stone's edges during printing. Another piece of paper or a piece of cardboard would be placed on top of the paper to protect it from tearing during the printing process, and the printer would pull the lever of the printing press, causing a rectangular bar at least the width of the piece of paper but less than the width of the stone to lower onto one end of the stone. Then with the turning of a crank (turned initially by hand and later by steam or electricity), the printer would roll the bed of the printing press, on which the

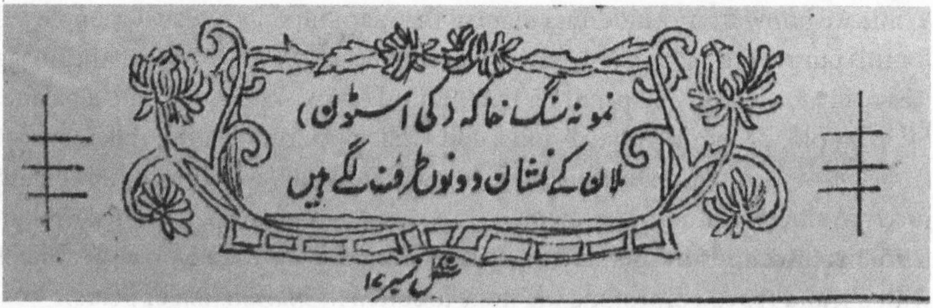

Figure 3.3 A sample image showing the use of *nishān*, or lines to assist in tracking the place of the paper when multiple runs of a single piece of paper were required. From: Muḥammad Aḥīuddīn, *Lithogrāfī, Fann ṯabāʿat par Urdū mein̠ kār-āmad aur pahalī kitāb* (Budaun: Maṯbuʿa Nizāmī Press, 1926), 81.

stone lay, underneath the rectangular bar to apply pressure evenly over the entire page of the newspaper. Once the bar had applied pressure to the whole page of text, then the bar would be released and the printing bed rolled back to allow the printer to peel back a corner of the newspaper page to examine the quality of the ink.[95] If satisfactory, the piece of paper would be lifted off the stone and placed separately to dry. Hints at the rhythms of the production process survive in the physical remains of the newspapers: there are countless examples of Urdu newspapers that show a ghost of an image of the same page of newspaper, suggesting that copies of the same page had been stacked on top of each other before they were fully dry.

In lithographic printing, the process for printing thousands of copies of one page could take several hours of labor or several laborers. The work force for the production of a weekly newspaper, and in the case of *Madīnah* even briefly a daily newspaper (in 1933), was formidable in size. Two men simultaneously worked at grinding each stone, speeding up the process. A team of workers folded, addressed, and prepared the newspapers for printing and mailing.[96] Perhaps as soon as the fresh copies of the newspaper were packed for transport, the long process of grinding away the surface of the stone began to make room for the next edition of the paper. Following the printing, drying, and stacking, the sheets of paper were taken into separate rooms of the press to be collated, stapled, and folded and sealed into packages for shipping. When *Madīnah* was ready for distribution, a piece of paper was printed via lithographic press with a gridded list of names of subscribers and their addresses (Figure 3.4); each subscription sheet would be placed manually into a corrugation machine so that the separate boxes in the subscription list grid were easy to tear off. Then each copy of *Madīnah* was folded in half, and the rectangle with the subscriber's information was pasted in a way that held the newspaper closed (see Figure 3.5 for an example of residue of a subscriber patch on an archived newspaper). Sample newspapers from Raza Library show that the stamps for shipping were placed directly onto the back sheet of newspapers for mailing.[97] The subscriber patch functioned simultaneously as an address and a method of protecting the cover page until it arrived in the hands of the reader. When the newspaper arrived at the home or office of the reader, the subscriber would break the seal by ripping in half the piece of pasted paper printed with his own name. This means the name of a subscriber is often left as residue on archived issues of particular newspapers. A surviving list of subscribers for another popular publication of Madīnah Press, *Ghunchah*, shows the format of these subscriber patches prior to cutting and shows that subscribers of an Urdu magazine communicated in English, Urdu, and Hindi.

No long-term records have been retained of subscribers in Madīnah Press; the names of the readers traveled with the paper itself, and we must uncover them one by one if we hope to recover them at all. Nevertheless, the hints that

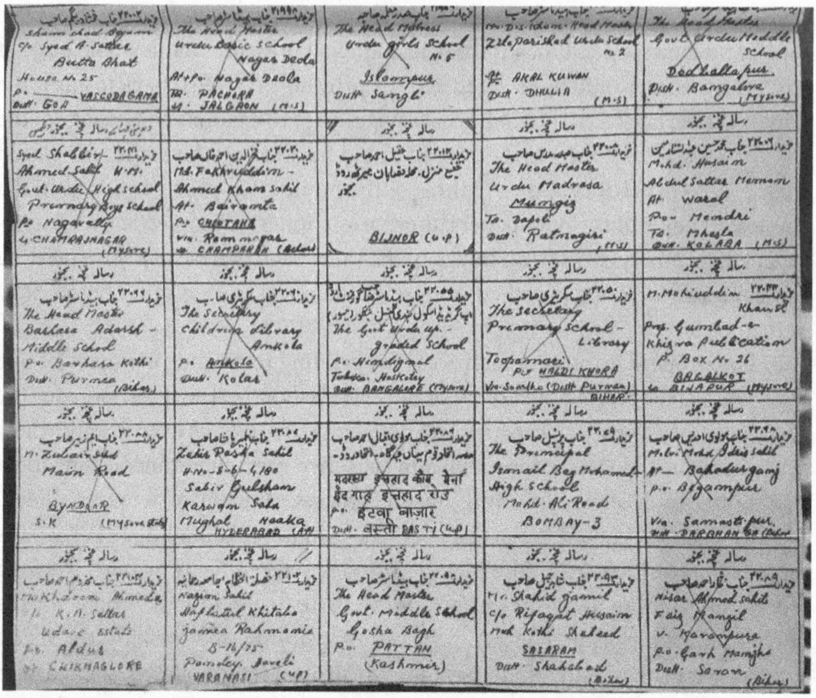

Figure 3.4 A surviving list of subscribers to Ghunchah, a children's magazine printed by Madīnah Press. Personal archive, Naginah, Bijnor district.

remain indicate a remarkable breadth of readership, spanning not only districts but also continents. The surviving grid of subscribers from *Ghunchah* (Figure 3.4) is significant in showing a wide geographic and linguistic spread in its subscriber base—on a single page, addresses appear from Kashmir to Varanasi, from Bombay to Purnea in Bihar.

The diaries of many prominent mid-twentieth-century figures include accounts of newspaper reading and meeting with newspaper owners. The physical papers themselves were often carefully preserved, indicating their significance. Ḥasrat Mohānī's diary described flurries of meetings with newspaper *wālās*, common parlance for journalists and editors. In early 1947 he worked on behalf of representatives of the Urdu newspaper *Hamdam* to negotiate a curfew pass.[98] It is clear from his diary that Ḥasrat Mohānī was dependent on newspapers to receive information about the movement of major political activists such as Jinnah in the days leading to independence and Partition. Ḥusain Aḥmad Madanī also kept a close eye on newspaper conversations, keeping careful records of each newspaper he read every day and packing them up carefully.[99] While most individual newspapers were passed around and read to tatters, reprinted anthologies

ڈاکٹر عبدالحکیم خانصاحب

ایم.بی. کے مذہبی و طبی جواہرا

تفسیر القرآن بالقرآن

دوم تجربات

تجربات خاصہ

مبارک برادرس پٹیالہ

یا

منیجر مطبع عزیزی تراوڑی

Figure 3.5 A back page of a 1921 copy of *Ahl-i Ḥadīth* showing a subscriber patch, printed in the same grid format as shown earlier, a postage stamp, and a postmark. Raza Rampur Library.

of Urdu newspapers are preserved in private family libraries in *qasbahs* scattered across North India. By the mid-twentieth century prominent public figures such as Ḥasrat Mohānī, the romantic poet and politician of the independence movement, kept records of his daily newspaper readings, keeping a copy of every paper he bought bound in steel cabinets labeled by year, to protect them from the ravages of time.[100]

The publications of Madīnah Press traveled the globe, and records of those subscriptions could be used to map an Urdu-speaking network. The nucleus of that network remained a small *qasbah* in the middle of nowhere, gesturing in its images of a holy city toward a space apart that the newspaper offered its readers far and wide.

Lithographic *Nastaʿlīq* as Visual Culture

Majīd Ḥasan saw Muslim values not only as a subject of his publication, but also as an integral component of the business. The virtues of a good Muslim, particularly calligraphy and a commitment to timeliness, were also the virtues that characterized his newspaper. *Madīnah* also saw itself, and the newspapers it was in conversation with, as a voice for Muslims and a guide for their faith. Defending the correct method of writing Persianized Urdu and Arabic was part of its responsibility to guide fellow Muslims in its subject matter. Calligraphers were well respected; their names were published next to the names of the editors and owners of the press, emphasizing their importance. The poet Zammarud-raqam—a pen-name, or *ta<u>kh</u>allus,* meaning "emerald pen"—was one such calligrapher (see Figure 3.6).[101]

Madīnah exhorted Muslims to bolster their faith by protecting writing in the Persian script—one issue included a diatribe against a press in Amritsar that published sections of the Qur'an written poorly or with errors included "from selfish concern with their own personal profit."[102] In the same article *Madīnah* recommended Muslims avoid publishing houses that employed sloppy publishing practices so that "there might not be weakness of faith from the publication." It further threatened to send a request to the government to protect the proper publishing of Islamic texts.[103] While it is unclear whether the paper followed up on this declaration, the threat demonstrates that the protection of correctly reproduced calligraphy (in this example, *nas<u>kh</u>* calligraphy) was one significant aspect of *Madīnah*'s commitment to fellow Muslims; the form of the written words was important along with their meaning.

Madīnah provides evidence that methods of safeguarding written transmission of knowledge—calligraphy, consistency in transcription—that previously had been secondary in importance compared to the oral tradition in Islam with the shift to the printed word became elevated as important to religious experience. This manifested itself in a reverence for the elegantly written and printed word. Newspapers appear to be disposable objects, often crumpled before the

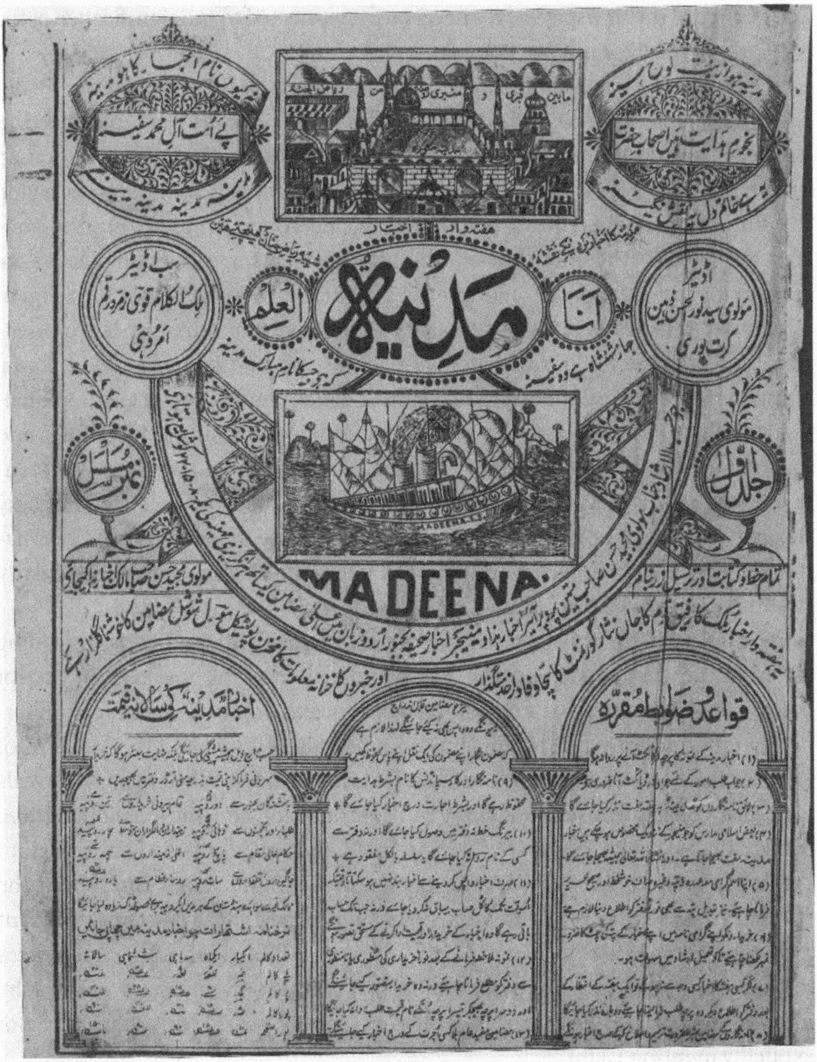

Figure 3.6 The first cover page of *Madīnah*. *Madīnah*, May 1, 1912. Library of Congress Microfilm Collections, Washington, DC.

ink is dry. Perhaps for this reason newspapers are used by historians only as records of fact or impression. But newspapers were also material extensions of the social networks that they sought to serve; they blurred content and form and shaped the "imaginary collectivity" in which they were immersed.[104] The physical appearance of the newspaper was necessarily connected to the significance of the networks of correspondence linked to it.

Where few were literate in Arabic, and where Persian literacy was on the decline, handwritten Urdu and the methods by which it was mass produced in newsprint became linked to piety. Scholarship on Islam in public life has focused on the political process through which this transformation occurred—decrying the shift from syncretism to communal alliances, and emphasizing the constructed nature of the shift.[105] While these approaches correctly acknowledge the constructivist nature of the language debate, there is the risk of positing religion as an essentialist category that functions separately from other aspects of identity. It is important not to restrict religion to the category defined by the colonial legislation dividing personal and secular law, which would obstruct serious analysis of religion in conversations about print publics in South Asia. Politics and material interests were coherent with religious sensibility. Islam was "polycentric," in the words of Margrit Pernau—constantly created and recreated not only through expressions of alterity but also through those of belonging.[106] The material Urdu newspaper was an important medium for Islam's recreation in early twentieth-century South Asia.

By considering ways of writing as somatic engagement, and ways of reading as visual culture, we move closer to an understanding of how *nasta'līq* script could become a symbol of a *certain* type of civic religion in British India, inherited in different ways by the Muslims of independent India and the Muslims of Pakistan. The visual culture of Urdu as expressed through the newspaper reveals a popular culture whose production and consumption constituted pious action. Subscribing to a newspaper, receiving it, reading it regularly, and entering into the newspaper conversation formed part of the cultural capital and indeed the "system of dispositions" of the *ashrāf*; through particular applications of print technology, Islam could become a part of that.[107] Along with explicit references to time and place, the visual aesthetic of a publication and use of calligraphy infused *Madīnah* with a Muslim flavor, even in sections where the paper did not explicitly mention Islam.

Attention to the materiality of Urdu newspaper production using lithography shows that the form of reproduction can be read alongside—sometimes tangential to and sometimes adjacent to—its discursive content. In chapters 4 and 5 I build on this methodology to consider visual and material evidence alongside the newspaper's discursive content. Through analysis of coverage of several historical flashpoints from the 1910s until the 1930s, I demonstrate how *Madīnah* newspaper invoked particular attitudes to time and space to establish narratives of belonging and difference. We begin this process by turning back to the newspaper's founding decade and the irruptive influence of World War I.

Notes

1. Ulrike Stark, *An Empire of Books: The Naval Kishore Press and the Diffusion of the Printed Word in Colonial India* (New Delhi: Permanent Black, 2008); Francis Robinson, "Technology and Religious Change: Islam and the Impact of Print," *Modern Asian Studies* 27, no. 1 (February 1993): 229–51; Francesca Orsini, "Introduction," in *Print and Pleasure: Popular Literature and Entertaining Fictions in Colonial North India* (Ranikhet: Permanent Black, 2009), 1–33; Graham Shaw, "Calcutta: Birthplace of the Indian Lithographed Book," *Journal of the Printing Historical Society* 27 (1998): 89–111.
2. Francesca Orsini, "Introduction" in *Print and Pleasure: Popular Literature and Entertaining Fictions in Colonial North India* (Ranikhet: Permanent Black, 2009), 1–33.
3. "We are grateful to exalted God that he has allowed us to live in a remote township to perform the duty (farẓ) of journalism," *Madīnah*, February 13, 1933. Translation published in Shabana Mahmud, "*Angāre* and the Founding of the Progressive Writers' Association," *Modern Asian Studies* 30, no. 2 (May 1996): 447–48.
4. Jamal Elias, *Aisha's Cushion: Religious Art, Perception, and Practice in Islam* (Cambridge, MA: Harvard University Press, 2012), 245.
5. Jamal Elias, *Aisha's Cushion: Religious Art, Perception, and Practice in Islam* (Cambridge, MA: Harvard University Press, 2012), 245.
6. David Morgan, "Notes on Meaning and Medium in the Aesthetics of Visual Piety," unpublished paper, 1998, cited in Peter Horsfield, "Media," in *Key Words in Religion, Media, and Culture*, ed. David Morgan (New York: Routledge, 2008), 121.
7. J. Baudrillard, *The System of Objects*, trans. James Benedict (London: Verso, 1996), 198, cited in Jamal Elias, *Aisha's Cushion: Religious Art, Perception, and Practice in Islam* (Cambridge, MA: Harvard University Press, 2012), 218.
8. Peter Burke, *Eyewitnessing: The Use of Images as Historical Evidence* (Ithaca: Cornell University Press, 2001); Ivan Gaskell, "Visual History," in *New Perspectives on Historical Writing*, ed. Peter Burke (Cambridge: Cambridge University Press, 2000), 187–217; David Morgan, *Sacred Gaze: Religious Visual Culture in Theory and Practice* (Berkeley: University of California Press, 2005).
9. David Morgan, *Visual Piety: A History and Theory of Popular Religious Images* (Berkeley: University of California Press, 1999).
10. Francis Robinson, "Technology and Religious Change: Islam and the Impact of Print," *Modern Asian Studies* 27, no. 1 (1993): 229–51.
11. While Muhammad Qasim Zaman does not contest the assertion that print challenged the authority of the *'ulamā*, he argues that a more critical area of investigation is the diverse ways that the *'ulamā* were defending and contested authority. Muhammad Qasim Zaman, *The Ulama in Contemporary Islam: Custodians of Change* (Princeton: Princeton University Press, 2002), 55.
12. "That different texts performed distinct functions in, say, the medieval Hanafi school, as noted at the outset of this chapter, is an important reminder that simultaneity of discourses, or their articulation at different levels, is, in itself, no novelty for the

ulama." Muhammad Qasim Zaman, *The Ulama in Contemporary Islam: Custodians of Change* (Princeton: Princeton University Press, 2002), 58–59.

13. Zaman's approach is distinct from linear approaches that recount how *'ulamā* accommodated print technologies or used them to great effect. Mamoun Fandy, *Saudi Arabia and the Politics of Dissent* (New York: St. Martin's Press, 1999); Mamoun Fandy, "CyberResistance: Saudi Opposition between Globalization and Localization," *Comparative Studies in Society and History* 41 (1999): 124–46, cited in Muhammad Qasim Zaman, *The Ulama in Contemporary Islam: Custodians of Change* (Princeton: Princeton University Press, 2002), 8, also see 40, 42, 49.
14. For more on newspaper content, see Asghar Abbas, *Print Culture: Sir Syed's Aligarh Institute Gazette, 1866–1897*, translated from Urdu by Syed Asim Ali (New Delhi: Primus Books, 2015); Aḥmed Sayed, "Tartīb o tadvīn," in *Roznamah Zamīndār: Moqālah hāe iftitāhiyah aur shazarāt* (Lahore: Maulana Zafar 'Ali Khan Trust, 2013). For work looking at print in general, see Ulrike Stark, *Empire of Books: Naval Kishore Press and the Diffusion of the Printed Word in Colonial India* (New Delhi: Permanent Black, 2008); Brannon Ingram, "Portable Madrasa: Print, Publics, and the Authority of Deobandi *Ulama*," *Modern Asian Studies* 48, no. 4 (2013): 845–71.
15. Laura Bear, "Doubt, Conflict, Mediation: The Anthropology of Modern Time," *Journal of the Royal Anthropological Institute* 20, no. S1 (2014): 3–30.
16. Peter Horsfield, "Media," in *Key Words in Religion, Media, and Culture*, ed. David Morgan (New York: Routledge, 2008), 111–22.
17. Annemarie Schimmel, *Calligraphy and Islamic Culture* (London: Tauris, 1990).
18. Franz Rosenthal, "Abū Ḥaiyān al-Tawḥīdī on Penmanship," *Ars Islamica* 13–14 (1948): 8–9.
19. Quoted in Franz Rosenthal, "Abū Ḥaiyān al-Tawḥīdī on Penmanship," *Ars Islamica* 13–14 (1948): 8–9, 13.
20. Franz Rosenthal, "Abū Ḥaiyān al-Tawḥīdī on Penmanship," *Ars Islamica* 13–14 (1948): 9.
21. V. Minorsky, *Calligraphers and Painters: A Treatise by Qadi Ahmad, Son or Mir Munshi*, trans. from Russian by B. N. Zakhoder (Washington, DC : Freer Gallery of Art Occasional Papers, 1959), cited in Seher A. Shah, "A History of Traditional Calligraphy in Post-Partition Lahore," PhD diss., George Washington University, 2016.
22. Shaikh Syed Manaẓir Aḥsan Gilānī, *Sawāniḥ-i qāsmī*, vol. 1 (Deoband: Daftar Dār ul-'Ulūm, 1955–1956), 1–4, 32, cited in Barbara Metcalf, *Islamic Revival in British India: Deoband, 1860–1900* (Princeton: Princeton University Press, 1982), 103.
23. Seher A. Shah, "A History of Traditional Calligraphy in Post-Partition Lahore," PhD diss., George Washington University, 2016, 26.
24. While I have not been able to find Urdu calligraphic manuals from prior to 1950, presumably because at that time personal transmission of calligraphic knowledge was paramount, manuals from the 1970s onward make a case for the connection between Urdu and Islam. Muḥammad 'Abdullāh Caghtā'ī, *Sarguzasht-i khaṭ-i nasta'līq* (Lāhaur: Kitāb Khānah-yi Nauras, 1970); Ibn-i Kalīm, *Tarīkh-i fanni khattātī: Nādir va nāyāb-i shāhkār-i khushnivīsī* (Multān: Ibn-i Kalīm, 1977); Shīmā Majīd, *Urdū rasmulkhat: Intikhāb-i maqālāt, ṭaba'-i 1* (Islāmābād: Muqtadirah-yi Qaumī Zabān,

1989). Seher A. Shah, "A History of Traditional Calligraphy in Post-Partition Lahore," PhD diss., George Washington University, 2016.

25. J. R. Osborn, *Letters of Light: Arabic Script in Calligraphy, Print, and Digital Design* (Cambridge, MA: Harvard University Press, 2017).
26. V. Minorsky, *Calligraphers and Painters: A Treatise by Qadi Ahmad, Son or Mir Munshi,* trans. from Russian by B. N. Zakhoder (Washington, DC: Freer Gallery of Art Occasional Papers, 1959), 100.
27. Qādī Aḥmad also described Maulānā Sultān-'Alī as one "whose writing [was] among other writings as the sun among the other planets." V. Minorsky, *Calligraphers and Painters: A Treatise by Qadi Ahmad, Son or Mir Munshi,* trans. from Russian by B. N. Zakhoder (Washington, DC: Freer Gallery of Art Occasional Papers, 1959), 102.
28. V. Minorsky, *Calligraphers and Painters: A Treatise by Qadi Ahmad, Son or Mir Munshi,* trans. from Russian by B. N. Zakhoder (Washington, DC: Freer Gallery of Art Occasional Papers, 1959), 122.
29. Mohammad Hukk, Herman Ethe, and Edward Robertson, *A Descriptive Catalogue of the Arabic and Persian MSS* (Edinburgh: University of Edinburgh Press, 1925), cited in Pares Islam Syed Mustafizur Rahman, *Islamic Calligraphy in Medieval India* (Bangladesh: University Press Limited, 1979), 46.
30. A. J. Arberry, M. Minovi, and E. Blochet, *The Chester Beatty Library: A Catalogue of the Persian Manuscripts and Miniatures*, vol. 1, *MSS 101–150*, ed. J. V. S. Wilkinson (Dublin: Hodges Figgis, 1959), cited in Pares Islam Syed Mustafizur Rahman, *Islamic Calligraphy in Medieval India* (Bangladesh: University Press Limited, 1979), 45.
31. W. M. Thackston, *Baburname*, 3 vols. (Cambridge, MA: Harvard University Press, 1993); Stephen Dale, "The Poetry and Autobiography of the Babur-nama," *Journal of Asian Studies* 55, no. 3 (August 1996): 635–64.
32. Pares Islam Syed Mustafizur Rahman, *Islamic Calligraphy in Medieval India* (Dacca: University Press, 1979), 93.
33. For instance, Mohammad Hukk, Herman Ethe, and Edward Robertson, *A Descriptive Catalogue of the Arabic and Persian MSS* (Edinburgh: University of Edinburgh Press, 1925), cited in Pares Islam Syed Mustafizur Rahman, *Islamic Calligraphy in Medieval India* (Bangladesh: University Press Limited, 1979), 46. It is not clear from Rahman's book which copy of *Ain-i Akbarī* given with diacritics earlier was used, but I include the page numbers that Rahman has cited here.
34. Brinkley Messick, *The Calligraphic State: Textual Domination and History in a Muslim Society* (Berkeley: University of California Press, 1996).
35. Brinkley Messick, "Print," in *The Calligraphic State: Textual Domination and History in a Muslim Society* (Berkeley: University of California Press, 1996), 115–16.
36. Zoe Griffith, "Calligraphy and the Art of Statecraft in the Late Ottoman Empire and Modern Turkish Republic," *Comparative Studies of South Asia, Africa, and the Middle East* 31, no. 3 (2011): 601–14.
37. "In particular, digital scanning techniques readily allow the reproduction and transmission of the authority's signature, seal, and handwriting where print did not." Morgan Clarke, "Neo-Calligraphy: Religious Authority and Media Technology in

Contemporary Shiite Islam," *Comparative Studies in Society and History* 52, no. 2 (2010): 351–83.

38. Jamal J. Elias, "Truck Calligraphy in Pakistan," in *The Aura of Alif: The Art of Writing in Islam*, ed. Jürgen Wasim Frembgen (New York: Prestel, 2010), 211–24; Jürgen Wasim Frembgen, "Calligraphy in the World of Sufi Shrines in Pakistan," in *The Aura of Elif: The Art of Writing in Islam*, ed. Jürgen Wasim Frembgen (New York: Prestel, 2010), 225–36.
39. Francis Robinson, "Strategies of Authority in Muslim South Asia in the Nineteenth and Twentieth Centuries," *Modern Asian Studies* 47, no. 1 (2013): 1–21.
40. Unani Tibb is a system of medicine with roots in the teachings of Hippocrates (c. 460–370 BCE) and Galen (c. 130–c. 216 CE) and developed by Ibn Sina (or Avicenna) (c. 980–1037). Tibb means "medicine" in Arabic.
41. Seema Alavi, *Islam and Healing: Loss and Recovery of an Indo-Muslim Medical Tradition, 1600–1900* (Basingstoke: Palgrave Macmillan, 2008), 43–53.
42. Frances Pritchett, *Nets of Awareness: Urdu Poetry and Its Critics* (Berkeley: University of California Press, 1994), 141, cited in Francis Robinson, "Strategies of Authority in Muslim South Asia in the Nineteenth and Twentieth Centuries," *Modern Asian Studies* 47, no. 1 (2013): 16–17.
43. Moḥammad Ḥusain Āzād, *Nazm-i Āzād* (The Poetry of Āzād), ed. Tabassum Kashmīrī (Lahore: Maktabah 'āliyah, 1978 [1899]), 46, cited in Frances Pritchett, "Introduction," in *Nets of Awareness: Urdu Poetry and Its Critics* (Berkeley: University of California Press, 1994), fn. 15.
44. Khvājah Alṭāf Ḥusain Ḥālī, *Hali's Musaddas: The Flow and Ebb of Islam*, ed. Christopher Shackle and Javed Majeed (New Delhi: Oxford University Press, 1997), 88–97, cited in Francis Robinson, "Strategies of Authority in Muslim South Asia in the Nineteenth and Twentieth Centuries," *Modern Asian Studies* 47, no. 1 (2013): 17.
45. David Washbrook, "After the Mutiny: From Queen to Queen-Empress," *History Today* 47, no. 9 (September 1997): 10–15.
46. Seher A. Shah, "A History of Traditional Calligraphy in Post-Partition Lahore," PhD diss., George Washington University, 2016, 27.
47. Interview with Irfan Ahmed Qureshi, reporting speech from Javed Iqbal, son of Muḥammad Iqbāl; Seher A. Shah, "A History of Traditional Calligraphy in Post-Partition Lahore," PhD diss., George Washington University, 2016, 27.
48. Margrit Pernau, "The Delhi Urdu *Akhbar*: Between Persian Akhbārāt and English Newspapers," *Annual of Urdu Studies* 18, no. 1 (2003): 105–31.
49. Michael H. Fisher, "The Office of Akhbār Nawīs: The Transition from Mughal to British Forms," *Modern Asian Studies* 27, no. 1 (1993): 47–48.
50. For more on the fluid boundaries between the *ashrāf* elite and other groups, see Imtiaz Ahmad, "The Ashrāf-Ajlaf Dichotomy in Muslim Social Structure in India," *Indian Economic Social History Review* 3 (1966): 268–78.
51. Michael H. Fisher, "The Office of Akhbār Nawīs: The Transition from Mughal to British Forms," *Modern Asian Studies* 27, no. 1 (1993): 54.
52. Michael H. Fisher, "The Office of Akhbār Nawīs: The Transition from Mughal to British Forms," *Modern Asian Studies* 27, no. 1 (1993): 20.

53. Michael H. Fisher, "The Office of Akhbār Nawīs: The Transition from Mughal to British Forms," *Modern Asian Studies* 27, no. 1 (1993): 20.
54. "*ʿĀm akhbār aur ʿām tār*," *Madīnah*, May 22, 1912, 10. Most issues of *Madīnah* between 1912 and 1924 have an identically titled section in each issue of the newspaper.
55. For an example of Persian poetry published in *Madīnah*, see Hasan Zahīr Kirātpurī, "*Akhbār Madīnah Bijnor*," *Madīnah*, May 1, 1912, 2.
56. *Madīnah*, June 21, 1917.
57. Margrit Pernau, "The Delhi Urdu Akhbar: Between Persian Akhbarat and English Newspapers," *Annual of Urdu Studies/Sālnāmah-i dirāsāt-i Urdū* 18, no. 1 (2003): 108.
58. These papers often earned the moniker "bigoted" according to colonial censor typologies, a term meant to refer to a communalist approach that stirred up trouble between Hindus and Muslims or between Sunnis and Shias, but that seemed more aptly applied to newspapers that discussed political issues in explicitly religious terms. *Madīnah* was described in its early years as "a somewhat bigoted Muhammadan organ, inclined to make trouble between Hindus and Muhammadans." The general remarks relevant to *al-Qāsim* newspaper published in Deoband indicated this unfavorable assessment: "It deals with educational and religious topics, and though somewhat bigoted, its tone is not objectionable." The editor of *al-Nāẓir* (The Overseer), Maulvī Abū Raḥmat was described as "very bigoted, and writes and preaches against the Arya Samaj. He attends Arya Samaj meetings and holds discussions, and has written books criticizing the Arya Samaj. He is much respected by the Muhammadans." Department of Criminal Intelligence, *Statement of Newspapers and Periodicals Published in the United Provinces during the Year 1912 [with Index]* (Simla: Government Central Branch Press, 1913), Uttar Pradesh State Archives.
59. Department of Criminal Intelligence, *Statement of Newspapers and Periodicals Published in the United Provinces during the Year 1912 [With Index]* (Simla: Government Central Branch Press, 1913), Uttar Pradesh State Archives.
60. Anūr ʿAlī Dihlavī, *Urdu Sahāfat* (New Delhi: Urdu Academy, 1987), 177–78.
61. E.g., on July 15, 1913, an editorial in *Madīnah* commented on a column printed in *Hamdard* proposing an Indian mission to Arabia; on September 15/22, 1913, *Madīnah* reprinted a poem from *Hamdard* (Delhi), encouraging Muslims to protest against the destruction of the mosque at Kanpur, and a poem in *Zamīndār* (Lahore), attributing the spread of atheism to modern science; on October 8, 1913, *Madīnah* reprinted a poem by Maulānā Shibli titled "Equality in Islam" from *al-Hilāl* (Calcutta), advocating the principle of equality in Islam, and another poem published in *Hamdard* objecting to the Nawab of Rampur's October 1913 meeting attempting to represent the voice of Muslims; on January 1, 1917, *Madīnah* reproduced an article from *Sadāqat* (*Candour*, Calcutta) in order to refute its claim that a Turkish court-martial had pronounced a death sentence on the Egyptian sultan.
62. "*Maslah-i Jazīrah ul-ʿArab aur Tiḥirīk-i Mafāhmat* [The Problem of the Arab Peninsula and the Movement for Understanding]," *Zamīndār*, November 16, 1923, reprinted in *Roznāmah Zamīndār Lāhor: September to December 1923*, ed. Aḥmad Saʿīd (Lahore: Maulana Zafar Ali Khan Trust, 2013).

63. October 1917 *Madīnah* reproduced a poem contesting the government's refusal to release Muḥammad ʿAlī and Shaukat ʿAlī. *Madīnah,* October 17, 1917.

64. Francis Robinson, *Separatism among Indian Muslims: The Politics of the United Provinces' Muslims 1860–1923* (Cambridge: Cambridge University Press, 1974), 365–415.

65. Rauf Parekh, "Allama Iqbal, Zafar Ali Khan, and Zamindar," *Dawn,* https://www.dawn.com/news/671867.

66. A *tazkirah* of newspapers published in the latter half of the eighteenth century identifies at least one *akhbār,* or newspaper, as focusing on agricultural issues; see, e.g., entries for *zarāʾyat* and *zamīndār. Savānih ʿumrī akhbārāt, ḥiṣṣah aval,* by Secretary of the Anjuman-i ʿilmi and the proprietor of the newspaper *Akhtar-i Hind* and Akhtar Press (Lucknow: Akhtar Press, June 1888), Raza Rampur Library, Rampur India, 143. *Dehātī,* a Hindi newspaper published from Benares by Gulāb Chānd, was a paper "containing subjects on agriculture beneficial to landholders and agriculturalists." Department of Criminal Intelligence, *Statement of Newspapers and Periodicals Published in the United Provinces during the Year 1911 [with Index]* (Simla: Government Central Branch Press, 1912), Uttar Pradesh State Archives.

67. Raza Rampur Library has a large collection of these lithographed newspapers, e.g., *Rampur State Gazette, Dabdabai Sekundaree, Ahl-i Ḥadīth,* and *Hamdard.*

68. This account is found in the autobiography of Muḥammad Zakarīyā Kāndhlavī, *Āp Bītī* (Lahore: Darul Ishaʾat, 2003). I am very grateful to Professor Mohammad Talib of the Oxford Centre for Islamic Studies for pointing me in the direction of this book.

69. Ḥāmidul Anṣārī Ghazī was another editor at the time. Parvez ʿĀdil, *Tārīkh-i Madīnah Bijnor* (Rampur: Applied Books, 2018), 339.

70. Muḥammad Zakarīyya Kāndhlavī, *Āp Bītī* (Lahore: Darul Ishaʾat, 2003).

71. Graham Shaw, "Calcutta: Birthplace of the Indian Lithographed Book," *Journal of the Printing Historical Society* 27 (1998): 89–111.

72. Lithography was invented in 1798 by German author and printer Alois Senefelder. The first lithographed books in Benares date from 1824 and in Agra and Calcutta from 1826. Olimpiada P. Shcheglova, "Lithography ii. in India," *Encyclopædia Iranica,* online edition, 2012, available at http://www.iranicaonline.org/articles/lithography-ii-in-india.

73. Francesca Orsini, "Introduction," in *Print and Pleasure: Popular Literature and Entertaining Fictions in Colonial North India* (Ranikhet: Permanent Black, 2009), fn. 18.

74. Gianni Seviers, "Learning How to Print: The Nizami Press in Badayun and the First Urdu Manual on the Art of Lithography," presentation at the British Library in July 2018. Script of draft article based on presentation shared with author January 2019.

75. "*Afsos ki hindūstān meiṉ yih fann usī purānī ṣūrat meiṉ jaisā ki sāṭh-satar sāl qabl thā ab bhī maujūd hai, tarqī kā to zikr hī kyā jo tarkībeiṉ sīnah-ba sīnah chalī ātī haiṉ* "(I regret that in India, this art even now exists in the old form that it took sixty or seventy years ago, and how can I even talk of progress when the training is conducted person to person)." Muḥammad Aḥiuddīn, *Līthogrāfī: Fann ṭabāʾat par Urdū meiṉ kār-āmad aur pahalī kitāb* (Budaun: Maṭbuʿa Nizāmī Press, 1926), alef.

76. Muḥammad Aḥīuddīn, *Līthogrāfī: Fann ṯabā'at par Urdū mein̲ kār-āmad aur pahalī kitāb* (Budaun: Maṯbu'a Nizāmī Press, 1926). Thanks to Gianni Sievers for sharing photographs of this book with me, obtained at the University of Lucknow.
77. Ulrike Stark, *Empire of Books: Naval Kishore Press and the Diffusion of the Printed Word in Colonial India* (New Delhi: Permanent Black, 2008); Barbara Metcalf, *Islamic Revival in British India: Deoband, 1860–1900* (Princeton: Princeton University Press, 1982).
78. Bijnor, which had a population of approximately 17,500 at the turn of the twentieth century, had at least five lithograph printing presses (some reports had the estimate as high as ten). By comparison, Lucknow, with a population of 264,000 in 1901, had twenty-five lithograph printing presses. We can see a small town with 6 percent of the population size of Lucknow had at least 20 percent of the lithographic printing presses of a major city, and almost a fourth the number of printing presses overall. In Bijnor, before *Madīnah*, these were *Qulqul*, *Ṣaḥīfa*, and *Tohfa-i hind*. There was also the weekly *Risāla-i Tāza Naẕā'ir* and the monthly magazine *Zamīndār wa Kāshtkar*, which, under the leadership of Muḥammad K̲h̲alīl-ur-Raḥmān of Mandawar, dealt with agricultural issues. H. R. Nevill, *Bijnor: A Gazetteer* (Allahabad: Supt., Govt. Press, 1928), 107.
79. Gianni Seviers, "Learning How to Print: The Nizami Press in Badayun and the First Urdu Manual on the Art of Lithography," presentation at the British Library in July 2018. Script of unpublished article based on presentation shared with author January 2019.
80. We know from work done by Ulrike Stark that a form of writing design for the lithographic stone called "mirror-writing" had been developed and was in use by Nawal Kishore press in Lucknow in the nineteenth century. However, it is clear that *Madīnah* newspaper, at least, used the egg-white emulsion technique described previously; it is likely that for everyday publications like *Madīnah* this was the more affordable and time-efficient technique. For more on mirror-writing, see Ulrike Stark, *Empire of Books: Naval Kishore Press and the Diffusion of the Printed Word in Colonial India* (New Delhi: Permanent Black, 2008).
81. Muneer Akhtar, interview, January 7, 2018, Bijnor, Uttar Pradesh, India.
82. Muḥammad Aḥīuddīn, *Līthogrāfī: Fann ṯabā'at par Urdū mein̲ kār-āmad aur pahalī kitāb* (Budaun: Maṯbu'a Nizāmī Press, 1926), 111.
83. Muḥammad Aḥīuddīn, *Līthogrāfī: Fann ṯabā'at par Urdū mein̲ kār-āmad aur pahalī kitāb* (Budaun: Maṯbu'a Nizāmī Press, 1926), 111.
84. Gianni Seviers, "Learning How to Print: The Nizami Press in Badayun and the First Urdu Manual on the Art of Lithography," presentation at the British Library in July 2018. Script of unpublished article based on presentation shared with author January 2019, forthcoming in the *Journal of the Royal Asiatic Society*.
85. Conversation with Muneer Akhtar, January 7, 2018, Bijnor, Uttar Pradesh, India.
86. This comment is based on an analysis of the physical stones still in the possession of now-defunct Madīnah Press. I thank Muneer Akhtar for his assistance in showing

me the stones still in the possession of Madīnah Press. Conversation with Muneer Akhtar, January 7, 2018, Bijnor, Uttar Pradesh, India.

87. A lithographic stone can have a rough or fine grain—a rough grain has a slightly more uneven surface that allows for a wider variation in the tonality of the image expressed (this unevenness would be invisible to the naked eye and imperceptible by touch). A rough grained stone is a poor fit for printing text in lithography, since one would be transferring text or even writing directly onto the stone using what is in modern printing parlance "full fill" images, or ones where the shape of the image matters more than variations of tonality in the image. A fine grain stone would have a smoother surface as well. I am grateful to the master lithographer Alexander Krillov for his instruction in fall 2017 on the lithographic print process.
88. In the 1830s there was a limestone mine discovered in Kurnool (written in this source Kulnoor) which was used for domestic mining and distribution of limestone. H. J. Carter, "Summary of the Geology of India, between the Ganges, the Indus, and Cape Comorin [With Map and Diagram]," *Journal of the Bombay Branch of the Royal Asiatic Society* (1854): 28–29.
89. See mention of lithographic stones from these three mines displayed in 1851. *Great Exhibition of the Works of Industry of All Nations: Official Descriptive and Illustrated Catalogue*, vol. 2 (London: Spicer Brothers, 1851), 868.
90. Interview, Alex Kirrilov, master lithographer, Philadelphia, October–November 2017.
91. While I was unable to measure precisely the weight of the two stones still in the possession of Madīnah Press, each stone was at least seventy pounds in weight and over two feet tall.
92. Muneer Akhtar, conversation, January 8, 2018, Bijnor, Uttar Pradesh, India.
93. Muḥammad Aḥīuddīn, *Līthogrāfī: Fann ṯabā'at par Urdū mein̲ kār-āmad aur pahalī kitāb* (Budaun: Maṯbu'a Nizāmī Press, 1926), chapter 5, cited in Gianni Seviers, "Learning How to Print: The Nizami Press in Badayun and the First Urdu Manual on the Art of Lithography," presentation at the British Library in July 2018. Script of draft article based on presentation shared with author January 2019.
94. In today's fine art market the substance is a specially prepared concoction called lithotine.
95. Many thanks to Muneer Akhtar for providing this particular detail of the process.
96. Muneer Akhtar, interview, April 2013.
97. *Ahl-i Ḥadīth*, January 7, 1921, 16, Raza Library Rampur. The subscription seal shows that each newspaper was sent directly to a man referred to as *Janāb Afsar Sāḥab* in Rampur. Issues of the *Aligarh Institute Gazette* sent in 1920 and stored in the Raza Library also still have this seal, although in such a state that it is not possible to see the name of the subscriber. *Aligarh Institute Gazette*, January 7, 1920, 1, Raza Library Rampur.
98. Hasrat Roznamah [Hasrat's Register of Daily Proceedings], March 23, 1947. Transcript of diaries provided in private correspondence by Francis Robinson, who has used the diaries in his book *Jamal Mian: The Life of Maulana Jamaluddin Abdul Wahab of Farangi Mahall, 1919–2012* (Karachi: Oxford University Press, 2017).

99. *Hazrat Ḥusain Aḥmad Madanī ki siyāsī dā'irī: Akhbār aur afkār kī raushnī mein* ("The Political Diary of the Revered Shaikhul Islam Maulānā Ḥusain Aḥmad Madanī: In the Light of Newspapers and Commentary"), 3 vols. (Karachi: Majlisi-i Yādgār-i Shaikhul Islam Pakistan), cited in Barbara Metcalf, "Introduction," in *Husain Ahmad Madani: The Jihad for Islam and India's Freedom* (Oxford: Oneworld, 2009), 6.
100. Diaries of Hasrat Mohānī in the Jamal Mian Papers (Karachi), translated by Mahmood Jamal, with the assistance of Francis Robinson. Francis Robinson generously shared translations of the diaries with me for this book. Additional detail on the content of the papers are available in Francis Robinson, *Jamal Mian: The Life of Maulana Jamaluddin Abdul Wahab of Farangi Mahall, 1919–2012* (Karachi: Oxford University Press, 2017), 405–7.
101. Raqamzadah Mulk ul-kalām Syed Muḥammad La'īq Ḥussain Ṣāḥab Qaumī "Zamarudraqam" "*Raftār-i zamānah* [Quickly Changing Times *or* The Speed of Time]," *Madīnah Akhbār*, May 1, 1912.
102. "*Apnī zātī manfa'at kī garaẓ se* [From Selfish Concern with Their Own Personal Profit]," *Madīnah*, May 1, 1912, 6.
103. "*Apnī zātī manfa'at kī garaẓ se* [From Selfish Concern with Their Own Personal Profit]," *Madīnah*, May 1, 1912, 6.
104. J. Baudrillard, *The System of Objects*, trans. James Benedict (London: Verso, 1996), 197, cited in Jamal Elias, *Aisha's Cushion: Religious Art, Perception and Practice in Islam* (Cambridge, MA: Harvard University Press, 2012), 236.
105. "Language and religion, however, would not have formed a mutually reinforcing vicious circle, sharply reinforced by separate scripts with all their social and religious connotations." Christopher King, *One Language, Two Scripts: The Hindi Movement in Nineteenth Century North India* (New Delhi: Oxford University Press, 1994), 188.
106. Margrit Pernau, *Ashrāf into Middle Classes: Muslims in Nineteenth-Century Delhi* (New Delhi: Oxford University Press, 2013), xix.
107. Pierre Bourdieu, *Outline of a Theory of Practice* (Cambridge: Cambridge University Press, 1977), 95.

4
Viewing the Map of Europe through the Lens of Islam

Hīch āfat nah rasad gausha-yi tanhā'ī rā[1]

During World War I, *Madīnah* published elaborate maps of the field of war, delineating the lines of control in Urdu.[2] With these intricate visuals, *Madīnah* instructed Muslims on their place in the world beyond the *qasbah*. Chapter 4 and chapter 5 delineate the interpretive lens *Madīnah* provided to its Muslim readers to demonstrate how the newspaper became a space of observation for the *ashrāf* of Turkey, Europe, and Britain. Rather than assuming a separation between spatial knowledge that is prior to and following experience, this chapter shows how spatial knowledge of Europe was influenced by the available methods for representing this spatial knowledge, by looking at *Madīnah* as one influential medium of spatial representation.[3] In this chapter I focus on the 1910s, when *Madīnah* became one of many viewfinders used by Muslims to train their eyes on a world that included Turkey, the Balkans, the European powers, and England. The history of the *qasbah* and the *ashrāf* were relevant to the shape and size of that viewfinder.

In the early twentieth century, the *ashrāf* Muslims descended from those Mughal retainers who had been exiled from Delhi in 1857 confronted a number of regional and international developments that gave them cause for anxiety. Religious buildings and the press took on new significance as possessions of the Muslim *qaum* under threat. As elites became aware of the increasingly precarious balance of power in Europe, support for the Caliph gave further clarity to expression of these anxieties. Elites became aware of the increasingly precarious balance of power in Europe in the early twentieth century. In the pages of *Madīnah* Muslim writers used discussion of warfare in Europe to hash out the boundaries of an Urdu public with global proportions. Through its coverage of the European martial and political landscape *Madīnah* focused attention on Islam as it vigorously debated the line between religious and political. In the 1910s, despite the nominal division between secular political objectives and the supposedly apolitical aims of the Deobandi *'ulamā*, in *Madīnah* the voices of *'ulamā* appeared

Print and the Urdu Public. Megan Eaton Robb, Oxford University Press (2021). © Oxford University Press.
DOI: 10.1093/oso/9780190089375.001.0001

alongside explicitly political discussions, visualizations of Europe and Turkey, and guidance on how to see the word as global Muslims. Chapters 2 and 3 established how the paper targeted Muslims as Muslims; this chapter discusses how the paper saw its relationship to the global political context and how it counseled Muslims to understand and act in the world in the early twentieth century.

From Time to Time: Mughal Dissolution to the Balkan Wars

Before 1857, Mughal emperors invoked the nominal authority of the Ottoman Caliphate, legitimizing Mughal rule as an extension of caliphate power. The dissolution of the Mughal Empire in 1857 not only deposed Bahadur Shah but also removed India's local link to the Caliphate of Islam. Indian Muslims in the second half of the century reforged that link symbolically; the name of the Ottoman sultan, the only remaining candidate for the position of caliph, was woven into Friday sermons across the subcontinent, binding those rituals to the fundament of Muslim tradition. This ritual link served as a vestigial reassurance to Indian Sunni Muslims of their rightful inheritance as theological and state leaders. Just as the Mughal emperors had issued currency in their names, the Ottoman sultan appeared on coins minted in the latter half of the nineteenth century.[4] The Ottoman sultan had taken up the mantle of symbolic power dropped by the Mughals.

Both the Turkish War of 1877–78 and the Greco-Turkish War of 1897 inspired Muslim fundraising and relief efforts in India.[5] Later the Agha Khan would cite the Greco-Turkish War as the initial awakening of an "essential unity" between Indian and Turkish Muslims.[6] When the Balkan Wars occurred, the caliph once again emerged as a symbol of Islam, this time under threat.[7] Because of the long-established links between Muslim temporal power in India and that in the Ottoman Empire, the plight of the Ottoman sultan resonated with Indian Muslims, particularly those *qasbatis* descended from servants of the then-defunct Mughal Empire.[8]

In early twentieth-century Europe, tension between Italy and Turkey rose to a fever pitch. Italian nationalists, unnerved by the Austrian acquisition of Bosnia-Herzegovina on October 6, 1908, in what came to be known as the Balkans Crisis, began to look toward Ottoman-controlled Libya as a way to help restore its influence.[9] What followed was a period of "peaceful penetration" by Italy comprising attempts to establish economic dominance in Libya via the Italian government's agent Banco di Roma.[10] By 1910 Banco di Roma, known as a purveyor of Italian influence in Libya as much as a financial institution, had attracted widespread ire among locals. Italy's surplus population and the growing trend of emigration among nationals also underlined the increasingly zealous press campaign for military action in Libya.[11] Despite the dramatic increase in Italy's share of the Libyan economic pie (from 5 percent of Tripolitania's international commerce in 1895 to 50 percent in 1910), Italy claimed obstructionist policies as justification for its invasion of Ottoman Libya in September 1911. The "Great Powers" of the Ottoman Empire and Italy saw their claims to influence steadily diminishing. With each determined effort to display dominance over the other, tensions escalated. The Italo-Turkish War, waged between September 1911 and October 1912, saw the transfer of the Ottoman provinces of Tripolitania, Fezzan, and Cyrenaica to Italian possession.

As a result of tensions leading to the outbreak of the Italo-Turkish War, Indian Muslims became increasingly concerned with the status of the Ottoman Empire. The Italo-Turkish War was one of the immediate catalysts for the founding of several politically oriented Urdu-language publications, including *Madīnah*. Maulānā Sirajjudīn Aḥmed's Lahore newspaper *Zamīndār* (re-est. May 1911) and Abul Kalam Āzād's Calcutta newspaper *al-Hilāl* (July 1912) also both built their reputations on coverage of Ottoman interests under threat.[12] The Italo-Turkish War, also known as the Tripolitan War, exposed the weakness of the Ottoman Empire and laid it open to challenges from the Balkans.

With the weakness of the Ottoman Empire exposed, the Balkan League (composed of Bulgaria, Greece, Montenegro, and Serbia) carried out an attack before the last shots of the Italo-Turkish War had been fired. The Indian Muslim press had been quick to pick up on the implications of the Italo-Turkish War; after the outbreak of the Balkan Wars on October 8, 1912, Muslim anxiety regarding the relationship between the British, the Ottomans, and the Balkan Allies increased tenfold. The First Balkan War ended in May 1913 with the Treaty of London. However, less than a month later internal rivalries in the Balkan League led to Bulgaria's invasion of its allies. Incensed at Serbia and Greece's attempts to hoard the territorial spoils of war, Bulgaria attempted to reclaim its rightful share of Macedonia. Serbia and Greece, along with Romania and the Ottoman Empire, effectively countered Bulgaria's offensive through separate attacks. The Second Balkan War spelled the end of the Balkan League, which Russia had employed as a diplomatic lever in pursuit of a warm water port and as a check on Austro-Hungarian power. After cessation of hostilities in August 1913, the Treaty of Bucharest deprived Bulgaria of almost all its territorial gains from the First Balkan War.

As long as Britain remained neutral in the Italo-Turkish and the Balkan Wars, newspapers such as *Madīnah* were free to express support for Turkey's Muslims and their state. When Britain's interests in the area took on greater complexity, attitudes in the Indian press also changed in tenor. During the Balkan Wars, England supported the integrity of the Ottoman Empire, since doing so prevented Russia from gaining access to warm water ports in the Mediterranean.

At the same time, England pragmatically accepted the advantage of Greek expansion into the Ottoman Empire as insurance against Russian dominance in the region.[13] In other words, prior to World War I, England's attitude toward the Ottoman Empire was characterized by extreme ambivalence (although its opposition to Italian expansionism was more definite[14]). It is perhaps for this reason that the Indian press's criticism of Italy, even when tinged with anti-Christian rhetoric, passed imperial censorship without comment in 1911 and 1912.

The government's decision in 1900 to accept Hindi along with Urdu as a language of the courts opened the playing field to Indians uneducated in Urdu, a change that seemed to threaten the threads binding contemporary *ashrāf* with their Mughal past.[15] British India conferred on Hindi symbolic status equal to Urdu with the Nagri Resolution, requiring all state employees to read and write both Devanagari and the Persian script fluently within a year of their appointment. This resolution placed Muslim intelligentsia unlettered in Hindi at a distinct disadvantage.[16] Those who knew Hindi as their mother tongue, on the other hand, usually had some passing knowledge of Urdu as a result of the long association between state power and the Persian script. After the passage of the Nagri Resolution, Muslims became increasingly concerned to preserve Urdu as a language of cultural and political importance, as a method of preserving the privileged status of the Muslim intelligentsia, status that, as long as their linguistic dominance had remained unchallenged, had in large part rested on ancestry in *qasbahs*.[17] Urdu Defense Associations began to crop up across the United Provinces, particularly in Allahabad and Lucknow.[18]

Despite a major boon in the form of the Morley-Minto reforms of 1909 awarding separate electorates, the revocation of the partition of Bengal in 1911 may have made the 1909 reforms seem like a Pyrrhic victory. Reversing the partition of Bengal not only revoked a guaranteed source of administrative appointments but also posed a symbolic challenge to Muslim efforts to protect their special interests. Until that point, Muslims, particularly those affiliated with the Muslim League, had used only expressions of loyalty to petition the government. The revocation of the partition of Bengal came about after extensive agitations from Hindu interest groups. In the words of Gail Minault, "[The] leadership of the League thus learned that agitation, as well as loyalty, got results."[19] This realization led to the founding of the League and the embrace of electoral politics by Muslim elites.

Changes to legislation governing censorship led to greater pressure on newspapers like *Madīnah*. Since 1867, the Press and Registration of Books Act had required keepers of book presses and publishers of newspapers to register the location of the physical press with the government, to provide the name of the press owner and editor on every newspaper copy, and to provide the Press Registrar with an annual statement.[20] The Vernacular Press Act of 1878 had created special restrictions and rights to censorship in papers printed in languages other than English. In particular, papers in vernacular languages were prohibited from impugning the motives of the British Raj. This was in response to the proliferation of criticism directed toward the British during the Anglo-Afghan War (1878–1880). While the law was repealed in 1881 after widespread protests, a precedent for the distinction between vernacular and English-language press policies had been established.[21] Some newspapers, among them *Amrita bazar patrika*, which had been bilingual until that time, became English-language publications as a result of the act. The Telegraph Act of 1885 quickly followed, allowing the government to monitor and intercept messages in public emergencies. In 1908 the Newspapers (Incitement to Offences) Act allowed the government to confiscate a printing press if its publications incited murder or any act of violence among its readership and allowed for the search and seizure of newspapers inciting violence.[22] The Indian Press Act of 1910 quickly followed, empowering the magistrate to require a deposit of between 500 and 2,000 Rupees from proprietors of newspapers, with the purpose of exerting more effective control over newspapers.[23] Later legislation affecting the press included the 1923 Official Secrets Act and the 1932 Foreign Relations Act. Each of these pieces of legislation contributed to a sense of beleaguerment among journalists not only in Urdu but in any so-called vernacular language.

Linking Urdu and Islam in Print

As is evident from the obvious reference to one of the holy cities of Islam in its name, *Madīnah* advertised itself as a newspaper for Muslim *ashrāf*. It is important to note that in any particular population, individuals claim identification simultaneously with a number of communities.[24] As Margrit Pernau has observed, personal identity for the *ashrāf* in the latter nineteenth century was multifaceted, formed through public interactions and points in common with any number of groups. The late nineteenth and early twentieth centuries saw some *ashrāf* make the decision to emphasize one particular facet of their identity, Islam. *Madīnah* was one of the most prominent public outlets enacting this decision. What was distinctive about *Madīnah*'s voice in comparison to Urdu newspapers of previous periods was its attempt to more closely connect Islam with both the *qasbah* context and specific political aspirations. It is crucial to note that there was nothing inevitable about this emphasis, just as there is nothing essentially Muslim about Urdu. Instead, the growing association of these elements in the early twentieth century was a product of social and political influence as well as the momentum of choices by individuals with measures of power.

The growing link between Urdu and Islam on the pages of *Madīnah* was in keeping with the trend found in other Urdu-language papers in Bijnor district, which had shifted from discussing issues of primarily local importance to issues of "general importance," particularly the Balkan Wars.[25] Before the founding of *Ṣaḥīfa* and *al-Khalīl*, which had been started in 1907 and 1909, respectively, Urdu-language newspapers in Bijnor tended to focus on local and agricultural matters. Two other established Urdu newspapers in the area, *Risāla-i Tāza Naẕā'ir* and *Zamīndār wa Kāshtkār* dealt with legal matters and agricultural questions specifically.[26] These would have been issues of importance to propertied Muslims and Hindus in Bijnor district. However, as pointed out in chapter 1, land ownership among Muslims was less prevalent in western United Provinces than eastern United Provinces; thus the shift from agricultural concerns to focus on other matters may be linked with the shift to a Muslim audience. *Zamīndār wa Kāshtkār* became *al-Khalīl* in 1909, with its subject matter changing significantly along with its name. The only other Urdu newspaper running in Bijnor before 1910 that we know of, *Qulqul*, had died out by the time *Madīnah* started publication. By the time the Balkan Wars conflict broke out, Urdu newspapers in Bijnor targeted an explicitly Muslim readership.

Europe on Its Own Terms

During the decade of the 1910s *Madīnah*'s journalists had cultivated the skill of adopting a "foreign" logic in order to effectively argue a point. Coverage of the March 1914 Muslim deputation to the Viceroy in Delhi demonstrates how the newspaper fought its battles through a combination of Qur'anic injunctions and English-style logic. It presented parallel conversations in order to demonstrate to the Raj how complying with the demands of the Muslim *qaum* would satisfy Western logic, while simultaneously voicing those demands in Islamic terms. This tactic demonstrated the awareness of *Madīnah*'s dual audience—both the Indian Muslim public and the colonial government.

This approach in *Madīnah* contrasted with the approach of Abul Kalam Āzād's well-known and short-lived newspaper *al-Hilāl*. In July 1912, after the conclusion of the Italo-Turkish Wars and just before the outbreak of the first Balkan War, Abul Kalam Āzād, who later became a senior leader of the Indian nationalist movement, founded the newspaper *al-Hilāl* published from Calcutta.[27] He named his publication for an Egyptian newspaper to cultivate sympathy among Indian Muslims for coreligionists in both Asia and Africa.[28] *al-Hilāl* emphasized Āzād's independence as a journalist from special interests. Like *Madīnah*, the paper sought to promote social and political awareness among Muslims and affirmed the importance of Islam as the foundation of any social or political action.[29] Popular in Bengal, the United Provinces, and Punjab, *al-Hilāl* was well known and cultivated a sense of the importance of the caliphate as a unifying power for the world's *ummah*.[30] The colonial government forced the newspaper to close, demanding large security deposits and finally confiscating the press in November 1914, after the start of World War I. Although Āzād attempted to revive the paper under the new banner *al-Balāgh*, it lasted a mere five months before closing.[31] Through the medium of *al-Hilāl*, Āzād promoted self-government, cooperation between Muslims and Hindus,[32] and a distinctively Muslim approach to Indian politics. He balanced these three priorities in a way analogous to that of *Madīnah*, although his paper's less carefully ambiguous approach to political action rendered his project anathema to colonial rule from the outset, while *Madīnah* succeeded in walking a finer line between nominal loyalism and fiery critique. In the *Times of India*, there appeared an article in August 1913 that revealed the preoccupation among the British with the question of Muslim loyalty, which in turn led to a powerful outcry in *Madīnah*. The *Times of India* article described the joyful reaction of Muslims around South Asia to the reclamation of Adrianople by Turkey at the end of the Balkan Wars. The reports of the most elaborate celebration came from Burma, with additional celebrations reported in Bombay, Madras, and Sholapur in India.[33] The *Times* also reported that the organization Anjuman-i Islam in Bombay had sent a crore of rupees and two medical support missions to assist the Turks. English-language press coverage of Muslims had been preoccupied with the question of Muslim loyalty; in that spirit this article explained there was a difference between Muslims' sending contributions in the spirit of *religious* duty and celebrating a *military* victory by the Turks. In 1914 an article in *Times of India* reported on an article written by the Agha Khan in the *Edinburgh Review* suggesting that Muslims' religious sentiments might be "inflamed" if the future brought Turkey and Britain into conflict.[34] The article ultimately affirmed the loyalty of the Muslims through a quote from the Agha Khan:

> They are not disloyal, and labelling criticism sedition can engender nothing but disloyalty. There is plenty of room in India for loyal and free criticism.

This general assertion of loyalty was not entirely effective. Despite the Agha Khan's contributions, articles in the *Times of India* revealed doubts about the validity of Muslims' professions of loyalty as tensions in Europe once again approached the breaking point. Two months before Gavrilo Princip assassinated archduke Franz Ferdinand, a Muslim deputation composed of *'ulamā*, rulers of princely states, and council members gained a private audience with the Viceroy in order to attest to Muslims' loyalty. Aware of the concern caused by the outpouring of support for the Ottoman Empire following its success in reclaiming

Adrianople, the deputation sought to assure the British of their fealty as the situation in Europe continued to disintegrate.

Madīnah, under the editorship of Āg͟hā Rafīq Bulāndshahrī, strongly objected to the *Times of India* questioning the loyalty of Muslims. Although Bulāndshahrī did not specify the publication dates, he certainly referred specifically to the series of articles published in the *Times of India* at the end of March and beginning of April 1914, beginning with the article described previously about the deputation to the Viceroy (in Delhi on Wednesday, March 25). Sarcastic and critical of the sincerity of the deputation, the *Times of India* columnist had joked:

> Having determined on an indirect reply of this nature to their calumniators, these Mahomedan gentlemen could scarcely adopt any other line than that of impassioned protestation, though the length at which they addressed His Excellency was slightly suggestive of the refrain "we are all honourable men." We trust they will not misunderstand us when we say that they might with equal propriety have protested their sanity, for disloyalty in a Mahomedan in India at the present time would be equivalent to insanity.[35]

Bulāndshahrī's editorial correctly surmised that Muslims were being accused of hiding their feelings of disloyalty,[36] but by the time Bulāndshahrī's diatribe appeared in the hands of his readers at the beginning of April, the drama in the *Times of India* had already run its course. Three days after the acerbic column hit the stands, a meek addendum had appeared in *Times of India*, affirming the diverse composition of the deputation and, ironically, warning "the English Press against the dangers of recklessly attacking a loyal community through the influence of misinformed and biased writers." In other words, it was *Times of India*'s turn to make the case for its own honor, possibly after receiving a slap on the wrist from censors who predicted a volatile response from the "vernacular" press.

Regardless, Bulāndshahrī went on to pen multiple editorials in response in the April issues of *Madīnah*, vehemently opposing not just the *Times*'s attitude but the existence of a deputation of Muslims formed to assure the government of the community's loyalty in the first place.[37] He quickly adapted his protest to the new idiom posed by *Times of India*, understanding that in the evolving political climate, the repeated panegyrics that characterized formal communication in the *qasbah* would be read as tantamount to disloyalty. He implicitly accepted the argument that protestations of loyalty could be misinterpreted and blamed both the Viceroy and the Muslim deputation for opening up the *qaum* to criticism by the English-language press, long viewed with suspicion in *Madīnah*. Turning the *Times of India* argument on its head, he accused the Viceroy of inconsistency in accepting a profession of loyalty after claiming to desire nothing of the sort. Here again, *Madīnah*'s editorial team quickly assessed the logical parameters of the controversy and built their argument in the context of its internal logic. Significantly, they were clearly aware of and conversant with the contents of not only other Urdu newspapers but also the English-language press.

Other Urdu-language newspapers weighed into the debate. Bijnor's *al-Khalīl* soon afterward suggested that such strenuous objections to the deputation from conservatives were due to the fact that English-educated liberals had organized and attended it. In other words *al-Khalīl* suggested that Bulāndshahrī's high-minded rhetoric was ultimately based on local factionalism.[38] Bulāndshahrī had argued that if such a gathering were necessary then the Muslim League should have organized it.[39] The "frivolous" deputation lowered the prestige of the League as the representative voice for Muslims by excluding them from the planning process. If *al-Khalīl* was correct, *Madīnah* sought to preserve a local political advantage through using a national event with global philosophical overtones as a straw man for local factional concerns. Much later, during the by-election of 1937, *Madīnah* would protest the League's claims for sole representation of Muslims based on similar concerns of local representation, an episode described in detail in chapter 5.

The Transformation of Imperial Loyalty through the Lens of Islam

While some scholarship has emphasized the Muslim press's view of the Balkan Wars as evidence of Christian conspiracy,[40] evidence in *Madīnah* paints a more complex picture. It demonstrates that parallel to a discourse concerned with competition between Islam and "the West" was a persistent attempt to reconcile two threads of identity: fealty to the British Empire and obedience to Islam. This attempt at reconciliation contributed to the delineation of a Muslim, Urdu-speaking public; in the process this public wove the threads of language choice, religion, and politics into a nationalist pattern equating those three categories.

Madīnah certainly presented the Ottoman Empire's military and political victories during the Balkan Wars as a victory for Islam. Reporting on an Ottoman general's hesitancy to employ firepower against airplanes, the correspondent reports that the enemy planes soon crashed of their own accord. God had defended the righteous, peace-loving Ottoman Muslims from the airplane attacks.[41] Meanwhile, according to *Madīnah*, internal developments within the Ottoman Empire, including but not limited to a departure from Sunni ideals, contributed to its decline in power.

On March 15, 1913, a poem titled "A Speech to India's Women" appeared, which talked about the Turks being driven out of their homeland.

> Look, look, what memories have come to them when they sit down
> The eyes fill with tears seeing the desolate, empty house
> [. . .]
> Who knows how those people can sleep
> When their neighbors' houses are going up in flames.

The poem, which focused on the plight of Turkish women and children, used pathos to invite the reader to sympathize with the Ottoman cause. Despite their many miseries, these fellow Muslims have enough strength to assert the need for patience. The last two lines are a direct plea to the readers to consider their obligations to their neighbors, the Ottomans. The newspaper placed its readers in direct proximity to the Turks, presenting them as neighbors whose needs were as immediate as if they lived in the house next door. This is an example of the paper's use of spatial imaginary to create the sense of a global *qaum*.

Nonetheless, during the Balkan Wars *Madīnah* went to elaborate lengths to insist that there was no tension between the heritage Indians claimed from European Christian nations on the one hand and their link to the Ottoman Empire on the other. *Madīnah* maintained this attitude even as its long-winded arguments threw into relief the intensity of the strain. The newspaper's methods of reconciliation were labyrinthine. First, *Madīnah* was careful to distinguish between England's policy priorities and those of other European powers. In an article discussing the progress of the war in the Dardanelles in May 1912, mention is made of a meeting between the English ambassador and the Ottoman foreign minister.[42] While the same article laments that "a truce [was] impossible" between Italy and the Ottoman Empire, this report of a collegial meeting between English and Ottoman officials served to emphasize the relative health of the relationship between those governments. The Dardanelles were closed in April 1912 in order to more effectively protect Turkey from attack, and although the English ship Rani suffered harm as a result of the closure, *Madīnah*'s report instead focused on England's polite submission of a petition to open the Dardanelles. It also maintained its conviction that Turkey had the matter firmly in hand.[43] Reports of an English officer Moṭonkū (perhaps an interpretation of the name Montague) with a wry sense of humor appeared in *Madīnah*:

> The current newspaper *Tansein* has written that an English officer whose name is Moṭonkū, who is in Algharab, Tripoli, after meeting with the Muslim warriors, was fighting the Italians. He has been present in our city for two days. Yesterday we sent a reporter to ask him about the state of the war but at the time of the arrival of the reporter the man was going to meet with the Minister of War. Therefore he was able to give answers to [only] a few short questions to the reporter. Our reporter asked the aforementioned officer the reason for his

> arrival, and he gave the response that he has come for a change of climate. After this he praised at length the bravery and courage of the Ottoman soldiers.[44]

This Englishman is self-deprecating about his own valor, yet quick to praise the bravery of the Ottoman soldiers. The story contributes to a narrative of universal appeal surrounding the Ottoman cause and complicates England's place in the Christian–Muslim world dichotomy.

Madīnah's attitude toward the British government remained ambiguous throughout its first decade. Rather than viewing the Christian world as a monolith, the paper tended to distinguish between different members of the "Christian powers" and portray them as having diverse motivations.[45] As opposed to Āzād's *al-Hilāl, Madīnah* refrained from criticizing the British government for refusing to provide support to the Ottoman Empire in 1912 and 1913 and occasionally praised it for its attempts to keep war out of India. But in 1914, *Madīnah* encouraged the allied forces to correct the veracity of their accounts of victories and defeats, implying that their numbers were misleading. As late as 1915 coverage in *Madīnah* tended to cast England's refusal to assist the Ottoman Empire as a persistent misunderstanding, repeatedly emphasizing that the interests of the Ottomans and the English, properly understood, would not come into conflict.[46] In fact in that period England, although neutral in the conflict, looked unfavorably on Italian military advances in Libya.[47]

The paper's support for the Ottoman Empire's alliance with the Central Powers rested on the assumption that an exchange of accurate information would reconcile loyalty to the British and the Ottomans. This search for reconciliation undermines assumptions that the Urdu press already saw the relationship between the Christian and Muslim worlds as one of irreconcilable conflict as early as the Balkan Wars.[48] On the contrary, these discussions in *Madīnah* gave shape to a new Urdu public of global proportions, a public that, while it built on a dichotomy between Christian and Muslim power, avoided relating Britain explicitly with the Christian half of that dichotomy.

World War I: Discussing Islam on the *Maidan* of Europe

Before Turkey's entrance into World War I, *Madīnah* had quickly affirmed her unbounded loyalty to Britain.[49] With Turkey's entrance into World War I on the side of the Central Powers in 1914, *Madīnah* continued to insist that England was a natural ally of the Turks. *Madīnah* expressed regret in February of 1915 that Germany had "alienated from Turkey the sympathies of her two best friends—England and France."[50] At the same time, when other newspapers such as *Mashriq* suggested that Turkey was forced to enter the war by Germany, *Madīnah* preferred to believe that Turkey must have chosen to do so of her own accord.[51] Turkey's complete surrender of her political agency to a European power was more disturbing than the prospect of her being in open opposition to Britain and her allies.

Expressing regret at Turkey's decision to join the war, *Madīnah* then laid out a detailed rationale for preserving loyalty toward the British government. The crux of the argument was the assumption that "the hostilities between the two states [are] not . . . of a religious nature."[52] When the colonial government proscribed a seditious pamphlet signed by *'ulamā* from Tunis, Sudan, Tehran, Morocco, Bukhara, Egypt, India, and Afghanistan in December 1914, *Madīnah* questioned the provenance of the signatures, suggesting that they were false. In a tactic that had become common in *Madīnah* by 1914, the editors sought to undermine proposed facts by suggesting the existence of counterfeit or intrigue.[53] In a period of time in which access to news was relatively infrequent and the provenance of that information not easily checked, questioning the truth of a published argument allowed a publication to save face and postpone the discussion of the issue at hand. Displaying an eagerness to defend Turkish virtue, *Madīnah* accused the Anglo-Indian press of propagating a deceptive news report and called the government to invoke strict measures of censorship.[54]

By late 1914, while *Madīnah*'s words remained primarily loyalist, an emphasis on Islamic imagery and Arabic ornamentations indicated increased solidarity with the Ottomans. Flags bearing the crescent of Islam, which bore a striking resemblance to the flag of the Ottoman Empire, marked the top of the cover, with increasingly large representations of the city of *Madīnah* accompanied by Arabic language embellishments (Figure 4.1). These embellishments had the added advantage of not being easily translated into surveillance reports by censors.

Madīnah had to walk the line between the necessity of professing loyalty and a compulsion to critique the British government, and it did so by framing its arguments against British policy in terms of internal consistency. *Madīnah* only asked Britain to maintain its own standards of propriety in terms of its dealings with the Ottomans. *al-Khalīl* chimed in on the same note; it specified that Indian Muslims' disappointment stemmed from the European powers' (specifically Britain's) failure to adhere to their declaration of neutrality.[55] According to the argument in local *qasbah* papers in Bijnor, it was Europe that had been disingenuous in its claims to neutrality. This argument placed the discussion firmly within the context of an internal political debate, measuring Britain's behavior by the metric of statesmanship rather than by the irrelevant concern of religious fealty. Rhetorically, it was a neat tactic that preempted accusations of religious bias, since the debate was conducted according to European political vocabulary. This is an illustration of the complex, flexible methods by which *Madīnah* established itself as an effective spokesperson for Muslims.

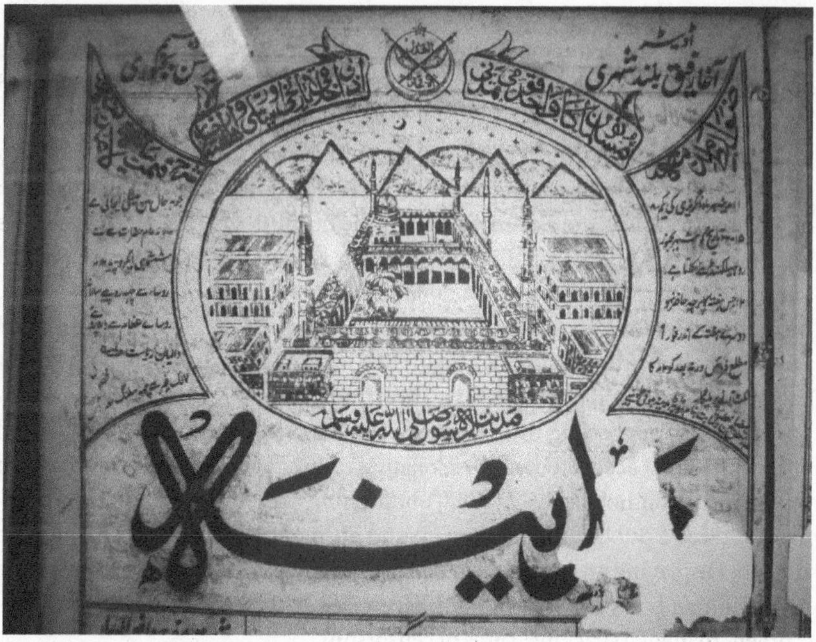

Figure 4.1 Cover of *Madīnah*, December 1914.

The British government specifically solicited statements of loyalty from moderate Muslims.[56] We know about *fatāwa* to attest loyalty issued by Aḥmad Raẓa Khān (Bareilly), ʻAbdul Ḥaq (Calcutta), ʻAbdul Ḥamīd (Farangi Mahal), ʻAbdul Majīd (Farangi Mahal), Pīr Mihr ʻAlī Shāh (Golra), and Maulvī Syed Muḥammad Razwī.[57] Other statements similarly engineered by the British would go beyond expressing loyalty to advocate British dominance in the Middle East. For example, Khān Bahādur Qāẓī ʻAzīz-ud-dīn, a deputy collector and therefore member of the *ashrāf*, published a pamphlet entitled "*Turkon kī himāqat*" or "Turkey's Follies," encouraging the British to take over the Hijaz and assert direct control.[58] *Madīnah*'s sister publication, *Ṣaḥīfa*, while proclaiming loyalty to Britain, called for proscription of Qāẓī ʻAzīz-ud-dīn's pamphlet on the grounds that it was unfavorably influencing Muslims.[59] The article expressed concern that Qāẓī, a government servant, was permitted to write in such an explicitly political manner. This mention of Qāẓī's affiliation with the government hints at suspicions regarding the true source of the article, while refraining from stating explicitly the cause of its objection. Less than a month later *Madīnah* published its own article attempting to shut down any discussion of the caliphate's validity.[60] The opposition to Qāẓī's pamphlet was based on objections to the conflict between the British profession to separate religion and government, and the way that the pamphlet troubled that binary regarding policies toward Turkey. Initially it was very important to *Madīnah* to explicitly distinguish between religious matters and political matters, as a way of balancing loyalty to Britain with concern for the caliphate. In the same way, according to histories published in *Madīnah*, Islamic rulers had distinguished between matters of religious observance and rulers' obligations to subjects of all faiths.[61] By this logic, the existence of the caliphate was a matter in which the British should bow to the sentiments of its Muslim population and protection of the caliphate was an act consistent with political economy that did not violate the British separation between state and religious matters. Increasingly, as the 1910s wound on and the importance of electoral politics for Muslims became entrenched, the abject professions of loyalty in *Madīnah* transformed to bold critiques, and the concern to separate religion and government grew less pronounced as the necessity for electoral participation became clear.

Madīnah's links to both Deoband and later on Jam'īat 'Ulamā-i Hind would only become clear later; in 1914 the paper had not yet risen to the prominence it would enjoy in the following decade. Therefore, we should read the loyalty statements crafted at the beginning of World War I, asserting the nonexistence of any tension between its religious and political loyalties, as the choices of a fledgling paper aware that it is at the mercy of colonial censorship. Certainly the British government remained suspicious about the purported loyalty of its Muslim subjects. Surveillance records from 1911 onward show a penchant for press clippings mentioning Muslim identity in the context of the Balkan Wars and World War I, reflecting an anxiety about the potential of unrest among Muslim subjects.[62] *Madīnah*, on its part, repeatedly expressed frustration at the government's unwillingness to accept the loyalty of Muslims. For instance, after a deputation of Muslims was gathered to address the accusations of disloyalty brought about by the English newspaper *Times*, *Madīnah* published a scathing opinion column on the subject that was picked up by government surveillance.[63]

Given that there were press laws in place that prohibited any accusation that the British were acting in bad faith, the tone of these statements should not necessarily be taken at face value. Nonetheless, while government pressure was undoubtedly a factor in editorial decisions, the creative balancing of seemingly distinct agendas in the Urdu press suggests that most of these statements were voluntarily crafted. Telegrams affirming loyalty included those from the Muslim League of Lucknow, the Trustees of Aligarh University, the Muslim League of Moradabad, the Anjuman-i Islam of Julbulpore, and the *Observer* newspaper.[64] Each of the Urdu-language papers in Bijnor, including *Madīnah*, *Ṣaḥīfa*, and *al-Khalīl*, among others, expressed their loyalty to the British Empire.[65] There is no suggestion in coverage of the Balkan Wars that religious concerns made the political failures of England more deplorable, even while Turkey's need for support from

India's Muslims became increasingly urgent. At the same time, these publications tried to shut down any attempts at undermining the caliphate and exhorted Indian Muslims to support Turkey. These appeals were carefully siloed in separate pieces from the arguments aimed at British policy makers.

Coverage of World War I in 1914 and at the beginning of 1915 tended to focus on timely coverage of action in the war, and complaints when timely, accurate information was not available. From the outbreak of the war in 1914, several pages of each issue of *Madīnah* were devoted to the nuances of military engagement and political machinations on both sides, republishing reports wired from London, Rome, Washington, and Paris.[66] Commentary certainly demonstrated support of the Ottoman Empire and its backers, as well as anxiety that it was under threat. At the same time, there was initially a concern, consistent with the approach the paper had cultivated throughout the Balkan Wars, to correct the misconception of an outright conflict between Muslim and Christian civilizations. Just how far the Urdu press was able to go in reconciling (or denying) such tensions can be seen in an article from another Bijnor paper, which proposed that the Christian population of Europe temporarily adopt the Muslim practice of polygamy for practical reasons:

> *al-Khalīl* of Bijnor, 16th May 1915, suggests that polygamy should be temporarily allowed in Christianity, due to the large loss of male life during World War I. He suggests that polygamy should be allowed on scientific principles, that is every fifth person, provided he is of sound physique, in the population should be allowed to have two wives or every tenth male be allowed to have three, so that the offspring should not be weak and degenerated.[67]

al-Khalīl evidently presented this proposal as though it would pose no particular difficulty. It is also only one of many examples of concerns about the status of European and Turkish women that appear in *Madīnah*, as ways of reflecting on the health and status of those communities.[68]

Such was the anxiety regarding the existence of tension between these two strands of identity, Muslim and British, and so high were the stakes of the conversation in terms of political fallout, that *Madīnah*'s editorial board sometimes denied the existence of conflict between religious and political "identities." This absence exaggerates the existence of the tension for the historian, who observes that the absence of the word left unspoken speaks loudest. On the other hand, *Madīnah* also commented explicitly on civilizational differences between Muslims and Europeans, although it was often implied that the British were excluded from the European category—through writing that emphasized differences between European and British political approaches to Turkey, for instance.[69] The growing emphasis on the connection of religion and politics as the

1910s continued was a product of a decade in which Muslims were realizing the necessity of electoral participation along lines defined by communal identity.

British surveillance picked up on some of the reflections on the civilizational conflict between Christianity and Islam that appeared in *Madīnah* and printed them in their records:

> Yea, you (Christians) must remember that in revenge for (the wrongs done to) Persia
> (We) will execute every individual,
> (You) have bombarded Meshed, and, remember,
> We (Muhammadans) have not forgotten it and will punish you for that also.
> Our Crescent will shine through all time,
> What care we if the enemy has raised a little dust.
> O *Qawi*, the world knows that we are true to our word:
> Whatever has passed from our lips will, without fail, be translated into action.[70]

Implied in the framing of this article in the surveillance records is the assumption that the "Christians" referred to included Britons; however, in *Madīnah* discussions of European Christians were siloed off from discussions of the English. Indeed, English attitudes were even occasionally invoked as authorities in international issues relevant to Muslims. Occasionally the English were enlisted to testify to the absence of "true" Muslim morals and culture in Iran, as had existed there previously.[71] While it was not surprising to see a Sunni newspaper critiquing Shīʿa Islam, what was more remarkable was the invocation of English authority to bring about that critique. In the same vein, we see articles affirming the rectitude of Afghanistan's loyalty to the British Empire, despite temptations placed on it to defect to the support of Germany.[72]

During the Balkan Wars and the first several months of World War I, a firm distinction was made between the needs of Indian Muslims and the motivation for assisting the failing Ottoman Empire. Two major issues for Indian Muslims, for instance, were the concerns of representation on municipal boards[73] and economic support for the poor to perform Hajj, which *Madīnah* framed in terms of British obligation to constituents.[74] By contrast, as we have seen, when addressing Britain's dealings with the Ottomans, *Madīnah* framed the issue deferentially as a matter of meeting Britain's own standards of statesmanship. It was in legislation of coverage of the state of the Ottoman, Empire where these two conversations—the domestic claims made on behalf of Indian Muslims and the concern for the failing Empire—uncomfortably overlapped. The result was that the newspaper conversation itself was framed as a Muslim interest.

Networks against Censorship

As a result of developments in legislation, newspapers and their proprietors faced constant threats of censorship, closure, and even arrest. *Madīnah*'s editors would have been aware of the threat of fines and arrest when publishing their articles. In this environment, *Madīnah*'s proprietor and editors regularly spoke out against the enforcement of the Press Act of 1910 targeting what they called the Muslim Press. Protection of sacred Muslim spaces had become a major concern, demonstrated poignantly by the riot at Kanpur mosque on August 3, 1913, and the ensuing firestorm of press coverage.[75] Telegrams flooded the Viceroy upon the entry of Turkey into World War I, imploring the government to "safeguard the holy places of Islam."[76] *Madīnah* presented the Muslim press as an important space worthy of protection.

Colonial administration shut down the English journal *Comrade* in November 1914, after Muḥammad 'Alī published a strongly worded editorial titled *The Choice of the Turks*, responding to a *Times* article of the same name. 'Alī Jauhar's column had expressed strong sympathies with Turkey and its loss of territory to the Allies.[77] *Comrade* was closed and a security demanded under the Press Act. *Hamdard* seems to have also ceased publication at the same time. Muḥammad 'Alī was arrested on May 15, 1915, and lobbying for his cause was a prominent topic in other newspapers such as *Madīnah* until his release in 1919. Rather than seeing themselves as competing against each other for circulation and income, the network of Muslim newspapers formed solidarity against censorship. The social connections among editors doubtless also contributed to the sense of a collective identity as "the Muslim Press."

Compared to other newspapers based in more central areas, such as *al-Hilāl* and *Urdu-i-Mu'alla, Madīnah* was initially careful to avoid major clashes with the British government. Maulānā Hasrat Mohānī, born in the United Province *qasbah* of Mohan (in Unnao district), started the newspaper *Urdu-i-Mu'alla* in Aligarh in July 1903. The newspaper focused on a combination of literature and politics and demonstrated a decidedly anti-English perspective to readers. Mohānī was arrested for sedition following the publication of an article titled "The Educational Policy of the English in Egypt."[78] The British labeled *Urdu-i-Mu'alla* a paper requiring "careful watching" in 1912. Mohānī was again arrested on April 13, 1916, for sedition; after his release, he continued to run his paper from 1918 until 1924, when his third arrest finally caused the paper to close permanently.[79] The threat of closure and arrest was persistent for journalists and proprietors alike.

While newspapers could not comment on censorship carried out on their own papers, they could comment on the censorship of others. They did so, often. When the *Zamīndār* (Lahore) lost its appeal against British censorship,

Madīnah published an energetic defense built on sewing the newspaper into the identity of the Muslim community, saying that *Zamīndār* "is the property of the Muhammadan [Muslim] community, and that any loss to the *Zamīndār* means loss to the community."[80] This sort of activism presented the newspaper conversation as an essential space for Muslims, public in the sense of providing a forum for open airing of views outside the limitations of the private correspondence networks. Indeed *Madīnah* portrayed not only *Zamīndār* but also the Urdu press as a whole as a representative voice of the *qaum*, or nation, community.

When requesting that the English government censor the "Anglo-India" press regarding its coverage of Turkey, the request was expressed as a veiled threat against "wounding the religious susceptibilities of Indian Muhammadans."[81] The tone of this coverage echoed the outrage in *Madīnah* surrounding the Kanpur affair of July 1913, when the acquisition of a portion of a mosque for destruction in Macchli Bazaar in Kanpur had inflamed the sentiments of Indian Muslims.[82] It also suggested a polarization, with English on the one side and Urdu and Islam paired on the other side. Public conversation about the Ottoman Empire in newspapers was framed in the same defensive terms as the coverage of the Macchli Bazaar mosque, a holy place of Islam. Even though the Ottoman Empire itself could not be tied explicitly to the needs of Indian Muslims, discourse around the Ottoman context was essential.

Some praised the government, emphasizing that British policies were protecting India's borders.[83] Other articles criticized the exploitation of Indian trade for the benefit of the English economy during wartime,[84] but only in terms of their effect on India. An exception to the general rule of avoiding grand global dichotomies appeared in *Madīnah* in May 1912, during the Balkan Wars. On this occasion, claims that Italy was inaccurately reporting casualties and losses provided the newspaper with an opportunity to criticize the failings of European civilization generally, without directly impugning the British:

> Europe, which claims to be civilized, and Italy is a part of it, so what can we say of that civilization when there is no distinction between truth and a lie. It is regretful that if the opposing sides and the quality of reporting about them remain like this, then it will be extremely difficult for the world to determine whether news of events is a truth or a lie.[85]

> *Yūrap jo tahazīb kā mudd'aī hai Iṭalī bhī usī kā eik juz'v hai to kyā uske nazdīk sivlazaishan isī ko kahate hain̲ kih sach aur jhūṭ mein̲ kuch bhī imtiyāz nahīn̲ rak̲h̲tā. Afsos hai kih agar farīqain kī aur un kī k̲h̲abar rasānī kī yahī ḥālat rahī to kisī vaqa'ah aur k̲h̲abar ke saḥīh yā g̲h̲alat k̲h̲ayāl karne mein̲ dunīyā ko baṛī muṣībat vaqa' hogī.*

While implicitly critiquing European civilization by referring to it as a mere petitioner, or *mudd'aī*, to that label, the coverage in *Madīnah* referred to Britain as though it stood on a continuum between the two poles of Christianity and Islam. Its readers, after all, were both Muslims and nominally loyal British citizens.

A combination of specific factors caused a change in tone in *Madīnah*, from professed loyalty to articulated skepticism, over the 1910s. The growing threat posed to the existence of the caliphate and the lack of consideration given the Turks by the British were foremost of these. Other Urdu newspapers such as *Comrade* and *al-Hilāl* began expressing concern regarding the integrity of the Ottoman Empire.[86] A summary of an article in *Madīnah* in the *Vernacular Newspaper Reports* reads:

> The *Medina* (*sic*) (Bijnor) of the 8th May 1915, objects to Sir Daniel Gourd's remarks that the Turks are but a band of robbers who exist at the sufferance of some European powers, and says that it is highly unbecoming of a responsible British official to give expression of sentiments that are calculated to wound the feelings of a large number of His Imperial Majesty's subjects.

These objections foreshadowed a concern of *Madīnah* to simultaneously identify South Asian Muslims with the Turks while establishing itself as a voice of authentic critique of British governance in India. The tone of critique would become sharper in the years following the conclusion of World War II.

Balancing Act: Establishing a Muslim Voice

Meanwhile, while maintaining a prudent degree of nominal loyalism or at least ambiguity in regard to Britain, *Madīnah* cultivated its approach as a Muslim paper. In particular, it focused on publishing and promoting *'ulamā*. Making special note of prominent *'ulamā* who came to Bijnor *qasbah* and neighboring districts to provide instruction, the newspaper also often published articles on religious subjects by *'ulamā* from Deoband, Nadwah, and *qasbahs* around North India. In one of many examples, a February 1917 issue mentions the arrival of Maulwī Faiz Muḥammad Ṣāḥab to the district Bhojīyān in order to provide religious instruction.[87] In another February 1917 issue, an article on the "Allurement of Islam" lays out the manifest attractions of religion.[88] Several other articles appeared on the subject of instruction in religious history, including the proper timing and physical comportment for prayers.[89] Perhaps needless to say, mentions of explicitly Hindu authorities did not appear at all.

The identification with a global Muslim community expressed through concern for the Turks and the Balkans[90] complemented the focus on local and regional Muslim authorities. This theme was developed in coverage ranging from a 1914 article that mentions Turkey as the seat of Islam[91] to accounts of Italy's 1917 victories that emphasize the persistence and heroism of Muslim Turks, even in defeat.[92] During the same period *Madīnah* also expressed interest in the development of Islam in other areas of the world, such as China.[93]

The question of the validity of the caliphate emerged for the first time in *Madīnah* in February 1915. In response to the appearance of challenges to the caliphate in English language newspapers in India, *Madīnah* attempted to stem the flood of discussion with an editorial asserting that any discussion on the subject was premature and risky. The *Vernacular Newspaper Report* summarizes the editor's article as follows:

> He remarks that Muhammadans are well aware of the fact that politics and religion are two distinctly separate things, and he impresses upon his readers the futility of raising the question of the Caliphate, which, he says, is only likely to flame fanaticism.[94]

The original version of the editorial, titled "The Religious Caliphate of Islam and an Intractable Political Issue,"[95] is much more vivid:

> In the world there are many different religions and communities. The foundation of every religion is distinct. And different behaviors predominate among different communities. And for many religions in Europe, in subordination to strong feelings, the governments have come near to trodding on religious foundations. Perhaps it is better to say they have become subordinate to the foundations of politics, which have themselves become religion. In this standing the status of religion and the religious community has become dependent on politics. Among Muslims religion is more predominant. . . . If this [Khilafat] issue comes to light then many opinions will be established, and many extreme difficulties will emerge. . . .
>
> The government does not know if I am Indian or European. There will be no profit in unearthing this problem. Religion is a thing separate from the individual, and politics is accepted as having the standing of overlord. . . . The issue of the Khilafat is only important because it relates to Muslim religious feelings, not worldly issues. It is connected to issues of both faith and worldly matters, so the issue of the Khilafat should be understood as a refuge not a source of harm. . . . In this way our religious emotions are connected to the Imam of the Caliphate and our feelings regarding worldly politics belong to the British Government.

Madīnah, along with other vernacular newspapers of the period, sought to argue that the issue of the Khilafat was a purely religious, not a political, matter. This was a pragmatic, even a necessary position to take: to let that particular cat out of the bag would spell disaster for India's Muslims, who would most certainly become caught in the crossfire. The issue of the caliphate temporarily fell off the public radar in India as World War I waged on. Then, as hostilities wound down, the readership of *Madīnah* began to peer ahead, trying to discern what lay at the end of the tunnel of war. The importance of the caliphate would return as justification for supporting Mohandas Gāndhī's noncooperation movement.

A New Tone: The End of World War I and the Khilafat Movement

The internment of Muḥammad and Shaukat 'Alī was a significant influence in transforming *Madīnah*'s tone regarding Muslims' relationship to the British government. *Ṣaḥīfa* and *al-Khalīl* had both expressed doubts as to the veracity of reports of Muḥammad 'Alī's prolonged internment before eventually expressing extreme regret at the confirmation of those reports in 1915.[96] As World War I entered its final year, *Madīnah* doubled down on its support for Muḥammad and Shaukat 'Alī, reporting on the movements and public speeches their mother gave in support of her sons while they were incarcerated.[97] On December 1, 1917, *Madīnah* reported on a meeting called by the Home Rule League in the Delhi Jama Masjid to petition for the release of the 'Alī brothers. According to the report, the meeting or *jalsah* included members of Congress, the Muslim League, and the Home Rule League and was led by Doctor Tej Bahadur Sapru, a Kashmiri Brahman and well-known moderate figure. Reporting on a speech given at the meeting, the article voiced a radical goal: "After this unexpected result, the patience of Hindustan's Muslims has already worn thin . . . in our opinion for us there is now only one option, to start a nation which will not follow India's historical approach." The article concluded with a request to readers to send a telegram with a scripted message to the Secretary of State in Calcutta requesting the release of Muḥammad 'Alī, Shaukat 'Alī, and Abul Kalam Āzād.[98] The message, written in both English and Urdu, is one of the few examples of any message, other than the title on the cover, printed in the English language in *Madīnah*. The calligraphy of the original author of the English wording was preserved through the lithographic medium. This image gave readers an exact model of how to write to the Secretary of State, presenting not only the message in Urdu translation, but the exact form of the English wording.

In 1918 Muḥammad 'Alī Jauhar was elected president of the All India Muslim League, elected in absentia since he was serving a prison sentence. In May 1919 *Madīnah* and other Urdu publications were sent a letter by the 'Alī brothers written from Chindwara, where they had been detained for seditious activities related to the famous publications *Hamdard* and *Comrade*. The copy sent to *Madīnah* was intercepted by British Central Intelligence and translated. In it, the ʿAlī brothers refer to a well-known memorandum they wrote addressed to the Viceroy of India on April 24, 1919, demanding the freedom of Indian Muslims to support the Turkish Khalifa.[99]

"I am being dragged for love of you and there is a great noise;
Do come to the roof yourself as it is a sight worth seeing."[100]

Dear Sir, Greetings.
We shall be grateful if you will by way of justice help the proclaiming of the word of truth by the publication of this letter. You might be knowing that we sent our last petition to the Viceroy on the 24th April, and in that letter we frankly stated all those religious ordinances the obedience of which was obligatory on every Musalman as a Musalman. We had hoped that the valid demands of the Musalmans would be attended to, and the stability of the Empire would be secured by a decision in respect of the demands in accordance with the Muslim desires. But we have come to know through newspapers that that letter has been proscribed (forfeited) in different Provinces under the Press Act. As that letter has probably not been seen by anyone, so there is a danger of mistrust and doubt. It is our duty to inform all our friends generally that that letter did not contain anything which could be objected to by any faithful Muslims or with which any just non-Muslim could not sympathise. In spite of our weakness and helplessness, we have such confidence in our truthfulness and love of justice that we shall shortly, with the help of God, gain success against this order of forfeiture in the High Courts of Nagpur and Bombay by appeal. May God help us and give us and all the country strength that we may not hesitate to utter words of truth and by serving truthfulness thus gain the blessings of religion and of the world. We are very sorry to hear that the security of Rs. 1,000 of the Mehri Nimroz Press, Bombay, has been confiscated for printing this letter and now a fresh security of Rs. 10,000 is demanded. We were never wealthy and now after four years' internment are destitute. Would that we were able to fully help Mr. Muhammad Yusaf Mazim. We request all truth-abiding friends to help them by a public subscription in which we shall take pride to join according to our ability. We request our Muslim and country brethren not to distrust us and to be the means of the betterment and improvement of religion and country after facing all the troubles and trials with endurance and truthfulness and patience. As for us

I after losing all the worldly gains for three (*sic*),
Thought that there was something better than this in store for me

Truly,
(Sd.) Shaukat 'Alī, servant of Kaaba
(Sd.) Muḥammad 'Alī, servant of Kaaba

This letter reassured its recipients, Majīd Ḥasan of *Madīnah* among them, that the letter sent to the Viceroy had been in the interests of Muslims. Since the April letter had been banned, and all issues of newspapers that published the Viceroy's letter had been proscribed, the 'Alī brothers first sought to provide reassurance to their friends in journalism of the letter's contents and their good intentions. Second, they sought to spur newspaper owners like Majīd Ḥasan to take up a collection of money for the support of Muḥammad Yusaf Mazim, of Mehri Nimroz Press in Bombay, who had been hit with an outlandish demand of a security of 10,000 rupees intended no doubt to drive him out of the business of journalism. The letter never reached Majīd Ḥasan, finding its way instead to the bowels of the Central Intelligence in the colonial archives and earning Ḥasan himself another black mark. It documents a clear sense of identification among a certain group of journalists with each other and with Islam. The 'Alī brothers certainly included *Madīnah* in a group of publications committed to a common cause. Rather than only competing with each other for the latest news, which they certainly did also, they were often publishing the same open letters with unique commentary. In this way, the Urdu newspaper conversation gathered around common nodes. It was through the efforts of the 'Alī brothers and the extensive interest in their trials that these nodes became increasingly associated with the interests of Islam.

After the end of the war in November 1918, *Madīnah* experienced an adjustment period in which it searched for new material to fill pages that had been devoted to battle updates and descriptions of casualties. Discussions of the state of Islam, coverage of national organizations such as the Home Rule Leagues, the Muslim League, and Congress, and coverage of internal district meetings all increased.[101] Gāndhī appeared in several of these articles.[102] In addition, discussions of the fallout in Turkey and the caliphate in particular took center stage.[103] On October 21, 1919, an article titled "Islam and Nationalism: The Muslim Community and Freedom and Equality" was published.[104] In it, the editors of *Madīnah* continued to outline a clear connection between the Muslim community in India and Muslims living in Turkey and other Muslim-dominated nations. In contrast to the tone of coverage prior to and during World War I, Britain had become entangled with what was by then a well-established Christian-Muslim dichotomy in Europe.

World War I had brought economic hardship to South Asia. India had contributed substantially to the war effort, and then starting in 1917 the country experienced several failed harvests. Simultaneously, the end of the war brought with it both a series of reforms that took seriously Indian claims to self-governance (the Montagu-Chelmsford Reforms) and legislation to crack down on political dissidents (the Rowlatt Act). The Montagu-Chelmsford Reforms took over a year to implement, the Rowlatt Act hardly any time at all. Had there been any doubt, this difference gave the clear impression that resistance to self-government still trumped support for it.[105]

One week after the passage of the Rowlatt Act, an editorial titled "The Difference between Peace and War: Is There Enmity between the East and West?" presented the political divide as indicative of differences between two conflicting cultures.[106] The article pointed out that the cessation of hostilities made the extension of the Rowlatt Act redundant and oppressive. The Montagu-Chelmsford Reforms were welcomed in the paper, particularly the decision to institute provincial elections. Majīd Ḥasan published an issue of the newspaper that informed readers that "the time has come for elections."[107] The word for "elections," *intikhāb*, also means "choice" in Urdu.

It arrived, the chance for elections,	the chance for the board's revolution
Like the day of reward, this election	is the day of reckoning
Every third year it returns,	a chance for the voter's proof
Congratulations today, all cities,	for old and young's chance to ask,
Venerable sir, for God's sake,	this is a chance to lose your title somewhere
Sir has arrived for inspection	This is the opportunity for victory
Use gentleness, oh Lord (sarkār)	Now is not the time for forcefulness.[108]

Ā gayā intikhāb kā moqa'	*bord ke inqilāb kā moqa'*
yih ilaikshan bhī misl-i roz-i jazā	*hai ḥisāb-o-kitāb kā moqa'*
tīsre sāl 'ūd kartā hai	*voṭron kā shabāb kā moqa'*
ho mubārak tamām shahr ko āj	*pursish-i shaikh-o shāb kā moqa'*
shaikh sāḥib kahīn khudā ke līye	*khonah duniyā khitāb kā moqa'*
sāhib ā'e hu'e hain daure mein	*hai yahī fata' bāb kā moqa'*
kām narmī se lījīye sarkār	*ab nahīn hai 'itāb kā moqa'*

The poem celebrated the advent of local elections as a result of both the Montagu-Chelmsford Report of 1918 and the Government of India Act of 1919, which established a diarchy at the provincial level. Directed at the government, it requested that leaders perform their work "gently."

As time wore on, after the passage of the Rowlatt Act, *Madīnah*, like most Urdu newspapers, grew increasingly critical of the government's failure to act with the requisite delicacy. The newspaper's tone toward the act became sardonic and indulged in sarcastic references to loyalty. In the month following the passage of the Rowlatt Act in March 1919 poetry and prose contributions described its many failings.

We have not complained—nor will we ever—about oppression,
For all our lives, whether you are loyal to us or not,
The Rowlatt Bill has been passed for India
It would be amiss if we did not divulge this secret.[109]

Shikvah-yi jaur-o jafā hamne kiyā thā nah kareiṉ
ʿumr bhar hamse vafā āp kareiṉ yā nah kareiṉ
Hind ke vāsṯe ab pās huʾā raulaṭ bil
nāmunāsib hai jo is rāz ko afshā nah kareiṉ

This poem expressed resignation at the paper's role as whistle-blower for the Rowlatt Act, which had extended wartime legislative measures, such as strict censorship practices and permitting detention without arrest, into peacetime.[110] Significantly, many prominent pieces criticizing the Rowlatt Bill were poems, all penned anonymously. Poetry may have been a more effective way of writing on sensitive topics, as Urdu verse lent itself to the emotive themes of suffering, oppression, and longing. Any attempts to avoid the ire of the censor through the use of poetry over prose were misguided, however. The *Vernacular Newspaper Reports* paid close attention to poetry as the *swadeshi* and noncooperation movements took flight.[111] Plenty of criticism appeared in prose, as well, albeit with disarmingly bland titles. One article, advertising itself as a record of governmental statistics, lambasted the Rowlatt Committee for spending 27,000 rupees transporting the president of the committee from London to India.[112] In a political environment in which increasing numbers of Indians were calling for greater participation in government, the casual expenditure of tens of thousands of rupees to outsource major governmental decisions to the British would have been profoundly unpopular.

Just as importantly, *Madīnah* capitalized at this time on its intricate knowledge of the state budget, building a reputation as a newspaper that, although ideologically rooted in a specific locality, Bijnor *qasbah*, had the expertise to bring national and international affairs into the local tea-stand or living room. In the meantime, the Khilafat Movement had begun, characterized by cooperation between Gāndhīan nationalists and British Muslims to agitate for the preservation of the authority of the Ottoman sultan as Caliph of Islam following the breakup of the Ottoman Empire at the end of World War I.

Following the passage of the Rowlatt Act, *Madīnah* became increasingly likely to express its objections as a clash between cultures, classing Hindus and Muslims together as groups whose interests were aligned in the Khilafat Movement. This attitude rested on dichotomies between European and Eastern culture, making use of the overstated reification of European culture as a method of agitating against specific abuses of the imaginary "East." A 1914 account of a lecture by Maulvī Ṣadr-ud-dīn in the United Kingdom discussing the conflicts between Islam and Christianity assisted in setting up a dichotomy between those two religions, and the theme continued to appear in the paper.[113] In 1919 Bal Gandaghar Tilak brought suit against the author Valentine Chirol for licentious statements against Indians in his book *Indian Unrest*.[114] Chirol had named Tilak "the father of Indian unrest" who manipulated the superstitions and "racial fanaticism" of India's Hindus.[115] *Madīnah*'s expression of open support for Tilak demonstrated the increasing boldness of the consolidating Urdu newspaper conversation, a solidarity that extended to a Hindu author. Both Gāndhī and the alliance with Congress were eagerly embraced in *Madīnah* in terms explicitly linked to the health of the Muslim community. *Madīnah* corrected the misconception that noncooperation was a Hindu religious concept after Gāndhī called those participating in the noncooperation protest to adhere to a 24-hour fast and day of prayer, arguing that cooperation with Gāndhī's movement was not in fact tantamount to a religious act but was rather an act of remembrance of a common cause.

> it is written that *khāmosh moqāblah* is a particular religious movement; instead it merely means tolerating difficulty, and it is a remembrance [*tazkirah*], conducted with the mind and heart. The motive of this movement is this that by tolerating oppressions [*sakhtīyān*] they should achieve reform and settle crises. In this movement it is necessary to take part in the actions of *khāmosh moqāblah* and other actions, which are taking part in all *qasbāt* and villages. In every gathering this reservation has been accepted, that the ominous laws number 1 and number 2 be taken back, in provision for freedom and life. If this is the object of desire, then this very path is the one to success.[116]

Madīnah emphasized the participation of all *qasbahs* in the action. Signficantly, it translated noncooperation or *asahayog* into the Urdu equivalent *khāmosh moqāblah* (or "silent opposition"), thus calling all *qasbahs* into a timescape in which these distinctive urban spaces stood together in solidarity with a movement that had an Urdu name.

Even while it became bold in the face of English surveillance, *Madīnah* continued to depend on news reports from English newspapers and Reuter's reports from Europe, which allowed it to provide timely international news to its readers.[117] The same technologies they depended on for access to fresh news ironically enabled effective surveillance by the British Raj central intelligence office. *Madīnah*'s contributors, who often contributed articles anonymously, commented on international news with the same tone of personal investment applied to local, Muslim affairs. For instance, *Madīnah* sharply criticized the continuation of Kaiser Wilhelm II's birthday commemoration in Holland, observing that as the monarchy had ended, so should its ceremonial trappings.[118] In this critique there were hints of a sense of propriety to the tradition of failed monarchies and empires; just as the Mughal imperial ceremonies had faded away after 1857, so should those of Kaiser Wilhelm II. Again we see the subcontinent's concerns mirrored in coverage of Europe. We also see that *Madīnah* saw itself as a commentator on world affairs, capable of documenting and commenting on global affairs as effectively as it did on local and national matters.

The Ottoman sultanate was abolished in 1922, and the caliphate abolished in 1924. Both *Madīinah*'s name and those of some of its prominent journalists had by now been established in the hearts and minds of Muslim readers throughout the Khilafat Movement. What became clear in retrospect—that the Khilafat Movement essentially ended in 1924—was not obvious at the time, as demonstrated by the continued focus on Khilafat issues that continued to animate *Madīnah* and its journalists. For years following the abolition of the caliphate, *Madīnah* and journalists who had worked on that paper continued to be preoccupied with Turkey's fate. A separate but connected legacy of this period was the fiery opposition to the government that had been kindled in the young journalists who began their journalism careers at *Madīnah* in this period. Editor Qāẓi Muḥammad 'Adīl "Abāsī" (1898–1980) had begun his life as a journalist in a fiery period of *Madīnah*'s legacy at the height of the Khilafat Movement. When he shifted to *Zamīndār* (Lahore), where the editorial team penned its columns with pens made of iron, his contributions were so extreme he once quipped "our government is very afraid of iron [*lūhe bahut ḍartī hai sarkār hamārī*]."[119] For Maulvī Nūr ul-Raḥmān (1894–1972), who would become the editor of *Madīnah* in 1928, his sympathies with the Khilafat movement were the key turning point in his intellectual life, forcing him to depart Aligarh for the life of a journalist in 1921.[120] Prior to the Khilafat Movement *Madīnah* had never been forced to yield its security deposit to the government; by the end of the 1920s Majīd Ḥasan would have had many brushes with the law. The Khilafat Movement of India had been remarkable as a moment when a nationalist movement saw the successful alliance of explicitly Muslim and Hindu voices for significant gains in the direction of self-rule. In the process of reorienting itself around involvement in the Khilafat Movement, *Madīnah* was building additional scaffolding to construct a roof of "Islam" over the houses of religious and political life.

Looking Forward from the Khilafat Movement

By the 1930s, *Madīnah* had developed an even greater degree of self-consciousness regarding its place as a world apart from urban South Asia. Upon the publication of *Angāre*, the Literary Progressive Movement's call to arms that lit the South Asian literary scene on fire, *Madīnah* retreated into its battlements and expressed gratitude for the boundaries of the *qasbah*. Perhaps the introduction of the railway in 1930 brought the inhabitants of Bijnor *qasbah* a fuller experience of the extent to which leaps in technology and shifting cultural sands could threaten their way of life. *Madīnah*'s commentary on *Angāre* is both an affirmation of the *qasbah* and its swan song to the *qasbah*'s place as a bastion for conservative Muslim ideals. While in its early years *Madīnah* had emphasized its broadening geographic horizons through international coverage, by the 1930s the newspaper was making an effort to shrink the boundaries of the *qasbah* once again.[121]

In that same decade *Madīnah* would shift permanently from its support for the Muslim League to the Congress Party, establishing links with the Jam'īat 'Ulamā-i Hind, which it would retain long after independence and the miseries of Partition. It is in the 1930s that the newspaper's *ashrāf* networks, its distinctive material and visual oeuvre, and the discourse it had developed about the difference between Muslim and European temporalities all consolidated to produce a coherent opposition to the Muslim League and even to Congress political agendas. Chapter 5 discusses how in the decade preceding independence *Madīnah* took the skills and political networks cultivated in its first two decades of publication and used them to construct alternatives to national political trends. Many of these alternatives were abortive, rendering a study of the Urdu newspaper conversation necessarily a study of forgotten remnants of a fragmented national imaginary.[122]

Notes

1. "No calamity can reach the place of solitude."
2. E.g., "*Naqshah-yi Yurop* [Map of Europe]," *Madīnah*, August 22, 1914, 8; "*Sarvīyā kā maidān-i jang*" [Serbia's Battlefield]," Madīnah, December 1, 1915; "*Naqsha-yi jang* [Map of War]," *Madīnah*, October 8, 1915.
3. Matthias Schemmel, "Preface," in *Spatial Thinking and External Representation* (Berlin: Edition Open Access, 2016). Immanuel Kant applied his argument that there was an a priori spatial knowledge to his studies of time. Matthias Schemmel, *Historical Epistemology of Space: From Primate Cognition to Spacetime Physics* (Cham: Springer, 2016); Immanuel Kant, *Metaphysische Anfangsgründe der*

Naturwissenschaft (Hamburg: Meiner, 1997), cited in Matthias Schemmel, "Towards a Historical Epistemology of Space: An Introduction," in *Spatial Thinking and External Representation: Towards a Historical Epistemology of Space*, edited by Matthias Schemmel (Berlin: Edition Open Access, 2016).

4. F. W. Buckler, "The Historical Antecedents of the Khilafat Movement," *Contemporary Review* 121 (1922), cited in Gail Minault, *The Khilafat Movement: Religious Symbolism and Political Mobilization in India* (New York: Columbia University Press, 1982), 4.
5. Gail Minault, *The Khilafat Movement: Religious Symbolism and Political Mobilization in India* (New York: Columbia University Press, 1982), 5.
6. "Indian Moslem Ideals," *Times of India*, February 4, 1914, 6.
7. Gail Minault, *The Khilafat Movement: Religious Symbolism and Political Mobilization in India* (New York: Columbia University Press, 1982), 6.
8. Margrit Pernau has written about the return to the *qasbah* context after 1857. Seema Alavi has traced the vibrant reformism inspired by the "spirit of 1857." See Margrit Pernau, *Ashraf into Middle Classes: Muslims in Nineteenth-Century Delhi* (New Delhi: Oxford University Press, 2013); Seema Alavi, *Muslim Cosmopolitanism in an Age of Empire* (Cambridge, MA: Harvard University Press, 2015).
9. Timothy Winston Childs, *Italo-Turkish Diplomacy and the War over Libya, 1911–1912* (Leiden: Brill, 1990), 29–30.
10. Timothy Winston Childs, *Italo-Turkish Diplomacy and the War over Libya, 1911–1912* (Leiden: Brill, 1990), 32–33.
11. Timothy Winston Childs, *Italo-Turkish Diplomacy and the War over Libya, 1911–1912* (Leiden: Brill, 1990), 32–33.
12. Rauf Parekh, "Allama Iqbal, Zafar Ali Khan and Zamindar," *Dawn*, July 7, 2011, http://beta.dawn.com/news/671867/allama-iqbal-zafar-ali-khan-and-zamindar; John Willis, "Debating the Caliphate: Islam and Nation in the Work of Rashid Rida and Abul Kalam Azad," *International History Review* 32, no. 4 (2010): 2.
13. Michael Llewellyn Smith, *Ionian Vision: Greece in Asia Minor, 1919–1922* (London: Allen Lane, 1973), 80.
14. Saho Matsumoto-Best, "British and Italian Imperial Rivalry in the Mediterranean, 1912–14: The Case of Egypt," *Diplomacy and Statecraft* 18, no. 2 (2007): 297–314.
15. Gail Minault, *The Khilafat Movement: Religious Symbolism and Political Mobilization in India* (New York: Columbia University Press, 1982), 10.
16. Amit Kumar Gupta, "Elitism, Factionalism and Separatism: Politics in the United Provinces, 1885–1920," *History and Sociology of South Asia* 4, no. 2 (2010): 118.
17. Christopher King, *One Language, Two Scripts: The Hindi Movement in Nineteenth Century North India* (New Delhi: Oxford University Press, 1994), 3.
18. Amit Kumar Gupta, "Elitism, Factionalism and Separatism: Politics in the United Provinces, 1885–1920," *History and Sociology of South Asia* 4, no. 2 (2010): 119.
19. Gail Minault, *The Khilafat Movement: Religious Symbolism and Political Mobilization in India* (New York: Columbia University Press, 1982), 10.
20. Press and Registration of Books Act, 1867, Act No. 25 of 1867 dated March 22, 1867, Advocate Khoj, http://www.advocatekhoj.com/library/bareacts/pressandregistration/index.php?Title=Press%20and%20Registration%20of%20Books%20Act,%201867.

21. East India (Native Press), *Copy of Opinions, and Reasons for the Same, Entered In the Minutes of Proceedings of the Council of India, Relating to the Vernacular Press Act, 1878* (Cambridge, UK: Proquest LLC, 2006).
22. Newspapers (Incitement to Offences) Act, 1908—Bare Act, LegalCrystal, https://www.legalcrystal.com/act/133985/newspapers-incitement-to-offences-act-1908-complete-act.
23. Press Act, 1910 Complete Act—Bare Act, *LegalCrystal*, https://www.legalcrystal.com/act/134062/press-act-1910-complete-act.
24. "To this heterogeneity within the community corresponds the existence of similarities between members of a community and non-members. These similarities may in turn lead to the formation of alternative communities and thus have the potential to be disruptive." Margrit Pernau, *Ashraf into Middle Classes: Muslims in Nineteenth-Century Delhi* (New Delhi: Oxford University Press, 2013), xvi.
25. Department of Criminal Intelligence, "*Al Khalil* (sic)," *Statement of Newspapers and Periodicals Published in the United Provinces during the Year 1912 [with Index]* (Simla: Government Central Branch Press, 1913), Uttar Pradesh State Archives.
26. H. R. Neville, *Bijnor: A Gazetteer* (Allahabad: Supt., Govt. Press, 1908), 107, University of Oxford, Bodleian Library.
27. Maulānā Abul Kalam Āzād, *India Wins Freedom* (New Delhi: Orient Longman, 1988).
28. John Willis, "Debating the Caliphate: Islam and Nation in the Work of Rashid Rida and Abul Kalam Azad," *International History Review* 32, no. 4 (2010): 712.
29. Abul Kalam Āzād, *al-Hilāl*, October 22, 1912, quoted (in Urdu) in Rihān Hasan, "Maulāna Āzād kī Urdu Sihāfat [The Urdu Journalism of Maulana Āzād]," *Nayā Daur* (Lucknow: Information and Public Relations Department, 2011), 31; for studies on *al-Hilāl* and Maulānā Āzād, see *The Dawn of Hope: Selections from the al-Hilāl of Maulana Abul Kalam Azad* (New Delhi: Indian Council of Historical Research, 2002).
30. Ayesha Jalal, "Striking a Just Balance: Maulānā as a Theorist of Trans-National Jihad," *Modern Intellectual History* 4, no. 1 (2007): 95–107; Ravindra Kumar, *Life and Works of Maulana Abul Kalam Azad* (New Delhi: Atlantic Publishers & Distributors, 1991); Ian Henderson Douglas, *Abul Kalam Azad: An Intellectual and Religious Biography*, ed. Gail Minault and Christian W. Troll (New Delhi: Oxford University Press, 1988); Syeda Saiyidain Hameed, *Islamic Seal on India's Independence: Abul Kalam Azad, a Fresh Look* (Karachi: Oxford University Press, 1998).
31. Syeda Saiyidain Hameed, *Islamic Seal on India's Independence: Abul Kalam Azad, a Fresh Look* (Karachi: Oxford University Press, 1998), 73.
32. Abul Kalam Āzād, *al-Hilāl*, October 22, 1912.
33. "Mahomedan Meetings: Turkey and the Powers," *Times of India*, August 4, 1913.
34. "Indian Muslim Ideals," *Times of India*, February 4, 1914.
35. "The Loyalty of Mahomedans," *Times of India*, March 27, 1914.
36. "*Vafādārī kī namāyesh: ek na'ūz be m'anī kār-ravāyī; līḏarān-i Islām kī be natījah harkat* [Professions of Loyalty: God Forbid, a Useless Action; the Pointless Action of Islamic Leaders]," *Madīnah*, April 8, 1914.
37. "*Musalmān-i hind kā vafad hiz eksalansī vāyisrāye kī khidmat meiṉ* [The Loyalty of the Muslims of India in the Service of His Excellency Vice Roy]," *Madīnah*, April 1, 1914.

38. "Medina, April 16, 1914." *Selections from Indian Owned Newspapers Published in the United Provinces 1914–1916* (Nainital: United Provinces Government, 1917), 461, Uttar Pradesh State Archives.
39. "Medina, April 15, 1914." *Selections from Indian Owned Newspapers Published in the United Provinces 1914–1916* (Nainital: United Provinces Government, 1917), 461, 472, Uttar Pradesh State Archives. "*Vafādārī kī namāyesh: eik be ma'nī kār-ravāyī; līḍarān-i islām kī be natījah ḥarkat II* [Professions of Loyalty: God Forbid, a Useless Action; The Pointless Action of Islamic Leaders: Installment II]," *Madīnah*, April 15, 1914.
40. "[The] Muslim press viewed the [Balkan] wars as evidence that the Christian powers were conspiring to crush the Ottoman Empire and the caliph of Islam." Gail Minault, *Khilafat Movement: Religious Symbolism and Political Mobilization in India* (New York: Columbia University Press, 1982), 10.
41. "*Jang-i Maidān* [Field of Battle]," *Madīnah*, May 12, 1912, 3.
42. "*Jang-i Maidān* [Field of Battle]," *Madīnah*, May 12, 1912, 3.
43. *Madīnah*, May 12, 1912, 3.
44. *Madīnah*, May 12, 1912, 11.
45. "*Raftār-i Jang* [The Speed of War]," *Madīnah*, February 25, 1917, 2.
46. "Medina, March 13, 1915." *Selections from Indian Owned Newspapers Published in the United Provinces 1914–1916* (Nainital: United Provinces Government, 1917), 298, Uttar Pradesh State Archives.
47. Timothy Winston Childs, *Italo-Turkish Diplomacy and the War over Libya, 1911–1912* (Leiden: Brill, 1990), 46.
48. Gail Minault reported that the "Muslim" press's view that the Balkan Wars and their impact on the Ottoman Empire were evidence of Christian conspiracy. While *Madīnah*'s content certainly reflected the view that political conflict involving the Ottoman Empire was indicative of a clash of civilizations, it also used access to news from Europe and the United States to establish prestige among the *qasbah* readership while successfully reaffirming its reformist principles in opposition to the "West." Gail Minault, *Khilafat Movement: Religious Symbolism and Political Mobilization in India* (New York: Columbia University Press, 1982).
49. "October 15, 1914; October 22, 1914," *Selections from Indian Owned Newspapers Published in the United Provinces 1914–1916* (Nainital: United Provinces Government, 1917), 1147, 1153, Uttar Pradesh State Archives.
50. "October 22, 1914," "Medina, April 15 1914." *Selections from Indian Owned Newspapers Published in the United Provinces 1914–1916* (Nainital: United Provinces Government, 1917), 298, Uttar Pradesh State Archives.
51. "December 1, 1914; November 8–9, 1914," *Selections from Indian Owned Newspapers Published in the United Provinces 1914–1916* (Nainital: United Provinces Government, 1917), 1215; 1316–17, Uttar Pradesh State Archives.
52. "November 8, 1914," *Selections from Indian Owned Newspapers Published in the United Provinces 1914–1916* (Nainital: United Provinces Government, 1917), 1214, Uttar Pradesh State Archives.
53. "December 8, 1914," *Selections from Indian Owned Newspapers Published in the United Provinces 1914–1916* (Nainital: United Provinces Government, 1917), 1347–48, Uttar Pradesh State Archives.

54. "December 28, 1914; January 4, 1915," *Selections from Indian Owned Newspapers Published in the United Provinces January–July 1915* (Nainital: United Provinces Government, 1917), 10, 35, Uttar Pradesh State Archives.
55. "March 8, 1913," *Selections from Indian Owned Newspapers Published in the United Provinces January–July 1913* (Nainital: United Provinces Government, 1917), 233, Uttar Pradesh State Archives.
56. Robinson has discussed the Farangi Mahalli Baḥru'l-'Ulūm Party's pro-government attitude following Turkey's entry into World War I, which it maintained in exchange for rewards from the government. Francis Robinson, *Separatism among Indian Muslims* (Cambridge: Cambridge University Press, 1974), 270–72.
57. M. Naeem Qureshi, *Pan-Islam in British Indian Politics: A Study of the Khilafat Movement, 1918–1924* (Leiden: Brill, 1999), 76.
58. M. Naeem Qureshi, *Pan-Islam in British Indian Politics: A Study of the Khilafat Movement, 1918–1924* (Leiden: Brill, 1999), 77.
59. "January 19, 1915," *Selections from Indian Owned Newspapers Published in the United Provinces January–July 1915* (Nainital: United Provinces Government, 1917), 77, Uttar Pradesh State Archives.
60. "February 1, 1915," *Selections from Indian Owned Newspapers Published in the United Provinces January-July 1915* (Nainital: United Provinces Government, 1917), 115, Uttar Pradesh State Archives.
61. "Since the time of the Prophet Muḥammad, may blessings be upon him, until recent times, all promises have been thoroughly fulfilled by Islamic rulers." See "*Jang-i Iṭalī-o Ṭurkī* [The War of Italy and Turkey], *Madīnah*, May 1, 1912, 3.
62. *Selections from Indian Owned Newspapers Published in the United Provinces January–July 1913; July–December 1913; January–July 1914* (Nainital: United Provinces Government, 1917), Uttar Pradesh State Archives.
63. "April 8, 1914," *Selections from Indian Owned Newspapers Published in the United Provinces January–July 1915* (Nainital: United Provinces Government, 1917), 431, Uttar Pradesh State Archives; *Madīnah*, April 8, 1914.
64. "Indian Muslims: Telegrams to the Viceroy," *Times of India*, November 7, 1914, 8.
65. "January–June 1915," *Selections from Indian Owned Newspapers Published in the United Provinces January - July 1915* (Nainital: United Provinces Government, 1917), 70–90, Uttar Pradesh State Archives.
66. E.g., "*Barqiyāt-i Jang* [War Telegrams]," *Madīnah*, March 13, 1917, 5.
67. "May 16, 1915," *Selections from Indian Owned Newspapers Published in the United Provinces January–July 1915* (Nainital: United Provinces Government, 1917), 506, Uttar Pradesh State Archives.
68. Megan Eaton Robb, "Women's Voices, Men's Lives: Masculinity in a North Indian Urdu Newspaper," *Modern Asian Studies* 50, no. 5 (2016): 1441–73.
69. E.g., "*Iṭalī ko eik aur mushkil darpeish* [One More Difficult Confrontation for Italy]," *Madīnah*, May 12, 1913, 3.
70. "Abu Sidq Qawi, Amrohi Correspondent," *Selections from Indian Owned Newspapers Published in the United Provinces January–July 1913* (Nainital: United Provinces Government, 1917), 107, Uttar Pradesh State Archives; Mulk ul-Kalām Abu Sidq Qauwī Amrohī, "*Nahīn̲ rahegā* [It Will Not Last]," Madīnah, February 8, 1913.

71. Sir John Malcom, "*Sache Musalmāno<u>n</u> kā tazkirah* [Lineage of True Muslims]," *Madīnah*, March 13, 1917, 3.
72. "*Īrān-o Kābul par Garmanī asar* [The Impact of Germany on Iran and Kabul]," *Madīnah*, March 5, 1917, 4.
73. "May 15, 1914," *Selections from Indian Owned Newspapers Published in the United Provinces January–July 1914* (Nainital: United Provinces Government, 1917), 585, Uttar Pradesh State Archives.
74. Much later *Madīnah* would publish glossy black-and-white advertisements for dedicated steamship lines for the performing of Hajj, *Madīnah Jūbalī Nambar 1939* [*Madīnah* Jubilee Number, 1939], Rampur Library, Akhbārāt-i Urdu Catalogue Number 533.
75. Spencer Lavan, "The Kanpur Mosque Incident of 1913: The North Indian Muslim Press and Its Reaction to Community Crisis," *Journal of the American Academy of Religion* 42, no. 2 (1974): 263–64.
76. "Indian Muslims: Telegrams to the Viceroy," *Times of India*, November 7, 1914, 8.
77. Syed Tanvir Wasti includes a quotation from Mahomed Ali's fiery response to a certain *Times* article in his piece: "Are not the Turks men? Do they not have feelings and sensibilities as other men? Look at France. Had she forgotten the claims of *revanche* nearly half a century after the loss of Alsace and Lorraine? . . . Has not the dome of its Aya Sofia, or the ancient pile of its Eski Juma or Old Mosque the same meaning for the Osmanli warrior or statesman that the Cathedral spire of Strassburg has for the French historian?" Syed Tanvir Wasti, "The Circles of Maulana Mohamed Ali," *Middle Eastern Studies* 38, no. 4 (2002): 51–62.
78. Department of Criminal Intelligence, *Statement of Newspapers and Periodicals Published in the United Provinces during the Year 1912 [with Index]* (Simla: Government Central Branch Press, 1913), 405, Uttar Pradesh State Archives.
79. Ḥasan 'Abāsur Fitrat, "*Urdu Ṣiḥāfat kī Nashīb-o Farāz*," *Nayā Daur* (Lucknow: Information and Public Relations Department, 2011), 81.
80. "July 1, 1914," in *Selections from Indian Owned Newspapers Published in the United Provinces January–July 1914; July–December 1914* (Nainital: United Provinces Government, 1917), 748, Uttar Pradesh State Archives.
81. "November 1, 1914," in *Selections from Indian Owned Newspapers Published in the United Provinces July–December 1914* (Nainital: United Provinces Government, 1917), 1192, Uttar Pradesh State Archives.
82. *Madīnah*, June 1, 1913; April 11, 1913.
83. "*Sab se zyādah us kā <u>kh</u>ayāl hai ki us daurān jang mei<u>n</u> ḥifāẓat-i hind kī tadbīrein mavāsir sābat ho<u>n</u> jis ke līye nayī faujī beheterī kī koshishei<u>n</u> ho rahī hai<u>n</u>*" (Above all there is the opinion that during that war the effect of policies for the protection of India are in evidence, for which attempts at new military improvements are occurring). "*Raftār-i jang* [Speed of War]," *Madīnah*, March 9, 1917, 2.
84. "*Inglistān kī bandash darāmad kā asar tajārat-i hind par* [The Impact of the Implementation of Prohibition on Indian Trade]," *Madīnah*, March 9, 1917, 4.
85. "*Jang-i Iṭalī-o Tarkī* [War of Italy and Turkey]," *Madīnah*, May 1, 1912, 3.
86. *Akhbar-i Islam* (Bombay), November 11, 1914; *Islamic Mail*, December 1, 1914, IOL&R, L/P&S/10/519, file 5061, cited in M. Naeem Qureshi, *Pan-Islam in British Indian Politics: A Study of the Khilafat Movement, 1918–1924* (Leiden: Brill, 1999), 75.

87. "*Maulvī Faiz Muḥammad Sāḥab*," *Madīnah*, February 17, 1917, 7.
88. "*Kashish-i Islām*," *Madīnah*, February 17,1917.
89. "*Salām Sha'ār Islām hai*," *Madīnah*, February 25, 1917, 2; "*Ādāb du'ā*," *Madīnah*, March 5, 1917, 3.
90. "*Tarkī-o Balqān*," *Madīnah*, February 25, 1917, 6.
91. "September 22, 1914," *Selections from Indian Owned Newspapers Published in the United Provinces July–December 1914* (Nainital: United Provinces Government, 1917), 1062, Uttar Pradesh State Archives.
92. "*Tarāblis mein̲ Itālvīyon kī fatah* [In the Balkans the Victory of the Italians]," *Madīnah*, February 25, 1917.
93. "*Chīn kī Islāmī Duniyā* [The Muslim World of China]," *Madīnah*, February 28, 1917, 4.
94. "February 1, 1915," *Selections from Indian Owned Newspapers Published in the United Provinces January–July 1915* (Nainital: United Provinces Government,1917), 115, Uttar Pradesh State Archives.
95. "*Khilāfat-i maz̲hab-i Islām aur Ṣiyāsī Mohār Bāt*," *Madīnah*, February 1, 1915, 3.
96. "May 16, 1915," *Selections from Indian Owned Newspapers Published in the United Provinces January–July 1915* (Nainital: United Provinces Government, 1917), 483, 530, Uttar Pradesh State Archives.
97. *Madīnah*, December 25, 1917, 4; Madīnah, January 1, 1918, 3, 5.
98. "[The Blessed Assembly of December 8]," *Madīnah*, December 3, 1917.
99. For a transcription of part of the letter to the Viceroy, see Gopal Krishna, "The Khilafat Movement in India: The First Phase (September 1919–August 1920)," *Journal of the Royal Asiatic Society of Great Britain and Ireland*, no. 1/2 (April 1968): 40.
100. The letter was written on May 22, 1919, and was circulated to several newspapers. The Persian couplet was apparently a well-known one at the time, in which the lover asks the beloved to come to the roof to watch him being killed. I have not been able to find the original letter in Urdu/Persian to determine which Persian couplet this is; I only have access to the English translation provided in the Central Intelligence File in the National Archives of India. Memorandum no. 5106, dated June 21, 1919, from the United Provinces Criminal Investigation Department, National Archives of India, Home Political Deposit 1921 SEP 50, 8–9.
101. "*Piyām-i Aman: Sulah Kānfarans kā In'eqād* [Message of Peace: The Holding of the District Conference]," *Madīnah*, January 25, 1919, 2; "*Āll In̲dia Muslim Līg aur Maslah-yi K̲h̲ilāf* [All India Muslim League and the Problem of the Caliphate]," *Madīnah*, October 9, 1919; "*Vafād Muslim Līg kī tāzah 'arzdāsht be-k̲h̲idmat vazīr-i 'azim* [Loyal Muslim League's New Appeal to the Prime Minister]," *Madīnah*, October 9, 1919, 5.
102. "*Gereftār aur Mahātmā Gāndhī ka Payām* [Arrest and the Message of Mahātmā Gāndhī], *Madīnah*, April 13, 1919, 7.
103. "*Maslah-yi Turkī* [The Problem of Turkey]," *Madīnah*, January 25, 1919, 4; "The Daily Life of the Current Kaiser of Germany," *Madīnah*, February 5, 1919, 4; "According to Turkey, the Opinion of Major Pībal," *Madīnah*, February 5, 1919, 5; "*Khilafah-yi aval kī tajārat-o sakhāvat* [The Business Generosity of the First Caliphate]," *Madīnah*, February 13, 1919, 1.

104. "*Islām aur Naishanalizam: Islāmī Qaumī-ye Hurriyat aur Musāvat* [Islam and Nationalism: The Freedom and Equality of the Muslim Community]," *Madīnah*, October 21, 1919, 2.
105. A. C. Niemeijer, *The Khilafat Movement in India* (The Hague: Martinus Nijhoff, 1972), 69–72; "[First Martyr in Freedom Movement]," *Madīnah*, November 5, 1918, 6.
106. "*Salah-o jang kī āvazaish* [The Difference between Peace and War]," *Madīnah*, March 17, 1919.
107. "*Ā gayā intikhāb kā moqa*ʿ [The Opportunity of the Election Has Arrived]," *Madīnah*, March 17, 1919.
108. "*Ā gayā intikhāb kā moqa*ʿ [The Opportunity of the Election Has Arrived]," *Madīnah*, 17 March 1919.
109. "*Raulaṭ bil aur ham* [The Rowlatt Bill and We]," *Madīnah*, April 19, 1919.
110. For other examples, see "*Qānūn-i raulaṭ bil: Eik sokhtah-dil ke qalam se* [The Rowlatt Bill Laws: From the Pen of a Grieved Heart]," *Madīnah*, April 9, 1919.
111. *Selections from the Vernacular Newspapers Published in the Punjab, North Western Provinces, Oudh, and the Central Provinces* (1900–25), National Archives of India.
112. "*B*ʿ*az sarkārī shamār vā'idād* [Some Governmental Considerations and Numbers]," *Madīnah*, April 5, 1919.
113. "October 18, 1914," *Selections from Indian Owned Newspapers Published in the United Provinces July-December 1914* (Nainital: United Provinces Government, 1917), 1114, Uttar Pradesh State Archives.
114. "*Misṭar tilak kā moqadamah-yi inglistān* [Mister Tilak's Case against England]," *Madīnah*, February 25 and March 1, 1919.
115. Valentine Chrol, "Brahmanism and Disaffection in the Deccan," in *Indian Unrest* (London: St. Martin's Street, 1910), accessed on Project Gutenberg, November 13, 2013, http://www.gutenberg.org/cache/epub/16444/pg16444.html.
116. "*Mahātmā Gāndhī aur du*ʿ*ā kā din* [Mahātmā Gāndhī and the Day of Prayer]," *Madīnah*, April 1, 1919, 3.
117. "*Barqīyāt*" [literally "Electricity," this title indicated news traveling by telegram], *Madīnah*, March 28, 1919; "*Boyir-yā aur jarman gavernmanṭ* [Boers and the German Government]"; "*Kainadā ne masāraf jang kā masūdah makamal kar līyā hai* [Canada Has Finished the Draft of War Expenditures]," *Madīnah*, April 1, 1919.
118. "*Kaisir-i jarmanī kā jashan sālgirah* [The German Kaiser's Birthday Celebration]," *Madīnah*, April 1, 1919.
119. Parvez ʿĀdil, *Tārīkh-i Madīnah Bijnor* (Rampur: Applied Books, 2018), 332.
120. Parvez ʿĀdil, *Tārīkh-i Madīnah Bijnor* (Rampur: Applied Books, 2018), 324–27.
121. *Madīnah*, February 13, 1933, 1. Translation published in Shabana Mahmud, "*Angāre* and the Founding of the Progressive Writers' Association," *Modern Asian Studies* 30, no. 2 (May 1996): 447–48.
122. Partha Chatterjee, *The Nation and Its Fragments: Colonial and Postcolonial Histories* (Princeton: Princeton University Press, 1993).

5
Provincializing Policies through the Urdu Public

In the case of Bijnor, the symbolic distance of the *qasbah* from the city allowed it first to promote League–Congress collaboration in terms of benefit to "all *qasbahs* and villages."[1] The *qasbah* timescape was significant in its distance from the city, but more importantly in its proximity to the units of community that mattered, communities crystallized by language, geography, and culture. *Madīnah*'s politics in the 1920s and 1930s were a mix of opposition to the Muslim League, support for Congress, suspicion of Westernization, and justified cooperation with Hindus, all in Islamic terms. The case study of the 1937 Bijnor by-elections demonstrates that conversations in one *qasbah* both exposed fault lines in Muslim identity and instituted a separation from the national matrix of Congress–Muslim League alignment. In the process, the paper sought to accommodate and report on a vast array of conversations relevant to Muslims, many of which have not received attention in the historiography of media prior to 1947 previously.

Newspaper Networks between *Qasbahs*

Colonial sources, even those whose purpose was surveillance, initially had dismissed local journalism in *qasbahs* as inconsequential. In Bijnor district, in 1906, the only publication distributed outside of the town of its publication was the *Upkār* of Naginah, owned and distributed by a Jat. But, as discussed in chapter 3, Bijnor district and *qasbah* invested heavily in journalism infrastructure. The district boasted six or seven lithographic presses by the end of the first decade of the twentieth century.[2] It was common for the publishers and journalists to shift from one *qasbah* to another; the proliferation of publications in this period illustrates a flourishing and flexible *ashrāf* network that stretched across communities in North India. As this network grew, it became a more significant part of the national conversation.

These papers presented a diversity of viewpoints, both individually and collectively, and could indeed appear in different political lights, depending on where they were being consumed. The *Z̲ulqarnain*, which began publication in 1905 at the Nizāmī Press in Sota Muhalla, was described by colonial surveillance

Print and the Urdu Public. Megan Eaton Robb, Oxford University Press (2021). © Oxford University Press.
DOI: 10.1093/oso/9780190089375.001.0001

as being "locally respectable, but [. . .] connected with an extreme section of Muhammadans elsewhere."[3] The isolation of the *qasbah* environment in some ways seemed to free the *qasbah* publication from identification with any specific political ideology, allowing it to adapt and contribute to several diverse contexts.

Post-Khilafat: *Madīnah* as a Member of the Nationalist Canon and Muslim Vanguard

From his humble origins on the staff of an unknown newspaper in the Punjab, followed by the family newspaper *Ṣaḥīfa*, Majīd Ḥasan had successfully capitalized on an increasing interest in national and international affairs to build his core readership in the Punjab (although only in the late 1920s and 1930s did his paper gain popularity and influence in its home district). By extension, its editors and managers gained influence as nationalist figures, in Bijnor *qasbah* and district. As early as 1919, *Madīnah*'s editor Manzuruddīn Shairkoṭī spoke at a harṭāl in the major gathering place, named Baṛa, in Bijnor *qasbah*. The meeting brought together *ta'ālīmyāftah* or educated Hindus and Muslims, with Shairkoṭī acting as a representative of the Muslim political voice in the city.[4] Even after Muslim control over the Congress party disintegrated, *Madīnah* remained the voice of both moderate and radical Muslims in the 1910s and 1920s. Although it was primarily influential as a Congress voice, it had a high degree of recognition and respect from Muslims generally, enough so that its failure to support the Muslim League after 1937 became a matter of public concern.

As a popular newspaper in the 1920s and 1930s, *Madīnah*'s political role was significant. It traced the development of the noncooperation movement, the Khilafat movement, and later the independence movement in minute detail. Its moderate stance in the late 1910s had evolved into a nationalist one in the 1920s–1930s. *Madīnah* shifted from displaying dual support for both Congress and the Muslim League to a loyalty to the Congress Party, which emphasized representing discrete Muslim interests within a Hindu-dominated political structure. *Madīnah*'s links with the branch of the Jam'īat 'Ulamā-i Hind opposed to Partition would remain long after independence and the miseries of Partition. Meanwhile, the government's increasingly oppressive attempts to clamp down on *Madīnah*'s antigovernment stance reveal, if nothing else, a colonial perception of its risk to government control (the newspaper was required to deposit a security twice, and forfeit it once, during the late 1920s and early 1930s).

As already acknowledged, it is notoriously difficult to measure the impact of words, written or spoken, on an individual or community. It is fair to say, however, that an awareness of *Madīnah* remains in the collective memory of Lucknawis, Lahoris, and *qasbatis* across North India and Pakistan. The delicate balancing act between expanding geographical horizons and an anxiety to police the boundaries of community identity persists among Muslims in South Asia today. *Madīnah* remains remarkable for its resourceful approach this challenge. *Madīnah* was adamant that local political dynamics be given priority in its pages. The following three examples of *Madīnah*'s engagement with local issues trace the way that newspaper attempted to offer viable alternatives to national political narratives over time. This attempt met with varying levels of success.

Madīnah and the Octroi Tax

Madīnah took a long time to gain traction in Bijnor *qasbah*—it was first popular in large cities, then as Majīd Ḥasan's profile increased the popularity filtered back into the locality where it was produced. Even before it gained national prominence the paper arbitrated controversy on local issues, by rallying support among *ashrāf* and presenting a unified front of Muslim opinion to government observers. *Madīnah*, when it concerned itself with local *qasbah* issues, tended to do so as means either to discuss issues of broader geographical importance or to influence local educational and electoral policies that might affect the daily life of the gentry. It also often published "local" news from other *qasbah*s, enacting its alliance with a broader *qasbah*-born community.

Between 1914 and 1916 *Madīnah* and Ḥasan's other publication *Ṣaḥīfa* both published editorials opposing the imposition of a municipal tax and the removal of an octroi duty.[5] The opposition was ultimately unsuccessful,[6] but in the midst of its efforts *Madīnah* printed an article by the joint secretary for the Public Committee in Moradabad, Mirzā Isḥāq Beg, opposing the imposition of a House Tax and requesting a rise in octroi duty instead.[7] Octroi duties were the main form of revenue collected by municipal councils in Bombay, Punjab, and the United and Central Provinces. It was a duty levied on the movement of goods into a district, town, or city, usually impacting the "tillers of land." The tax could be paid either in the form of cash or goods, and it dated from the Mughal period. By the beginning of the nineteenth century, when Bijnor district came into British ownership, the octroi tax instead began to be used for municipal purposes.[8] However, in the early 1910s the Bijnor municipal board proposed to shift from octroi duty, which targeted landowners importing goods into cities and towns, to a house tax, which would provide a direct form of taxation on all members of the *qasbah*, instead of only landowners. Providing a more stable revenue stream to municipal board members was one of the stated aims.

An editorial in *Madīnah* portrayed the act as a sign of municipal members' greed, proclaiming a gap between the will of "the people of Bijnor" and "the ears of government."[9] The editorial's aim was twofold: first, to mobilize readers to "use the power they possess"—in this context probably leveraging connections and bending the ears of influential people—in order to work against the proposed house tax. Second, however, *Madīnah*'s editors spoke over the heads of lay readers directly to the censors who were monitoring the Indian vernacular press. The editorial, anonymously penned by a member of the small editorial board, represented its views as those of the Muslim population. Because of *Madīnah*'s circulation, the editorial had the potential to influence policy not only locally but also in *qasbah*s across the western United Provinces (UP). On the one hand, it is clear from surveillance records that the British government registered *Madīnah* and *Ṣaḥīfa*'s opposition to the replacement of the octroi tax with a house tax.[10] However, the tide against the octroi was too strong for protests to register. Although the octroi had been levied in seventy-seven towns in 1874–1875, by 1914–1915 the government only levied the tax in thirty-seven towns in the United Provinces.[11] That form of taxation was on its way out, and the house tax remained in force in Bijnor. Nevertheless the surveillance demonstrates that *Madīnah* had already become, in the eyes of surveillance officials, one of a number of voices representative of the local concerns of northwest United Provinces. *Madīnah* and *Ṣaḥīfa* both embraced and cultivated this role, not only calling for changes to Bijnor's local policies but also insisting, even when the case was hopeless, that exceptions made for Bijnor should be applied to the national context as a rule.[12] While in this case *Madīnah*'s efforts to retain the octroi tax failed, the paper would be more successful in its next major attempt to influence national policy: when it took up the issue of local access to affordable grain.

Local Grain for Local Gain

Madīnah and other *qasbah* newspapers were successful in pressuring the government to change local policies regarding grain prices in Bijnor during World War I. Media coverage in *Madīnah* during World War I reflected a concern with exploitation of local grain markets. Complaints opposed the government's refusal to fix rates of interest and their allowing the private export of grain at the expense of local need.[13] *Madīnah*'s objections to grain prices, along with the protestations of other newspapers, regularly appeared in British surveillance records. Bijnor district was not alone in suffering high grain prices. The 1909 Settlement Report for neighboring Moradabad mentions the drastic transformation occurring in rental systems as a result of skyrocketing grain prices.[14] The initial cause of rising prices in Bijnor in 1908 would have been flooding from the monsoon, which also contributed to fatalities from waterborne illnesses. Although the harvests in the first years of World War I were better, war conditions and inadequate internal transportation kept prices high.[15] The government-supported transition from grain to cash rents, implemented in Amroha in this period, had not yet taken hold in Bijnor.[16] While sugarcane and cotton crops were administered using cash rents, other crops in Bijnor were split between the landlord and the tenant. This made it difficult to assess agricultural revenue in the district, and may have slowed the process of developing adequate protections for landowners and tenants alike after the start of World War I. Regardless of the reason, government protections failed to solidify. Editorials in *Madīnah* included suspicion of corruption and typical references to the threat of "disturbances" if no action were taken.[17] By early 1915, the British had prohibited private exports of grain and published a *communiqué* on the subject of grain prices. *Madīnah* published an editorial praising governmental efforts, affirming its own influence as a key factor in the legislation as well as providing the British with proof of its responsiveness to the threat of instability. Along with praise, however, *Madīnah* pushed the government to follow through on the results of the *communiqué*, expressing fears that it would find the same fate as the Articles of Commerce Ordinance, which the government had failed to translate into practice.[18] *Madīnah*'s coverage of the controversy regarding grain prices in Bijnor not only reflected the perception among Indians that the government was exploiting local economies for the benefit of the international market. The coverage also demonstrated *Madīnah*'s role as watchdog for the *qasbah*'s immediate locality when its concerns intersected with those of the *ashrāf* without landholdings. The voices in the newspaper reminded readers of the *qasbah* locality, where educated and landless elite stood watchful over government policies threatening to disenfranchise them. Closer to the sources of agricultural production than papers in large cities, which commented less frequently on these issues, papers like *Madīnah* deployed their far-flung status as a bid to authentic representation. *Madīnah* further identified itself as a representative voice of "the Muslim Press" from an early stage.[19]

Bijnor and the Redrawing of Electoral Lines, 1913–1931

Elections were a controversial issue in Bijnor district, as in other cities and municipalities around India. The year 1910 saw national recommendations to limit voting to Muslims who could meet a certain bar of wealth. Muslim *ashrāf* in Bijnor objected to the disadvantage that such rules would pose to Muslims in the *qasbah*. After a subsequent enquiry, the Commissioner of Rohilkhand ruled, "under the higher standard of qualifications the Muhammadans would be at a disadvantage for orders."[20] The table in Appendix II demonstrates the process of negotiation that the Muslim gentry of Bijnor undertook in order to maintain the influence of their numerical majority in the *qasbah*. The discussion in the UP Municipal Records reveals that Muslims crafted their objections in order to maintain a numerical majority of Muslims among the electorate. At the time of the proposed alterations to voter eligibility, the population of Bijnor *qasbah* was 53 percent Muslim and 45 percent Hindu. Under the proposed amendment, Bijnor would have 227 Hindu electors and 405 Muslim electors. Under the conditions the Muslim negotiators proposed, the number of *qasbati*s eligible to vote would amount to 167 Hindus and 418 Muslims. The objection resulted in the interpretation most favorable to Muslims, with the larger majority retained.

Later, controversy surrounding the redrawing of electoral districts motivated Majīd Ḥasan to file an official objection to a 1931 proposal to separate the electorate of Bijnor *qasbah* into nine districts, five Muslim and four non-Muslim, to reflect the distribution of the population. Although at the time of the proposal's passage, the municipality board had five Muslim and four non-Muslim members, local authorities were concerned that "[this] system has had the effect of creating inter-*moḥalla* (neighborhood) rivalries and animosities due obviously to there being only one constituency for the whole municipality." Colonial officials were eager to prove that the distribution of electoral seats would not change with census results; the delineation of electoral wards would stand regardless of the relative growth of each religious community's population.[21] The reconstitution of electoral districts in Bijnor mirrored a similar process occurring in *qasbah*s and cities across North India in 1931. Colonial officials scrambled to put the orders into effect before the elections of the same year,[22] in order to successfully establish divisions between religious communities, reduce the risk of communal violence, and undermine collective action.

Manuscript accounts of Majīd Ḥasan's objections mention how a small section of the *qasbah* called Civil Lines, where Hindus lived, was bestowed with its own electoral district under the new system. The suggestion seems to be that the districts had been gerrymandered to privilege Hindus. The section of Bijnor where a large concentration of Muslims, including Majīd Ḥasan, lived was referred to as the "mohalla *Qasbah*."[23] This section of Bijnor had been divided into three sections under the new system, weakening its collective power, according to Majīd Ḥasan. The internal papers regarding the issue were dismissive of Majīd Ḥasan's objections, declaring there to be no case for any amendment to the process.

The description of the Muslim and non-Muslim neighborhoods offers some information about the composition of the *qasbah*. Muslims and Hindus lived in separate sections of the *qasbah*; the *moḥallas* surrounding the Jama Masjid and the Idgah were predictably Persian in character, sporting the names "Kazipara" and "Shimali." *Moḥallas* in non-Muslim voter areas included more areas ending in "ganj," a Hindi suffix indicating a market area. However, another Kazipara mohalla cropped up in the first non-Muslim voting ward, and a mohalla named

Palmerganj remained in the third Muslim voting ward. Furthermore, officials were forced to use markers as arbitrary as a flight of stairs or pillars in personal gardens to separate a Muslim mohalla from a Hindu one.[24] By using a road bordering the Jama Masjid, or Bijnor's largest mosque, as one of the dividing lines between the first and second voting wards, the plan drew an invisible division through the heart of the Muslim *qasbah* community, which formed the heart of Majīd Ḥasan's opposition to the proposal. However, Majīd Ḥasan was not the only *qasbati* to weigh in on the debate regarding the election wards, and attitudes varied. Nawab Mohammad Yusuf, a minister for local self-government in Nainital, wrote a letter in support of the electoral districts.[25]

These electoral tensions were rooted in the late eighteenth and early nineteenth centuries. As the princely states had declined with the advent of the East India Company, Muslim *t'āluqdārs* and *zamīndārs* had emerged as a force to be reckoned with in Awadh, but to a much lesser extent in Rohilkhand.[26] While these landed elites in general embodied aspects of Indo-Persian culture, their demographics in Awadh were more heavily Muslim than in Rohilkhand. In both regions, *t'āluqdārs*' influence was rooted in their majority ownership of land, which they then leased to laborers in exchange for rent and a share in the profits. The *t'āluqdār*'s emergence as a powerful figure started with the award of land grants in 1859, commissioned by Governor-General Charles Canning (1811–1879).[27] These administrators became allied with the British to obtain new sources of income, which contributed to the vitality of *qasbah* culture. The exact conditions of tenures varied in each district, as did the demographic composition of *t'āluqdārs*.

The resulting difference in distribution of land between west and east UP was stark. In west UP, Hindu moneylenders gained ownership over land at rates that far outstripped Hindu moneylenders in east UP. This meant that Muslim *zamīndārs* and other members of the so-called conservative classes felt a greater pinch from the inroads into land ownership made by Hindus in west UP, which explained in part the greater tendency toward communal attitudes regarding land ownership in that half of the province. Here competition for power tended to fall along communal lines.[28]

Perhaps because of the success that Muslims had in redrawing voting district lines to Muslim advantage in other districts,[29] *Madīnah* was very involved in the debates to redraw election lines in the 1910s—ultimately with little success. In Bijnor, "where Hindus dominated the board" in 1903 the Hindu kotwal (chief police officer or town magistrate) arranged for the thrashing of Muslim butchers who sold beef in the marketplace.[30] The limited success of Muslims in preventing the shift of power to Hindu traders and landowners in Bijnor may explain why in that *qasbah* it was important to present newspapers as part of a Muslim public sphere.

Madīnah and the Election of 1937

Bijnor *qasbah*'s isolation, its aura of authenticity, and its Muslim character all came under the microscope during the election of 1937, when Ḥāfiẓ Ibrāhīm switched party affiliations from the Muslim League to Congress and was forced to run for re-election as a result. It is in the by-election of 1937 that we see most clearly the power of the discursive distance separating *qasbah* from city, demonstrating that the force of authentic isolation is strongest in times of extended intimacy or overlap.

The late 1930s famously saw a series of elections that provoked UP nationalists to hash out their approaches to the Muslim League and Congress. Recent scholarship has brought to light a number of new sources that highlight the centrality of the categories of "Muslim," "Hindu," and even "apostate" in these electoral battles.[31] In 1937 one of the most prominent politicians in Bijnor briefly became one of the most controversial politicians in the UP, as the link between Islam and political identity became a point of contention the first of four by-elections that occurred late in the year. Ḥāfiẓ Ibrāhīm had won his provincial seat on a Congress ticket, running unopposed in late 1936 and early 1937. After his victory, he defected from the Muslim League to Congress, earning a minister position in the process.[32] After Ḥāfiẓ Ibrāhīm switched party affiliations from the Muslim League to Congress, his appointment to a Minister position caused an outcry, which several months later led to his resignation and pursuit of re-election on the Congress ticket proper.[33] He was opposed by a League candidate and local lawyer, Khān Bahādur ʻAbduṣ Samiḥ. The coverage of the election by national English-language papers like the *Times of India* and Hindi-language papers like *Hindustan* naturally varied. The narrative transmitted by national news sources emphasized the uncertainty of the election and the role of religion in determining the result. The coverage in the nationally oriented papers posed a contrast to the coverage of the *qasbah* newspaper network, which at this point was definitively led by *Madīnah*.

Ḥāfiẓ Ibrāhīm was the central figure in the 1937 election upset. Newspaper evidence indicates that Congress embraced Ibrahim's success as a "test case" for their mass contact campaign, while the League demurred, citing a lack of League infrastructure in the district.[34]

If we look at Ḥāfiẓ Ibrāhīm not only as a test case for the mass contact campaign, but also as a test case for local *qasbah* political norms, analysis of the by-election demonstrates that the *qasbah* was one of the crucial spaces where Muslim support for Congress and opposition to the League gained a robust theorization. A significant aspect of the norms of the political *qasbah* was temporal; by this I mean that authoritative and institutional representations of time produced social rhythms in the *qasbah* that stood at odds with the national, urban space. This temporality was characterized not by the "abstract time-reckoning of capitalism," in the words of Laura Bear,[35] but instead by habits and everyday occupations. Time in the *qasbah* was grounded in the everyday, continuously sewn together with the past.

Coverage of the election suggested that the majority rural population of the district (70 percent as opposed to 30 percent of the population considered urban) were "people to which politics means very little."[36] This external coverage was dismissive of political alliances in such a far-flung place as Bijnor and dovetailed with the suspicion, widespread in the national press, that religion, defined as affiliation with an *'alim* and his following, was all that mattered in the election. National coverage speculated about who would be able to mobilize religious affiliation among the presumably uneducated and uninformed voters. Details reported are unusual to the point of being questionable in veracity. For instance, supporters of both Congress and the Muslim League were reported to wear green shorts with the inscription "Allahu Akbar"—Congress shorts having a Congress flag, and League shorts having an image of a crescent and star in place of the flag.[37] Urban journalists indicated that the small town, the village, or the *qasbah* was seen by Congress supporters a symbol of a backward insistence on the importance of religion over national unity, or as simply politically irrelevant. The election coverage in local Urdu press, in contrast, was far less focused on competition between rival *'ulamā* and more on retaining the local freedom to determine the role of religion in public life. It was also characterized by a derision for the idea that the League could win in two weeks of campaigning an influence comparable to that which Ḥāfiẓ Ibrāhīm had secured over many years of service. Depth of service and embedding in the timescape of the *qasbah* correlated with power.

Before Ḥāfiẓ Ibrāhīm announced that he was running for re-election under the auspices of Congress, he was heavily criticized for failure to do so.[38] *Madīnah*, having the reputation of being pro-Congress, published an article including a statement by Ḥāfiẓ Ibrāhīm himself, written in response to the concerns of Jinnah,[39] and in its introduction to Ibrahim's statement, *Madīnah* observed that the politician did seem to be tacitly indicating he was ready to run against Jinnah. The matters of direct concern for Ḥāfiẓ Ibrāhīm included the Muslim League's new policy of opposition to Congress and a related issue, the Muslim League's claim to represent Muslims exclusively. Ḥāfiẓ Ibrāhīm also emphasized the shift in leadership away from those individuals in whom Ḥāfiẓ Ibrāhīm had placed trust, among them Chaudhri Khaliquzzaman.

In opposing Jinnah and favoring Ḥāfiẓ Ibrāhīm, the local Urdu press focused on Jinnah's attempt to elide the boundary between public life and private religious life. In this context, the way Ḥāfiẓ Ibrāhīm's statement in *Madīnah* characterized Jinnah's approach focuses on the public/private distinction in politics, making use of the English term *pablik*:

> Pandit Jawaharlal and other Congress leaders were in favor of the League candidates, but even before the end of the election Mr. Jinnah and the president of Congress had become opponents regarding who would contest the Muslim seat of Congress. So one fine morning Mr. Jinnah, in front of the whole world, presented this view, that Muslim political science (*siyāsiyāt*) is a thing particularly his and his alone (*un kī ma<u>kh</u>ṣuṣ chīz hai*) and whoever will challenge him (*us kī ṯaraf naẕar uṭhākar deikhe gā*) is both his personal enemy as well as the public's enemy (*ẕātī aur pablik*). This is a strange view and absolutely contrary to the principles of political science. Congress is a political organization and its policy has an effect on every Indian and every Hindu and Muslim, and it is its duty to try to build support for its policy among all without discrimination for color and race; this thing is the root of the current fight.[40]
>
> *Panḍit Jawāharlāl aur dīgar kāngrisī līḍron̲ ke umīdvāron̲ kī ta'īd bhī kī magar aleikshan ke i<u>kh</u>titām se qabl hī misṯar jinnāḥ aur ṣadr kāngris mein̲ kāngris kī muslim staiṭ par laṛne ke līye i<u>kh</u>tilāf ho gayā chunānchah eik <u>kh</u>ush-gavār ṣubḥ ko misṯar jinnāḥ ne dunīyā ke sāmne yih naẕar yih peish kīyā kih muslim sīyāsat un kī ma<u>kh</u>ṣuṣ chīz hai aur jo ko'ī bhī us kī ṯarf naẕar uṭhākar deikhe gā voh un kā ẕātī aur pablik donon̲ kā dushman hai. Yih eik 'ajīb-o <u>gh</u>arīb naẕariyah hai aur sīyāsīyāt ke uṣūlon̲ ke bilkul <u>kh</u>ilāf hai. Kāngris eik sīyāsī anjuman hai aur uskī pālīsī se hindū-musulmān aur har hindūstānī par a<u>s</u>ar paṛtā hai aur* (word illegible) *yih uskā farẕ hai kih voh har hindūstānī ko bilā imtīyāz-i rang-o nasl apnī pālīsī kā hamnawā banānekī koshish kare goyā maujūdah jhagṛe kī binā yahī chīz hai.*[41]

It is important to understand what Ḥāfiẕ Ibrāhīm meant by the term "*ẕātī*"—it meant personal or intimate, probably alluding to personality politics. To Ibrahim, Jinnah had dyed his forceful political persona a religious hue, running contrary to the ideals of *adab*, which emphasized intellect and even self-effacement. *Ẕātī* also referred to a distinction between public politics, in which religion had a limited role, and private life, where religion was paramount. The mention of Chaudhri Khaliquzzaman was significant, since his name was synonymous with the height of *adab*.[42] Implicit in Ḥāfiẕ Ibrāhīm's critique is the accusation that Jinnah lacked the leadership quality and indeed the respectability of a man like Chaudhri Khaliquzzaman or Ḥāfiẕ Ibrāhīm's own mentor, Maulānā Ḥusain Aḥmad Madanī.

1937 was a turning point for Madanī, who began the year campaigning heavily for the League in his capacity as representative of the Jam'iat 'Ulamā-i Hind, but by the end of the year became disappointed at the League's thankless attitude after the Jam'iat 'Ulamā-i Hind had helped it win the election. Madanī had received assurances that the League would defer to the Jam'iat in religious matters following the election and therefore expected there to be no conflict in his maintaining a relationship with both the League and the Congress. The League ultimately did not honor the promise it had made to defer to *'ulamā* in religious matters.[43] And, as is well known, following the election, the League insisted that Congress should not nominate any Muslims to its ministries, seeking to appoint only those Muslims who were League representatives. Congress declined this request, in effect refusing to form an alliance with the League, and the League as a result embarked on its "mass contact" campaign. At this point, the battle lines were drawn and Muslims like Ḥāfiẓ Ibrāhīm were increasingly pressured to choose between alliance with Congress or the League. Metcalf has written that Jinnah's failure to honor his promise to defer to *'ulamā* in relevant issues before the legislature after the 1937 elections, and his dismissive attitude to the concerns about his broken promises, in Madanī's estimation demonstrated a flawed character. By the end of the year, Madanī had become a proponent of Composite Nationalism. In the statement that Madanī's protégé Ḥāfiẓ Ibrāhīm penned in *Madīnah*, he criticized his opponent.

> Mr. Jinnah is now trying by every method to safeguard his "rights" [to represent Muslims], but we people who want to look at the events without any bias cannot obtain correct guidance from the personal political theory of Mr. Jinnah. Even now we will abide by some principles.[44]
>
> *Misṭar jinnāḥ ab apne "ḥaqūq" ke ḥifẓ ke līye har koshisein̲ kar rahe hain̲, magar ham log jo bag̲h̲air kisī jānibdārī ke vāqi'āt ko dek̲h̲nā chāhtī hain̲ misṭar jinnāḥ kī z̤ātī sīyāsīyāt se hidāyat nahīn̲ ḥāṣil kar sakte. Hamārī ba'ẓ uṣūl hain̲ ham ab bhī un par qāyim hain̲.*

Ḥāfiẓ Ibrāhīm's letter in *Madīnah* was his attempt to speak directly to voters, to explain his decision and his willingness to seek an additional mandate in the face of "Mr. Jinnah's" anger, but his disdain for Jinnah's character seeped through. Even the repeated appellation of "Mister" before Jinnah, with no appellation after, much less a *nisba*, seemed designed to paint Jinnah as Westernized, and by extension an outsider to the *adab* of the local politician.

In the same issue of *Madīnah* there was an article titled "Mahatma Gāndhī's Newest Guidance (*hidāyāt*) for Congress Ministers."[45] The implication was clear: the paper supported Mahātmā Gāndhī's authority to issue guidance and considered Mr. Jinnah patently unqualified. *Madīnah* also published responses to Jinnah's protests against Ḥāfiẓ Ibrāhīm from Rajendra Prasad[46] and Maulānā Āzād.[47] Prasad and Āzād focused not on the issue of Ḥāfiẓ Ibrāhīm's campaign—*Madīnah* and many locals remained confident that the long-entrenched public servant would win the day—but instead on the general issue of the Muslim

League's claim to a monopoly on issues of Muslim representation. Rajendra Prasad in particular stated that Jinnah had agreed that each appointment or officeholder should be determined on the basis of "*infirādī haiṣīyat*," or "individual standing." Individual standing referred to records of service (*k͟hidmāt*), not only to the Muslim *qaum* but to the *mulk*—which could mean nation, but which probably in this case was intended to refer to territory or region. Prasad stated that Jinnah had agreed that they would decide together which Muslims should take office in government, and he echoed Congress's rejection of the Muslim League's claim to preside over appointments for any Muslim members of the Congress majority government as an exclusive right of Muslim representation.[48]

This newspaper conversation was not only a rebellion against being compelled to choose between Congress and the League but also a debate about the nature of political authority. *Madīnah*'s coverage tended to argue that political authority should reside in the individual and his qualities, and his service to a locality above all, rather than primarily in his religious label. Adherence to a primary concern with religion, it was suggested, would be both ideologically incorrect and counterproductive to UP's Muslims, who had long accepted that they must work either alongside or against Hindus and had determined that working alongside was preferable. Shortly after this conversation appeared in *Madīnah* Ḥāfiẓ Ibrāhīm resigned and fulfilled his promise to seek a new mandate from his Congress voters—once he was reasonably confident he could win re-election. 'Abduṣ Samiḥ' was nominated on October 8 for an election on October 27.

Bijnor *qasbah* was a strong influence in the outcome of the Bijnor district election. In the last few days before the election, the *qasbah* that the *Times of India* referred to as "the small town of Bijnor" became ground zero for political activity in the district. Its streets experienced a parade of national figures and the daily chanting of slogans[49]—causing enough disturbance that *Madīnah*'s election coverage section was "On the Election Tumult (*Hangāmah*)." On October 20, Muḥammad 'Alī Jinnāh stopped by on his way to Calcutta.[50] On October 21, a band of Khudai Khidmatgars came to Bijnor and were targeted by an alleged bomb attack—later proven to be a stray firecracker that fell from the roof of a neighboring house. The rumor of the attack, along with a report that a Congress worker had been stabbed on a train running between Bijnor and Najibabad,[51] only served to increase the popularity of Congress before the arrival of 'Abdul G͟haffār K͟hān on October 24.[52] Immediately before this, on October 22, two competing rallies were held in Bijnor *qasbah*. The Congress meeting boasted Maulānā Ḥusain Aḥmad Madanī, Sir Wazīr Ḥasan, and Pandit Jawaharlal Nehru (who motored in to speak and then left immediately for Chandpur to speak again) and attracted 8,000 people.[53] The *qasbah* was crawling with special police assigned to prevent more incidents of violence, as "feelings [were] running high."[54]

The English-language press, primarily the *Times of India*, reported as if the ʻ*ulamā* were the primary influencers of the 1937 election. In one corner, fighting on the side of Congress, were the Jamʻīat ʻUlamā-i Hind of Delhi, led by Maulānā Ḥusain Aḥmad Madanī, Maulānā Aḥmad Saʻīd, Muftī Kifāyatullah, and Maulānā Hifẓur Raḥmān Sīyuhārvī (early that year in the 1937 elections proper Madanī had been campaigning for the League).[55] In the other corner, fighting on the side of the Muslim League, were the ʻ*ulamā* of Farangi Mahal, including Muftī Inayātullah, Maulānā Sibghatullah, and Jamāluddīn Mīyān, as well as Maulānā Shaukat ʻAlī, Maulānā Ḥasrat Mohānī, and Khwāja Ḥasan Nizami.[56] In the lead-up to the election, in response to the mobilization of ʻ*ulamā* by Congress, the Muslim League were said in some news reports to have imported their own false mystic from Lahore, Ferozuddīn, who pretended to be a saint in order to win over the inhabitants of Chandpur to the League cause. News reports in the *Times* claimed "all [Ferozuddin] does is to sit under a tree dressed in saffron clothes and tell beads from sunrise to sunset and wear a false beard to cover up the fact that he was clean-shaven.[57] This account portrayed the Muslim League as engaged in an embarrassingly last-ditch effort to shore up its false claim to authenticity—attempting to offer a make-believe front of piety designed to appeal to locals. This urban newspaper also reported that the faux shaikh had already gathered a handful of followers, suggesting the gullibility of Bijnor locals. This account, like the account of shorts printed with a badge of *Allahu-Akbar*, may have been embellished by reporters. Since the same reporting indicated that a pro-Congress ʻ*alim* in Kiratpur had threated to "excommunicate" any followers who did not vote for Congress, this sort of coverage about ʻ*ulamā* did not seem to undermine any particular political party, but instead it seemed calculated to characterize the electorate of Bijnor as biddable and overdependent on religious leaders for political stances in general.[58]

National-level English-language media were understandably concerned with the role of the by-election in the fate of the national parties. However, by this point *Madīnah* was a national newspaper in its own right, being distributed across India as well as internationally.[59] So *Madīnah* was a new kind of national paper, one targeted to the masses in Urdu, which simultaneously served as a medium by which the ʻ*ulamā* exercised its influence and offered a space for reflection and conversation by leaders and common Muslims in Bijnor district on the important issues. *Madīnah*'s inclusion of first-person essays from prominent political as well as religious figures makes it clear that it had the prestige to host interactions among important contributors.

It is difficult to determine how much of a role the press played in Congress's victory in Bijnor district. In practical terms, the Muslim League district division had neither a secretary nor president, and the national leadership had been busy planning their central meeting in Lucknow, while Congress leadership was putting effort into the groundwork for Ḥāfiẓ Ibrāhīm's campaign.[60] *Madīnah*'s coverage may have contributed to the evolution of attitudes toward Congress and the League as much as it sought to report on them. The word *ẕātī* emerged repeatedly, either to describe the limited influence of the challenger Abid Sami',[61] or as a term that undermined the credibility of Jinnah's approach to politics.[62] What *Madīnah* newspaper emphasized repeatedly was the importance of considering Ḥāfiẓ Ibrāhīm's individual role in the district: his connections, his service to community, and his previous electoral successes. *Madīnah* predicted two weeks before the election that without a doubt Ḥāfiẓ Ibrāhīm would win; its prediction was of course correct.

Once *Madīnah*'s prediction of Ḥāfiẓ Ibrāhīm's victory in the by-election came to pass, disgruntled League supporters complained that the five-month delay before he resigned had allowed Ḥāfiẓ Ibrāhīm to consolidate his support in the district before standing for election under the auspices of Congress.[63] Congress and the League moved on quickly to three December by-elections in other UP districts—Moradabad, Saharanpur, and Bulandshahr—which the League won.[64]

Some Muslim League slogans and reports from this by-election suggested Ḥāfiẓ Ibrāhīm had committed apostasy by going to temple and applying Hindu marks to his forehead and that he was committed to shutting down mosques.[65] The League was attempting to deploy its supposed monopoly on Muslim representation by assuming the authority to brand Muslim Congress members apostates, or *kufr*. But their attempts were undercut by pro-League leaders' extensive experience fostering and selling inter-religious collaboration during the Khilafat movement. Significantly, *Madīnah* published articles by the pro-League Shaukat 'Alī that laid out theological grounding for working with nonbelievers.[66] It is unclear why Shaukat 'Alī would make the pronouncement that "*dushman bhī dost ho saktā hai* [even an enemy can be a friend]" in the context of Muslim cooperation with Congress, with the Bijnor election so close, and with his own party actively discouraging cooperation with a Hindu-dominated Congress. It is possible that this article was taken out of context from earlier writings by Shaukat 'Alī, since its pro-cooperation stance doesn't fit with his commitment to the League as of late 1937.[67] At any rate, the article raised the possibility of working with Congress members *even if* they might be *kufr* and underlined the perceived hypocrisy of League leaders in previously supporting cooperation between Muslims and Congress before suddenly closing ranks in the 1937 by-elections. This observation complicates Venkat Dhulipala's argument that the League used the label *kufr* as a polarizing mechanism; in fact, pro-Congress as well as pro-Muslim League leaders were concerned to discuss the implications of cooperating with non-Muslims, employing the term *kufr* in that open-air discussion.[68]

Whose Islam? Whose Culture?

Reading *Madīnah*'s election coverage complicates our picture of the identities and alignments at play during this period. It shows that Islam was the language not only of Muslim League proponents but also of influential supporters of Congress, including *Madīnah*'s writers and editors. And those writers and editors did not appreciate the League's tactics. This was made abundantly clear when, during the election, Khwaja Ḥasan Nizami published leaflets asserting that Muslims would be untouchables under a Hindu Raj: the newspaper *Madīnah* had taken him to court.[69] While it is clear that religion was of paramount importance to the voters of Bijnor district that *Madīnah* claimed to represent, they did not subscribe to the constraints of Jinnah's definition of Islamic "culture." Instead, they were fiercely defensive of the legitimacy and importance of a range of local variations of Islam.

> After all, *which* culture is this whose slogans are raised [emphasis mine]? Often the name of Islamic culture is invoked. In "culture" [*kalchar*] there is an extremely important thing, language. All of us—Bengali, Hindustani, Pashto, Balochi, Mandhi, Marathi, Gujarati, Punjabi, Telugu, Malayali—we all speak the language of our linguistic circle. And Islamic culture's language is Arabic. Even if we accept that the culture that is associated with Hindustani Muslims is indeed *the* Islamic Culture (*Islāmī Kalchar*), even then there is no single culture of Muslims. The language, lifestyle (*ṯarz-i rehā'ish*), and socialization (*mo'āsharat*) of Muslims of every province are distinct; every person's economic, political and social background is different and opposed. The people who invoke the name culture, what type or which mode of culture do they want to protect after all? Perhaps it is that very one in which Muḥammad 'Alī Jinnāh has been raised, that which Muḥammad 'Alī Jinnāh has managed to protect. If the common Muslim has any connection to this culture and if indeed this culture is the same as "Islamic culture," then by all means lend Mister Jinnāh a hand in its protection.[70]

Āk̲h̲ir yih kaunsā kalchar hai jis ki na're boland hote haiṉ. Aks̲ar islāmī kalchar kā nām bhī līyā jātā hai. Kalchar meiṉ eik bahut hī ahim chīz zabān hai. Āp aur ham sāre Bingālī, Hindūstānī, Pashto, Balochī, Sindhī, Marhaṭī, Gujrātī, Panjābī, Teileigū, Malāyām y'anī apne lisānī ḥalqah kī zabān bolte haiṉ. Aur islāmī kalchar kī zabān 'Arbī hai. Agar ham yih bhī mān leṉ kih joh kalchar Hindūstānī musalmānoṉ se vābastah hai usī kā nām islāmī kalchar hai, jab (sic)[71] *bhī musalmānoṉ kā eik kalchar nahiṉ hai. Har ṣūbah (sic) ke musalmānoṉ kī zabān, ṯarz-i rahā'ish, mo'āsharat judā judā; har shak̲h̲s kā ma'āshī, sīyāsī, aur samājī pas manẓar muk̲h̲talif aur mutaẓād (hai). Kalchar ke yih nām laivā āk̲h̲ir kis qism aur kis ṭarz ke kalchar kī ḥifāẓat karnā chāhte hain̲? Shāyad yih kalchar vahī hogā jis mein̲ misṭar Muḥammad 'Alī Jinnāh ne parvarish pā'ī hai. Is kalchar se agar 'ām musalmānon̲ ko ko'ī ta'lūq hai aur isī kalchar kā nām agar islāmī kalchar hai to us kī ḥifāẓat mein̲ misṭar Jinnāh kā hāth ẓarūr baṭā'ein̲.*

What is most significant about this article is the prominence it gives to language as a marker of place. The article, written by Kanwar Muḥammad Shaukat, stated that in UP wherever you go to the fields then you will see people wearing *dhotis*, and speaking "*dihātī*," or "rural" language. In contrast, wherever you go in cities, you will hear "Hindustani."[72] A range of authentic and politically significant regional cultures lay beyond the Hindu/Muslim dichotomy and the equally notable urban/rural dichotomy. As a multidimensional approach to time and geographic location, the concept of the timescape captures the richness of this variety, punctuated by the distinctive temporal rhythms of Muslim life.

Salil Misra has observed that work dealing with the League and Congress alike has "tended to be oblivious to any regional variations that may have existed in the structure of Muslim League politics."[73] It seems to have been this intolerance for regional variation in the face of national policy priorities that was a matter of frustration for *qasbatis*, who remained acutely aware of the political importance of Islam but simultaneously expressed suspicion at the demand that Muslims had to equate their Muslim identity with a particular party or oppose any other party purely on the basis of religious affinity. From their point of view, decades of conversation and policy supporting collaboration between the parties had laid the foundation for unified political action.

By all accounts, Partition was a death knell for *Madīnah*'s literary following and to a great extent the influential corner of the public it had nourished from the period of the Khilafat movement. *Madīnah* newspaper and its press continued publishing until the early 1970s, and there are many even today who remember that *Madīnah* was necessary reading among the urban *ashrāf* of both India and Pakistan in early years of independence. However, within two years of 1947 Urdu was demoted from its place as an official language in what had become Uttar Pradesh, in one fell swoop removing the incentive to study in Urdu and depriving future generations of Indian Urdu speakers of erstwhile interlocutors. While Madīnah Press distributed its newspaper and a popular children's literary magazine, *Ghunchah*, in both North India and Pakistan as late as the 1950s, shrinking audiences and the increasing bureaucratic difficulties of communication with kin and kind across the newly forged national borders took their toll. Many had relocated to Pakistan, and those that were left behind faced a future in which knowledge of Urdu bore little promise of professional advancement. There are still many who remember reading *Madīnah* with fondness and nostalgia; I have spoken to several of these men, who have now grown old. In Lucknow, Delhi,

Kandhla, and Karachi these men can speak of *Madīnah* and lively Urdu journalism as legacies of nationalism, the memory of broken extended family networks, a growing sense of a worldwide community linked over time and space. However, the legacy of newspapers like *Madīnah* is perhaps more poignantly felt in the daily rhythms of newspaper consumption and discussion over cups of chai, punctuating the day as habitually as the sound of the *āzān*.

Notes

1. "*Mahātmā Gāndhī aur du'ā kā din* [Mahātmā Gāndhī and the Day of Prayer]," *Madīnah*, April 1, 1919, 3.
2. In Bijnor, before *Madīnah* the newspapers distributed locally were *Qulqul*, *Ṣaḥīfa*, and *Tohfa-i Hind*. There was also the weekly *Risāla-i Tāza Naẓā'ir* and the monthly magazine *Zamīndār wa Kāshtkar*, which, under the leadership of Muḥammad Khalīl-ur-Raḥmān of Mandawar, dealt with agricultural issues. H. R. Nevill, *Bijnor: A Gazetteer* (Allahabad: Supt., Govt. Press, 1908), 107.
3. Department of Criminal Intelligence. *Statement of Newspapers and Periodicals Published in the United Provinces during the Year 1912 [with Index]*. Simla: Government Central Branch Press, 1913, 411, Uttar Pradesh State Archives.
4. "*Harṭal* [Strike]," *Madīnah*, April 5, 1919.
5. *Ṣaḥīfa*, "February 26, 1914; March 5, 1914," *Selections from Indian Owned Newspapers Published in the United Provinces January–July 1914* (Nainital: United Provinces Government, 1917), 274, 301, Uttar Pradesh State Archives.
6. *Madīnah*, "January 15, 1916," *Selections from Indian Owned Newspapers Published in the United Provinces January–July 1916* (Nainital: United Provinces Government, 1917), 64, Uttar Pradesh State Archives.
7. *Madīnah*, "January 15, 1916," *Selections from Indian Owned Newspapers Published in the United Provinces January–July 1916* (Nainital: United Provinces Government, 1917), 64, Uttar Pradesh State Archives.
8. Henry Herbert Dodwell, *The Cambridge History of the British Empire*, vol. 5. (Cambridge: Cambridge University Press, 1929), 535; H. R. Nevill, *Bijnor: A Gazetteer* (Allahabad: Supt., Govt. Press, 1908), 127.
9. *Madīnah*, "March 15, 1914," *Selections from Indian Owned Newspapers Published in the United Provinces January–July 1914* (Nainital: United Provinces Government, 1917), 329, Uttar Pradesh State Archives.
10. *Selections from Indian Owned Newspapers Published in the United Provinces January–July 1916* (Nainital: United Provinces Government, 1917), 64, 249, Uttar Pradesh State Archives.
11. Francis Robinson, "Municipal Government and Muslim Separatism in the United Provinces, 1883–1916," *Modern Asian Studies* 7, no. 3 (1973): 389–441.
12. *Vernacular Newspaper Reports*, January–July 1916, 300, Uttar Pradesh State Archives.

13. *Madīnah*, "August 1, 1914; August 15, 1914," *Selections from Indian Owned Newspapers Published in the United Provinces January-July 1914* (Nainital: United Provinces Government, 1917), 906, 925, Uttar Pradesh State Archives.
14. H. J. Boas, *Final Report on the Eleventh Settlement of the Moradabad District* (Allahabad: Supt., Govt. Press, 1909), 15.
15. Ira Klein, "Population and Agriculture in Northern India, 1872–1921," *Modern Asian Studies* 8, no. 2 (March 1974): 204.
16. Justin Jones, "The Local Experiences of Reformist Islam in a 'Muslim' Town in Colonial India: The Case of Amroha," *Modern Asian Studies* 43, no. 4 (2009): 898; William Stevenson Meyer et al., *Imperial Gazetteer*, vol. 8 (Oxford: Clarendon Press, 1911), 200.
17. *Madīnah*, "November 22, 1914; August 15, 1914," *Selections from Indian Owned Newspapers Published in the United Provinces July-December 1914* (Nainital: United Provinces Government, 1917), 925, 1270, Uttar Pradesh State Archives.
18. *Madīnah*, "March 8, 1915," *Selections from Indian Owned Newspapers Published in the United Provinces January—July* 1915 (Nainital: United Provinces Government, 1917), 258, Uttar Pradesh State Archives.
19. "July 5, 1914," *Selections from Indian Owned Newspapers Published in the United Provinces July-December 1914* (Nainital: United Provinces Government, 1917), 748, Uttar Pradesh State Archives.
20. *Amendments of Election Rules Bijnor 1913*, Uttar Pradesh State Archives, 1.
21. *Notes and Orders: Reconstruction of the Municipal Board of Bijnor* (Uttar Pradesh: Administrative Correspondence, 1931), Uttar Pradesh State Archives.
22. "It is for consideration and orders if the proposal of the board may be notified first allowing two weeks only for receiving objections in view of the fact that time is short within which to bring about the change desired and also that the board had already invited objections and after fully going through them rejected finally." From *Notes and Orders: Reconstruction of the Municipal Board of Bijnor* (Uttar Pradesh: Administrative Correspondence, 1931).
23. *Notes and Orders: Reconstruction of the Municipal Board of Bijnor* (Uttar Pradesh: Administrative Correspondence, 1931).
24. *Notes and Orders: Reconstruction of the Municipal Board of Bijnor* (Uttar Pradesh: Administrative Correspondence, 1931).
25. *Notes and Orders: Reconstruction of the Municipal Board of Bijnor* (Uttar Pradesh: Administrative Correspondence, 1931).
26. Rahman, *Locale, Everyday Islam, and Modernity: Qasbah Towns and Muslim Life In Colonial India* (Oxford: Oxford University Press, 2015), 8.
27. Mushirul Hasan, "Qasbas: A Brief in Propinquity," in *A Leaf Turns Yellow: The Sufis of Awadh*, ed. Muzaffar Ali (New Delhi: Rumi Foundation / Bloomsbury Publishing India 2013), 110.
28. Francis Robinson, "Municipal Government and Muslim Separatism in the United Provinces, 1883–1916," *Modern Asian Studies* 7, no. 3 (1973): 409.
29. Francis Robinson, "Municipal Government and Muslim Separatism in the United Provinces, 1883–1916," *Modern Asian Studies* 7, no. 3 (1973): 411.

30. Francis Robinson, "Municipal Government and Muslim Separatism in the United Provinces, 1883–1916," *Modern Asian Studies* 7, no. 3 (1973): 413.
31. Venkat Dhulipala, *Creating a New Medina* (Cambridge: Cambridge University Press, 2015).
32. "Who's Who in the United Provinces Cabinet: First Woman Minister in India: Two Muslim Members: Premier's Long Legislative Experience," *Times of India* (1861–current), August 3, 1937, ProQuest Historical Newspapers.
33. "Who's Who in the United Provinces Cabinet: First Woman Minister in India: Two Muslim Members: Premier's Long Legislative Experience," *Times of India* (1861–current), August 3, 1937, 6, ProQuest Historical Newspapers.
34. "The Importance of Bijnor: And Its Reactions; Sind Gives Lead in Communal Amity. Our Political Correspondent," *Times of India*, November 8, 1937, 9, ProQuest Historical Newspapers.
35. Laura Bear, "Doubt, Conflict, Mediation: The Anthropology of Modern Time," *Journal of the Royal Anthropological Institute* 20, no. S1 (2014): 3.
36. "The By-Election at Bijnor: Congress & League Chances," *Times of India*, October 18, 1937, 14, ProQuest Historical Newspapers.
37. "The feature of the election is that even in Congress meetings the *Allaho Akbar* cry is raised along with *Vande Mataram*. Both Ḥāfiẓ Ibrāhīm's and the League volunteers are dressed in green short, but whereas the former have the Congress flag with *Allaho Akbar* inscribed on it, the League volunteers have the crescent and *Allaho Akbar* on their badge. In the Congress election meetings Hindus are predominant as the speeches have a common appeal." "Bijnor By-Election Campaign: In Full Swing," *Times of India*, October 25, 1937, ProQuest Historical Newspapers.
38. "His joining the Congress Party in the Assembly without resigning his seat and seeking re-election on the Congress ticket has evoked very considerable criticism." "Who's Who in the United Provinces Cabinet: First Woman Minister in India: Two Muslim Members: Premier's Long Legislative Experience," *Times of India*, August 3, 1937, 6, ProQuest Historical Newspapers.
39. Ḥāfiẓ Ibrāhīm, "*Ḥāfiẓ Muḥammad Ibrāhīm kā Misṭar Jinnāḥ ko dandā̱n-i shikan javāb* [Ḥāfiẓ Ibrāhīm's Crushing Reply to Mister Jinnāh]," *Madīnah*, August 9, 1937, 5.
40. Ḥāfiẓ Ibrāhīm, "*Ḥāfiẓ Muḥammad Ibrāhīm kā Misṭar Jinnāḥ ko dandā̱n-shikan javāb* [Ḥāfiẓ Ibrāhīm's Crushing Reply to Mister Jinnāh]," *Madīnah*, August 9, 1937, 5.
41. Ḥāfiẓ Ibrāhīm, "*Ḥāfiẓ Muḥammad Ibrāhīm kā Misṭar Jinnāḥ ko dandā̱n-shikan javāb* [Ḥāfiẓ Ibrāhīm's Crushing Reply to the Mister Jinnah]," *Madīnah*, August 9, 1937, 5.
42. C. M. Naim, "The Muslim League in Barabanki, 1946," in *A Desertful of Roses*. http://www.columbia.edu/itc/mealac/pritchett/00litlinks/naim/txt_naim_muslimleague.pdf.
43. Barbara Metcalf, "Who Speaks for Muslims? The Challenges of the 1930s," in *Husain Ahmad Madanī: The Jihad for Islam and India's Freedom* (London: Oneworld, 2009), 97.
44. Ḥāfiẓ Ibrāhīm, "*Ḥāfiẓ Muḥammad Ibrāhīm kā Misṭar Jinnāḥ ko dandā̱n-shikan javāb* [Ḥāfiẓ Ibrāhīm's Crushing Reply to Mister Jinnah]," *Madīnah*, August 9, 1937, 5.
45. "*Kāngrisī vazīro̱n ke līye Mahātmā Gāndhī kī tāzah hidāyāt* [Mahātmā Gandhi's Recent Guidance]," *Madīnah*, August 8, 1937, 5.

46. "*Misṭar Jinnāḥ kī javāb mein̲ bābū rājindra parshād* (sic) *kā tāzah bīyān* [In Response to Mister Jinnah, Rājindra Prasād's New Announcemẹnt]," *Madīnah*, August 13, 1937, 5. Rajendra Prasād argued that the masses should make their own decision regarding representation.
47. "*Maulānā Āzād Rājindra Bābū kī ḥimāyat mein̲* [Maulānā Āzād in Defense of Rājindra Bābū]," *Madīnah*, August 13, 1937, 5. Maulānā Āzād defended Rājindra Prasād's argument against the appointment of a Muslim member of Orissa's provincial cabinet.
48. "*Misṭar jinnāḥ kī javāb mein̲ bābū rājindra parshād (sic) kā tāzah bīyān* [In Response to Mister Jinnah, Rājindra Prasād's New Announcement]," *Madīnah*, August 13, 1937, 5.
49. "Bijnor By-Election Campaign: In Full Swing," *Times of India*, October 25, 1937, 10.
50. "Mr Jinnah for Bijnor," *Times of India*, October 20, 1937, 9.
51. "From Our Special Correspondent: Congress Worker Stabbed: Attack in Train: Sequel to Bijnor By-Election," *Times of India*, October 29, 1937, 11.
52. "Frontier Workers," *Times of India*, October 23, 1937, 14, ProQuest Historical Newspapers; "Khan Abdul Ghaffar Khan," *Times of India*, October 25, 1937, 1, ProQuest Historical Newspapers.
53. The League meeting included Maulānā Shaukat 'Alī, Syed Zākir 'Alī, Mr. A. B. Habībullah Jamāluddīn Mīnā, and Mukhtar Ahmad Āzād. That same evening a League mass meeting featured Chaudhrī Khāliquzzaman, Muftī Ināyatullah, the Raja of Mahmudabad, Maulānā Hasrat Mohānī, and Maulānā Sibghatullah. Dr. Syed Maḥmud, the Bihar minister, arrived in Bijnor early on October 26, the day before the election (*Times of India*, October 25, 1937, 10, ProQuest Historical Newspapers). These are only a few figures mobilized to travel to Bijnor in the lead-up to the election. Also documented as traveling to Bijnor, Nagina, and Najibabad were MLA (Member of the Legislative Assembly) Sherwani and MLC (Member of the State Legislative Council) Tufail Ahmad on October 15, 1937. See "Support for Nehru Report," *Times of India*, October 18, 1928, 11, ProQuest Historical Newspapers.
54. "Sharp Division in Muslim Ranks: Bijnor By-Election Bid for Last Minute Advantage," *Times of India*, October 26, 1937, 10, ProQuest Historical Newspapers.
55. "Bijnor By-Election Campaign: In Full Swing," *Times of India*, October 25, 1937, 10, ProQuest Historical Newspapers.
56. "Bijnor By-Election Campaign: In Full Swing," *Times of India*, October 25, 1937, 10, ProQuest Historical Newspapers.
57. "Sharp Division in Muslim Ranks: Bijnor By-Election Bid for Last Minute Advantage," *Times of India*, October 26, 1937, 10, ProQuest Historical Newspapers.
58. M. Van Zeeland, "Current Topics: Bijnor By-Election Politics Strange Tactics," *Times of India*, October 27, 1937, 10, ProQuest Historical Newspapers.
59. *List of Newspapers and Periodicals in the United Provinces* (United Provinces: United Provinces Government, 1926, 1927, 1928, 1929, 1934, 1936, 1937, 1948); Gyanendra Pandey, *The Ascendancy of the Congress in Uttar Pradesh, 1926–34: A Study in Imperfect Mobilization* (New Delhi: Oxford University Press, 1978), 64; Furqān Aḥmad Ṣiddīqī, *Ẓila' bijnor ke jauvāhir* [The Jewelry of Bijnor] (New Delhi: Jade Press, 1991), 40; conversation with Muneer Akhtar and Parvez 'Ādil, June 2012, Bijnor, India.

60. "The By-Election at Bijnor: To the Editor of 'The Times of India,'" *Times of India*, November 13, 1937, 22, ProQuest Historical Newspapers.
61. "*Bijnor mein̲ hangāmah-yi intik̲h̲āb* [In Bijnor an Election Tumult]," *Madīnah*, October 13, 1937, 7.
62. Ḥāfiẓ Ibrāhīm, "*Ḥāfiẓ Muḥammad Ibrāhīm kā Misṭar Jinnāḥ ko dandān̲-shikan javāb* [Ḥāfiẓ Ibrāhīm's Crushing Reply to Mister Jinnah]," *Madīnah*, August 9, 1937, 5.
63. "The By-Election at Bijnor: To the Editor of 'The Times of India,'" *Times of India*, November 13, 1937, 22, ProQuest Historical Newspapers.
64. Venkat Dhulipala, *Creating a New Medina* (Cambridge: Cambridge University Press, 2015), 93. "U.P. By-Election Result: League Success," *Times of India*, December 17, 1937, 13, ProQuest Historical Newspapers.
65. K. M. Ashrāf, "Congress aur Muslim League ka Doosra Election: Bijnor Ke Intekhabaat Par Ek Nazar," *Hindustan*, November 28, 1937, cited in Venkat Dhulipala, *Creating a New Medina* (Cambridge: Cambridge University Press, 2015), 91.
66. "*Kangris mein̲ musalmānon̲ kī sharkat: Islāmī aur sharī'a noqt̲ah-yi naẓar se* [The Participation of Muslims in Congress: From the Perspective of Islam and the Shariah]," *Madīnah*, October 12, 1937.
67. In this article, Shaukat 'Alī quoted the Surah Al-Mumtahanah 60:8, "Allah does not forbid you from those who do not fight you because of religion and do not expel you from your homes—from being righteous toward them and acting justly toward them." See "*Kangris mein̲ musalmānon̲ kī sharkat: Islāmī aur sharī'a noqt̲ah-yi naẓar se* [The Participation of Muslims in Congress: From the Perspective of Islam and the Shariah]," *Madīnah*, October 12, 1937.
68. "Some Notes on the General Approach and Propaganda Methods of the AIML with Special Reference to Communal Relations," cited in Venkat Dhulipala, *Creating a New Medina* (Cambridge: Cambridge University Press, 2015), 92.
69. "Some Notes on the General Approach and Propaganda Methods of the AIML with Special Reference to Communal Relations," cited in Venkat Dhulipala, *Creating a New Medina* (Cambridge: Cambridge University Press, 2015), 92.
70. Kanwar Muḥammad Shaukat, "*Muslim līg mein̲ hai kaun*? [Who Is in the Muslim League?]," *Madīnah*, October 25, 1937, 7, 10.
71. This is a grammar error and should be "tab."
72. Kanwar Muḥammad Shaukat, "*Muslim līg mein̲ hai kaun?* [Who Is in the Muslim League?]," *Madīnah*, October 25, 1937, 7, 10.
73. Salil Misra, "Muslim League in UP in 1937: Understanding Muslim Communalism," *Proceedings of the Indian History Congress* 60 (1999): 765–73.

Conclusion
The Public as a Timescape

This book has illustrated the importance of considering time and space in studies of the public. To do so, this study has told the story of *Madīnah* newspaper and Madīnah Press, a small lithographic printing press that fashioned itself out of the intersection of a handful of local characteristics into a global voice for Muslims. Out of the intersection of a modernity that shrank miles into minutes with a disjointed temporality preserved by the limitations to fast travel, it defined a new space and time. It transformed its geographic isolation into a source of moral authenticity for the modern age, and as a modern Islamic voice it wove its local public into the fabric of a history being lived by Muslims in many places. From the fusion of the telegraph and the printing press with centuries-old social and communication networks it fashioned credibility and accessibility; with Western print technology, it preserved the religious significance of traditional calligraphy; with this religious visual authority it elevated the aesthetic of the newspaper form. Embodying as a business the virtuous rhythms of Muslim devotion, it became an indelible part of the life rhythm of its home *qasbah* and of communities far beyond, vividly remembered to this day.

Pious Publics

The consolidation of public spheres coded to language in South Asia has received increased attention, as this history has proven relevant to contemporary discussions of nationalism. This work has established the influential role of language and linguistic divisions in reflecting and constructing community identities in South Asia.[1] Influenced by the vernacularization of language in the nineteenth century, print capitalism, and wider dissemination of religious knowledge and authority, Urdu speakers increasingly identified with other speakers of Urdu through the medium of print. For some Muslims, the emergence of Urdu as an aspect of *ashrāf* identity manifested itself in an emphasis on Islam. *Madīnah*, a *qasbah* newspaper, showed this consolidation in process. While initially maintaining a clear bias toward the old guard of the All-India Muslim League as a result of links to the landed elite, and later on to Congress, *Madīnah* simultaneously balanced its political objections with its perceived duty to provide a public forum for all Muslims. This approach succeeded in conflating *ashrāf* and Muslim

Print and the Urdu Public. Megan Eaton Robb, Oxford University Press (2021). © Oxford University Press.
DOI: 10.1093/oso/9780190089375.001.0001

identities, reflecting a broader shift among *ashrāf* at the time; Urdu print was a glue that held a new orientation of values together.

Madīnah newspaper demonstrated the expanding geographic horizons of the *qasbah*. Expansion of technologies, or lack of this expansion, influenced the material fate of individual *qasbah*s such as Bijnor. Revolutionary technologies such as the telegraph and the railway did not result in the wholesale adoption of the same political and social views that were prevalent in the political centers. Instead, inhabitants of *qasbah*s used the technologies to petition colonial bodies, and increasingly to petition the Indian National Congress and All-India Muslim League, for access to institutions and funding, as well as to promote local priorities on the national stage. The *qasbah*'s anxiety to access knowledge and interpret it to the advantage of the local environment using the newspaper demonstrates that the newspaper was an increasingly important stage on which battles of lasting importance were fought, won, and lost.

This book's reading of *Madīnah* mirrors well-documented historical trends, but it also complicates existing narratives. *Madīnah* underlined the connection between Islam and gentlemanly behavior; it expressed early ambivalence regarding the nationalist project and eventually became opposed to the Muslim League's voice as representative of Muslims; after coming out as decidedly pro-Congress, it discussed the implications of cooperating with Hindu compatriots, referring to them as *kufr*—all trends that have broader implications for Indian history. This indicates that the small-town newspaper may have been a key vector by which these political orientations were incubated, nourished, and maintained. The expansion of the newspaper conversation into *qasbah*s broadened the base of the Urdu public sphere, which increasingly became synonymous with the Muslim *qaum* as print capitalism spread into these areas. The early twentieth-century Urdu public sphere, it bears repeating, was not at all synonymous with the separatist movement or the call for a separate homeland for Muslims, even though Pakistan would ensure a future for Urdu after 1947 by adopting it as the official language of government. These *ashrāf*, who associated religious and national identity with the Indo-Persian ideals for which the *qasbah* stood as a paradigm, would be as likely to remain in India as they would to relocate to Pakistan following Partition. As demonstrated by the appendix, several of *Madīnah*'s editors and writers (Maulānā Naṣrullah Kh̲ān "'Azīz," Abū Sa'īd "Bazmī," and "Māhir" ul-Qādrī to name only a few), despite vigorously opposing the foundation of Pakistan, remained in Lahore or Karachi following Partition. Even following Partition, the gravity of the local city—the familial, heritage, and career ties woven into the fabric of either of those two cities—won out over national politicking.

The analysis of *Madīnah* and Bijnor is rich with additional implications. Lightly scratch the surface, and the pieces of this story challenge many common narratives: the assumption that proponents of the old guard of the All-India Muslim League were all landed elites; that *'ulamā* and "secular" politicians did not participate in the same conversations regarding public and political life; perhaps most importantly, that the *qasbah* newspaper culture was a secondhand version of English-language models echoing the concerns of Indian-language papers in large cities.

As a *qasbah* newspaper, *Madīnah* demonstrates the importance of translating national trends to the local context and exposes the risk of eliding *qasbah*s into other types of urban life. Indeed the unique nature of Bijnor's narrative cautions against treating *qasbah*s as a homogeneous category. In the contemporary moment, when India demonstrates one of the highest rates of urbanization in the world, a better understanding of the thinnest layers of urban life offers insight into the transformations urbanization imparts.

On the one hand, histories of Islam in South Asia have argued that print disembeds individuals from cultural contexts and necessarily promotes individuation among religionists. On the other hand, recent histories of print and language in South Asia have generally discounted or avoided the analytical category of religion. By recognizing a discursive relationship between printed Urdu, material production and papers, and construction of religious identity, this book has also demonstrated that lithographic technology did not arrive in the subcontinent infused with liberal values but instead contributed to the continuation, consolidation, and transformation of existing networks of meaning and authority. Through lithographic technology, Urdu newspapers actually crystallized an association between printed language and religion. Local manifestations of Urdu print in the early twentieth century demonstrate that print interacted with other modes of communication to facilitate community formation at the local level. The consideration of how time and space are formed through social acts complicates assumptions about the division between public and religious life. Adding evidence for the relevance of Islam in these studies, it encourages a renewed attention to the utility of the term "religion" in studies of the public sphere.

The public sphere has become a space of contention for scholars of India seeking to understand the specific character of India's remarkably numerous, overlapping publics in the century before Independence and Partition.[2] Amir Ali has cited the development path of India's public sphere, and its tendency to normalize majoritarian views, as partially responsible for the contemporary dominance of Hindutva policies.[3] The issue is as much contemporary as historical: in a contemporary context where Islam is linked with issues of public safety and migration, definitions of a "Muslim public" promise to offer non-Muslim intellectual and political leaders guidance in how to interact with the Muslim world.[4] Thus recent studies are often situated in Western, European perspectives where Islam is linked with international security concerns and concerns about migration. The pressure to predicate the discussion on the existence of a single, albeit diverse Islamic public sphere, however, obscures the complexity of grounded historical narratives. It is not desirable or even possible to separate the Urdu and Hindi public spheres during the first decades of the twentieth century; nor was either linguistic tradition simply and cleanly linked to a single religion. In fact, it was in the early twentieth century that the links between language and religion were being transformed substantially, with newspapers playing a key role.[5] *Madīnah* is an important example of a voice that actively emphasized the connection between Islam and Urdu at a time when many Urdu newspapers were owned by Khatris, Kayasths, and other Hindu members of the elite. Grappling with the concept of a public that may or may not be inflected by religion has the potential to open up new ways of understanding the evolution of nationalisms inflected by Islam.

An alternative to generalization has emerged in the mapping of dominant trends onto heterogeneous expressions of political Islam in local contexts, focusing on Urdu and Muslims as inhabiting linked but separate public spaces.[6] Terenjit Sevea and Akbar Zaidi, working in the colonial context, discuss intellectuals of the late nineteenth and early twentieth centuries employing a "Muslim hermeneutic," or a distinctively Islamic mode of interpreting texts, as an alternative to the imposition of a set of global trends. Essential to this interpretation is the role of local context in relation to religion.[7] Akbar Zaidi's thesis localizes the character of the Muslim *qaum* in the latter half of the nineteenth century, resisting the imposition of a single, normative Muslim public in that period. His work emphasizes difference over uniformity, encouraging a return to local nuance.[8] In the context of this work, a study of the timescape calls for an accounting of space and time in the public. When we do this, piety, ritual, and even religion may come into focus, as these categories are often fundamental to the daily experience of social time. In the case of *Madīnah* and Bijnori *ashrāf*, Islam comes to the fore.

This book has made two theoretical interventions: First, public spaces are not purely figments of an abstract discourse but may be built on key geographic hearthstones. And second, it demonstrates that a necessary component of a common language must be a coherent cosmology of time. These are to be considered productively together as a timescape, a way of grounding public discussions in time and space. In turn, this approach opens up the possibility of taking emotions and embodiment more seriously in studies of the public sphere.

The Alternative *Qasbah*

In the last three decades, while much scholarship has made mention of *qasbahs* as significant players in nineteenth- and twentieth-century economic and intellectual life, there have been only a few attempts to examine the *qasbah* as a category of urban life in the context of South Asia.[9] The newspaper *Madīnah* self-consciously defined Bijnor against the "Westernized" city, engaging in what Justin Jones calls in Amroha "a constant process of negotiation between broader, standardized agendas and local distinctiveness."[10] As work on Amroha suggests, this type of negotiation was not unique to Bijnor, underlining the importance of the context of each particular *qasbah*. What is fascinating about *Madīnah*, and useful for broader understandings of the period, is how Bijnor *qasbah*'s timescape as produced and reflected in the newspaper became influential outside the *qasbah*.

The growth of urban studies scholarship in South Asia previously has tended to overlook *qasbah*s, emphasizing concentrated populations in prominent cities such as Lucknow, Calcutta, Lahore, Bombay, and of course Delhi.[11] Works that focus on Bijnor district and the *qasbah*s within it, including Bijnor *qasbah*, are overwhelmingly focused on themes of migration and economic prosperity in the context of contemporary concepts of development.[12] This has left *qasbah*s on the margins of the social and cultural history of South Asia, limiting our understanding of the crucial role these spaces have played. In contrast to characterizations of the *qasbah* as largely derivative of larger urban centers[13] or of their agricultural environs,[14] Bijnor *qasbah* derived its significance in the early twentieth century from its place as an alternative to urban life.[15] This alternative status became key to the development of an identity as an advocate and protector of Islam. Scholarship in urban studies has tended to assume a binary relationship between urban and rural life, encouraged by the Gāndhīan conception of the village as the Indian heartland and the city as an externally imposed Western convention.[16] Other work has either focused on the differing impact of first- and second-tier cities, focusing on colonial perceptions of the city as structured by a racial duality that gradually gave way to divisions based on class,[17] or emphasized the city's overweening influence on the development of religious thought at the margins of urban life.[18] Research on *qasbah*s has for the most part, however, fallen by the wayside in this shift toward urban studies.[19] Interest in the category of urban life encompassed by the term *qasbah* in South Asia has remained limited to cultural historians of South Asian Islam, focusing almost exclusively on its contribution to intellectual, rather than political and cultural, life in the late nineteenth and early twentieth centuries.[20] This book has been an attempt to fill that gap, demonstrating the possibility of alternate currents of knowledge and influence involving the *qasbah* and the city.

This book has addressed M. Raisur Rahman's call for work on how "*qasbahs* tell a story different from the nationalized narrative."[21] It has argued that *qasbati* life could be simultaneously both a form of opposition to the life of the city and a microcosm of the relationship between modernity and Islam in South Asia.

Newspapers in Bijnor contributed to the creation of the *qasbah* as an alternative to the life of the colonial city; in turn the *qasbah* derived a new form of cultural power from this otherness that enabled it to influence political and social discourse in the *qasbah* network and beyond. This otherness was different in form from the distinctions that had once been made between *qasbah*s and the imperial centers of the Mughal and British colonial empires. It was its new, carefully crafted cultural location that lent the *qasbah* distinctive power in the first half of the twentieth century. In slight counterpoint to Rahman, this book does not suggest that all *qasbah*s are essentially different from the large city in the same way. The risk of depending so heavily on an *essential* difference between the *qasbah* and urban centers is the temptation to downplay important overlaps. *Madīnah* was part of the process of appropriating the *qasbah* space to create a sense of belonging around Urdu, Islam, and the *qasbah*.

Madīnah Remembered

The remnants of *Madīnah* continue to intersect with the past and the present simultaneously. Majīd Ḥasan's grandson, Muneer Akhtar, still lives in the house where Majīd Ḥasan ran Madīnah Press until the 1960s. In the lower level of the expansive *haveli* (mansion) rests a large portico that housed the printing machinery, including an offset lithography machine imported from Britain.[22] Upstairs, Muneer Ḥasan and his two sons stay in the high-ceilinged rooms where *Madīnah*'s editors and proprietor used to gather together to work. Across from the portico is a separate room where staff used to fold the freshly printed pages before delivery by railway post. On my first visit in 2012, the alcove where the printing press had stood housed only a few chickens, a goat, and a rooster.

By late 2017, the veranda and the old press office had been cleared out and repainted in preparation for a family wedding. Old machinery and a few massive lithographic stones belted with metal had emerged during the renovation. There stood an ancient manual corrugation machine that had been used to punch lines of corrugation into paper for easier tearing; it still worked, as Muneer A<u>kh</u>tar showed me. The office where *Madīnah* had been folded and labeled for postage also boasts a box of telephone wires from the first telephone connection in Bijnor. Muneer A<u>kh</u>tar, trained in the press office before it closed in the 1970s, remembers well the stories of *Madīnah* passed down through the family and his early training in the lithographic printing methods used to print the newspaper and books. During my last visit there were discussions about restarting the family printing business to produce books on Islamic subjects. As interest in the newspaper has increased, the descendants of Majīd Ḥasan have engaged with that interest and now highlight that heritage as part of the family's vision for the future.

In doing this, they manifest the keen talent for perceiving and adapting to the times that Majīd Ḥasan demonstrated when he built *Madīnah* into a surprisingly wild success. If, as this book has argued, the public is understood best through consideration of geography and temporality, the cohabitation of the present and the future in a far-flung location like Bijnor continues to mark features characteristic of a *qasbah* context. Traces of the timescape remain, even if its explicit influence seems to have disappeared.

Notes

1. For general discussions of language and nationalism, see Francesca Orsini, *The Hindi Public Sphere, 1920–1940: Language and Literature in the Age of Nationalism* (Oxford: Oxford University Press, 2002), 5. For a study linking literature and nationalism, see Sudhir Chandra, *The Oppressive Present: Literature and Social Consciousness in Colonial India* (New Delhi: Oxford University Press, 1992).
2. For studies attempting to focus on regional or South Asian trends, see Isabel Hofmeyr, Preben Kaarsholm, and Bodil Folke Frederiksen, "Introduction: Print Cultures, Nationalisms and Publics of the Indian Ocean," *Africa* 81, no. 1 (2011): 1–22; Vinay Lal and Gita Rajan, "Ethnographies of the Popular and Public Sphere in India," *South Asian Popular Culture* 5, no. 2 (2007): 87–95; Rizwan Qaiser, *Resisting Colonialism and Communal Politics: Maulana Azad and the Making of the Indian Nation* (New Delhi: Manohar, 2011).
3. Amir Ali, "Evolution of Public Sphere in India," *Economic and Political Weekly* 36, no. 26 (June–July 2001): 2419–25.
4. For a study of the public sphere of Islam in Europe, see Ralph Grillo, "Islam and Transnationalism," *Journal of Ethnic and Migration Studies* 30, no. 5 (2004): 861–78.
5. Christopher King, *One Language, Two Scripts: The Hindi Movement in Nineteenth Century North India* (New Delhi: Oxford University Press, 1994), 130–45.
6. For an illustrative example of this approach applied to an example of the transition from childhood to womanhood in the nineteenth-century context, see Ruby Lal, *Coming of Age in Nineteenth-Century India: The Girl-Child and the Art of Playfulness* (New York: Cambridge University Press, 2013).
7. Terenjit Sevea, "Islamist Questioning and [C]olonialism: Towards an Understanding of the Islamist Oeuvre," *Third World Quarterly* 28, no. 7 (October 2007): 1375–99.
8. S. Akbar Zaidi, "Contested Identities and the Muslim *Qaum* in Northern India, c. 1860–1900," DPhil thesis, University of Cambridge, 2009, 1–35.
9. For work that has mentioned *qasbahs* as significant players, see Anand Yang, *Bazaar India: Markets, Society, and the Colonial State in Bihar* (Berkeley: University of California Press, 1998); Peter Reeves, *Landlords and Governments in Uttar Pradesh: A Study of Their Relations until Zamindari Abolition* (New Delhi: Oxford University Press, 1991). For studies that have considered the *qasbah* as a category of urban life, see Mushirul Hasan, *A Leaf Turns Yellow: The Sufis of Awadh*, ed. Muzaffar Ali (New Delhi: Rumi

Foundation / Bloomsbury Publishing India, 2013); Justin Jones, "The Local Experiences of Reformist Islam in a 'Muslim' Town in Colonial India: The Case of Amroha," *Modern Asian Studies* 43, no. 4 (2009): 871–908; M. Raisur Rahman, *Locale, Everyday Islam and Modernity: Qasbah Towns and Muslim Life in Colonial India* (New Delhi: Oxford University Press, 2015).

10. Justin Jones, "The Local Experiences of Reformist Islam in a 'Muslim' Town in Colonial India: The Case of Amroha," *Modern Asian Studies* 43, no. 4 (2009): 871–908.
11. William J. Glover, *Making Lahore Modern: Constructing and Imagining a Colonial City* (Minneapolis: University of Minnesota Press, 2008); Kenneth R. Hall, ed., *Secondary Cities and Urban Networking in the Indian Ocean Realm, 1400–1800* (Lanham, MD: Lexington Books, 2008); Eric Lewis Beverley, "Colonial Urbanism and South Asian Cities," *Social History* 36, no. 4 (2011): 482–97; Sandeep Hazareesingh, *The Colonial City and the Challenge of Modernity: Urban Hegemonies and Civic Contestations in Bombay City, 1900–1925* (New Delhi: Orient Black Swan, 2007). An exception to this trend is work by Douglas E. Haynes. See Douglas E. Haynes, *Small Town Capitalism in Western India: Artisans, Merchants and the Making of an Informal Economy, 1870–1960* (Cambridge: Cambridge University Press, 2012).
12. Mashkoor Ahmed's doctoral work explores migratory patterns in Bijnor district from 1960 to the present to understand the impact of migration on economy and society. Mashkoor Ahmed, "Structural Analysis of Internal Migration and Socio-Economic Transformation in Bijnor District, Uttar Pradesh," MPhil thesis, Aligarh Muslim University, 2008. Syed Matanat Husain Zaidi focused on the efforts of the Anṣārīs of Bijnor to improve their social and economic condition by the assertion of a collective identity—namely by adopting the *ashrāf* appellation Anṣārī despite being weavers descended from Hindu converts. Syed Matanat Husain Zaidi, "A Socio-Economic Study of the Ansaris of Bijnor District," DPhil thesis, Aligarh University, 1988.
13. For instance, see Margrit Pernau, *Ashraf into Middle Classes: Muslims in Nineteenth-Century Delhi* (New Delhi: Oxford University Press, 2013), 272. In her analysis, the founding of the madrasah at Deoband was a relocation of the tradition of Delhi, particularly that of the Madrasah Rahimiya in Delhi.
14. Thomas Metcalf, *Land, Landlords, and the British Raj: Northern India in the Nineteenth Century* (Berkeley: University of California Press, 1979), 281–305. Metcalf's concern is how the influence of the *t'āluqdār*s and the British government combined to form local government in towns, in Oudh.
15. Chris Bayly and Francis Robinson have already pointed out *qasbahs*' distinctive roles from the eighteenth to the twentieth century, although neither scholar discusses the ways that the *qasbah* began to view itself as an alternative to the large city. Bayly highlighted the power of the *qasbah* towns as "the repository of aristocratic and courtly values in north India" and the future "seed-beds of Muslim political movements towards the end of the century." C. A. Bayly, *Rulers, Townsmen, and Bazaars: North Indian Society in the Age of British Expansion, 1770–1870*, 3rd ed. (New Delhi: Oxford University Press, 2012), 348. Francis Robinson pointed out that changes in municipal governance in the towns in the late nineteenth century led to a divergence in attitudes toward communalism between *qasbahs* in East and west UP. Francis Robinson,

"Municipal Government and Muslim Separatism in the United Provinces, 1883 to 1916," *Modern Asian Studies* 7, no. 3 (1973): 389–441. The urban studies turn has resulted in a renewed attention to cities that underestimates the significance of *qasbahs* and their inhabitants.

16. Prashant Kidambi, *The Making of an Indian Metropolis: Colonial Governance and Public Culture in Bombay, 1890–1920* (Aldershot: Ashgate, 2007); Eric Lewis Beverley, "Colonial Urbanism and South Asian Cities," *Social History* 36, no. 4 (2011): 483–84.
17. Eric Lewis Beverley, *Hyderabad, British India, and the World: Muslim Networks and Minor Sovereignty, c. 1850–1950* (Cambridge: Cambridge University Press, 2015). Also see Sandip Hazareesingh, *The Colonial City and the Challenge of Modernity: Urban Hegemonies and Civic Contestations in Bombay City, 1900–1925* (New Delhi: Orient Black Swan, 2007); Prashant Kidambi, *The Making of an Indian Metropolis: Colonial Governance and Public Culture in Bombay, 1890–1920* (Aldershot: Ashgate, 2007); Stephen Legg, *Spaces of Colonialism: Delhi's Urban Governmentalities* (Oxford: Blackwell, 2007).
18. Janel L. Abu-Lughod, "The Islamic City—Historic Myth, Islamic Essence and Contemporary Relevance," *International Journal of Middle East Studies* 19, no. 2 (1987): 156, cited in Justin Jones, "The Local Experiences of Reformist Islam in a 'Muslim' Town in Colonial India: The Case of Amroha," *Modern Asian Studies* 43, no. 4 (2009): 872.
19. Eric Beverley's recent, rich historiography of urban studies makes little mention of the *qasbah* as an urban category in the recent flood of scholarship related to the urban environment in South Asia. Eric Beverley, "Colonial Urbanism and South Asian Cities," *Social History* 36, no. 4 (2011): 483–84.
20. M. Raisur Rahman, *Locale, Everyday Islam and Modernity: Qasbah Towns and Muslim Life in Colonial India* (New Delhi: Oxford University Press, 2015), 6, 128. For studies discussing *qasbahs*' contribution to education, see Gail Minault, *Secluded Scholars: Women's Education and Muslim Social Reform in Colonial India* (Delhi: Oxford University Press, 1998); Barbara Metcalf, *Islamic Revival in British India: Deoband, 1860–1900* (Princeton: Princeton University Press, 1982), 125–37; David Lelyveld, *Aligarh's First Generation: Muslim Solidarity in British India* (Princeton: Princeton University Press, 1978); Francis Robinson, *The 'Ulama of Farangi Mahall and Islamic Culture in South Asia* (New Delhi: Permanent Black, 2001).
21. M. Raisur Rahman, *Locale, Everyday Islam, and Modernity: Qasbah Towns and Muslim Life in Colonial India* (New Delhi: Oxford University Press, 2015), 7, 14. The conclusion of Rahman's analysis mirrors similar conclusions arrived at by existing studies on the nation, cities, and *qasbahs*. For instance, Muhammad Qasim Zaman has spoken at length against the assumption that tradition and modernity are at odds, highlighting the selective appropriation of some aspects of "the modern" while retaining a sense of identity rooted in faith. Muhammad Qasim Zaman, *The Ulama in Contemporary Islam: Custodians of Change* (Princeton: Princeton University Press, 2002). David Lelyveld has talked at length about the ways that the Anglo-Oriental College mediated "the modern" in their own lives, in great measure

by selective appropriation and participation. For instance, "To Sayyid Ahmad the truth of Islam was always prior; modern scientific ideas were either consistent with Islamic doctrine, or they had to be refuted." E.g., David Lelyveld, *Aligarh's First Generation: Muslim Solidarity in British India* (Princeton: Princeton University Press, 1978), 110. Some of the figures that Ayesha Jalal discusses practice this selective appropriation. Ayesha Jalal, "Negotiating Colonial Modernity and Cultural Difference: Indian Muslim Conceptions of Community and Nation, 1878–1914," in *Modernity and Culture: From the Mediterranean to the Indian Ocean*, ed. Leila Tarazi Fawaz and C. A. Bayly (New York: Columbia University Press, 2002), 230–60.

22. Muneer Akhtar, conversation, Bijnor, India, April 14–16, 2013.

Transliteration and Citation Method

In this book I use an altered version of the transliteration system developed by Steingass, using some alterations to accommodate sounds that appear only in Urdu and not in Persian or Arabic.[1] Where a retroflex vowel appears, it is usually signified by a dot or line below the letter (e.g., d̲ for ڈ). The Urdu character ث is represented as "s̲."

In this descriptive system, as in the Steingass system, there are three "elementary vowels" represented by the letters *a, i,* and *u,* which correspond to the equivalent sounds in the English words *son, sick*, and *pull.* These sounds correspond to the Urdu characters *zabar* (َ), *zer* (ِ), and *pesh* (ُ). The long forms of these vowels are represented by the roman characters *ā, ī, ū,* which correspond to the equivalent sounds in the American English words *tall, creep*, and *tube.* There are also the sounds *o* and *e*, which correspond to the sounds in the English words *home* and *hay.* While these are diphthongs in construction (*o* etymologically combines the sounds *a* and *u*, and *e* combines *a* and *ī*), Urdu does not pronounce these vowels as diphthongs. They are here referred to as diphthongs etymologically, with the understanding that Urdu pronounces these sounds as pure vowels. Other diphthongs include *ai* (representing the sound ā + i) and *au* (representing the sound ā + u). These two diphthongs are roughly captured in the American English words *fail* and *stout.*

As in the Library of Congress scheme, any word-final nasalized sound is represented by n̲. 'Ain appears as '.

Place names are spelled according to the contemporary accepted English spelling, with diacritics included in cases where clarification is necessary. Names of people are transliterated to make pronunciation and spelling clear, for ease of reference by scholars.

When writing proper names, while I have erred on the side of using diacritics for clarity, I occasionally do not include diacritics when writing common words or proper names, on the assumption that eliminating these clues will not impede the reader's understanding.

Transliterated Urdu words are capitalized according to English convention. This means that transliteration is capitalized at the beginning of sentences, in titles, and for proper names. There is a glossary of terms in Appendix I.

Urdu Transliteration Table

ṣ	ص	a, ā	آ, ا
ẓ	ض	b	ب
t̲	ط	p	پ
z̤	ظ	t	ت
ʿ	ع	ṭ	ٹ
g̲h̲	غ	s̱	ث
f	ف	j	ج
q	ق	ch	چ
k	ک	ḥ	ح
g	گ	k̲h̲	خ
l	ل	d	د
m	م	ḏ	ڈ
n	ن	ẕ	ذ
w (v)	و	r	ر
h	ہ, ﮨ, ﮩ	ṛ	ڑ
h	ھ	z	ز
ʾ	ء	zh	ژ
ī	ی	s	س
e	ے	sh	ش

Note

1. Francis Joseph Steingass, *A Comprehensive Persian-English Dictionary, Including Arabic Words and Phrases to Be Met with in Persian Literature*, 2nd ed. (London: Kegan Paul, Trench, Trubner & Co., 1930), vii–viii.

APPENDIX I

General Glossary

ʿalim (pl. ʿulamā)—a learned man, usually used to denote a man with significant learning in Islamic religious and legal studies

anjuman—association, usually of Muslims

ashraf (ashrāf)—noble by birth or status; usually used in reference to one of four communities, including Syed, Shaikh, Pathan, and Mughal

darbar (darbār)—a public gathering in honor of an Indian ruler or high-ranking British official during the colonial period

dars-i nizami (dars-i niẓāmī)—a syllabus of religious education influential among Muslims from the eighteenth century, with origins among the Farangī Mahallīs of Lucknow

fatwa (pl. fatāwā)—a decision on a point of Islamic law, delivered by an *ʿalim*

hadith (ḥadīs̤)—the reported sayings or actions of the Prophet Muḥammad

hafiz (ḥāfiẓ)—a person who has memorized the Qur'an

haftahvār—weekly

hakīm (ḥakīm)—physician practicing traditional medicine or Unani Tibb in South Asia

idārah—institution, organization, administration

idārat—editorship

idāriyyah—editorial; leading article

ijazat (ijāzat)—permission granted by one with authority to teach a subject, usually a religious or legal text

khilafat (khilāfat)—successorship

khwajah (khwājah)—honorific title

māhnāmah—monthly

maktab—primary school

masjid—mosque

maulana (maulānā)—a title usually applied to an *ʿalim*, but during the Khilafat movement extended to, or assumed by, the politically influential[1]

mudīr—editor

mudīr-i moʿāvin—assistant editor

Nadwat-ul-'ulamā—literally "congress of scholars," this is the name given to the educational institution founded for Muslims in Lucknow in the late nineteenth century

nā'ib mudīr—assistant editor

namaz (namāz)—prayers

pir (pīr)—spiritual guide and master

qasbah (qaṣbah)—a town usually characterized by a significant Muslim minority or majority, with historical ties to Sufi ritual, Mughal patronage, and colonial administration

qasbati (qaṣbātī)—a resident of a qasbah, townsperson

roznāmah—daily

ṣaḥāfat—journalism

sharif (sharīf)—an adjective describing those noble by birth or status; usually used in reference to one of four communities: Syed, Shaikh, Pathan, and Mughal

subah (ṣuba')—a district or province (a Mughal term, also applied during the colonial period)

tahsil (tihsīl)—revenue district held by a tahsildar

tahsildar (tihsīldār)—one who holds rights over a revenue district

takhallus (takhalluṣ)—a pen-name attached to a poet, used to sign literary works

t'āluqdār (tāluqdār)—landowner with proprietory rights to the revenue of lands

waqf—a trust set aside for charitable purposes, to be maintained in perpetuity

zenana (zināna)—the section of a Muslim home where only women may enter, or their immediate male relatives

Note

1. This definition draws on Francis Robinson, *Separatism among Indian Muslims: The Politics of the United Provinces' Muslims 1860–1923* (Cambridge: Cambridge University Press, 2007), 437.

APPENDIX II

Proposal for Qualifications for Electors in Bijnor, 1913

Qualifications of electors	Existing	Proposed	Proposed in Sec. 25 to meet objections from Muhammadans
Ownership	Rs. 24 a year rental of houses owned	Rs. 48 a year	Rs. 24 a year
Rental	Rs. 2 per mensem	Rs. 4 per mensem	Rs. 2 per mensem
Land Revenue	Rs. 50 a year	Rs. 100 a year	Rs. 50 a year
Muafi	Nil	Rs. 100 a year inserted by Govt.	Rs. 50 a year
Tenant	Nil	Nil	Rs. 100 a year to meet the case of agriculturalists
Income	Rs. 200 a year	Rs. 300 a year	Rs. 200 a year
Office holder	Nil	As generally passed for other places	No change suggested
Degree	Nil	Graduate of the Allahabad University	No change suggested
Tax	Rs. 2 a year	Rs. 5 a year	No change suggested

Table reproduced from "Amendments of Election Rules Bijnor 1913," Municipal Records, Uttar Pradesh State Archives, 2–3.

APPENDIX III

Editors and Journalists of *Madīnah*, 1912–1948

Most Prominent Editors and Journalists

Maulvī Syed Nūr ul-Ḥasan Ẕahīn Karatpūrī (1888–1939)
Editor 1912, 1916–1917
Birthplace
Kiratpur *qasbah*
Education
Local madrasah
Career
Boasting only limited education, Nūr ul-Ḥasan Ẕahīn Karatpūrī established his reputation in his journalistic endeavors. Blind, he also became a noted dream interpreter.

Syed Muḥammad La'iq Ḥussain Qavī "Zamurrud-raqam" Amrohavī
Assistant editor, 1912–1915
Birthplace
Amroha
Education
Local madrasah
Journalism Career
His *takhallus* translated as "emerald-pen," signifying his fame as a calligrapher, which became a trademark for *Madīnah*.

M. Āg͟hā Rafīq Bulandshahrī
Editor, 1913–1915
Birthplace
Bulandhshahr city, Bulandhshahr district
Education
Local madrasah
Journalism Career
He presided over *Madīnah*'s involvement in the Kanpur Mosque uproar.

Maulānā Maẓhar ud-Dīn Shairkoṭī (1888–1939)
Editor, 1917–1921
Birthplace
Shairkoṭ *qasbah*, Bijnor district
Education

Deoband. Initially educated by Maulānā 'Abdul Qayūm Arshāq and Miyānji Sa'ad Allah Sahib, he went on to attend Deoband, where he was a pupil of Maulānā Maḥmud ul-Ḥasan Asīr Mālṭā, known as Shaikh ul-Hind.

Journalism Career

After completing his education at Deoband, he worked on a newspaper in Dastūr in Shairkoṭ *qasbah* and then edited *Nagīnah* in the city of the same name. After leaving *Madīnah* in 1921 he went on to edit the Naginah-based paper *Almān*. Ultimately he became close to the Muslim League leadership, leaving *Madīnah* to found a paper *Vaḥdat* (*Unity*) to assist in the propounding of Muslim League policies.

Maulānā Amīn Aḥsan Iṣlāḥī (1904–1989)

Assistant editor, 1922–1924

Birthplace

Bamhaur Village, Azimgarh, UP

Education

Educated in a government school in his village for his earliest years, Iṣlāḥī entered Madrasatul Iṣlāḥ in 1914, when Maulānā Shiblī No'mānī (1857–1914) was heavily involved in the foundation of that institution. He remained at Madrasatul Iṣlāḥ until 1922.

Journalism Career

Iṣlāḥī's journalism career centered in Bijnor and Lucknow. He was an assistant editor with *Madīnah* and also worked with the children's magazine *Ghunchah*. His name appeared as a third-in-command "joint editor" in December 1922 at the young age of eighteen. He was so young, in fact, that when he started work in Bijnor, many were of the opinion that he did not look the part of a scholar of Arabic.[1] After leaving Bijnor, he worked on the editorial board of *Sach* (Lucknow). However, his true passion was theological research, and he eventually left journalism behind to focus on that passion.

Maulānā Badrul Ḥasan "Jalālī," B.A. (1891–1956)

Editor, 1921–1924, 1924–1927

Birthplace

Qānūn Goyān neighborhood, Moradabad

Education

He received his BA from Aligarh University, and also earned his MA.

Journalism Career

Jalālī was prosecuted in 1924 under section 124A for an article related to Kabul. He apologized and resigned his editorship, but soon resumed his position. He had a reputation as a "noncooperator," according to British newspaper surveillance.[2] After leaving the newspaper in 1927, he joined Muḥammad 'Alī Jauhar on the staff of the newspaper *Khilāfat* in Bombay. In this period he became close to Maulānā Āzād, Rafi' Aḥmed Qidwai, and Lal Bahādur Shāstrī. After some time Jalālī left Bombay to join Rafi' Aḥmed Qidwai in working on the newspaper *Vakīl*. Then he shifted to Hyderabad, where he worked on the paper *Vaṭan*. After this, he returned to Delhi at the invitation of Muḥammad 'Alī Jauhar to take up a place as professor in Jamia Millia Islamia. He also did editing work for *Jang* prior to 1947. In 1947 he returned to Moradabad for a few years, before he began editing the daily newspaper *Nāẓim* (Rampur) in 1952.

Maulvī Nūr ul-Raḥmān, B.A. (1894–1972)

Editor 1928; reporter for an unspecified period of time prior

Birthplace
Bacchraon *qasbah*, Amroha district
Education
Madrasa Awliyā Rampur, followed by Muslim High School Utavah and Aligarh Muslim University; in 1920 he separated himself from the institution over differences in opinion related to the Khilafat movement.
Background
Shaikh
Journalism Career
He worked first as a reporter. After leaving *Madīnah* he joined Jamia Millia Islamia's library and became the head editor of the periodical *Jām'ah*. He was the Secretary for the Muslim Chairman of Commerce, Calcutta and Joint Secretary for the Anjuman-i Taraqqī-yi Urdū.

Muḥammad Aḥsan Morādabādī
Assistant editor, 1928–1930
Birthplace
Bacchraon *qasbah*, Amroha district
Education
local madrasah
Background
Shaikh
Journalism Career
Aḥsan was also an administrative clerk in government service.

Maulānā Naṣrullah Khān "'Azīz" (1897–1967)
Assistant editor, 1924–1928; editor, 1929–1930, 1932–1936
Birthplace
Gujranwala, Panjab
Education
Educated until 10th class in Gujranwala, then enrolled in Āzād High School.
Background
Son of Moḥammad Sharīf Ullah Khān
Journalism Career
Naṣrullah Khān 'Azīz, B.A., is mentioned as an editor in the 1924 *Statement of Newspapers and Periodicals,* the same year that 'Azīz started work for *Madīnah* as his first job in journalism. Convicted under section 124A of the Indian Penal Code by the District Magistrate of Bijnor on April 15, 1930. Sentenced to fifteen months' rigorous imprisonment and an additional fine of Rs. 500 (or three months' further rigorous imprisonment). He entered jail on March 31, 1930. It is not known whether he paid the additional fine or whether he was imprisoned for a total of eighteen months, although we know he was in prison in the Bijnor and Gonda jail.[3] He was later listed in *Madīnah* as one of three "*idārah-yi mas'ūl*," or those responsible for the administration of the newspaper, on the title page of *Madīnah* in September 1935. After he left *Madīnah* in late 1935 or early 1936 he worked for *Zamīndār* (Lahore), *Pasbān* [Sentinel] (Lahore), *Zamzam* (Lahore), *Musulmān* (Lahore), *Kauṡar* (Lahore), *Tasnīm* (Lahore), and published his own weekly publication, *Aishīyā*; he published a consistent satirical column named "*tīr-o nashtar*" [arrows and lancets] in each of these newspapers. He was not done with imprisonment in the independence period; he

again spent a period in jail in 1953, presumably for his inflammatory journalist activities that targeted the Pakistani government after independence.[4]

Ḥamīd Ḥasan "Fakīr" Bijnorī (1903–1991)
Assistant editor, January 1930–1935; editor, January 1, 1945–April 5, 1945
Education
Ḥamīd Ḥasan "Faqīr" Bijnorī received his early education in Arabic, Persian, and Urdu at home through private instruction.
Background
Son of Moḥammad Muẓaffar Ḥasan, Shaikh, of Bijnor
Journalism Career
Ḥamīd Ḥasan "Fakīr" Bijnorī had his poetry published in *Madīnah* from an extremely young age, perhaps as early as the newspaper's first issues. He married one of Majīd Ḥasan's daughters in the 1910s, suggesting that perhaps he was already a member of Majīd Ḥasan's extended family. Ḥamīd Ḥasan is listed as assistant editor on the title page of *Madīnah* from January 1930; he appears third in the list of *idārah-yi mas'ūl* from January 1932 to 1935. This listing appears to be an extension of recognition for his role as the editor of *Ghunchah*, the weekly magazine for children, soon after its inception in 1922 (probably from the mid-1920s).[5]

M. Shabbīr Beg
Editor, April 6, 1945–December 31, 1945
Birthplace
Bareilly

Maulānā Ḥāmidul Anṣārī "Ghāzī" (1906–1992)
Chief editor, 1931–1937, 1945–1950
Birthplace
Ambhattā *qasbah* in Saharanpur district
Education
Dar ul-'Ulūm Ma'īnīyah, Ajmer; Dar ul-'Ulūm Deoband; received instruction from Anwar Shāh Kashmīrī, Maulānā Shabīr Aḥmed 'Usmānī, Maulānā Ibrāhīm Balīyavī, and Maulānā 'Azaz 'Alī Amrohavī Shaikh ul-Adab.
Background
Shaikh and son of M. Manṣūr Anṣārī
Journalism Career
During his studies Anṣārī worked at the weekly periodical *Gul bāgh* (later to be renamed *Bahār bāgh*) and on the staff of *al-Mahmūd*, a weekly periodical in honor of Shaikh ul-Hind Maḥmūd ul-Ḥasan. After completing his Deoband qualifications quickly in 1926, he worked on the publications *Muhājir* and *al-Jamiyat*, the paper of Jam'iat 'Ulamā-i Hind, until he took up his position with *Madīnah* in 1931. Ghazī was *Madīnah*'s chief editor from 1935 to 1937, and again from 1945 until 1950. In the interim he briefly edited the Najibabad publication *Adabī dunīyā* before shifting to Delhi and founding the Delhi publisher Nadwatul Muṣannifīn. Following his final departure from *Madīnah* in 1950, Anṣārī shifted to Bombay and became the chief editor of the daily *Jamhūrīyat* there; in 1956 he left that paper and founded his own weekly version of *Jamhūrīyat*, which ran until 1962.

Abū Sa'īd "Bazmī" (1910–1951)
Chief editor, 1937–1940, 1942–1945
Birthplace
Bhopal
Education
Passed exams in Farsi, Arabic, Urdu, and English. BA and MA in English.
Career
Government service; editor of newspaper in Bhopal called *Rehnumā*, which was shut down by the British government. Arrived in Bijnor in 1937, promoted to head editor in May 1937. His articles were also published in *Nigār* while he worked for *Madīnah*. He also worked on the staff of Madinah Press's children's magazine *Ghunchah*. He was arrested in 1940 under the "Defense of India Act." After leaving *Madīnah*, he worked for two other Urdu newspapers in Lahore: *Zamzam* and *Shahbāz*. After Partition he was the editor of the Pakistan publications *Zamzam* and *Shihāz*. He died in the United States and was buried in Lahore.

Maulānā Abūllais Iṣlāḥī Nadvī (1913–1990)
Worked at *Madīnah* from approximately 1934 until the late 1930s
Education
He was a graduate from Madrasatul Islāḥ in Sarai Mir in the Azamgarh district of UP. This madrasa had been founded by Maulānā Muḥammad Shāfi in 1908 with reformist aims. He was also a graduate of Nadwatul 'Ulamā in Lucknow, where he taught following his graduation. He was literate in English.
Journalism Career
The man who would become the first Amīr of the Jamā'at-i Islāmī Hind after independence became an assistant editor of *Madīnah* shortly before 1935, probably initially under the editorial leadership of Naṣrullah Khān, and remained an assistant editor when Bazmī took over the editorial board.[6] During his tenure at the newspaper Nadvī's calling card was writing scholarly articles in an accessible style, not only for *Madīnah* but also for Nīyāz Fatehpūrī's newspaper *Nigār*.

Other Influential Contributors

Maulānā Syed Abūl A'la Maudūdī (1903–1979)
Worked as a journalist from 1918 to 1923
Birthplace
Aurangabad
Education
He gained his metric qualification in Aurangabad, after which he continued his education in Bhopal and Delhi.
Journalism Career
From 1918 to 1923 Maudūdī worked as a journalist for the following publications: *Madīnah* (Bijnor), *Tāj* (Jabalpur), and *Muslim* (Delhi). He became an editor of the Jam'īat 'Ulamā's newspaper *al-Jam'īat* in 1925.[7]

Qāẓi Muḥammad 'Adīl "Abāsī" (1898–1980)
Member of *Madīnah* Editorial Board, 1921–1922

Birthplace
The village Biyara, then part of district Basti in UP
Education
A member of a middling *zamīndār* family, he received his primary education in the village Kotli near his birthplace. Then he attended middle school in a nearby *qasbah,* Hallaur, where he graduated in 1911. He attended high school in Basti's capital city, then attended college at Saint Andrew's College in Gorakhpur, where he received his BA in 1920.[8] After receiving his BA he enrolled in the University of Allahabad and became involved in the Khilafat movement.[9]
Journalism Career
Joined *Madīnah* in 1921 as part of its editorial board briefly before leaving for Lahore, where he eventually became chief editor of *Zamīndār*.

Maulānā Muḥammad Us̱mān Fāraqlaiṯ (1897–1967)
Worked on the editorial board of *Madīnah* for one year in the 1920s, probably 1927
Birthplace
Born in Delhi, his ancestral *qasbah* was Pilkhuwa of Ghaziabad district in the then-United Provinces. While he was raised in Delhi, he considered himself to be from Pilkhuwa and was buried there.
Education
At the age of seven or eight he entered into a madrasah named Zīnat Gul, where he received his foundational education. He was strongly influenced by the novels of ʻAbdul Halīm Sharar, particularly the novel *Florā Florinḏa*. He also studied at the madrasah at the Hājī ʻAlī Jān *masjid* in Bombay and Masjid Fatehpūrī. He engaged Nawab Ẓamīr Mirzā as a private tutor.
Journalism Career
At the beginning of his career he wrote for the publication *Ahl-i Ḥadīth*, working with the famous dialectician Maulānā S̱anā'ullah Amritsarī. His journalistic ambition sparked, he began working for the Karachi publication *Al-Wahīd* in 1926; there he translated Arabic articles into Urdu, before their translation into Sindhi. Fāraqlaiṯ became editor of *al-Jamʻīat* after Maudūdī's departure from that publication. Concerned that associations like the Jamʻīat ʻUlamā-i Hind had become targets for imprisonment, he fled to Bijnor, where he oversaw the publications *Fārān* and then the newspaper *Madīnah*, where he was an assistant editor during Jalālī's editorial tenure, perhaps in 1927. He served on the editorial board for one year, contributing to *Madīnah*'s strengthening reputation as a newspaper by writing editorials. After a year Maulānā Ḥusain Aḥmad Madanī traveled to Bijnor in person to ask Majīd Ḥasan to give Fāraqlaiṯ permission to return to his work on *al-Jamʻīat*, after which Fāraqlaiṯ returned to Delhi to work on that publication. In 1939, Fāraqlaiṯ arrived in Lahore, where he oversaw editorials at the publication *Zamzam*, which ran afoul of the colonial government until it was closed for a year in the early 1940s. In Lahore, Fāraqlaiṯ continued to be renowned for his fiery, anticolonial rhetoric. In 1947 he returned to Delhi to edit *al-Jamʻīat*, where he continued working until his resignation in 1963.[10] Even after retirement he continued writing, publishing a column called "*Nayā Dunīyā* [*New World*]" and a popular novel titled *Izābilā*.[11]

Maulvī Shabīr ul-Raḥmān Chāndpūrī (1886–1980)
Birthplace
Chandpur, Bijnor district

Education
He was educated at home by this mother before being sent to Aligarh University to complete his education, becoming Chandpur's first Aligarh graduate. In Aligarh he received an MA in Philosophy. He received an LT (Licenciate in Teaching) from Allahabad University.
Journalism Career
He briefly worked with *Madīnah* in 1925 but left soon after to take up a place in Aligarh as a professor.

"Māhir" ul-Qādrī (1906–1978)
Birthplace
Bulandshehr
Education
He received his foundational education at home. His father, M'ashūq 'Alī "Ẓarīf," was a poet, so he was educated in poetry as well as in Urdu, Persian, and Arabic from a young age. He traveled widely to Hyderabad, Bombay, and Delhi for his studies.
Journalism Career
He worked for three publications put out by Madīnah Press: the newspaper *Madīnah*, the children's journal *Ghunchah*, and the journal *Fārān*. He worked on the newspaper from 1932 until 1947, when he relocated to Karachi following Partition.[12]

Qadūs Ṣahbā'ī (c. 1900–c. 1960)
Wrote for *Madīnah* pre-1947
Birthplace
Unknown
Education
He studied journalism with Maulānā Shaukat 'Alī, gaining his passion for the career from that man's influence.
Journalism Career
He first worked on the newspaper *Khilāfat* (Bombay), and prior to independence he worked for *Madīnah* (Bijnor), *Āzād Hind* (Calcutta), *Musulmān* (Delhi), *Ṣobaḥ vaṯan* (Bhopal), and *Niẓām* (Delhi). After independence, he shifted to Pakistan and edited the papers *Navā'e vaqt* and *Qandīl*, which were published from Lahore. In Pakistan he also became attached to prominent English language newspapers.[13] He died in Karachi.

Notes

1. Parvez 'Ādil, *Tārīkh-i Madīnah Bijnor* (Rampur: Applied Books, 2018), 361.
2. Department of Criminal Intelligence, *Statement of Newspapers and Periodicals Published in the United Provinces 1926* (Allahabad: Supt., Govt. Press, 1927), British Library.
3. Home Political 1930 F-173-1, Part li, National Archives of India.
4. Gurbachan Chandan, *Urdū Ṣaḥāfat kā Safar* [Journey of Urdu Journalism] (New Delhi: Educational Publishing House, 2007), 3, 273; cited in Parvez 'Ādil, *Tārīkh-i Madīnah Bijnor* (Rampur: Applied Books, 2018), 368–70.
5. Majīd Ḥasan, "Ẓarūrī guzārish [Necessary Announcement]," *Madīnah*, September 21, 1927; Parvez 'Ādil, *Tārīkh-i Madīnah Bijnor* (Rampur: Applied Books, 2018), 358.
6. Parvez 'Ādil, *Tārīkh-i Madīnah Bijnor* (Rampur: Applied Books, 2018), 352.

7. Raḥīm Ba<u>kh</u>sh Shāhīn, *Maulānā Maudūdī* (unpublished manuscript), 118–19; cited in Parvez ʿĀdil, *Tārī<u>kh</u>-i Madīnah Bijnor* (Rampur: Applied Books, 2018), 335–38.
8. Mumtāz Aḥmed Makkī, *Teḥrīk-i Āzādī ke numā'indah Muslim mujāhidīn*, 70; cited in Parvez ʿĀdil, *Tārī<u>kh</u>-i Madīnah Bijnor* (Rampur: Applied Books, 2018), 328–29.
9. Muḥammad Adīl ʿAbāsī, "*Dībāchah* [Preface]," *Teḥrīk-i <u>Kh</u>ilāfat* (Lahore: Jumhoori Publications, 2009).
10. Note that ʿĀdil lists this retirement date as 1973, which is likely a clerical error, since ʿĀdil records that Fāraqlai<u>t</u> died in 1967. Parvez ʿĀdil, *Tārī<u>kh</u>-i Madīnah Bijnor* (Rampur: Applied Books, 2018), 349.
11. Source of this entry is Parvez ʿĀdil, *Tārī<u>kh</u>-i Madīnah Bijnor* (Rampur: Applied Books, 2018), 346–50.
12. Parvez ʿĀdil, *Tārī<u>kh</u>-i Madīnah Bijnor* (New Delhi: Applied Books, 2018), 366.
13. ʿĀrif ʿAzīz, *Ẓikr-i Jamīl* (Bhopal: Madhīyah Pradīsh urdū ākādamī, 1995), 72; cited in Parvez ʿĀdil, *Tārī<u>kh</u>-i Madīnah Bijnor* (New Delhi: Applied Books, 2018), 321–23.

APPENDIX IV

Spring Season

The following are the translations provided in file Home Political NA 1930 NA F-173-1 Part li, pp. 196–208 in the National Archives of India, recording the two articles that led to the conviction of *Madīnah* editor Naṣrullah Khān in 1930.

SPRING SEASON
Days of verdure for the autumn-affected garden of our motherland.
Tell the tavern-keeper to open the doors of the public house
The jolly fellows have left their homes on seeing the clouds of the spring season.

Full eleven years ago, the Indian world was convulsed with the tumultuous agitation against the Rowlatt Act. With the advent of the spring season spring had also visited afresh the autumn-affected garden of the oppressed mother-land (sic). It was exactly on March 13 that the greatest rum-guzzler of the public house of freedom was arrested and it is exactly on March 12 that the same brave cavalier of the field of independence again marches into the battlefield with a handful of his followers, saying "Bismillah o Mujraha" (lit. in the name of God and relying on his mercy).

I will come out with my weary caravan in the darkness of night.
My sigh will give forth sparks and my breath will emit flames.

The old sky is asking Venus and Jupiter in a state of astonishment whether the people of India have not gone mad and whether this old and lean Gandhi particularly, who is a mere handful of bones, has not lost his senses and who despite the extreme lack of resources and even giving up the thought of violence and use of force and absolutely unarmed intends to oppose a power which has defeated the armed and powerful powers of Germany, Austria, Turkey and Bulgaria, which possesses lakhs of airships which devastate habitations by dropping bombs, lakhs of machine guns which shower fire like rain and in the twinkling of the eye can turn a vast jungle of humanity into a cemetery, which has shell-proof motor cars of steel on the occupants of which it is believed that even the angel of death cannot lay his hands, which possesses army and police out of number, whom even the angels hesitate to offer battle. Has this lean and thin old man left his home to encounter that power? Let us see how many lakhs of troops, how many thousands of armoured cars, how many thousands of cannon, how many lakhs of machine-guns and how many hundreds of airships are accompanying him? Only 72 men! Unarmed! Pledged to non-violence! Resolved upon putting up with all the abuses of tyranny and oppression with a smiling face? Great God! What a spectacle!

Doubtless, it is a wonderful spectacle but it is not an unparalleled and unprecedented one. Whenever there has been a clash between right and wrong the right has always had to encounter the wrong in a similarly unequal state from the standpoint of strength and power. The best and greatest number of instances of this are found in the life of that perfect man (the Prophet)—may God confer peace and blessing upon him—whose every action is an ideal for men and whose every gesture is a laudable example for God's creatures.

If Mahatma Gandhi has today, in such a helpless state, come out to break the laws of the British Government, long before this the Prophet had gone with 313 crusaders in a state of extreme helplessness to fight an armed and militant power. The last mentioned event is but an imitation of this 1300 years old event and no one who is acquainted with the result of the battle of Badr should express surprise at Gandhi's self-sacrificing resolve. Right is always helpless and wrong powerful in the beginning but in the end right alone gets the upper hand and wrong is always defeated. The right always triumphs and the wrong is always vanquished.

However with the advent of the spring season the dead agitation of India has also begun to revive. That which could not even be thought of a few months ago has come before our eyes. The trumpet of war has been sounded. Troops have begun to array themselves. The battle is about to be started. The sentiments of crusade and martyrdom which having been fostered in the hearts were agitating the minds of the people are now impatient to come out and circumstances for their satisfaction have also been brought about. Happy is the man who risking his life and property manfully joins this battle of right and wrong. The time for apologies and excuses is over. This is the time for fighting and action alone. The arguments are over. The time for action has begun. It is for the cowards and eunuchs to discuss its failure or success. The duty of the brave is only to sacrifice themselves like moths on the candle of the crusade for independence.

The historic letter which Mahatmaji has written to Lord Irwin is praiseworthy in every respect. This letter truly represents the heart of India which has been placed before the assassin so that he may see what painful sights of ruin and devastation of India lie concealed in the drops of its warm blood. It is a very accurate picture of the economic, political, moral, and educational ruin of India on reading which the heart of even the most evil-minded person trembles and the fact is that this letter itself justifies the campaign of civil disobedience started by Mahatma Gandhi. In this letter Mahatmaji has given this reason for stepping into the thorny valley of breaking laws that under the present system of Government crores of God's creatures are undergoing the sufferings of poverty and starvation and that it ought to be the duty of every good-hearted Indian to emancipate them from these calamities. From this standpoint Mahatma Gandhi has won over to his side every noble, self-respecting and philanthropic human being and only a very hard-hearted man can keep aloof from him on the basis of political difference of opinion. The object of removing the hardships of God's creatures is in itself so magnificent, so sacred and so holy that no one can avoid taking part in this war. Lord Irwin has also given a very decisive reply to this challenge. Rather the Government of India has by arresting Sardar Patel really announced what its policy would be towards civil disobedience. On the one hand Mahatma Gandhi's object is so magnificent and sacred, on the other the Government of India's reply is so impetuous and haughty that by comparing the two, no noble-minded Indian who believes in God and has sympathy for God's creatures can remain aloof from this movement.

The Position of Muslims

The position of Muslims is quite clear. The Muslims are a brave and proud race. As soon as a battle begins it is compelled by its warlike nature and self-sacrificing disposition and raising the cry of "Allah-o-Akbar" joins it. To prevent a Muslim from joining a battle is like preventing a Sufi from joining a Qawwali party. Moreover the sentiment of the strong hatred towards the British Government which is surging in his heart does not allow him to sit idle. He is compelled to join every movement which proclaims the destruction of this Government. As soon as he hears the name of the British Government his body is inflamed. The terrible ruins of the Islamic Empire in India on the destruction of which has been reared the lofty edifice of the British Government, present themselves before his eyes. The story of the helplessness of the Islamic world and of the oppression to which it has been subjected becomes fresh. He (Muslim) sees in its pomp and splendor the ruin of Islam and Islamic power. No inhabitant of India bears such hatred towards the British Government as the Muslim does. And when he sees that a brave man is out to oppose this Government then he forgets all his differences and reaches the field of battle. This is why every Muslim barring a few extremely shortsighted and selfish persons, is praying for the success of Mahatmaji, so much so that Maulana Hasrat Mohani, who, not only from the time of the Nehru Report, but also from that of the Ahmedabad Congress, is the bitterest opponent of Mahatma Gandhi on matters of principles, declares his warm sympathy for the civil disobedience movement. And the fact is that every Muslim who fears God and in whose heart is surging the love of the Prophet cannot forsake that person who risks his life to help the oppressed creatures of God. The history of the Muslim is replete with sacrifices and martyrdom and he is an unbought slave of every self-sacrificing man.

Call to Action

The manner in which the moths burn themselves on the candle,
In the same way self-sacrificing people lay down their lives for the sake of their country.
Brave to the intoxication of the wine of patriotism.
I go about in such a way as if I were carrying a public house on my shoulders.
The door of the public house has opened, come ye who may like to have a drink.
This is what the old tavern-keeper is telling those who drink.
Come. Young men, there is again a stir in the field of action.
How long is this merry-making to go on? How long this indulgence in drinking?
The garden of our country has been laid waste through plunder,
The country now possesses neither that bloom nor glory.
May, O Lord! the tree of the objects of him who has in this way devastated the garden of (our) country be also cut out by the root.
Captivity in English prison is a prelude to the joys of heaven,
That is to say the door of the jail of the country opens in Paradise.
Is there any enjoyment or pleasure even greater than martyrdom?
What are you thinking? Arise young men of the country.
May spring come afresh over the garden of liberty.
O, blood of martyrs of the country, flow like a river.

Bibliography

Archives Consulted and Abbreviations

British Library—BL
National Archives of India—NAI
Raza Rampur Library—RRL
University of Cambridge—Cambridge
University of London, Royal Holloway—ULRH
University of Oxford, Bodleian Library—Bodleian
US Library of Congress—USLC
Uttar Pradesh State Archives—UPSA

Newspapers

Ahl-i Ḥadīth (1920–1921). RRL.
al-Hilāl (1912–1914). RRL.
Aljami'at (Delhi 1920–1948, 1948–1953). University Library, Cambridge.
The Dabdabai Sekundaree (1920–1922). RRL.
Hamdard (1924). RRL.
Madīnah (Bijnor 1913–1947). Microfilm, Royal Holloway, University of London Library.
Milap (Delhi 1923–1948). University Library, Cambridge.
Times of India (Delhi 1912–1926). ProQuest Online Archive, Bodleian.
Zamānah (Kanpur 1906–1908). University Library, Cambridge.
Z̲ulqarnain (Badaun 1910–1944). University Library, Cambridge.

Unpublished Government Records

Administrative Reports of the Indo-European Telegraph Department, 1872–3 to 1894–5. V/ 24/ 4289. Bodleian.

Amendments of Election Rules Bijnor 1913. Nainital, 1913. UPSA.

Confiscations and Disposal of Confiscated Lands. Board of Revenue, Miscellaneous Department, 1902. UPSA.

Control and Management of Nazul Property in Badaun District. Miscellaneous Department, 1902. UPSA.

Home Political Records [Confidential], 1910–1924. NAI.

Memorandum Submitted by the Government of the United Provinces to the Indian Statutory Commission, vol. 9. London: Indian Statutory Commission, 1930. UPSA.

Notes and Orders: Reconstruction of the Municipal Board of Bijnor. Uttar Pradesh: Administrative Correspondence, 1913. UPSA.

"Petition from the Inhabitants of Bijnor." Department: Railway Department, Branch: Railway Construction, 1907–10. File No. 79–84. National Archives of India.

Robinson, D. G., Colonel. *Correspondence between D. G. Robinson, Colonel, R.E., Director General of Telegraphs in India and the Secretary to the Government of India, Public Works Department*, 1871. Bodleian.

Official Publications

1931 Census Report Uttar Pradesh. UP Government Press, 1931. UPSA.

Appendix to the 1906 Census of Uttar Pradesh. UP Government Press, 1914.

Department of Criminal Intelligence, *Statements of Newspapers and Periodicals Published in India and Burma during the Year 1914* (Delhi: Supt., Govt. Printing, India, 1916). National Archives of India.

Department of Criminal Intelligence. *Statement of Newspapers and Periodicals Published in the United Provinces. Allahabad: Sup., Govt. Press, 1927–1948*. British Library.

Department of Criminal Intelligence. *Statement of Newspapers and Periodicals Published in the United Provinces during the Year 1911, 1912 [with Index]*. Simla: Government Central Branch Press, 1912, 1913. UPSA.

East India (native Press). *Copy of Opinions, and Reasons for the Same, Entered in the Minutes of Proceedings of the Council of India, Relating to the Vernacular Press Act, 1878*. Cambridge, UK: Proquest LLC, 2006.

Gazetteer of the Province of Oudh. Vol. 11. Lucknow: Oudh Government Press, 1877–1878. Bodleian.

History of Indian Railways. Simla: India Railway Dept., 1919. Bodleian.

Indian Newspaper Reports, c. 1868–1942, UPSA, BL.

India Post Office. *Annual Report of the Post Office of India: 1902–1903* (Calcutta: Supt., Govt. Press, 1903). Bodleian.

Meyer, William Stevenson, Richard Burn, James Sutherland Cotton, and Herbert Hope Risley. *Imperial Gazetteer*. Vol. 8. Oxford: Clarendon Press, 1911.

Nevill, H. R. *Bara Banki: A Gazetteer*. Allahabad: Supt., Govt. Press, 1904. Bodleian.

Nevill, H. R. *Bareilly: A Gazetteer*. Allahabad: Supt., Govt. Press, 1911. Bodleian.

Nevill, H. R. *Bijnor: A Gazetteer*. Allahabad: Supt., Govt. Press, 1908. Bodleian.

Nevill, H. R. *Bijnor: Supplementary Notes and Statistics to Volume XIV of the District Gazetteers of the United Provinces of Agra and Oudh*. Allahabad: Supt., Govt. Press, 1914. Bodleian.

Nevill, H. R. *Budaun: A Gazetteer*. Allahabad: Supt., Govt. Press, 1907. Bodleian.

Nevill, H. R. *Bulandshahr: A Gazetteer*. Allahabad: Supt., Govt. Press, 1903. Bodleian.

Nevill, H. R. *Lucknow: A Gazetteer*. Allahabad: Supt., Govt. Press. Archive.org.

Nevill, H. R. *Moradabad: A Gazetteer*. Allahabad: Supt., Govt. Press, 1911. Bodleian.

Nevill, H. R. *Muzaffarnagar: A Gazetteer*. Allahabad: Supt., Govt. Press, 1903. Bodleian.

Nevill, H. R. *Rai Bareli: A Gazetteer*. Allahabad: Supt., Govt. Press, 1905. Bodleian.

Pert, Frederick James. *Final Settlement Report of the Bijnor District (Eleventh Revision)*. Allahabad: North-Western Provinces and Oudh Government Press, 1899. Bodleian.

Press and Registration of Books Act, 1867. Act No. 25 of 1867 dated March 22, 1867. Advocate Khoj Website: Law Library. Accessed August 28, 2018. http://www.advocatekhoj.com/library/bareacts/pressandregistration/index.php?Title=Press%20and%20Registration%20of%20Books%20Act,%201867.

"Public and State Abbreviated Addresses, 1923." In *Post Office Guide: India*. Calcutta: Government Press, 1910–1920. 680, British Library, IOR/V/25/760.

Report of the Telegraph Committee. Calcutta: Supt., Govt. Press, 1907. British Library.

Selections from Indian Owned Newspapers Published in the United Provinces 1914–1916. Nainital: United Provinces Government, 1914. UPSA.

Selections from the Vernacular Newspapers Published in the Punjab, North Western Provinces, Oudh, and the Central Provinces (1900–1925). NAI.

UP Government Poll: Report for Fortnight Ending 30-4-1919. Internal Government Correspondence, 1919. NAI.

Varun, Dangli Prasad. *Uttar Pradesh District Gazetteers: Bijnor*. Lucknow: Government of Uttar Pradesh, Dept. of District Gazetteers, 1981. Bodleian.

Official Maps

India Office of the Accountant General, Posts, and Telegraphs. *Skeleton Map of India Illustrating the Lines of Telegraph in 1870*. Dehra Dun: Survey of India, 1870. Bodleian.

Prepared in accordance with Govt. N.W.P., P.W. Dept. *Map of Rohilkhand*. Circular No. E dated May 16, 1872. Dehra Dun: Survey of India, 1891. Bodleian.

Survey of India. *India Showing Telegraphs. Map*. Dehra Dun: Survey of India, 1892. Bodleian.

Survey of India. *Telegraph Map of India: Corrected to Sept 30th 1914*. Dehra Dun: Survey of India, 1914. Bodleian.

Urdu Secondary Sources

ʿAbdullāh Cag͟htāʾī, Muḥammad. *Sarguẕasht-i k͟haṭ-i nastaʿlīq*. Lāhaur: Kitāb K͟hānah-yi Nauras, 1970.

ʿĀdil, Parvez. *Tārīk͟h-i Madīnah Bijnor*. Rampur: Applied Books, 2018.

ʿĀdil, Parvez. "Madīnah Ak͟hbār." Ph thesis, University of Najibabad, 2013.

Aḥīuddīn, Muḥammad. *Līthogrāfī: Fann tabāʿat par Urdū mein kār-āmad aur pahalī kitāb*. Budaun: Matbuʿa Nizāmī Press, 1926.

Aḥmed, Ashfāq ʿAzmī. *Nazīr Aḥmed: Shakṣīyat aur kārnāme*. Delhi: Muktabah Shāhirāh, 1974, 9.

Aḥmed, Nazīr. *Mirāt-ul ʿUrūs*. Lucknow: Nawal Kishore Press, 1881.

Aḥmed, Nazīr. *Mirāt ul-ʿUrūs*. Dihlī: Kitābī Dunīyā, 2003.

Aḥsan, Gilānī Shaik͟h Syed Manaẓir. *Sawāniḥ-i qāsmī*. Deoband: Daftar Dār ul-ʿUlūm, 1955–56.

al-Wahhab, Muḥammad ʿAbd. *Kitāb al-Tawhīd*. Riyadh: International Islamic Publishing House, 1994.

Anṣārī, Muḥammad Ināyatullah. *Taẕkira-i ʿulamā-yi Farangī Maḥalī*. Lucknow: Ishaat al-Uloom Barqi Press, 1930.

Anṣārī, Muḥammad Walī ul-Ḥaq. "Farangī Mahal kī ʿilmī, Adabī aur Siyāsī K͟hidmāt." *Nayā Daur* (February–March 1994): 48.

ʿĀrif ʿAzīz Maṯbūʿa, *Ẕikr-i jamīl*. Bhopal: Madhīyah Pradīsh Urdū Ākādamī, 1995.

Artemidorus, Daldanius. *Kitāb Taʿbīr al-rūʾyā*. Edited by ʿAbd al-Munʾim al-Hafni and Ḥunayn bin Isḥāq. Cairo: Dar al-Rashad, 1991.

Āzād, Muḥammad Ḥusain. *Nazm-i ʿĀzād* (The Poetry of Āzād). Edited by Tabassum Kashmīrī. Lahore: Maktabah ʿāliyah, 1978 [1899].

Azīz, ʿĀrif. *Ẕikr-i Jamīl*. Bhopal: Madhīyah Pradīsh Urdū Akādamī, 1995.

Barasawī, Shai<u>kh</u> Muḥammad Akram ibn Shai<u>kh</u> Muḥammad ʻAlī. *Iqtibās al-Anwar*. Lahore: Bazm-i Ittiḥad-ul-Muslimīn, compiled in 1130 AH / 1717–1718.

Bilgrāmī, Hosh (Nawāb Hosh Yār Jang Bahādur). *Mushāhidat*. Hyderabad, 1960.

Bilgrāmī, Maulvī ʻAbdul Ḥaq. *Māsir al-ikram*. Hyderabad: n.p., 1910.

Chandan, Gurbachan. *Urdū Ṣaḥāfat kā Safar*. New Delhi: Educational Publishing House, 2007.

Delanoue, G. "ʻAl-I<u>kh</u>wān Al-Muslimūn." *Ei^2* 3 (1971): 1068–71.

Dihlavī, Anūr ʻAlī. *Urdu Ṣaḥāfat*. New Delhi: Urdu Academy, 1987.

Farūqī, Ẓīyā ul-Ḥasan. *Risālah Do-māhī*. Lucknow: Uttar Pradesh Urdu Academy, 1981.

Fitrat, Ḥasan ʻAbāsur. "Urdū Ṣaḥāfat kī Nashīb-o Farāz." In *Nayā Daur: Urdū Ṣaḥāfat*. Vol. 66. No. 403. Lucknow: Information and Public Relations Department, June/July 2011: 64–74.

Ghazzālī. *Imām Ghazzālī's Iḥyā Ulūm-Id-Dīn*. Edited by Fazlul Karim. New Delhi: Published by Nusrat, Alī Nasrī for Kitāb Bhavan, 1982.

Ḥaidar, Syed ʻAqīl. "Uttar Pradesh mei<u>n</u> Urdū Ṣaḥāfat." *Nayā Daur: Urdū Ṣaḥāfat* 66, no. 403 (June/July 2011): 144–46.

Ḥasan, Rihān. "Maulānā Āzād kī Urdū Ṣaḥāfat." *Nayā Daur: Urdū Ṣaḥāfat*. Vol. 66. No. 403. Lucknow: Information and Public Relations Department. June/July 2011: 30–32.

Hāshmī, Syed Nūr ul-Ḥasan. *Eik Nādir Roznāmchah*. Lucknow: n.p., 1954.

Ḥaẓrat Ḥusain Aḥmad Madanī ki siyāsī dā'irī: A<u>kh</u>bār aur afkār kī raushnī mei<u>n</u> ("The Political Diary of the Revered Shaikhul Islam Maulana Husain Aḥmad Madanī: In the Light of Newspapers and Commentary"). 3 vols. Karachi: Majlisi-i Yādgār-i Shai<u>kh</u>ul Islām Pakistan, 2002–11.

Ismāʻīl, Muḥammad. *Taqwīyat-ul-Imān*. Riyadh: Dar-us-Salam Publications, 1995.

Kalīm, Ibn-i. *Tarī<u>kh</u>-i fann-i <u>kh</u>aṭṭāṭī: Nādir va nāyāb-i shāhkār-i <u>kh</u>ushnivīsī*. Multān: Ibn-i Kalīm, 1977.

Kaẓmī, Muḥammad Aḥmad. *Niẓāmī Badāyūnī: Yʻanī Sawāniḥ Ḥayāt Maulānā Niẓāmuddīn Ḥusain Niẓāmī Badāyūnī*. Badayun: Nizāmī Press, 1949.

<u>Kh</u>ān, Sir Syed Aḥmed. *Map of the Zila of Bijnor, 1863*. Delhi: Sharāfat Ḥusain Mirzā, 1964.

<u>Kh</u>ān, Sir Syed Aḥmed. *Tārī<u>kh</u>-i Sarkashī-i Ẓilaʻ-yi Bijnor (1858)*. Translated by Ḥāfiẓ Malik and Morris Dembo. Delhi: Idārah-i Adabīyat-i Dihli, 1982.

Madīnah Jūbalī Nambar. 1939. Rampur Library. A<u>kh</u>bārāt-i Urdu Catalogue Number 533.

Majīd, Shīmā. *Urdū Rasmul<u>kh</u>aṭ: Inti<u>kh</u>āb-i Maqālāt, ṭabaʻ-i 1*. Islāmābād: Muqtadirah-yi Qaumī Zabān, 1989.

Manṭo, Saʻādat Ḥasan. "Nayā Qānūn." In *Readings in Urdu: Prose and Poetry*, ed. C. M. Naim, 49–64. Honolulu: East-West Center Press, 1965. Digital South Asia Website. Accessed July 2013. http://dsal.uchicago.edu/digbooks/dig_toc.html?BOOKID=PK1975.N18.

Manṭo, Saʻādat Ḥasan. "Nayā Qānūn [New Law]." In *Manṭo ke numāyanda afsāne*, 13–45. Aligarh: Ejūkeshnal Buk Hā'us, 1977.

Nadwī, Muḥammad Isḥāq Jalīs. *Tārī<u>kh</u>-i Nadwat ul-ʻulamā*. Vol. 1. Lucknow: Lucknow Daftar-i niẓāmat-i Nadwat al-ʻUlamā, 1983–1984.

Nadwī, Sayyid Abu ʻl-Ḥasan ʻAlī. *Karwān-i Zindagī*. 5 vols. Lucknow and Karachi: Majlis-i nashrīyyat-i Islām, 1983–1994.

Nadwī, Sayyid Sulayman. *Ḥayāt-i Shiblī*. Azamgarh: Maṭbaʻ-i maʻārif, 1970.

Qāsmī, 'Atā ur Raḥmān. *Alwāḥ us-Ṣanādīd*. Delhi: Maulānā Āzād Akaidamī, 1991.
Qatīl, Muḥammad Ḥasan. *Haft Tamāshā-yi Mirzā Qatīl*. Lucknow: Maṯba'-i Nawal Kishor, 1875.
Qidwai, Sh. "Maulānā Muḥammad 'Alī Jauhar aur Hamdard." In *Nayā Daur: Urdū Ṣaḥāfat*. 66, no. 403 (June/July 2011): 29.
Rizvī, Syed Muḥammad Aqīl, ed. *Intikhāb-i Madīnah Bijnor*. Lucknow: Uttar Pradesh Urdu Academy, 1988.
Sabrī, Imdād. *Urdū ke akhbār navīs / Imdād Ṣābirī*. Dihlī: Ṣābirī Akaiḍmī, 1973.
Sa'īd, Aḥmad. *Roznāmah Zamīndār Lāhor: September to December 1923*. Lahore: Maulana Zafar Ali Khan Trust, 2013.
Savāniḥ 'umrī akhbārāt, ḥissah aval, by Secretary of the Anjuman-i 'ilmī and the proprietor of the newspaper Akhtar-i Hind and Akhtar Press. Lucknow: Akhtar Press, June 1888. Raza Rampur Library.
Sayed, Aḥmed. "Tartīb-o tadvīn." In *Roznamah Zamīndār: Maqālah hā'e iftitāhiyah aur shazarāt*. Lahore: Maulana Zafar 'Ali Khan Trust, 2013.
Shāhīn, Raḥīm Bakhsh. "Maulānā Maudūdī." Unpublished manuscript, n.d.
Sherwānī, Mohd 'Abdul Shāhīd Khān, ed. *Karvān-i Khayāl*. Bijnor: Madīnah Press, 1946.
Ṣiddīqī, Furqān Aḥmad. *Ẓila' Bijnor ke Jauvāhir*. Delhi: Jade Press, 1991.
Syed, Tāj, comp. *Kulliyāt-i majrūh sultānpūrī*. Lahore: Al-Hamd Publications, 2003.
Zakarīyā Kāndhlavī, Muḥammad. *Āp Bītī*. Lahore: Darul Ishā't, 2003.
Zarnūjī, Burhān al-Dīn. *Ta'līm al-muta'allim-tarīq at-ta'allum*. Edited by Theodora Mead Abel. New York: Published under the auspices of the Iranian Institute and School of Asiatic Studies by King's Crown Press, 1947.

English Secondary Sources

Abbas, Ashgar. *Print Culture: Sir Syed's Aligarh Institute Gazette, 1866–1897*. Translated from Urdu by Syed Asim Ali. Delhi: Primus Books, 2015.
Abbas, K. A. *I Am Not an Island: An Experiment in Autobiography*. New Delhi: Vikas, 1977.
Abdulrazak, F. A. *The Kingdom of the Book: The History of Printing as an Agency of Change in Morocco between 1865 and 1912*. Boston: Boston University Press, 1990.
Abdus, Salam Khurshid. *Journalism in Pakistan: First Phase, 1845 to 1857*. Lahore: Lahore Publishers United, 1964.
Abrahamov, B. *Islamic Theology: Traditionalism and Rationalism*. Edinburgh: Edinburgh University Press, 1998.
Abu-Lughod, Janel L. "The Islamic City—Historic Myth, Islamic Essence and Contemporary Relevance." *International Journal of Middle East Studies* 19, no. 2 (1987): 155–76.
Adam, Barbara. "Of Timescapes, Futurescapes and Timeprints." Lecture at Lüneburg University, June 17, 2008.
Aftab, Tahera. "Negotiating with Patriarchy: South Asian Muslim Women and the Appeal to Sir Syed Ahmed Khan." *Women's History Review* 14, no. 1 (2005): 75–98.
Aguiar, Marian. *Tracking Modernity: India's Railways and the Culture of Mobility*. Minneapolis: University of Minnesota Press, 2011.
Ahmad, Imtiaz. "The Ashraf-Ajlaf Dichotomy in Muslim Social Structure in India." *Indian Economic Social History Review* 3 (1966): 268–78.

Ahmad, Irfan. *Islamism and Democracy in India: The Transformation of Jamaat-e-Islami*. Princeton: Princeton University Press, 2009.

Aḥmad Khān, Sayyid. *Causes of the Indian Revolt: Three Essays*. Edited by Salim al-Din Quraishi. Lahore: Sang-e-Meel Publications, 1997.

Ahmad, Mumtaz. *Urdu Newspaper Reader*. Kensington, MD: Dunwoody Press, 1985.

Ahmad, S. Maqbul. *Historical Geography of Kashmir, Based on Arabic and Persian Sources from AD 800 to 1900*. New Delhi: Ariana Publishing House, 1984.

Ahmed, Akbar S. *Discovering Islam: Making Sense of Muslim History and Society*. London: Routledge, 1989.

Ahmed, Mashkoor. "Structural Analysis of Internal Migration and Socio-Economic Transformation in Bijnor District, Uttar Pradesh." Dissertation, Master of Philosophy. Aligharh Muslim University, 2008.

Ahmed, Safdar. "Literary Romanticism and Islamic Modernity: The Case of Urdu Poetry." *South Asia: Journal of South Asian Studies* 35, no. 2 (2012): 434–55.

Ahvenainen, Jorma. *The History of the Near Eastern Telegraphs: Before the First World War*. Edited by Suomalainen Tiedeakatemia. Helsinki: Academia Scientiarum Fennica, 2011.

Alam, Asiya. "Polygyny, Family and Sharafat: Discourses amongst North Indian Muslims, circa 1870–1918." *Modern Asian Studies* 45, no. 3 (May 2011): 631–68.

Alam, Muzaffar, and Sanjay Subrahmanyam. "The Making of a Munshi." *Comparative Studies of South Asia, Africa and the Middle East* 24, no. 2 (2004): 61–72.

Alam, Muzaffar, and Sanjay Subrahmanyam. "Witnesses and Agents of Empire: Eighteenth-Century Historiography and the World of the Mughal Munshi." *Journal of the Economic and Social History of the Orient* 53, nos. 1–2 (2010): 393–423.

Alam, Muzaffar, and Sanjay Subrahmanyam. *Writing the Mughal World*. New York: Columbia University Press, 2012.

Alam, Muzaffar. "The Culture and Politics of Persian in Precolonial Hindustan." In *Literary Cultures in History: Reconstructions from South Asia*, edited by Sheldon I. Pollock, 191–98. London: University of California Press, 2003.

Alam, Muzaffar. "The Debate Within: A Sufi Critique of Religious Law, *Tasawwuf* and Politics in Mughal India." *South Asian History and Culture* 2, no. 2 (2011): 138–59.

Alam, Rafat. "Qazi Abdul Ghaffar—My Maternal Grandfather (Nana Abba)." Rafat Alam's Blog. Accessed August 8, 2018. http://www.rafatalam.com/Qāẓī-abdul-ghaffar-my-maternal-grandfather-nana-abba.

Alavi, Seema. *Islam and Healing: Loss and Recovery of an Indo-Muslim Medical Tradition, 1600–1900*. Basingstoke: Palgrave Macmillan, 2008.

Alavi, Seema. *Muslim Cosmopolitanism in an Age of Empire*. Cambridge, MA: Harvard University Press, 2015.

Alavi, Seema. "Unani Medicine in the Nineteenth-Century Public Sphere: Urdu Texts and the Oudh Akhbar." *Indian Economic and Social History Review* 42 (March 2005): 101–29.

Algar, Hamid. "Political Aspects of Naqshbandi History." In *Naqshbandis: Cheminements et situation actuelle d'un ordre mystique musulman = Historical Developments and Present Situation of a Muslim Mystical Order*, edited by Institut français d'études anatoliennes d'Istanbul, 123. Istanbul: Isis, 1990.

Ali, Amir. "Evolution of Public Sphere in India." *Economic and Political Weekly* 36, no. 26 (June–July 2001): 2419–25.

Ali, Azra Asghar. "Recovery of the Female Voice through Women's Journals in Urdu in British India 1898–1947." *South Asia: Journal of South Asian Studies* 21, no. 2 (1998): 61–87.

Ali, Mohamed. *My Life, a Fragment: An Autobiographical Sketch of Maulana Mohamed Ali*. Edited by Mushirul Hasan. New Delhi: Manohar, 1999.

Allievi, S. "Islam in the Public Space: Social Networks, Media and Neo-Communities." In *Muslim Networks and Transnational Communities in and around Europe*, edited by S. Allievi and J. S. Nielsen, 1–27. Leiden: Brill, 2003.

Al-Shaibi, Kamil M. *Sufism and Shi'ism*. Surbiton: LAAM, 1991.

Amanullah, M. "Islamic Dreaming: An Analysis of Its Truthfulness and Influence." In *Dreaming in Christianity and Islam: Culture, Conflict, and Creativity*, edited by Kelly Bulkeley, Kate Adams, and Patricia M. Davis, 98–110. New Brunswick, NJ: Rutgers University Press, 2009.

Anderson, Benedict. *Imagined Communities: Reflections on the Origin and Spread of Nationalism*. Rev. ed. London: Verso, 1991.

Ansari, K. H. "Pan-Islam and the Making of the Early Indian Muslim Socialists." *Modern Asian Studies* 20, no. 3 (1986): 509–37.

Appadurai, Arjun. *Modernity at Large: Cultural Dimensions of Globalization*. London: University of Minnesota Press, 1996.

Arberry, A. J., M. Minovi, and E. Blochet. *The Chester Beatty Library: A Catalogue of the Persian Manuscripts and Miniatures*, vol. 1, *MSS 101–50*. Edited by. J. V. S. Wilkinson. Dublin: Hodges Figgis, 1959.

Ariès, Philippe. *Centuries of Childhood*. New York: Vintage Books, 1962.

Asad, Talal. "The Idea of an Anthropology of Islam." Presentation at the Center for Contemporary Arab Studies, Georgetown University, Washington, DC, 1986.

Assad, Muhammad, trans. *The Message of the Qur'an: Bilingual Edition*. Watsonville, CA: The Book Foundation, 2003.

Attewell, Guy. *Refiguring Unani Plural Healing in Late Colonial India*. New Delhi: Orient Longman, 2005.

Āzād, Abūlkalām. *The Dawn of Hope: Selections from the Al-Hilal of Maulana Abul Kalam Azad*. New Delhi: Indian Council of Historical Research, 2002.

Āzād, Maulānā Abul Kalam. *India Wins Freedom*. New Delhi: Orient Longman, 1988.

Bagchi, Barnita. "Two Lives: Voices, Resources, and Networks in the History of Female Education in Bengal and South Asia." *Women's History Review* 19, no. 1 (2010): 51–69.

Baldick, Julian. *Mystical Islam: An Introduction to Sufism*. London: London: Tauris, 1989.

Bang, Anne K. "Pondering the Text as Change Maker." *Comparative Studies of South Asia, Africa, and the Middle East* 35, no. 2 (2015): 375–81.

Bannerjee, Mukulika. *Muslim Portraits: Everyday Lives in India*. New Delhi: Yoda Press, 2008.

Basu, Suhbho. "Workers' Politics in Bengal, 1890–1929: Mill Towns, Strikes, and Nationalist Agitations, 1890–1929." DPhil thesis, University of Cambridge, 1994.

Baudrillard, J. *The System of Objects*. Translated by James Benedict. London: Verso, 1996.

Bayly, C. A. *Empire and Information: Intelligence Gathering and Social Communication in India, 1780–1870*. Cambridge: Cambridge University Press, 1996.

Bayly, C. A. *Rulers, Townsmen and Bazaars: North Indian Society in the Age of British Expansion, 1770–1870*. 3rd ed. New Delhi: Oxford University Press, 2012.

Bayly, C. A. "The Small Town and Islamic Gentry in North India: The Case of Kara." In *The City in South Asia: Pre-Modern and Modern*, edited by Kenneth Ballhatchet and John Harrison. London: Curzon, 1980.

Bear, Laura. "Doubt, Conflict, Mediation: The Anthropology of Modern Time." *Journal of the Royal Anthropological Institute* 20, no. S1 (2014): 3–30.

Bear, Laura. *Lines of the Nation: Indian Railway Workers, Bureaucracy, and the Intimate Historical Self*. New York: Columbia University Press, 2007.

Bendix, Reinhard. *Max Weber: An Intellectual Portrait*. London: Heinemann, 1960.

Berkey, Jonathan Porter. *The Formation of Islam: Religion and Society in the Near East, 600–1800*. Cambridge: Cambridge: Cambridge University Press, 2003.

Berkey, Jonathan Porter. *Popular Preaching and Religious Authority in the Medieval Islamic Near East*. Seattle: University of Washington Press, 2001.

Berkey, Jonathan Porter. *The Transmission of Knowledge in Medieval Cairo: A Social History of Islamic Education*. Princeton: Princeton University Press, 1992.

Beverley, Eric Lewis. "Colonial Urbanism and South Asian Cities." *Social History* 36, no. 4 (2011): 482–97.

Beverley, Eric Lewis. *Hyderabad, British India, and the World: Muslim Networks and Minor Sovereignty, c. 1850–1950*. Cambridge: Cambridge University Press, 2015.

Bhattacharya, Arnav. "Sexual Science and Unani Medicine: Exploring Islam, Gender and Sexuality in Abul Hasanat's *Sachitra Jouno Bigyan* [Illustrated Sexual Science]." Unpublished paper, 2018.

Birchok, Daniel Andrew. "Sojourning on Mecca's Verandah: Place, Temporality, and Islam in an Indonesian Province." PhD dissertation, University of Michigan, 2013.

Blake, Stephen P. *Shahjahanabad: The Sovereign City in Mughal India 1639–1739*. Cambridge: Cambridge University Press, 2010.

Blank, Jonah. *Mullahs on the Mainframe: Islam and Modernity among the Daudi Bohras*. Chicago: University of Chicago Press, 2001.

Blunt, Edward. *The Caste System of Northern India: With Special Reference to the United Provinces of Agra and Oudh*. London: Oxford University Press, 1931.

Boas, H. J. *Final Report on the Eleventh Settlement of the Moradabad District*. Allahabad: Supt., Govt. Press, 1909.

Bonea, Amelia. "Telegraphy and Journalism in Colonial India, c. 1830s to 1900s." *History Compass* 12, no. 4 (2014): 387–97.

Bose, Sugata, and Ayesha Jalal. *Modern South Asia: History, Culture, Political Economy*. Delhi: Oxford University Press, 2004.

Bourdieu, Pierre. *Outline of a Theory of Practice*. Cambridge: Cambridge University Press, 1977.

Brace, Catherine, Adrian R. Bailey, and David C. Harvey. "Religion, Place and Space: A Framework for Investigating Historical Geographies of Religious Identities and Communities." *Progress in Human Geography* 30, no. 1 (2006): 28–43.

Brass, Paul R. "Elite Groups, Symbol Manipulation and Ethnic Identity among the Muslims of South Asia." In *Political Identity in South Asia*, edited by David Taylor and Malcolm Yapp, 35–77. London: Curzon Press, 1979.

Brass, Paul R. *Language, Religion and Politics in North India*. London: Cambridge University Press, 1974.

Breckenridge, Carol Appadurai, ed. *Consuming Modernity: Public Culture in a South Asian World*. Minneapolis: University of Minnesota Press, 1995.

Buckler, F. W. "The Historical Antecedents of the Khilafat Movement." *Contemporary Review* 121 (1922): 603–11.

Buehler, Arthur F. *Sufi Heirs of the Prophet: The Indian Naqshbandiyya and the Rise of the Mediating Sufi Shaykh*. Columbia: University of South Carolina Press, 1998.

Bunt, Gary R. *Islam in the Digital Age: E-Jihad, Online Fatwas and Cyber Islamic Environments*. London: Pluto, 2003.

Bunt, Gary R. *Virtually Islamic: Computer-Mediated Communication and Cyber Islamic Environments*. Cardiff: University of Wales Press, 2000.

Burgess, Adam. *Cellular Phones, Public Fears, and a Culture of Precaution*. Cambridge: Cambridge University Press, 2004.

Burke, Peter. *Eyewitnessing: The Use of Images as Historical Evidence*. Ithaca: Cornell University Press, 2001.

Carter, H. J. "Summary of the Geology of India, between the Ganges, the Indus, and Cape Comorin [With Map and Diagram]." *Journal of the Bombay Branch of the Royal Asiatic Society* (1854). London: British Library, Historical Print Editions, 2011.

Chakrabarty, Dipesh. "Open Space/Public Place: Garbage, Modernity, and India." *South Asia: Journal of South Asian Studies* 14, no. 1 (June 1991): 15–31.

Chakrabarty, Dipesh. *Provincializing Europe: Postcolonial Thought and Historical Difference*. Princeton: Princeton University Press, 2000.

Chakrabarty, Dipesh. *Rethinking Working-Class History: Bengal, 1890–1940*. Princeton: Princeton University Press, 1989.

Chakravarty, Gautam. *The Indian Mutiny and the British Imagination*. Cambridge: Cambridge University Press, 2005.

Chamberlain, Michael. *Knowledge and Social Practice in Medieval Damascus, 1190–1350*. Cambridge: Cambridge University Press, 1994.

Chandavarkar, Rajnarayan. *The Origins of Industrial Capitalism in India: Business Strategies and the Working Classes in Bombay, 1900–1940*. Cambridge: Cambridge University Press, 1994.

Chandra, Sudhir. *The Oppressive Present: Literature and Social Consciousness in Colonial India*. Delhi: Oxford University Press, 1992.

Chatterjee, Partha. "Colonialism, Nationalism, and Colonialized Women: The Contest in India." *American Ethnologist* 16, no. 4 (1989): 622–33.

Chatterjee, Partha. *Nationalist Thought and the Colonial World: A Derivative Discourse*. Minneapolis: University of Minnesota Press, 1993.

Chatterjee, Partha. *The Nation and Its Fragments: Colonial and Postcolonial Histories*. Princeton: Princeton University Press, 1993.

Chatterjee, Partha. *Our Modernity*. Rotterdam: SEPHIS and CODESRIA, 1997.

Childs, Timothy Winston. *Italo-Turkish Diplomacy and the War over Libya, 1911–1912*. Leiden: Brill, 1990.

Chittick, William C. *Sufism: A Short Introduction*. Oxford: Oneworld, 2000.

Chodkiewicz, Michel. *An Ocean without Shore: Ibn ʿArabî, the Book, and the Law*. Edited by David Streight. Albany: State University of New York Press, 1993.

Choudhury, D. K. L. "Sinews of Panic and the Nerves of Empire: The Imagined State's Entanglement with Information Panic." *Modern Asian Studies* 38, no. 4 (2004): 965–1002.

Christopher King. *One Language, Two Scripts: The Hindi Movement in Nineteenth Century North India*. New Delhi: Oxford University Press, 1994.

Chrol, Valentine. "Brahmanism and Disaffection in the Deccan." In *Indian Unrest*, 37–63. London: St. Martin's Street, 1910.

Chugtai, Ismat. *A Life in Words: Memoirs*. Translated by M. Asaduddin. New Delhi: Penguin, 2012.

Clarke, Morgan. "Neo-Calligraphy: Religious Authority and Media Technology in Contemporary Shiite Islam." *Comparative Studies in Society and History* 52, no. 2 (2010): 351–83.

Cooke, Miriam, and Bruce Lawrence, eds. *Muslim Networks from Hajj to Hip Hop*. Chapel Hill: University of North Carolina Press, 2005.

Dale, Stephen. "The Poetry and Autobiography of the Babur-nama." *Journal of Asian Studies* 55, no. 3 (August 1996): 635–64.

Dalmia, Vasudha. *The Nationalization of Hindu Traditions: Bhāratendu Hariśchandra and Nineteenth-Century Banaras*. Delhi: Oxford University Press, 1999.

Das-Chaudhuri, R. "The Nationalist Imagination." In *A South Asian Nationalism Reader*, 68–69. New Delhi: Worldview, 2007.

Dasgupta, Rohit K. "Remembering Benedict Anderson and his Influence on South Asian Studies." *Theory, Culture, and Society* 33, no. 7 (2016): 334–38.

Day, Upendra Nath. *Medieval Malway: A Political and Cultural History, 1401–1562*. Delhi: Munshi Ram Manohar Lal, 1965.

Dehejia, Vidya. *The Body Adorned: Sacred and Profane in Indian Art*. New York: Columbia University Press, 2009.

Deol, Harnik. *Religion and Nationalism in India: The Case of the Punjab*. London: Routledge, 2000.

Devji, Faisal. "Apologetic Modernity." *Modern Intellectual History* 4, no. 1 (2007): 61–76.

Devji, Faisal. "Gender and the Politics of Space: The Movement for Women's Reform in Muslim India, 1857–1900." *South Asia: Journal of South Asian Studies* 14, no. 1 (1991): 141–53.

Dhulipala, Venkat. *Creating a New Medina*. Cambridge: Cambridge University Press, 2015.

Digby, Simon. "The Sufi Shaikh and the Sultan: A Conflict of Claims to Authority." *Iran: Journal of Persian Studies* 28, no. 1 (1990): 71–74.

Dodwell, Henry Herbert. *The Cambridge History of the British Empire*. Vol. 5. Cambridge: Cambridge University Press, 1929.

Douglas, Ian Henderson. *Abul Kalam Azad: An Intellectual and Religious Biography*. Edited by Gail Minault and Christian W. Troll. Delhi: Oxford University Press, 1988.

Douglas, J. "Anglo-Indian Ghosts." In *Bombay and Western India: A Series of Stray Papers*, 363–66. 2 vols. London: S. Low, Marston & Company, 1893.

Duara, Prasenjit. *Rescuing History from the Nation: Questioning Narratives of Modern China*. Chicago: University of Chicago Press, 1995.

Dubrow, Jennifer. *Cosmopolitan Dreams: The Making of Modern Urdu Literary Culture in Colonial South Asia*. Honolulu: University of Hawai'i, 2018.

Dubrow, Jennifer. *Urdu Cosmopolis*. Honolulu: University of Hawai'i Press, 2018.

Dudney, Arthur. "Keeping the Magic Alive: How Devakīnandan Khatrī's Chandrakāntā, the First Hindi Best-Seller, Navigates Western Modernity and the Fantastical." Unpublished paper. Academia.edu. Accessed May 2017.

Durkheim, Emile. *The Elementary Forms of Religious Life*. Translated and with an introduction by Karen E. Fields. New York: The Free Press, 1995.

Dwyer, R. *Filming the Gods: Religion and Indian Cinema*. Abingdon: Routledge, 2006.

Eaton, Richard M. "The Political and Religious Authority of the Shrine of Baba Farid." In *Moral Conduct and Authority: The Place of Adab in South Asian Islam*, edited by Barbara Metcalf, 333–56. Berkeley: University of California Press, 1984.

Eickelman, D. F. "The Art of Memory: Islamic Education and Its Social Reproduction." *Comparative Studies in Society and History* 20, no. 4 (1978): 485–516.

Eickelman, Dale F., and Jon W. Anderson. "Print, Islam, and the Prospects for Civic Pluralism: New Religious Writings and Their Audiences." *Journal of Islamic Studies* 8, no. 1 (1997): 43–62.

Eickelman, Dale F., and James Piscatori. *Muslim Politics*. Princeton: Princeton University Press, 1996.

Eisenstein, Elizabeth. *The Printing Presses as an Agent of Change*. First ed. Vol. 1. Cambridge: Cambridge University Press, 1979.

Elias, Jamal. *Aisha's Cushion: Religious Art, Perception, and Practice in Islam*. Cambridge, MA: Harvard University Press, 2012.

Elias, Jamal J. "Truck Calligraphy in Pakistan." In *The Aura of Alif: The Art of Writing in Islam*, edited by Jürgen Wasim Frembgen, 211–24. New York: Prestel, 2010.

Ernst, Carl. "Islam and Indian Regions." In *Islam and Indian Regions*, edited by Anna Dallapicrola and Stephanie Lallemant, 169–73. Stuttgart: Franz Steiner, 1993.

Ernst, Carl. *Eternal Garden: Mysticism, History, and Politics at a South Asian Sufi Center*. Albany: State University of New York Press, 1992.

Ernst, Carl. *The Shambhala Guide to Sufism*. Guide to Sufism. Boston, MA: Shambhala, 1997.

Erskine, K. D. *The Western Rajputana States Residency and the Bikaner Agency: Text*. Vol. 3-A. Allahabad: The Pioneer Press, 1909.

Fandy, Mamoun. "CyberResistance: Saudi Opposition between Globalization and Localization." *Comparative Studies in Society and History* 41 (1999): 124–46.

Fandy, Mamoun. *Saudi Arabia and the Politics of Dissent*. New York: St. Martin's Press, 1999.

Farouqui, Ather. "The Emerging Dilemma of the Urdu Press in India: A Viewpoint." *South Asia: Journal of South Asian Studies* 18, no. 2 (1995): 91–103.

Faruqui, Munis D. "At Empire's End: The Nizam, Hyderabad and Eighteenth-Century India." *Modern Asian Studies* 43, no. 1 (2009): 5–43.

Finkelstein, David, and Alistair McCleery. *An Introduction to Book History*. New York: Routledge, 2012.

Fischer, Claude S. *America Calling: A Social History of the Telephone to 1940*. Berkeley, University of California Press, 1992.

Fisher, Michael H. "The Office of Akhbār Nawīs: The Transition from Mughal to British Forms." *Modern Asian Studies* 27, no. 1 (1993): 45–82.

Flechon, Dominique. *The Mastery of Time: A History of Timekeeping, from the Sundial to the Wristwatch: Discoveries, Inventions, and Advances in Master Watchmaking*. Paris: Flammarion, 2011.

Florida, Nancy K. *Writing the Past, Inscribing the Future: Exile and Prophecy in an Historical Text of Nineteenth-Century Java*. Durham: Duke University Press, 1995.

Foucault, Michel. "The Unities of Discourse." In *Archaeology of Knowledge*. New York: Routledge, 1972. Accessed online August 7, 2017. https://www.marxists.org/reference/subject/philosophy/works/fr/foucault.htm.

Fraser, Nancy. "Rethinking the Public Sphere: A Contribution to the Critique of Actually Existing Democracy." *Social Text*, no. 25/26 (1990): 56–80.

Freitag, Sandra B., ed. "Aspects of 'the Public' in Colonial South Asia," Special issue, *South Asia: Journal of South Asian Studies* 14, no. 1 (June 1991).

Freitag, Sandria B. *Culture and Power in Banaras: Community, Performance, and Environment, 1800–1980*. Berkeley: University of California Press, 1992.

Frembgen, Jürgen Wasim. "Calligraphy in the World of Sufi Shrines in Pakistan." In *Aura of Alif: The Art of Writing in Islam*, edited by Jürgen Wasim Frembgen, 225–36. New York: Prestel, 2010.

Friedmann, Yohanan. "The Jam'iyyat' al-'Ulama-i Hind in the Wake of Partition." *Asian and African Studies* 11 (1976): 181–211.

Friedmann, Yohanan. *Prophecy Continuous: Aspects of Aḥmadī Religious Thought and Its Medieval Background*. Oxford: Oxford University Press, 2003.

Friedmann, Yohanan. *Shaykh Aḥmad Sirhindī: An Outline of His Thought and a Study of His Image in the Eyes of Posterity*. New Delhi; Oxford: Oxford University Press, 2000.

Frost, Mark R. "Pandora's Post Box: Empire and Information in India, 1854–1914." *English Historical Review* 131, no. 552 (2016): 1043–73.

Gaffney, Patrick D. *The Prophet's Pulpit: Islamic Preaching in Contemporary Egypt*. London: University of California Press, 1994.

Gait, Edward. *Census of India, 1911: United Provinces of Agra and Oudh*. Vol. 15. Part 2. Calcutta: Supt., Govt. Press, 1911.

Gaskell, Ivan. "Visual History." In *New Perspectives on Historical Writing*, edited by Peter Burke, 187–217. Cambridge: Cambridge University Press, 2000.

Gaur, Krishna Deo. *Textbook on the Indian Penal Code*. Delhi: Universal Law Publishing, 2009.

Geertz, Clifford. "'Internal Conversion' in Contemporary Bali." In *The Interpretation of Culture: Selected Essays*. 3rd ed, 170–92. London: Fontana Press, 1973.

Gellner, Ernest. *Saints of the Atlas*. Chicago: University of Chicago Press, 1969.

Ghose, Sarat Chandra. *A Monograph on Indian Railway Rates*. Calcutta: Supt. Govt. Press, 1918.

Gilliot, Clande. "Exegesis of the Qur'an: Classical and Medieval." In *Encyclopaedia of the Qur'an: Vol V*, edited by J. D. McAuliffe, 99–124. Leiden: Brill, 2002.

Gilliot, Clande, et al. "'Ulamā'." *Encyclopedia of Islam*. 2nd ed. edited by P. Bearman, Th. Bianquis, C. E. Bosworth, E. van Donzel, and W. P. Heinrichs, Brill Online, 2014.

Gilmartin, David. *Empire and Islam: Punjab and the Making of Pakistan*. London: Tauris, 1988.

Glover, William J. *Making Lahore Modern: Constructing and Imagining a Colonial City*. Minneapolis: University of Minnesota Press, 2008.

Goodman, Matthew. *Eighty Days: Nellie Bly and Elizabeth Bisland's History-Making Race around the World*. New York: Ballantine Books, 2013.

Gooptu, Nandini. *The Politics of Urban Poor in Early Twentieth-Century India*. Cambridge: Cambridge University Press, 2004.

Goswami, Manu. *Producing India: From Colonial Economy to National Space*. Chicago: University of Chicago, 2004.

Graham, William A. *Beyond the Written Word: Oral Aspects of Scripture in the History of Religion*. Cambridge: Cambridge University Press, 1987.

Graham, William A. "Traditionalism in Islam: An Essay in Interpretation." *Journal of Interdisciplinary History* 18, no. 3 (1993): 495–522.

Green, Nile. *Bombay Islam: The Religious Economy of the West Indian Ocean*. Cambridge: Cambridge University Press, 2011.

Green, Nile. "Mystical Missionaries in Hyderabad State: Mu'in Allah Shah and His Reform Movement." *Indian Economic and Social History Review* 41, no. 2 (2005): 187–212.

Green, Nile. "Persian Print and the Stanhope Revolution: Industrialization, Evangelicalism, and the Birth of Printing in Early Qajar Iran." *Comparative Studies of South Asia, Africa, and the Middle East* 30, no. 3 (2010): 473–90.

Green, Nile. "The Propriety of Poetry: Morality and Mysticism in the Nineteenth Century Urdu Religious Lyric." *Middle Eastern Literatures: Incorporating Edebiyat* 13, no. 3 (December 16, 2010): 299–314.

Grewal, Zareena A. "Imagined Cartographies: Crisis, Displacement, and Islam in America." PhD dissertation, University of Michigan, 2006.

Griffith, Zoe. "Calligraphy and the Art of Statecraft in the Late Ottoman Empire and Modern Turkish Republic." *Comparative Studies of South Asia, Africa, and the Middle East* 31, no. 3 (2011): 601–14.

Grillo, Ralph. "Islam and Transnationalism:" *Journal of Ethnic and Migration Studies* 30, no. 5 (2004): 861–78.

Growse, Frederic Salmon. *Indian Architecture of to-Day as Exemplified in New Buildings in the Bulandshahr District*. Allahabad: North-Western Provinces and Oudh Government Press, 1885–1886.

Guhin, Jeffrey. "Religion as Site Rather Than Religion as Category: On the Sociology of Religion's Export Problem." *Sociology of Religion* 75, no. 4 (2014): 579–93.

Gupta, Amit Kumar. "Elitism, Factionalism and Separatism: Politics in the United Provinces, 1885–1920." *History and Sociology of South Asia* 4, no. 2 (2010): 103–28.

Gupta, Babu Lal. *Trade and Commerce in Rajasthan during the 18th Century*. Jaipur: Jaipur Publishing House, 1989.

Habermas, Jürgen. "Notes on a Post-Secular Society." signandsight.com. Accessed January 8, 2018.

Habermas, Jürgen. *The Structural Transformation of the Public Sphere: An Inquiry into a Category of Bourgeois Society*. Cambridge: Polity, 1989.

Habib, Rafey. *An Anthology of Modern Urdu Poetry*. New York: Modern Language Association, 2003.

Hagen, Gottfried. "Dreams in Biographical, Historical, Theological, Poetical, and Oral Narratives, and on the Internet." In *Dreams and Visions in Islamic Societies*, edited by Özgen Felek and Alexander D. Knysh. Albany: State University of New York Press, 2012.

Haider, Qurratulain. *River of Fire*. Translated by Haider, Qurratulain. New Delhi: Kali for Women, 1998.

Haider, Qurratulain. *The Sound of Falling Leaves*. Translated by Qurratulain Haider. New Delhi: Sahitya Akademi, 2007.

Ḥālī, K͟hvājah Alṭāf Ḥusain. *Hali's Musaddas: The Flow and Ebb of Islam*. Edited by Javed Majeed and Christopher Shackle. Delhi: Oxford University Press, 1997.

Hall, Kenneth R., ed. *Secondary Cities and Urban Networking in the Indian Ocean Realm, 1400–1800*. Lanham, MD: Lexington Books, 2008.

Hall, Richard. *The Balkan Wars 1912–1913: Prelude to the First World War*. London: Routledge, 2000.

Hameed, Syeda Saiyidain. *Islamic Seal on India's Independence: Abul Kalam Azad, a Fresh Look*. Karachi: Oxford University Press, 1998.

Hamilton, Charles, comp. and ed. *Historical Relation of the Origin, Progress, and Final Dissolution of the Government of the Rohilla Afgans in the Northern Provinces of Hindostan*. 2nd ed. London: J. Debrett, 1788.

Handbook of Twentieth-Century Literatures of India. Edited by Nalini Natarajan. Westport, CT: Greenwood Press, 1996.

Hansen, Kathryn. "Theatrical Transvestism in the Parsi, Gujurati and Marathi Theatres (1850–1940)." In *Sexual Sites, Seminal Attitudes: Sexualities, Masculinities and Culture in South Asia*, edited by Sanjay Srivastava, 99–122. London: Sage, 2004.

Haque, Misbahul. "Darul Uloom Nadwatul Ulama." Accessed June 8, 2011. http://www.nadwatululama.org.

Hardy, Peter. *Partners in Freedom and True Muslims: The Political Thought of Some Muslim Scholars in British India 1912–1947*. Lund: Studentlitteratur, 1971.

Hardy, Peter. *The Muslims of British India*. Cambridge: Cambridge University Press, 1972.

Hasan, Mushirul. *From Pluralism to Separatism: Qasbahs in Colonial Awadh*. New Delhi: Oxford University Press, 2004.

Hasan, Mushirul. *Introduction to Delhi in Transition*. Oxford: Oxford University Press, 2007.

Hasan, Mushirul. *Nationalism and Communal Politics in India: 1916–1928*. 2nd ed. New Delhi: Manohar, 1994.

Hasan, Mushirul. "The Qasbah Culture." *The Hindu*, July 22, 2002.

Hasan, Mushirul. "Qasbas: A Brief in Propinquity." In *A Leaf Turns Yellow: The Sufis of Awadh*, edited by Muzaffar Ali, 110–12. New Delhi: Rumi Foundation / Bloomsbury Publishing India, 2013.

Hasanat, Abul. *Sachitra Jouno Bigyan* [Illustrated Sexual Science]. Vols. 1 and 2, Kolkata: Mullick Brothers, 1936.

Hassan, Riffat. "Islamic Modernist and Reformist Discourse in South Asia." In *Reformist Voices of Islam: Mediating Islam and Modernity*, edited by Shireen Hunter, 159–86. Armonk, New York: M.E. Sharpe, 2009.

Haynes, Douglas E. *Small Town Capitalism in Western India: Artisans, Merchants and the Making of an Informal Economy, 1870–1960*. Cambridge: Cambridge University Press, 2012.

Hazareesingh, Sandip. *The Colonial City and the Challenge of Modernity: Urban Hegemonies and Civic Contestations in Bombay City, 1900–1925*. Delhi: Orient Black Swan, 2007.

Hazareesingh, Sandip. "Colonial Modernism and the Flawed Paradigms of Urban Renewal: Uneven Development in Bombay, 1900–25." *Urban History* 28, no. 2 (2001): 235–55.

Headrick, Daniel. "Double-Edged Sword: Communications and Imperial Control in British India." *Historical Social Research* 35, no. 1 (2010): 51–65.

Heathorn, Stephen. "The Absent Site of Memory: The Kanpur Memorial Well and the 1957 Centenary Commemoration of the Indian Mutiny." In *Memory, History and Colonialism: Engaging with Pierre Nora in Colonial and Postcolonial Contexts*, edited by Indra Sengupta, 73–116. London: German Historical Institute London, 2009.

Heitzman, James. *The City in South Asia*. New York: Routledge, 2008.

Hermansen, Marcia. "Imagining Space and Citing Collective Memory in South Asian Muslim Biographical Literature (Tazkirah)." *Studies in Contemporary Islam* 4, no. 2 (2002): 1–21.

Hirschkind, Charles. *The Ethical Soundscape: Cassette Sermons and Islamic Counterpublics*. New York: Columbia University Press, 2006.

Ho, Engseng. *The Graves of Tarim: Geneaology and Mobility across the Indian Ocean*. Berkeley: University of California Press, 2006.

Hodgson, Marshall G. S. *Rethinking World History: Essays on Europe, Islam, and World History*. Edited by Edmund Burke. Cambridge: Cambridge University Press, 1993.

Hofmeyr, Isabel, Preben Kaarsholm, and Bodil Folke Frederiksen. "Introduction: Print Cultures, Nationalisms and Publics of the Indian Ocean." *Africa* 81, no. 1 (2011): 1–22.

Hofmeyr, Isabel. *Gāndhī's Printing Press*. Cambridge, MA: Harvard University Press, 2013.

Holmström, Mark. *Industry and Inequality: The Social Anthropology of Indian Labour*. Cambridge: Cambridge University Press, 1984.

Horsfield, Peter. "Media." In *Key Words in Religion, Media, and Culture*. New York: Routledge, 2008.

Hukk, Mohammad, Herman Ethe, and Edward Robertson. *A Descriptive Catalogue of the Arabic and Persian MSS*. Edinburgh: University of Edinburgh Press, 1925.

Husain, Mahdi. *The Rehla of Ibn Battuta: India, Maldive Islands and Ceylon*. 2nd ed. Baroda: Oriental Institute, 1976.

Ibn Khaldū. *The Muqaddimah: An Introduction to History*. London: London: Routledge & K. Paul, 1958.

Ingram, Brannon. "Crises of the Public in Muslim India: Critiquing 'Custom' at Aligarh and Deoband." *Journal of South Asian Studies* 38, no. 3 (2015): 403–18.

Ingram, Brannon. "The Portable Madrasa: Print, Publics, and the Authority of the Deobandi 'Ulama." *Modern Asian Studies* 48, no. 4 (2014): 845–71.

Ingram, Brannon. *Revival from Below: The Deoband Movement and Global Islam*. Berkeley: University of California Press, 2018.

Ingram, Brannon, J. Barton Scott, and SherAli K. Tareen. *Imagining the Public in Modern South Asia*. New York: Routledge, 2016.

Jaʿfar Sharīf. *Qanoon-e-Islam, Or, the Customs of the Moosulmans of India: Comprising a Full and Exact Account of Their Various Rites and Ceremonies, from the Moment of Birth till the Hour of Death*. Edited by Herčklots, G. A. London: Parbury, Allen, and Co, 1832.

Jalal, Ayesha. "Negotiating Colonial Modernity and Cultural Difference: Indian Muslim Conceptions of Community and Nation, 1874–1914." In *Modernity and Culture: From the Mediterranean to the Indian Ocean*, edited by Leila Tarazi Fawaz and C. A. Bayly, 230–60. Columbia: Columbia University Press, 2002.

Jalal, Ayesha. *Self and Sovereignty: Individual and Community in South Asian Islam since 1850*. Leiden: Brill, 1996.

Jalal, Ayesha. "Striking a Just Balance: Maulana Azad as a Theorist of Trans-National Jihad." *Modern Intellectual History* 4, no. 1 (2007): 95–107.

Jeffrey, Robin. "Urdu: Waiting for Citizen Kane?" *Economic and Political Weekly*, March 29, 1997, 631–36.

Johns, Adrian. *The Nature of the Book: Print and Knowledge in the Making*. Chicago: University of Chicago Press, 1998.

Jones, Justin. "The Local Experiences of Reformist Islam in a 'Muslim' Town in Colonial India: The Case of Amroha." *Modern Asian Studies* 43, no. 4 (2009): 871–908.

Kaifi, Shaukat. *Kaifi & I: A Memoir*. New Delhi: Zabaan, 2010.

Kant, Immanuel. *Metaphysische Anfangsgründe der Naturwissenschaft*. Hamburg: Meiner, 1997.

Karnik, V. B. *Indian Trade Unions: A Survey*. Bombay: Labour Education Service, 1960.

Kavuri-Bauer, Santhi. *Monumental Matters: The Power, Subjectivity, and Space of India*. Durham: Duke University Press, 2011.

Kazim, Lubna. *A Woman of Substance: The Memoirs of Begum Khurshid Misra*. Karachi: Oxford University Press, 2006.

Khalid, Adeeb. "Printing, Publishing, and Reform in Tsarist Central Asia." *International Journal of Middle East Studies* 26, no. 2 (1994): 187–200.

Khalidi, Omar. "Urdu Language and the Future of Muslim Identity in India." *Institute of Muslim Minority Affairs* 7, no. 2 (1986): 395–403.

Khan, Gulfishan. *Indian Muslim Perceptions of the West during the Eighteenth Century*. Karachi: Oxford University Press, 1998.

Khan, Razak. "The Social Production of Space and Emotions in South Asia." *Journal of the Economic and Social History of the Orient* 58, no. 5 (2015): 611–33.

Khan, Syed Ahmad. *Tārīkh-i sarkashī-yi ẓilaʿ-yi Bijnor* [The History of the Rebellion of the District of Bijnor]. Translated by Hafiz Malik and Morris Dembo. Delhi: Idarah-i Adabiyat Dilli, 1982.

Khosla, G. S. *A History of Indian Railways*. New Delhi: Ministry of Railways, 1988.

Kidambi, Prashant. *The Making of an Indian Metropolis: Colonial Governance and Public Culture in Bombay, 1890–1920*. Aldershot: Ashgate, 2007.

Klein, Ira. "Population and Agriculture in Northern India, 1872–1921." *Modern Asian Studies* 8, no. 2 (March 1974): 191–216.

Kolff, D. H. A. *Naukar, Rajput, and Sepoy: The Ethnohistory of the Military Labour Market in Hindustan, 1450–1850*. Cambridge: Cambridge University Press, 1990.

Krishna, Gopal. "The Khilafat Movement in India: The First Phase (September 1919–August 1920)." *The Journal of the Royal Asiatic Society of Great Britain and Ireland*, no. 1/2 (April 1968): 37–53.

Kugle, Scott. *Sufi and Saints' Bodies: Mysticism: Corporeality, and Sacred Power in Islam*. Chapel Hill: University of North Carolina Press, 2007.

Kumar, Ravindra. *Essays in the Social History of Modern India*. Delhi: Oxford University Press, 1983.

Kumar, Ravindra. *Life and Works of Maulana Abul Kalam Azad*. New Delhi: Atlantic Publishers & Distributors, 1991.

Lahiri, Nayanjot. "Commemorating and Remembering 1857: The Revolt in Delhi and Its Afterlife." *World Archaeology* 35, no. 1 (2003): 35–60.

Lal, Ruby. *Coming of Age in Nineteenth-Century India: The Girl-Child and the Art of Playfulness*. New York: Cambridge University Press, 2013.

Lal, Vinay, and Gita Rajan. "Ethnographies of the Popular and the Public Sphere in India." *South Asian Popular Culture* 5, no. 2 (2007): 87–95.

Lambert-Hurley, Siobhan. *Muslim Women, Reform and Princely Patronage: Nawab Sultan Jahan Begam of Bhopal*. Vol. 4. New York: Routledge, 2007.

Lapidus, Ira. "Knowledge, Virtue, and Action: The Classical Muslim Conception of Adab and the Nature of Religious Fulfillment in Islam." In *Moral Conduct and Authority: The Place of Adab in South Asian Islam*, edited by Barbara Metcalf, 38–61. London: University of California Press, 1984.

Larsson, Göran. *Muslims and the New Media: Historical and Contemporary Debates*. Farnham: Ashgate, 2011.

Lavan, Spencer. "The Kanpur Mosque Incident of 1913: The North Indian Muslim Press and Its Reaction to Community Crisis." *Journal of the American Academy of Religion* 42, no. 2 (1974): 263–79.

Lawrence, Bruce. "Introduction." In *Sharafuddin Maneri: The Hundred Letters*, edited by Paul Jackson, 1–6. New York: S.J. Paulist Press, 1980.

Lefebvre, Henri. *The Production of Space*. Hoboken, NJ: Wiley-Blackwell, 1992.

Legg, Stephen. *Spaces of Colonialism: Delhi's Urban Governmentalities*. Oxford: Blackwell, 2007.

Lelyveld, David. *Aligarh's First Generation: Muslim Solidarity in British India*. Princeton: Princeton University Press, 1978.

Lelyveld, David. "Sir Sayyid's Public Sphere: Urdu Print and Oratory in Nineteenth Century India." *Cracow Indological Studies* 11, no. 11 (2009): 237–67.

Liebeskind, Claudia. *Piety on Its Knees: Three Sufi Traditions in South Asia in Modern Times*. Oxford: Oxford University Press, 1998.

Llewellyn-Jones, Rosie. *The Great Uprising in India, 1857–58: Untold Stories, Indian and British*. Vol. 2. Rochester, NY: Boydell & Brewer, 2007.

Mahdi, Muhsin. *Ibn Khaldun's Philosophy of History*. London: George Allen and Unwin Ltd., 1957.

Mahmood, Saba. *Politics of Piety: The Islamic Revival and the Feminist Subject*. Princeton: Princeton University Press, 2005.

Mahmud, Shabana. "*Angāre* and the Founding of the Progressive Writers' Assocation." *Modern Asian Studies* 30, no. 2 (May 1996): 447–67.

Makdisi, George. *The Rise of Humanism in Classical Islam, with Special Reference to Scholasticism*. Edinburgh: Edinburgh University Press, 1990.

Malik, Jamal. *Islam in South Asia: A Short History*. Leiden: Brill, 2008.

Malik, Jamal. *Islamische Gelehrtenkultur in Nordindien: Entwicklungsgeschichte und Tendenzen am Beispiel von Lucknow*. Leiden: Brill, 1997.

Malik, Jamal. "The Making of a Council: The Nadwat Al-'Ulama." *Zeitschrift Der Deutschen Morgenlandischen Gesellschaft* 144 (1994): 60–90.

Mandaville, P. "Reimagining Islam in Diaspora: The Politics of Mediated Community." *Gazette* 63, nos. 2–3 (2001): 169–86.

Marsden, Magnus. *Living Islam: Muslim Religious Experience in Pakistan's North-West Frontier*. Cambridge: Cambridge University Press, 2005.

Masud, Muhammad Khalid. "Trends in the Interpretation of Islamic Law as Reflected in the Fatawa of Deoband School." MA thesis, McGill University, 1969.

Matsumoto-Best, Saho. "British and Italian Imperial Rivalry in the Mediterranean, 1912–14: The Case of Egypt." *Diplomacy and Statecraft* 18, no. 2 (2007): 297–314.

Maudoodi, Syed Abul 'Ala. *Towards Understanding Islam*. Edited by Khurshid Ahmad. Leicester: Islamic Foundation, 1980.

Mayaram, Shail. *Against History, against State: Counterperspectives from the Margins*. New York: Columbia University Press, 2003.

McLuhan, Marshall. *Letters of Marshall McLuhan*. Edited by William Toye. Oxford: Oxford University Press, 1987.

Mehta, N. B. *Indian Railways: Rates and Regulations*. London: P. S. King & Son, Ltd. 1927.

Mehta, Makrand, ed. *Urbanization in Western India: Historical Perspective*. Ahmedabad: Gujurat University, 1988.

Messick, Brinkley. *The Calligraphic State: Textual Domination and History in a Muslim Society*. Berkeley: University of California Press, 1993.

Messick, Brinkley. "On the Question of Lithography." *Culture and History* 16 (1997): 158–76.

Metcalf, Barbara. "Introduction." In *Moral Conduct and Authority*, edited by Barbara Metcalf, 1–22. London: University of California Press, 1984.

Metcalf, Barbara. *Islamic Contestations: Essays on Muslims in India and Pakistan*. Delhi: Oxford University Press, 2006.

Metcalf, Barbara. *Islamic Revival in British India: Deoband, 1860–1900*. Princeton: Princeton University Press, 1982.

Metcalf, Barbara, ed. *Moral Conduct and Authority: The Place of Adab in South Asian Islam*. London: University of California Press, 1984.

Metcalf, Barbara. "Nationalist Muslims in British India: The Case of Hakim Ajmal Khan." *Modern Asian Studies* 19, no. 1 (1985): 1–28.

Metcalf, Barbara. "Weber and Islamic Reform." In *Max Weber and Islam*, edited by Toby E. Huff and Wolfgang Schluchter, 217–30. London: New Brunswick, 1999.

Metcalf, Barbara. "Who Speaks for Muslims? The Challenges of the 1930s." In *Husain Ahmad Madani: The Jihad for Islam and India's Freedom*, 97–125. London: Oneworld, 2009.

Metcalf, Thomas. *Land, Landlords, and the British Raj: Northern India in the Nineteenth Century*. Berkeley: University of California Press, 1979.

Minault, Gail. "Begumati Zaban." *India International Center Quarterly* 11, no. 2 (June 1984) 155–70.

Minault, Gail. *Gender, Language, and Learning: Essays in Indo-Muslim Cultural History*. Bangalore: Permanent Black, 2009.

Minault, Gail. *The Khilafat Movement: Religious Symbolism and Political Mobilization in India*. New York: Columbia University Press, 1982.

Minault, Gail. *Secluded Scholars: Women's Education and Muslim Social Reform in Colonial India*. Delhi: Oxford University Press, 1998.

Minault, Gail. "Urdu Political Poetry during the Khilafat Movement." *Modern Asian Studies* 8, no. 4 (1974): 459–71.

Minault, Gail, and David Lelyveld. "The Campaign for a Muslim University, 1898–1920." *Modern Asian Studies* 8, no. 2 (1974): 145–89.

Minorsky, V. *Calligraphers and Painters: A Treatise by Qadi Ahmad, Son or Mir Munshi*. Translated from Russian by B. N. Zakhoder. Washington, DC: Freer Gallery of Art Occasional Papers, 1959.

Mir, Farina. *The Social Space of Language: Vernacular Culture in British Colonial Punjab*. London: University of California Press, 2010.

Misra, Salil. "Muslim League in UP in 1937: Understanding Muslim Communalism." *Proceedings of the Indian History Congress* 60 (1999): 765–73.

Mitchell, R. P. *The Society of the Muslim Brothers*. Oxford: Oxford University Press, 1993.

Mittal, S. C. *Freedom Movement in Punjab, 1905–29*. Delhi: Concept Publishing Company, 1977.

Moin, A. Azfar. *The Millennial Sovereign: Sacred Kingship and Sainthood in Islam*. New York: Columbia University Press, 2012.

Moosa, Ebrahim. *Ghazālī and the Poetics of Imagination*. Chapel Hill: University of North Carolina Press, 2005.

Morgan, David. "Notes on Meaning and Medium in the Aesthetics of Visual Piety." Unpublished paper, 1998.

Morgan, David. *Sacred Gaze: Religious Visual Culture in Theory and Practice*. Berkeley: University of California Press, 2005.

Morgan, David. *Visual Piety: A History and Theory of Popular Religious Images*. Berkeley: University of California Press, 1999.

Mowlana, H. "Radio and Television." In *The Oxford Encyclopedia of the Modern Islamic World*, vol. 3, edited by J. Esposito, 405–7. New York: Oxford University Press, 1995.

Mujtaba, Syed Ali. "Hyderabad's Fall and Sunderlal Report." CounterCurrents.org. Accessed August 8, 2018. https://www.countercurrents.org/mujtaba290913.htm.

Mukarram, Ahmed. "Some Aspects of Contemporary Islamic Thought: Guidance and Governance in the Work of Mawlana Abul Hasan Ali Nadwi and Mawlana Abul Aala Mawdudi." DPhil thesis, University of Oxford, 1992.

Mukherjee, Soma. *Royal Mughal Ladies and Their Contributions*. Delhi: Gyan Books, 2001.

Mukhopadhyay, Aparajita. "No Land for Muslims: Railway Travel and Imagining India." Presentation, SOAS, London, October 28, 2013.

Mushtaq, Faiza. "New Claimants to Religious Authority: A Movement for Women's Islamic Education, Moral Reform and Innovative Traditionalism." PhD dissertation, Northwestern University, 2010.

Naim, C. M. "How Bibi Ashraf Learned to Write." *Annual of Urdu Studies* 6 (1987): 99–115.

Naim, C. M. "The Muslim League in Barabanki, 1946." *A Desertful of Roses*. DPhil thesis, 2017. http://www.columbia.edu/itc/mealac/pritchett/00litlinks/naim/txt_naim_muslimleague.pdf

Naim, C. M. ed. *Readings in Urdu: Prose and Poetry*. Honolulu: East-West Center Press, 1965.

Naim, C. M. "Transvestic Words? The Rekhti in Urdu." *Annual of Urdu Studies* 16 (2001): 3–26.

Nandy, Ashis. *The Intimate Enemy*. Delhi: Oxford University Press, 1989.

Narain, Kirti. *Press, Politics and Society in Uttar Pradesh, 1885–1914*. New Delhi: Manohar, 1998.

Naregal, Veena. *Language, Politics, Elites and the Public Sphere: Western India under Colonialism*. London: Anthem, 2002.

Nelson, K. *The Art of Reciting the Qur'an*. Cairo: American University in Cairo Press, 2001.

Newman, Richard K. *Workers and Unions in Bombay, 1918–1929: A Study of Organisation in the Cotton Mills*. Canberra: Australian National University, 1981.

Niemeijer, A. C. *The Khilafat Movement in India*. The Hague: Martinus Nijhoff, 1972.

Nijhawan, Shobna. *Women and Girls in the Hindi Public Sphere: Periodical Literature in Colonial North India*. Oxford: Oxford University Press, 2012.

Nizami, Farhan. "Madrasahs, Scholars, and Saints: Muslim Response to British Presence in Delhi and the Upper Doab, 1803–1857." DPhil thesis, University of Oxford, 1983.

Nizami, Khaliq Ahmad. *On History and Historians of Medieval India*. New Delhi: New Delhi: Munshiram Manoharlal, 1983.

O'Hanlon, Rosalind. "Manliness and Imperial Service in Mughal North India." *Journal of the Economic and Social History of the Orient* 42, no. 1 (1999): 47–93.

O'Hanlon, Rosalind, and David Washbrook. "After Orientalism: Culture, Criticism, and Politics in the Third World." *Contemporary Studies in Society and History* 34, no. 1 (1992): 141–67.

Olsen, Elizabeth, Peter Hopkins, and Lily Kong. "Introduction—Religion and Place." In *Religion and Place: Landscape, Politics and Piety*, edited by Peter Hopkins, Lily Kong, and Elizabeth Olson, 1–20. New York: Springer, 2013.

Ong, Walter J. *Orality and Literacy: The Technologizing of the Word*. London: Routledge, 2002.

Ong, Walter J. "Writing is a Technology that Restructures Thought." In *The Written World: Literacy in Transition*, edited by Gerd Baumann, 23–50. Oxford: Clarendon Press, 1986.

Orsini, Francesca. *The Hindi Public Sphere, 1920–1940: Language and Literature in the Age of Nationalism*. Oxford: Oxford University Press, 2002.

Orsini, Francesca. *Print and Pleasure: Popular Literature and Entertaining Fictions in Colonial North India*. Ranikhet: Permanent Black, 2009.

Osborn, J. R. *Letters of Light: Arabic Script in Calligraphy, Print, and Digital Design*. Cambridge, MA: Harvard University Press, 2017.

Pandey, Gyanendra. *The Ascendancy of the Congress in Uttar Pradesh, 1926–34: A Study in Imperfect Mobilization*. Delhi: Oxford University Press, 1978.

Pandey, Gyanendra. *The Construction of Communalism in Colonial North India*. New Delhi: Oxford University Press, 2006.

Pandey, Gyanendra. "'Encounters and Calamities': The History of a North Indian Qasba in the Nineteenth Century." In *Selected Subaltern Studies*, edited by Ranajit Guha, and Gayatri Chakravorty Spivak, 89–128. Oxford: Oxford University Press, 1988.

Pandey, Shiva Mohan. *As Labour Organizes: A Study of Unionism in the Kanpur Cotton Textile Industry*. New Delhi: New Delhi: Shri Ram Centre for Industrial Relations, 1970.

Parekh, Rauf. "Allama Iqbal, Zafar Ali Khan and Zamindar." *Dawn*, July 7, 2011.

Peabody, Norbert. *Hindu Kingship and Polity in Precolonial India*. New York: Cambridge University Press, 2003.

Perkins, C. Ryan. "From the Meḥfil to the Printed Word: Public Debate and Discourse in Late Colonial India." *Indiana Economic and Social History Review* 50, no. 1 (January–March 2013): 47–76.

Pernau, Margrit. *Ashraf into Middle Classes: Muslims in Nineteenth-Century Delhi*. New Delhi: Oxford University Press, 2013.

Pernau, Margrit. "The Delhi Urdu Akhbar: Between Persian Akhbarat and English Newspapers." *Annual of Urdu Studies* 18, no. 1 (2003): 105–31.

Petievich, Carla. "Rekhti: Impersonating the Feminine in Urdu Poetry." In *Sexual Sites, Seminal Attitudes: Sexualities, Masculinities and Culture in South Asia*, edited by Sanjay Srivastava, 75–90. London: Sage, 2004.

Platts, John T. *A Dictionary of Urdu, Classical Hindi, and English. Digital Dictionaries of South Asia*.

Pritchett, Frances. *Marvelous Encounters: Folk Romance in Urdu and Hindi*. New Delhi: Manohar, 1985.

Pritchett, Frances. *Nets of Awareness: Urdu Poetry and Its Critics*. Berkeley: University of California Press, 1994.

Pritchett, Frances. *The Romance Tradition in Urdu: Adventures from the Dastan of Amir Hamzah*. New York: Columbia University Press, 1991.

Qaiser, Rizwan. *Resisting Colonialism and Communal Politics: Maulana Azad and the Making of the Indian Nation*. New Delhi: Manohar, 2011.

Qasmi, Ali Usman, and Megan Eaton Robb. "Introduction." In *Muslims against the Muslim League*, edited by Ali Usman Qasmi and Megan Eaton Robb, 1–34. New Delhi: Cambridge University Press, 2017.

Qureshi, M. Naeem. *Pan-Islam in British Indian Politics: A Study of the Khilafat Movement, 1918–1924*. Leiden: Brill, 1999.

Raheja, Gloria, and Ann Gold. *Listen to the Heron's Words: Reimagining Gender and Kinship in North India*. Berkeley: University of California Press, 1994.

Rahman, M. Raisur. *Locale, Everyday Islam, and Modernity: Qasbah Towns and Muslim Life in Colonial India*. New Delhi: Oxford University Press, 2015.

Rahman, M. Raisur. "Qasbah: Network, Everyday Islam, and Modernity in Colonial India." PhD dissertation, University of Texas at Austin, 2008.

Rahman, Munibur. "The Musha'irah." *Annual of Urdu Studies* 3 (1983): 75–84.

Rahman, Pares Islam Syed Mustafizur. *Islamic Calligraphy in Medieval India*. Bangladesh: University Press Limited, 1979.

Rahman, Tariq. *From Hindi to Urdu: A Social and Political History*. New York: Oxford University Press, 2012.

Raipuri, Hameeda Akhtar Husain. *My Fellow Traveller: A Translation of Humsafar*. Karachi: Oxford University Press, 2006.

Ramadan, Tareeq. *To Be a European Muslim: A Study of Islamic Sources in the European Context*. Leicester: The Islamic Foundation, 2002.

Ramadan, Tareeq. *Western Muslims and the Future of Islam*. Oxford: Oxford University Press, 2004.

Ramaswamy, Sumathi. *Goddess and the Nation: Mapping Mother India*. Durham: Duke University Press, 2010.

Rankin, Reginald, Bart. *The Inner History of the Balkan War*. London: Constable, 1914.

Ray, Anniruddha. *Bareilly Rising of 1857–1859 and the Bengali Babu*. Kolkata: Progressive Publishers, 2010.

Raza, Muhammad Ali. "Interrogating Provincial Politics: The Leftist Movement in Punjab, c. 1914–1950." DPhil thesis, University of Oxford, 2011.

Reetz, Dietrich. *Islam in the Public Sphere*. Delhi: Oxford University Press, 2006.

Reeves, Peter. *Landlords and Governments in Uttar Pradesh: A Study of Their Relations until Zamindari Abolition*. Delhi: Oxford University Press, 1991.

Richards, J. F. *The Mughal Empire*. Cambridge: Cambridge University Press, 1993.

Robb, Megan Eaton. "Women's Voices, Men's Lives: Masculinity in a North Indian Urdu Newspaper." *Modern Asian Studies* 50, no. 5 (2016): 1441–73.

Robinson, Francis. "Education." In *New Cambridge History of Islam*, vol. 4, edited by Robert Irwin, 495–531. Cambridge: Cambridge University Press, 2010.

Robinson, Francis. "Fundamentalism: Tolerance and India's Heritage." *Journal of the Asiatic Society* 45, no. 3 (2003): 5–13.

Robinson, Francis. "Islamic Reform and Modernities in South Asia." *Modern Asian Studies* 42, nos. 2–3 (2008): 259–81.

Robinson, Francis. *Jamal Mian: The Life of Maulana Jamaluddin Abdul Wahab of Farangi Mahall, 1919–2012*. Karachi: Oxford University Press, 2017.

Robinson, Francis. "Municipal Government and Muslim Separatism in the United Provinces, 1883 to 1916." *Modern Asian Studies* 70, no. 3 (1973): 389–441.

Robinson, Francis. "Religious Change and the Self in Muslim South Asia since 1800." *Journal of South Asian Studies* 20, no. 1 (1997): 1–15.

Robinson, Francis. *Separatism among Indian Muslims: The Politics of the United Provinces' Muslims 1860–1923*. 2nd ed. Cambridge: Cambridge University Press, 2007.

Robinson, Francis. *Separatism among Indian Muslims: The Politics of the United Provinces' Muslims 1860–1923*. Cambridge: Cambridge University Press, 1974.

Robinson, Francis. "Strategies of Authority in Muslim South Asia in the Nineteenth and Twentieth Centuries." *Modern Asian Studies* 47, no. 1 (2013): 1–21.

Robinson, Francis. "Technology and Religious Change: Islam and the Impact of Print." *Modern Asian Studies* 27, no. 1 (February 1993): 229–51.

Robinson, Francis. *The 'Ulama of Farangi Mahall and Islamic Culture in South Asia*. New Delhi: Permanent Black, 2001.

Robinson, Francis. "The Ulama of Farangi Mahall and Their Adab." In *Moral Conduct and Authority: The Place of Adab in South Asian Islam*, edited by Barbara D. Metcalf, 152–83. Berkeley: University of California Press, 1984.

Rogozen-Soltar, Mikaela. "Managing Muslim Visibility: Conversion, Immigration, and Spanish Imaginaries of Islam." *American Anthropologist* 114, no. 4 (2012): 611–23.

Roschanack, Shaery-Eisenlohr. "Territorializing Piety: Genealogy, Transnationalism, and Shi'ite Politics in Modern Lebanon." *Comparative Studies in Society and History* 51, no. 3 (July 2009): 533–62.

Rosenthal, Franz. "Abū Ḥaiyān al-Tawḥīdī on Penmanship." *Ars Islamica* 13–14 (1948).

Rosenthal, Franz. *Knowledge Triumphant*. Leiden: Brill, 1970.

Roznamah, Hasrat. *Jamal Mian: The Life of Maulana Jamaluddin Abdul Wahab of Farangi Mahall, 1919–2012*. Karachi: Oxford University Press, 2017.

Rugberg Rasmussen, T. "The Ideology of Gharbzadegi." In *Middle East Studies in Denmark*, edited by L. Erslev Andersen, 171–79. Odensen: Odense University Press, 1994.

The Ruling on Tasweer. Riyadh: Darussalam, 2002.

Russell, Ralph, and Khurshidul Islam. *Ghalib, 1797–1869: Life and Letters*. Delhi: Oxford University Press, 1994.

Sa'dī. *The Gulistan (Rose Garden) of Sa'di: Bilingual English and Persian Edition with Vocabulary*. Edited by W. M. Thackston. Bethesda, MD: Ibex Publishers, 2008.

Sadiq, Mohammed. *A History of Urdu Literature*. 2nd ed. London: Oxford University Press, 1964.

Sahai, Nandita Prasad. *Politics of Patronage and Protest: The State, Society, and Artisans in Early Modern Rajasthan*. New Delhi: Oxford University Press, 2006.
Sahni, Jogendra Nath. *Indian Railways: One Hundred Years, 1853–1953*. New Delhi: Ministry of Railways, 1953.
Salvatore, Armando, and Dale F. Eickelman. *Public Islam and the Common Good*. Leiden: Brill, 2004.
Sanyal, Nalinaksha. *Development of Indian Railways*. Calcutta: University of Calcutta, 1930.
Sanyal, Usha. *Ahmad Riza Khan Barelwi: In the Path of the Prophet*. Makers of the Muslim World Series. London: Oneworld, 2005.
Sanyal, Usha. "Al-Huda International: How Muslim Women Empower Themselves through Online Study of the Qur'an." *Hawwa* 13, no. 3 (2015): 440–60.
Sarkar, Sumit. *Writing Social History*. Delhi: Oxford University Press, 1997.
Sato, Manasori, and B. L. Bhadani, eds. *Economy and Polity of Rajasthan: Study of Kota and Marwar*. Jaipur: Publication Scheme, 1997.
Schacht, Joseph. "'Ashab Al-Ra'y." *Encyclopedia of Islam* 2 (1960): 692.
Schemmel, Matthias. *Historical Epistemology of Space: From Primate Cognition to Spacetime Physics*. Cham, Switzerland: Springer, 2016.
Schemmel, Matthias. "Preface." In *Spatial Thinking and External Representation: Towards a Historical Epistemology of Space*, edited by M. Schemmel, xi–xii. Berlin: Edition Open Access, 2016.
Schemmel, Matthias. "Towards a Historical Epistemology of Space: An Introduction." In *Spatial Thinking and External Representation: Towards a Historical Epistemology of Space*, edited by Matthias Schemmel, 1–33. Berlin: Edition Open Access, 2016.
Schimmel, Annemarie. *And Muhammad Is His Messenger: The Veneration of the Prophet in Islamic Piety*. Chapel Hill: University of North Carolina Press, 1985.
Schimmel, Annemarie. *Calligraphy and Islamic Culture*. London: Tauris, 1990.
Schimmel, Annemarie. *Mystical Dimensions of Islam*. Chapel Hill: University of North Carolina Press, 1978.
Schofield, Katherine Butler. "The Courtesan Tale: Female Musicians and Dancers in Mughal Historical Chronicles, c. 1556–1748." *Gender and History* 24, no. 1 (2012): 150–71.
Scott, J. Barton, and Brannon Ingram. "What Is a Public? Notes from South Asia." *South Asia: Journal of South Asian Studies* 38, no. 3 (2015): 357–70.
Sedgwick, Mark J. *Sufism: The Essentials*. Cairo: American University in Cairo Press, 2000.
Sehrwarwi, Siddiqa B. "Adab-e-Latif." WordPress. Accessed August 1, 2013. http://www.adab-e-latif.com.
Sender, Henriette. *The Kashmiri Pandits: A Study of Cultural Choice in North India*. New Delhi: Oxford University Press, 1988.
Sevea, Terenjit. "Islamist Questioning and [C]olonialism: Towards an Understanding of Islamist Oeuvre." *Third World Quarterly* 28, no. 7 (October 2007): 1375–99.
Seviers, Gianni. "Learning How to Print: The Nizami Press in Badayun and the First Urdu Manual on the Art of Lithography." Presentation at the British Library in July 2018. Script of draft article based on presentation shared with author January 2019.
Shah, Mihir, Rangu Rao, and P. S. Vijay Shankar. "Rural Credit in 20th Century India: Overview of History and Perspectives." *Economic and Political Weekly* 42, no. 15 (2007): 1351–64.
Shah, Seher A. "A History of Traditional Calligraphy in Post-Partition Lahore." PhD dissertation, George Washington University, 2016.

Sharar, Abdul Halim. "Scripts—Calligraphy and the Urdu Press." In *Lucknow: The Last Phase of an Oriental Culture*, edited by E. S. Harcourt and Fakhir Hussain, 102–9. London: Paul Elek, 1975.

Sharma, Karuna. "A Visit to the Mughal Harem: Lives of Royal Women." *South Asia: Journal of South Asian Studies* 32, no. 2 (2009): 155–69.

Shaw, Graham. "Calcutta: Birthplace of the Indian Lithographed Book." *Journal of the Printing Historical Society* 27 (1998): 89–111.

Shaw, Graham. *Printing in Calcutta to 1800: A Description and Checklist of Printing in Late 18th-Century Calcutta*. London: Oxford University Press, 1981.

Shcheglova, Olimpiada P. "Lithography ii. in India." *Encyclopædia Iranica*, online edition, 2012. Accessed June 30, 2012. http://www.iranicaonline.org/articles/lithography-ii-in-india.

Shinar, P. "Salafiyya." In *Encylopedia of Islam*, 2nd ed., vol. 8, edited by P. Bearman, Th. Bianquis, C. E. Bosworth, E. van Donzel, and W. P. Heinrichs, 900–909. Leiden: Brill, 2012.

Shridharani, Krishnalal Jethalal. *Story of the Indian Telegraphs: A Century of Progress*. New Delhi: India Posts and Telegraphs Department, 1953.

Siddiqi, Majid Hayat. "History and Society in a Popular Rebellion: Mewat, 1920–1933." *Comparative Studies in Society and History* 28, no. 3 (1986): 442–67.

Singh, Chetan. *Region and Empire: Punjab in the Seventeenth Century*. Delhi: Oxford University Press, 1991.

Sinha, Mrinalini. *Colonial Masculinity: The 'Manly Englishman' and the 'Effeminate Bengali' in the Late Nineteenth Century*. Manchester: Manchester University Press, 1995.

Skovgaard-Peterson, J. "Fatwas in Print." *Culture and History* 16 (1997): 73–88.

Smith, Michael Llewellyn. *Ionian Vision: Greece in Asia Minor, 1919–1922*. London: Allen Lane, 1973.

Smith, Wilfred Cantwell. "The Historical Development in Islam of the Concept of Islam as an Historical Development." In *Historians of the Middle East*, edited by Bernard Lewis and P. M. Holt, 484–502. Oxford: Oxford University Press, 1962.

Srivastava, Sanjay. *Passionate Modernity: Sexuality, Gender, Class and Consumption in India*. New Delhi: Routledge India, 2007.

Stark, Ulrike. *An Empire of Books: The Naval Kishore Press and the Diffusion of the Printed Word in Colonial India*. New Delhi: Permanent Black, 2008.

Stark, Ulrike. "Politics, Public Issues and the Promotion of Urdu Literature: Avadh Akhbar, the First Urdu Daily in Northern India." *Annual of Urdu Studies* 18 (2003): 66–94.

Stark, Ulrike. "Publishers as Patrons and the Commodification of Hindu Religious Texts in Nineteenth-Century North India." In *Patronage and Popularisation, Pilgrimage and Procession: Channels of Transcultural Translation and Transmission in Early Modern South Asia; Papers in Honour of Monika Horstmann*, edited by Heidi Rika Maria Pauwels, 189–204. Wiesbaden: Harrassowitz Verlag, 2009.

Stein, Burton. *Thomas Munro: The Origins of the Colonial State and His Vision of Empire*. Delhi: Oxford University Press, 1989.

Steinfels, Amina. "His Master's Voice: The Genre of Malfuzat in South Asian Sufism." *History of Religions* 44, no. 1 (2004): 56–69.

Steingass, Francis Joseph. *A Comprehensive Persian-English Dictionary, Including the Arabic Words and Phrases to Be Met with in Persian Literature*. 2nd ed. London: Kegan Paul, Trench, Trubner & Co., 1930.

Subramanayam, K. G., and Muzaffar Alam. *Writing the Mughal World*. New York: Columbia University Press, 2012.

Sweeny, Stuart. "Financing Indian Railways in the Period of High Imperialism, 1875–1914: War, Famine, and Gentlemanly Capitalism." DPhil thesis, University of Oxford, 2008.

Talwar, Vir Bharat. "Feminist Consciousness in Women's Journals in Hindi, 1910–1920." In *Recasting Women: Essays in Indian Colonial History*, edited by Kumkum Sangari and Sudesh Vaid. New Brunswick, NJ: Rutgers University Press, 1990.

Tetzlaffi, Stefan. "The Motorisation of the 'Mufassil': Automobile Traffic and Social Change in Rural North India, c. 1925–70." PhD dissertation, University of Gottingen, 2015.

Thackston, W. M. *Baburname*. 3 vols. Cambridge, MA: Harvard University Press, 1993.

Thānvī, Ashraf ʿAlī. *Perfecting Women: Maulana Ashraf ʿAli Thanawi's Bihishti Zewar: A Partial Translation with Commentary*. Edited by Barbara Daly Metcalf. Delhi: Oxford University Press, 2002.

Tsafrir, Nurit. *The History of an Islamic School of Law: The Early Spread of Hanafism*. Cambridge, MA: Islamic Legal Studies Program, Harvard Law School, 2004.

Tuan, Yi-Fu. *Space and Place: The Perspective of Experience*. Minneapolis: University of Minnesota Press, 1977.

Tymieniecka, Anna-Teresa. *Timing and Temporality in Islamic Philosophy and Phenomenology of Life*. Dordrecht: Springer, 2007.

van Gelder, G. J. H. "Hearing and Deafness." In *Encyclopaedia of Islam*, vol. 2, edited by J. D. McAuliffe, 405–6. Leiden: Brill, 2002.

Vanita, Ruth. "'Married among Their Companions': Female Homoerotic Relations in Nineteenth-Century Urdu Rekhti Poetry in India." *Journal of Women's History* 16, no. 1 (2004): 12–53.

Vanita, Ruth. *Gender, Sex, and the City: Urdu Rekhti Poetry in India, 1780–1870*. Palgrave Macmillan, 2012.

Varady, Robert Gabriel. "Rail and Road Transport in Nineteenth Century Awadh: Competition in a North Indian Province." PhD dissertation, University of Arizona, 1981.

Walker, J., and C. Walker. *India*. London: Edward Stanford, Society for the Diffusion of Useful Knowledge, 1861.

Washbrook, David. "After the Mutiny: From Queen to Queen-Empress." *History Today* 47, no. 9 (September 1997): 10–15.

Wasti, Syed Tanvir. "The Circles of Maulana Mohamed Ali." *Middle Eastern Studies* 38, no. 4 (2002): 51–62.

Wasti, Syed Tanvir. "The Indian Red Crescent Mission to the Balkan Wars." *Middle Eastern Studies* 45, no. 3 (2009): 393–406.

Weiss, B. "'Al-Mushaf Al-Murattal: A Modern Phonographic 'Collection' (Jam') of the Qur'an." *The Muslim World* 64, no. 20 (1974): 134–40.

Weller, Edward. *India*. London: Weekly Dispatch Magazine, c. 1859.

Werbner, Pnina. *Imagined Diasporas among Manchester Muslims*. London: James Currey, 2002.

Werbner, Pnina. *Pilgrims of Love: The Anthropology of a Global Sufi Cult*. London: Hurst, 2003.

Wheeler, Geoffrey. "Modernization in the Muslim East: The Role of Script and Language Reform." *Asian Affairs* 61, no. 2 (2007): 157–64.

Wiebe, D. "Modernism." In *Guide to the Study of Religion*, edited by W. Braun and R. T. McCutcheon, 351–64. London: I.B. Tauris, 2000.

Willis, John. "Debating the Caliphate: Islam and Nation in the Work of Rashid Rida and Abul Kalam Azad." *International History Review* 32, no. 4 (2010): 711–32.

Winkelmann, Mareike Jule. *"From behind the Curtain": A Study of a Girls' Madrasa in India*. Amsterdam: Amsterdam University Press, 2005.

Winkelmann, Mareike Jule. *Reaching the Minds of Young Muslim Women: Girls' Madrasas in India*. Gurgaon: Hope India Publications, 2007.

Yang, Anand. *Bazaar India: Markets, Society, and the Colonial State in Bihar*. Berkeley: University of California Press, 1998.

Yaqin, Amina. "Truth, Fiction, and Autobiography in the Modern Urdu Narrative Tradition." *Comparative Critical Studies* 4, no. 3 (2007): 379–402.

Yildirim, Sajjad Hyder. "Mirza Phoya Aligarh College Mein." In *Armughan-i Aligarh*, edited by K. A. Nizami, 224–28. Aligarh: Educational Book House, 1974.

Zaidi, S. Akbar. "Contested Identities and the Muslim *Qaum* in Northern India, c. 1860–1900." DPhil thesis, University of Cambridge, 2009.

Zaidi, Syed Matanat Husain. "A Socio-Economic Study of the Ansaris of Bijnor District." DPhil thesis, Aligarh University, 1988.

Zaman, Faridah. "Beyond Nostalgia: Time and Place in Indian Muslim Politics." *Journal of the Royal Asiatic Society* 27, no. 4 (October 2017): 627–47.

Zaman, Faridah. "The Future of Islam, 1672–1924." *Modern Intellectual History* 5, no. 1 (2008): 1–31.

Zaman, Muhammad Qasim. *Ashraf Ali Thanawi: Islam in Modern South Asia*. Oxford: Oneworld, 2007.

Zaman, Muhammad Qasim. "Commentaries, Print and Patronage: Hadith and Madrasas in Modern South Asia." *Bulletin of the School of Oriental and African Studies* 62, no. 1 (1999): 60–81.

Zaman, Muhammad Qasim. "Consensus and Religious Authority in Modern Islam: The Discourses of the 'Ulama." In *Speaking for Islam: Religious Authorities in Muslim Societies*, edited by Sabine Schmidtke, 153–80. Leiden: Brill, 2006.

Zaman, Muhammad Qasim. *The Ulama in Contemporary Islam: Custodians of Change*. Princeton: Princeton University Press, 2002.

Index